G000071042

*Pelican Books*

*SUN TRAPS*

After postgraduate research at the School of Environmental
Studies, University College, London, John Elkington joined
Transport and Environment Studies (TEST) and worked as a
planning consultant for such clients as the Organization for
Economic Co-operation and Development (OECD), the United
Nations Development Programme and the World Bank. During
this period he was a regular contributor to *New Scientist*, focusing
on environmental and development issues. In 1978 he was
appointed editor of the ENDS Report and, late in 1980, managing
director of Environmental Data Services (ENDS) Ltd. His book
*The Ecology of Tomorrow's World* was published in 1980 and
focused on the environmental strategies adopted by governments
and by industry in response to the concerns which emerged in
the 1960s and 1970s. Increasingly, his work has concentrated on
the environmental and resource implications of structural and
technological change in the industrialized economies. A report
he prepared for the Department of the Environment during 1981
was published as *Pollution 1990: The Environmental Implications
of Britain's Changing Industrial Structure and Technologies*. He
played a leading role in the development of the UK response
to the World Conservation Strategy. His report *Seven Bridges
to the Future: Industrial Growth Points for a Sustainable Economy*
was published in 1983. He is a Director of Earthlife UK Ltd and
of Bioresources Ltd, editor of *Biotechnology Bulletin* and writes
regularly for the *Guardian*.

John Elkington

# SUN TRAPS

The Renewable Energy Forecast

Penguin Books

Penguin Books Ltd, Harmondsworth, Middlesex, England
Penguin Books, 40 West 23rd Street, New York, New York 10010, U.S.A.
Penguin Books Australia Ltd, Ringwood, Victoria, Australia
Penguin Books Canada Ltd, 2801 John Street, Markham, Ontario, Canada L3R 1B4
Penguin Books (N.Z.) Ltd, 182–190 Wairau Road, Auckland 10, New Zealand

First published 1984

Copyright © John Elkington, 1984
All rights reserved

Filmset in Monophoto Sabon by
Northumberland Press Ltd, Gateshead
Made and printed in Great Britain by
Richard Clay (The Chaucer Press) Ltd, Bungay, Suffolk

*Dedicated to John Lennon (1940–80)*

*and to*
*Elaine, Gaia and Hania*

# Contents

# Preface

Trailing a scintillating tail almost five million kilometres long and as bright as Venus, the comet was a sight to see; but it streaked on unseen. Then, on 30 August 1979, a United States Air Force satellite, code P78–1, was training its telescope on the gaseous upper regions of the sun when it picked up the comet, racing in towards our local star at nearly one million kilometres an hour. A few hours later, it tore into the sun and a shimmering cloud of debris erupted millions of kilometres into space.

The extraordinary thing is that no one knew that the sun, a yellow dwarf star, had received a black eye – even though the energy given off in the collision would have met the total energy needs of the United States, that notoriously profligate consumer of energy, for a thousand years. And then, something over a year later, Dr Donald Michels of the US Naval Research Laboratory began to analyse the pictures returned by satellite P78–1 for evidence of solar storms and stumbled across this enormous and previously unseen event.

The sun is inconceivably large, something like 1.3 million times bigger than our home planet, so large that even such gigantic phenomena as this cometary collision can almost escape notice. It is 400,000 times brighter than the moon, radiating energy at a rate of 400,000,000,000,000,000,000,000,000 watts into space. Less than one billionth (used here in the American sense of one thousand-millionth) of that energy actually strikes the earth, a third of which is promptly reflected back out into space. Yet what remains is sufficient to drive our climatic system and fuel the vast web of life.

Not surprisingly, the sun's rays have fascinated our species for as long as it has walked on the earth. Maxim Gorky recalled seeing the Russian playwright Anton Chekhov, 'while sitting in his garden, try unsuccessfully to catch a sunbeam with his hat and put it on his head. The would-be sun-catcher became more and more angry. Finally, after tapping his hat disconsolately on his knee, he abruptly rammed it on to his head'.

Chekhov died in 1904, some sixty-three years before Harold W.

Dahly was issued US Patent No. 3,353,191 for a hat which might have restored the playwright's humour. The idea was ingenious, involving the use of the sun's rays to keep the wearer's head cool. It worked like this: a cluster of photovoltaic cells (of which more in Chapter 9) sited on top of the hat would convert sunshine into electric current, which, in turn, would drive a small electric motor. The motor would spin a fan, according to the design filed in the patent application, forcing cool air through a screen on to the scalp below.

Mr Dahly may have been an eccentric, or he may have wanted to keep his patented approach to solar cooling, quite literally, under his hat. Whatever his motives, a few short years after he walked into the patents office the first oil crisis sent pulses racing and temperatures soaring throughout the world. While it is fair to say that there was no discernible rush for solar-cooled hats, many of the oil companies were soon investing in solar insurance policies, funding a growing number of renewable-energy research and development programmes.

But what, in the meantime, has been happening in Chekhov's homeland? By the time I started to write this book, news was emerging from the Soviet Union that a pilot solar power plant was being built in the Crimea, with completion expected during 1985. The plant, which was being designed for a power output of 5 million watts (or 5 *megawatts*, hereafter abbreviated to 5 MW), will use parabolic mirrors to focus the sun's rays to super-heat water, with the resulting steam being used to generate electricity.

The striking thing about the plant, though, was the projected cost of the power it was being built to produce. As the comet streaked in towards the centre of our solar system, the Soviet Ministry of Energy was busy calculating that the production cost of 1 kilowatt-hour (abbreviated to 1 kWh, and representing a steady output of 1,000 watts for one hour) was 0.752 kopeks for electricity generated by conventional, fossil-fuel-fired thermal stations, 0.786 kopeks for nuclear power, and a low 0.149 kopeks for hydroelectricity. At these prices, Chekhov would have been well advised to hang his hat on the hydro peg, had he been around. But, as we shall see in Chapter 12, there are limits to the hydro resource, even in a massive country like the Soviet Union.

The Crimean solar power plant, by contrast, was expected to produce electricity at *1.5–2.0 rubles* per kWh. On these figures, at least, solar energy in the USSR is going to be almost two hundred times as expensive as nuclear energy – and more than a thousand times dearer than hydropower. It would be no surprise to hear that energy planners in the Soviet Union had been displaying the same irritation that Gorky witnessed in that failed sun-trapper, Chekhov. But, it appears, renewable energy has an important place in the appropriate Five-Year Plan. The technology is evolving so rapidly, in fact, that there is a very good chance indeed that the cost of some forms of solar energy will fall dramatically in the near future.

The Soviet Union may be in no immediate danger of running out of fossil fuels and uranium, of which it has enormous reserves, but it is stressing the use of fossil fuels as feedstocks for industry in the longer term. A great deal of work is going on around the world on solar energy, and the Soviet Union is at least keeping its options open. Among the projects the Russians have under way at the Alushta research centre, in the Crimea, is a village of single-storey cottages, used to test solar-powered heating and air-conditioning units, while the experimental metallurgy centre at Karsiveli has been using parabolic mirrors (see Chapter 8) to smelt metals at temperatures of up to 3,500°C.

West Germany's Dresdner Bank, meanwhile, had estimated that the West would have to spend about $10 trillion (million million) on new energy equipment by the end of the century, if it were to achieve the necessary transition away from oil. The Secretary of the Treasury in the United States also went on record arguing that the capital needed to wean his country away from oil 'will dwarf the Marshall Plan and the Apollo Space program combined'.

We are seeing, according to Roy Jenkins, speaking when President of the European Commission, 'no less than the break-up of the established economic and social order on which post-war Europe was built. It is now certain,' Mr Jenkins continued, 'that if we do not change our ways while there is still time, our society will risk dislocation and eventual collapse.' Everyone has his or her own idea as to how this transition might be executed, and the various energy-supply lobbies have been pressing their cases in every available forum.

Speaking as executive director of the International Energy Agency, for example, Dr Ulf Lantzke has claimed that a failure to meet the targets set for nuclear-energy capacity would result in 'still lower economic growth, with the unemployment, the hardships and the instability this entails'. So Dr Lantzke called not for a doubling of nuclear capacity by the year 2000, nor a tripling or a quadrupling, but a *five-fold* increase in the nuclear capacity of the IEA nations. This is not an anti-nuclear book, but it is fair to say that the nuclear industry has been finding it difficult to live up to the expectations expressed on its behalf (see Chapter 5). Nuclear power will be an important element in the future energy picture (see p. 361), but nuclear fission now seems very unlikely ever to be the dominant energy source, even in the developed nations.

We have, of course, been through energy transitions before. By the early years of the eighteenth century, for example, the British iron industry, which was then at the cutting edge of the Industrial Revolution, was facing imminent extinction because the pace of industrial development was exhausting supplies of the traditional fuel, charcoal, with the government refusing to permit further inroads on the country's timber for fear that it would have none left for building ships of the line.

Charcoal, as we see in Chapter 10, is still an important fuel in many countries, and one derived from a renewable resource. But, in England, ironmaster Abraham Darby of Coalbrookdale treated coal in the same way that the charcoal burners treated wood and ended up with a new fuel: coke. What he had in effect done was to give industry a new set of keys to Nature's energy deposit account – the fossil fuels. By consuming this energy capital, our industrial societies have enjoyed a new lease of life and the major oil discoveries of the twentieth century have fuelled unparalleled economic growth.

The next energy transition, however, a process upon which we are already embarked, will almost certainly need to be executed on an almost inconceivably larger scale and over a shorter time-span. The sun is, of course, the central character in *Sun Traps*, and solar energy will unquestionably play a vital role in the transition away from oil. But its role is constantly being rewritten by events, with the dramatic fluctuations in the price of oil during the prolonged world recession of the early 1980s creating moments of high drama – and, at times, near-farce – in the embryonic solar industry. Around the world, planners and pundits have been tearing up their energy forecasts and sitting down with clean sheets of paper.

Like that theatrical evergreen *The Mousetrap*, which opened in 1952 and was still running at the time of writing, the basic solar plot has become something of a standard. While the cast may change, the main dramatic interest lies in the continuing search for economic means of extracting energy from renewable sources. Cynics may say that the long run of Dame Agatha Christie's thriller reflected the small capacity of the Ambassadors Theatre, where the play spent the first twenty-two years of its life, but this argument does not hold as far as the energy transition is concerned. Here, as *Sun Traps* shows, the whole world is the stage – and the cast and the audience, who will become increasingly indistinguishable as the transition takes hold, are no less than the world's human population, currently estimated to number about 4.5 billion people.

*Sun Traps* is divided into four main sections. In the first, which includes Chapters 1 to 3, we look at some of the rival solar scripts which have been proffered in recent years. The second section, by contrast, steps back and looks at the competition, with a particular emphasis on the sunshine stored in fossil fuels (Chapter 4), on nuclear power (Chapter 5) and on geothermal energy (Chapter 6). The third section, running from Chapters 7 to 13, returns to the main dramatic interest, highlighting the successes and failures of some of the energy-capture technologies which are currently being used to harness the sun. Finally, Chapter 14 considers the rich interplay between the various members of the solar cast – and their prospects for the future.

*London, June 1983*

# Acknowledgements

Directly or indirectly, knowingly or unknowingly, many people have contributed to the shaping of this book. Anyone who attempts to understand and keep abreast of such a wide range of activity must read a great deal and talk to a considerable number of people. I have done both. What follows is a highly selective listing of some of those who have helped, giving freely of their time, expertise and contacts.

First and foremost, I owe a considerable debt of gratitude to the Winston Churchill Memorial Trust. As a 1981 Churchill Fellow, I was able to visit corporations, research facilities, energy organizations of many kinds and a wide range of individuals in pursuit of my raw material. While in America, my Fellowship took me to Washington, D.C., Pennsylvania, Colorado, Utah, California, Oregon and Washington State. And all this at a critical time for renewable-energy research and development, with public-sector funding being cut throughout the western world.

According to the International Energy Agency, its twenty-one member countries spent $198 million on renewable energy in 1976, a figure which grew to $1,102 million in 1980 – but slipped slightly to $1,076 million in 1981 (all in 1981 dollars). This was due partly to the worldwide recession and partly to the economic problems facing the renewable-energy technologies as the price of oil sagged. Shell underlined the basic problem in 1982 when it pointed out that the technical production cost for a barrel of Middle East oil was $1.1–4.5, compared with $5.7–22.8 for North Sea oil, $17.1–45.5 for shale oil, $51.2–74.0 for substitute natural gas made from coal in north-west Europe, $51.2–113.8 for crops grown for fuel, $91.0–135.0 for electricity from solar, wind or tidal sources, and $91.0–135.0 for solar heat.

Oil, Shell was saying, would still be the world's most important energy source by the turn of the century, accounting for 35–45 per cent of world energy needs, compared with about 45 per cent today. This is a very different picture from that painted by the Worldwatch Institute (see p. 361) – and it underscores the problems faced by anyone writing about the future. I personally am convinced that the future of oil supplies will be rather more precarious than companies like Shell hope. We have enormous quantities of oil, as Figure 4.3 (p. 74) shows, but the cheapest reserves are concentrated in an extremely volatile region of the world. In a recent survey of energy economists, a revolution in Saudi Arabia was seen as the most likely trigger for another major oil crisis, but it is by no means the only potential trigger.

And, while the price of a barrel of oil was certainly slipping as the recession bit, you still had to pay a great deal more than the production cost for your barrel. As *Sun Traps* shows, the renewable-energy prospect may not currently look as rosy as enthusiasts might hope, but the various technologies are developing very fast – and are finding a wide range of applications where economic circumstances are favourable.

In forming my views on the energy prospect, I have had a great deal of help from industrial scientists and engineers working on renewable energy. Conspiracy theorists continue to argue that the big industrial corporations have invested in solar energy to redirect and stifle it, yet most of the people I have spoken to have been genuine enthusiasts for the particular technology or application they were working on. Big industry certainly plays power games, but the renewable-energy lobby has a strong fifth column there, and its potential contribution should not be overlooked.

I should particularly like to thank Lynne Welte of the Acurex Solar Corporation; Dr Reinhard Dahlberg of AEG-Telefunken; Ray Burge and Elizabeth Muckle of Atomic Energy of Canada; Jim Dangerfield of the Billings Energy Corporation; Roger Gillette, Joe Holmes, Arved Plaks and Lee Salter of the Boeing Engineering and Construction Company; Neville Chapman and Dr Anthony Payne of Alcon Biotechnology; Rolf Carlstrom of Alfa-Laval; J. L. Malagarriga of Du Pont de Nemours International; Geoffrey Pardoe and Paul White of General Technology Systems; T. J. Ind of Lucas BP Solar Systems (now BP Solar Systems); Julia Hubbel of Martin Marietta Aerospace Solar Energy Systems; Dorothy Bergin of the Mobil Tyco Solar Energy Corporation; Tim Halford, Susan McClain and Marney Talbert of Occidental International Oil and Occidental Oil Shale; Jacob Bjornson of Iceland's Orkustofnun; Janice Miller of Pacific Gas & Electric; Dr J. M. Waalwijk of Philips; Mary Holden of Solar

Economy; Dominic Michaelis and Laurie Vowler of Solar Energy Developments; Dr Laurie Jones of Unilever; Wendy Peters of Westinghouse Electric; and Dr David Lindley of the Wind Energy Group.

Denis Hayes pulled out the stops for me at the Solar Energy Research Institute in Colorado, during a period when SERI was on the verge of major cuts. Among those who helped me at SERI were Norman Avery, Karel Grohmann, Bill Hunt, Dr Lawrence Kazmerski, Kate Kramer, Sylvia Ranes and Dr Tom Reed. But I owe a special debt of gratitude to Judith Morrison for orchestrating the exercise.

I should also like to thank Todd Bartlam (who has been studying the transfer of solar-energy technology to the developing countries), Gerald Leach and Richard Sandbrook of the International Institute for Environment and Development (IIED); Ashley Bruce; Thomas Canby and Polly McRee Brown of the National Geographic Society; Robin Clarke; Patrick Collins of Imperial College of Science and Technology, London; Kathleen Courrier and Kevin Finneran of the US Solar Lobby; Charles Schiffner of the Frank Lloyd Wright Foundation; Chris Dodson of Helix Multi-Professional Services; Thomas Johansson of the University of Lund; Professor Robert Jungk; Hans Landsberg of Resources for the Future; George Moody of the National Engineering Laboratory; Professor John Page; Christopher Palmer of the National Audubon Society; and Judith Stammers of the Solar Trade Association.

I have drawn on briefing documents prepared both by Earthscan and by the Worldwatch Institute. Particularly helpful were two briefing documents on the new and renewable-energy technologies, edited by Jon Tinker; one on carbon dioxide and climatic change, by Dr John Gribbin; and one on fuel alcohol, by Bill Kovarik. All are available from Earthscan, 10 Percy Street, London W1P 0DR, England.

Bruce Stokes of Worldwatch ensured that I plugged into the relevant streams of work within the Institute. Among its more recent publications in this field have been *Food or Fuel: New Competition for the World's Cropland*, by Lester Brown (Worldwatch Paper 35); *Wood: An Ancient Fuel with a New Future*, by Nigel Smith (Worldwatch Paper 42); *Rivers of Energy: The Hydropower Potential*, by Daniel Deudney (Worldwatch Paper 44); *Wind Power: A Turning Point*, by Christopher Flavin (Worldwatch Paper 45); *Electricity from Sunlight: The Future of Photovoltaics*, by Christopher Flavin (Worldwatch Paper 52); and *Building a Sustainable Society*, the book in which the Institute's director Lester Brown pulled these and many other themes together (W. W. Norton, New York, 1981). And, more recently, Daniel Deudney and Christopher Flavin have published *Renewable Energy: The Power to Choose* (W. W. Norton, 1983). The Worldwatch Institute can be reached at 1776 Massachusetts Avenue, N.W., Washington, D.C. 20036, USA.

Some elements of *Sun Traps* have already been published by the *Architectural Association Quarterly*, the *ENDS Report*, the *Guardian, Management Today* and *New Scientist*. I should like to thank all five publications for their help in supporting my renewable-energy habit – and particularly Tim Radford of the *Guardian*. Peter Clarke of the *Guardian* produced the four drawings on the splitter pages between the main sections of the book.

John Roberts, director of TEST, has been a constant inspiration, as have David Layton and Max Nicholson – who were the intellectual godfathers of Environmental Data Services (ENDS) Ltd. Marek Mayer, who took over from me as Editor of the *ENDS Report*, and Georgina McAughtry both helped to make it all possible. As Editor of *Biotechnology Bulletin*, with responsibility for producing a monthly publication covering another rapidly evolving field, I have been able to tap into a considerable number of projects with direct or indirect implications for the energy future – and would like to thank Nick Coles, Catherine O'Keeffe and Sue Whittaker for their support.

In working on the industrial components of the UK Conservation and Development Programme, in response to the publication in 1980 of the World Conservation Strategy by IUCN, the World Wildlife Fund and the United Nations Environment Programme, a significant proportion of the thought process underpinning this book has been financed by the World Wildlife Fund – and supported in other ways by the other sponsors of the Programme: the Council for Environmental Conservation; the Countryside Commission and the Countryside Commission for Scotland; the Nature Conservancy Council; and the Royal Society of Arts. I have had useful discussions with many members of both the Programme Organizing Committee and the Industrial Review Group, but am particularly grateful to Joan Davidson for her efforts on my behalf in Nairobi.

And, by no means finally, there are my colleagues at Earthlife, particularly Phil Agland and Nigel Tuersley; Michael Dover, Peter Carson and Eleo Gordon of Penguin Books; Alda Angst, Chuck and

Jeanne Branson, and Ian Keay, for their hospitality in San Francisco and Seattle; and Elaine, Gaia and Hania, who have accompanied me on some of the visits and have supported me in so many ways during the writing of the book. Thank you all.

# Solar Plots

# 1 ☉ *Competing Scripts*

Halfway through President Carter's solar sermon, delivered atop South Table Mountain, near Denver in Colorado, it began to pour with rain. The mountain enjoys an average 300 days of sunshine a year, but 4 June 1978, the day that the ill-fated President flew 500 miles from Washington, D.C., to launch America's first 'Sun Day', was clearly not going to be one of them. As he began his speech, grey clouds were already lowering over the foot-hills of the Rockies and, as he forecast that solar energy would meet a quarter of America's energy needs by the end of the century, the skies opened and a heavy downpour fell upon the faithful.

'Nobody can embargo sunlight,' the President persevered. 'No cartel controls the sun. Its energy will not run out. It will not pollute our air or water. The sun's power need only be collected, stored and used.' Which made it all sound relatively easy, indeed almost inevitable. The President, in fact, had omitted only one word: the sun's power need only be collected, stored and used *economically*. At the time, it was generally accepted that oil prices would continue to rise, year in, year out, an assumption which made a wide spectrum of new, alternative and often renewable energy technologies look a good deal more attractive than they otherwise would have done.

In retrospect, that downpour on South Table Mountain looks like something of an omen: in retrospect, at least, it presaged the cold shower forced on an overheated alternatives-to-oil industry by slumping oil prices. Few experts now doubt that the transition away from oil has begun, but they are very much at odds over how far we can expect that transition to go, in which directions and over what period of time.

Even among the most optimistic proponents of renewable-energy technologies, there have been dramatic differences of opinion over which technologies are likely to be desirable or, for that matter, economically feasible. Often it has seemed that a variety of casts have been rehearsing markedly different scripts, built around innumerable adaptations of the same basic plot, yet all using the same title. It is all too easy, however, to forget the singular revolution in attitudes

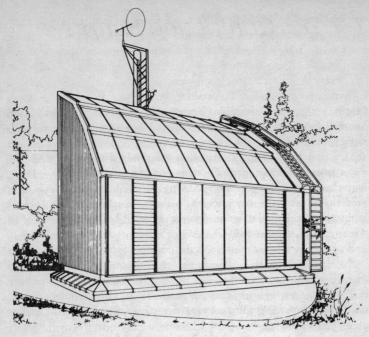

Figure 1.1 Solar laboratory built for the Calor Group
(source: Solar Energy Developments).

wrought in the process, with previously unacceptable energy 'heresies' transformed into near-orthodoxy in a remarkably short period of time. What, we might ask, induced a President of the United States to tread the 'soft-energy' path?

## Hard or Soft?

One of the most effective publicists of soft-energy paths has been Amory Lovins. As far as he was concerned, when writing *Soft Energy Paths* (Penguin, 1977) and later *Brittle Power* (Brick House, 1982), soft-energy technologies have five main characteristics. First, he suggested, 'they rely on renewable energy flows that are always there, whether we use them or not, such as the sun and wind and vegetation: on energy income, not on depletable energy capital'.

They will also, secondly, tend to be highly diverse. Lovins compared renewable-energy budgets with the operation of most national treasuries, suggesting that just as a treasury 'runs on many small tax contributions, so national energy supply is an aggregate of very many individually modest contributions, each designed for maximum effectiveness in particular circumstances'.

So far, so good. But companies and corporations like Boeing, British Aerospace, Grumman, Interatom, Lockheed or Rockwell, all of which have renewable-energy programmes, parted company when Lovins outlined the third characteristic. Soft-energy technologies, he argued, 'are flexible and relatively low technology – which does not mean unsophisticated, but rather, easy to understand and use without esoteric skills, accessible rather than arcane'. This requirement would rule out most of the solar technologies pursued by such industrial groups, including the solar 'power towers' and space satellites described in Chapters 8 and 9 below.

And, while most of the big solar industrialists were thinking in terms of plugging into electricity grids, Lovins continued to say that a fourth characteristic of soft-energy technologies is that 'they are matched in scale and in geographic distribution to end-use needs, taking advantage of the free distribution of most natural energy flows'.

There were many who saw – indeed still see – renewable-energy technologies as intrinsically revolutionary, facilitating the break-up of highly centralized societies, bound together with high-voltage energy grids and supply lines tapping into the coal, uranium and oilfields of the Middle East and elsewhere. The blueprints for survival put forward by such groups as the New Alchemists are reviewed in Chapter 7; their common thread is a vision of an increasingly decentralized settlement pattern, tapping into renewable-energy flows and, in the process, dispensing with the services of the conventional electricity supply industry.

The fifth, and final, characteristic advanced by Amory Lovins as a qualification for soft-energy technologies is their ability to achieve a close match between energy *quality* and end-use needs. The importance of energy quality derives from the Second Law of Thermodynamics and the fact that, as Lovins put it, 'people do not want electricity or oil, nor such economic abstractions as "residential services", but rather comfortable rooms, light, vehicular motion, food, tables and other real things.'

Hard-energy paths, by contrast, promote the use of wasteful energy consumption practices and high-technology energy supply methods. At the time Lovins was writing, for example, 8 per cent of all energy use in the United States required electricity for purposes other than low-temperature heating and cooling, but, he pointed out, electricity was already meeting 13 per cent of US end-use needs, and its generation accounted for 29 per cent of that country's consumption of fossil fuels.

'A hard energy path,' Lovins argued, 'would increase this 13 per cent figure to 20–40 per cent (depending on assumptions) by the year 2000, and far more thereafter. But this is wasteful because the laws of physics require, broadly speaking, that a power station change three units of fuel into two units of almost useless waste heat plus one unit of electricity. This electricity can do more difficult kinds of work than can the original fuel, but unless this extra quality and versatility are used to advantage, the costly process of upgrading the fuel – and losing two-thirds of it – is all for naught.'

The industrial nations, then, are using premium fuels and electricity for many tasks for which their high-energy qualities are superfluous. Hard-energy paths aggravate this mismatch between the quality of the energy required and consumed. Instead, it was argued, where we want to create temperature differences of only tens of degrees, we should meet the need with energy sources whose potential is tens or hundreds of degrees, not with a flame temperature of thousands of degrees or a nuclear reaction whose temperature equivalent is almost off the scale. This, Lovins concluded in a memorable phrase, is rather like 'cutting butter with a chainsaw'.

Sunshine, by contrast, arrives on earth at a relatively low temperature, making it highly suitable for tasks requiring low-quality energy – such as the heating of water or of buildings. However, the nature of solar radiation is such that it can be upgraded for tasks where high-quality energy is indispensable. Streaming out from the sun, sunshine is not degraded as it travels through space, being instead simply dispersed as it streaks along its radial routes away from the solar reactor.

In fact, as Barry Commoner, another long-standing supporter of solar energy, put it, 'the supposed disadvantages of solar energy – its diffuse nature and the economics of constructing solar devices – turn out, when properly understood, to be precisely the reverse: just because it is diffuse, solar energy has certain major thermodynamic advantages over conventional sources of energy.'

To demonstrate the intrinsic high quality of solar radiation, Commoner recalled a familiar experiment. 'If sunlight is sharply focused with a lens,' he pointed out, 'it will set paper or wood aflame (at ignition temperatures of 400–450°F). All that is required to deliver solar energy at any desired temperature is to concentrate it from a sufficiently large area. A three-inch lens will gather enough light to produce a temperature of a few hundred degrees, and the huge parabolic mirror of the French solar furnace in the Pyrenees will gather enough to melt tungsten, at a temperature of nearly 6,000°F.'

Renewable-energy technologies, then, typically focus the diffuse energy flows in the environment just as a lens focuses sunlight or a dam 'focuses' the diffuse potential energy in rain falling over an extensive water-catchment area. The greater your energy needs, the more extensive your catchment area must be. The problem here is that some of the methods now being used to concentrate solar energy, as at France's solar furnace near Odeillo, involve high technology. Indeed, it is often extremely hard to discern just where the soft-energy paths shade over into the hard.

Soft-energy technologists like Amory Lovins have insisted that the soft and hard paths are mutually exclusive, but it is fair to say that there are soft and hard paths within the renewable-energy field itself – paths which need not be mutually exclusive, if carefully balanced and sensitively managed. Yet, while the developed countries have lauded the renewable energies as morally superior, dubbing them 'green', 'appropriate' or 'soft', Third World countries, noting the continued dependence of these same developed countries on fossil fuels and nuclear power, have been intensely suspicious of their motives in promoting renewable energy.

## Second-class Technologies?

'We think new and renewable energy sources will survive this conference,' quipped one UN official in the wake of the UN Conference on New and Renewable Sources of Energy (UNERG), held in Nairobi, Kenya, between 10 and 21 August 1981. Once again, delegates from the developing nations had put forward the view that the renewable-energy technologies are 'second-class' technologies, designed to keep the developing nations in economic and technological subjection.

Despite the claim by UNERG secretary-general Enrique Iglesias that the occasion had put the renewables on the map in the same way that the 1972 Stockholm Conference on the Human Environment put environment on the international agenda, there were some critics who felt that the billions of sheets of paper used during UNERG would have been better employed on the cooking fires of the Third World.

Meanwhile, the plight of the developing countries was highlighted in figures published by the US oil company Texaco. These showed that they spent nearly $50 billion on imported oil during 1980, and the World Bank was forecasting that this import bill, which was already crippling some countries, could rise to $110 billion by 1990. Third World energy demand was expected to increase annually by 4.5 per cent during the 1980s and 1990s, twice the rate then expected for the non-communist world as a whole.

But Texaco pointed out that the developing countries have a long way to go before they begin to rival the energy usage in the industrial nations. Whereas the average US citizen was using about 63 barrels of oil a year, a figure expected to grow to 67.9 barrels a year by 1990, and while the figure for the industrialized world as a whole was 38.5 barrels a year per head (expected to grow to 44.9 a year by 1990), the per-capita consumption in the Third World was only about 3.2 barrels a year, a figure expected to grow to perhaps 4.7 barrels a year by 1990.

The Third World, however, had been much harder hit by rising oil prices than these figures would suggest. At a time when the world economy was depressed and inflation rampant, the commodity prices on which many developing countries were forced to depend for foreign currency had fallen significantly in real terms. In 1975, for example, a tonne of copper bought 115 barrels of oil, whereas by 1981 it bought only 57 barrels. Put another way, 101 per cent more copper was needed in 1981 than in 1975 to purchase a barrel of oil. The same depressing trend held true for other commodities too: by 1981, developing countries had to export 79 per cent more coffee, 180 per cent more sugar, 250 per cent more jute and 175 per cent more maize than in 1975 when buying a barrel of oil on the world market.

The World Bank had been urging that increased financial support for Third World energy developments should be given priority status, estimating that $54 billion a year would be needed in the period to

1985 alone. But there seemed to be little chance that this sort of money would be available, and UNERG signally failed to establish the financial mechanisms needed to meet its objectives.

Canada, however, impressed the delegates by announcing that it would make C$1 billion (then valued at £454 million) available to fund energy programmes in developing countries over the following five years. A further C$25 million, it said, had been earmarked for energy developments in Africa's drought-stricken Sahel region, while C$25 million more was promised for renewable-energy research and development the following year. And then, to cap it all, prime minister Pierre Trudeau was also able to announce that Canada was allocating another C$5 million to help private Canadian companies to tailor renewable-energy technologies to the needs of the Third World.

Compared with all this, the contributions of most other countries looked distinctly pale. The United States, for instance, announced that its Agency for International Development (AID) would double its budget for Third World energy development to $76 million (or about £42 million) a year, an increase which, it appeared, would be achieved by the simple expedient of cutting the funding for other AID programmes. Britain, represented by energy minister David Howell, promised a mere £2 million a year in total – which provoked one delegate to comment privately that this sum might just cover the cost of the paperwork likely to be involved in processing the aid.

Yet all the time the delegates sat and wrangled in the conference rooms, solar energy continued to fall on the earth – some 170 million million kilowatts ($170 \times 10^{12}$ kW), equivalent to an estimated 40,000 one-bar electric fires burning constantly for every man, woman and child of the earth's population. And how much of this vast flow of energy was being harnessed by the new solar technologies? By the time the conference closed its doors, all the world's solar collectors were believed to be yielding energy equivalent to a mere 400,000 tonnes of oil a year – about one ten-thousandth (or 0.01 per cent) of the world's annual oil consumption at the time.

Around the world, however, different countries and experts had very different ideas about what constituted a solar technology – and about the probable significance of the competing solar-energy capture technologies in the transition away from oil, differences which are illustrated in considerable detail in Chapters 3 and 7–14. Indeed, the solar contribution looks very much more convincing if you begin to wrap in some of the less obvious methods of harnessing sunshine, such as the 'biomass' option, involving the exploitation of the photo-synthetic ability of plants (see Chapter 10). But before we begin to look at the successes and failures of particular countries in harnessing their renewable-energy resources, it may help to take a closer look at the sun itself, and at some of the technologies which have been developed to harness its prodigious energy output.

# 2 ⊙ A Growing Cast

It is a strange thought that the earth and the other endlessly circling planets of our solar system began their long evolution in pitch darkness. Whatever triggered the process by which a cold cloud of gas began to collapse in on itself, condensing into our local star and its faithful planetary retainers, when those retainers first began to emerge out of that swirling nebula their Sun King was still fast asleep.

The explosive death throes of at least one massive star, it is thought, a supernova flaring in the dark distances of space, served as a cosmic alarm-clock. The blast wave searing out from the dying star collided with our own stellar nebula, seeding it with all the chemical elements formed during its long life and violent death, and starting – or accelerating – the process of centripetal collapse within that massive gas cloud.

While the matter in the outlying areas of cloud began to form into planets and asteroids, their size and spacing determined by the ebb and flow of what physicists call 'gravitational resonance', something even stranger was going on at the heart of this embryonic solar system. An observer, had there been one, would have noticed that although the emerging planets were continuing to sweep up any matter they

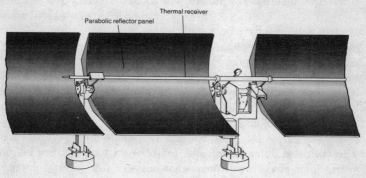

Figure 2.1: Parabolic-trough collector
(source: Acurex Solar Corporation).

encountered in their orbits with their ever stronger gravitational fields, very considerable quantities of matter were condensing in towards the most massive accumulation of matter in the system, the spherically symmetrical cloud of matter which was already acting as the emerging system's gravitational pivot.

Things really began to hot up, however, when this solar cloud became sufficiently dense for the internal motions of its particles to produce a gathering crescendo of collisions, each collision exciting and fuelling new collisions, each raising the cloud's internal temperature. At this stage, the outer boundary of the cloud was probably still as far out as the emerging orbit of Mars, but once the collisions became so violent that hydrogen began to be ionized, energy was soaked up by the ionization process and the cloud collapsed rather like a punctured balloon. Our solar system's first fusion reactor, in which matter is converted into energy according to Einstein's $E = mc^2$ formula, had switched itself on, banishing the dark.

## The Prodigal Sun

Anyone who is nervous about the risk involved in the operation of this planet's nuclear reactors might like to consider the following information about the fusion reactor which rises every morning and sets every evening of their lives. The English astronomer Sir James Hopwood Jeans, who died in 1946, once estimated that if a piece of the sun's core the size of a pinhead were to be placed on the earth's surface, its intense heat would be fatal to human beings over 90 miles away.

Jeans may well have been slightly out in his calculations, but the message was clear enough: the sun is a far deadlier piece of energy-conversion apparatus than the nuclear reactors which so concern us here on earth. Unlike most man-made reactors, however, the sun has operated within very fine tolerances for most of its operational life – but we can thank our lucky stars that we live 93 million miles (or 150 million kilometres) away.

The sun has, in fact, been burning five million tonnes of hydrogen a second, and doing so reliably, for between four and five billion years. Solar physicists estimate that our star still contains enough hydrogen to burn for another 100 billion years, but believe that most of the hydrogen lies near the sun's core, well below the outer shell of active thermonuclear reactions, suggesting that we have a guaranteed future of perhaps five billion years at current levels of output.

We know that the sun is nowhere near as solid as it looks. The bright outer layer, or photosphere, from which the light we see emerges, is composed of hot gases so rarified that the photosphere is technically a vacuum. However, as one approaches the heart of the sun, the force of gravity increases, and with it the density and temperature of the gases. One-tenth of the way in towards the sun's core, then, the density of the solar gases reaches that of air at sea level on our own planet, while by halfway it has reached the density of water. At the centre of the sun, by contrast, the density rises to ten times that of ordinary metals, and computations suggest that the gravitational force acting on atoms there is some 250 billion times that we experience here on earth.

While the temperature of the seething, if rarified, clouds of gas which make up the photosphere is about 6,000°C, core temperatures may be as high as 15,000,000°C. Given our distance from the sun, and the inhospitable conditions prevailing there, it is quite extraordinary how much we know about our star's inner workings. But, at the same time, it is also extraordinary how much we still have to learn about the operations of the reactor on whose continued reliable performance our lives so totally depend.

We are fairly sure we know how the reactor is fuelled, although there may be several fusion processes involved. The current favourite is a three-stage process, starting with a hydrogen nucleus, or, to be more accurate, with two hydrogen nuclei (or protons). In fusing together to form a single nucleus of heavy hydrogen, or deuterium, these protons emit a 'positron' (an electron with a positive electrical charge) and a 'neutrino', a tiny particle thought to have little or no mass and no electrical charge. The resulting 'deuteron' then combines with another proton, forming a rare variety of helium called helium 3 – and emitting a gamma ray in the process. The third stage involves the fusion of two of these helium 3 nuclei to form a single helium 4 nucleus, with two extra protons and another gamma ray being emitted during this reaction.

The result of all this is that four hydrogen nuclei have been transformed into a single helium nucleus. This nucleus, however, weighs less (about 0.7 per cent less) than did the original four hydrogen atoms. The missing mass has been converted into energy.

One of these so-called 'proton-chain' reactions produces a very,

very small amount of energy – about 0.00004 of an erg. Even an erg is an infinitesimal amount of energy; a one-watt current flowing for a single second delivers an astonishing 10 *million* ergs. But for every gram of the sun's mass, estimated to be $1.958 \times 10^{27}$ tons or $1.989 \times 10^{30}$ tonnes, two ergs are radiated every second. This, as the figures above suggest, is because there are something like $2 \times 10^{33}$ grams of mass in the sun.

The extraordinary thing, though, is that any one of the sun's protons might last for between 5 and 14 billion years before being captured by another proton, forming a deuteron, and any single pair of helium 3 nuclei would meet and fuse only once in a million years. Yet even these unimaginably infrequent reactions happen often enough to keep the atomic furnace blazing.

Fusion reactions do, of course, take place around the centre of the sun as well – and they do so furiously. Indeed, if the blaze of gamma rays and fast electrons they emit were to reach the surface of the earth in their raw state, life as we know it would be sizzled off the face of the planet. What happens, in fact, is that this 'first-generation' radiation is forced to make its way up out of the core and, finally, through the sun's outer layers, many of which are opaque to gamma rays, filtering out a large proportion of these rays and 'sweetening' the sunshine which finally emerges into space.

Interestingly, today's sunshine was generated in 8000 B.C., at the latest, having taken nearly 10,000 years to make its way up through the 480,000 miles of inferno between the sun's core and the photosphere.

With operating temperatures in the region of 15,000,000°C, the sun is obviously best left where it is. The solar power supply system is, in any event, extremely efficient, with sunlight covering the distance to earth in a little over eight minutes. But, since there are no power lines plugging us directly into the solar reactor, solar energy arrives all over the place.

The sun radiates something like 400,000,000,000,000,000,000,000,-000 watts, each watt representing 10 million ergs. Earth intercepts a very small proportion indeed of this prodigious amount of energy: the maximum amount of the sun's output which we could hope to harness at the moment, which would be the amount of solar radiation arriving in the uppermost reaches of the atmosphere, represents about one part in a billion of the sun's total output.

For many years, solar physicists tried to work out what they called the 'solar constant', or the average amount of solar energy available above the atmosphere. Our best estimates today suggest that an area of one square centimetre placed 150 million kilometres away from the sun would receive two calories per minute of solar energy – equal to about 1,400 joules per second per square metre.

Since, on average, any square metre of the upper atmosphere only receives sunlight for half of a twenty-four-hour cycle, it is fair to assume that it would receive something like 14.4 million calories each day – or 5.25 billion calories a year. About one third of this energy is promptly reflected back into space by cloud cover, and, as the remaining energy cascades down through the atmosphere, it is reduced almost exponentially by clouds, water vapour and other gases. These losses, however, are not losses to the system. They drive the earth's climate, powering the winds and the water cycle, systems which are harnessed by some of the technologies described in Chapters 12 and 13. A useful indicator of the size of our solar budget is the fact that the sunshine entering our atmosphere every year is roughly equivalent to 500,000 billion barrels of oil. This, in turn, is equivalent to perhaps 800,000 billion tonnes of coal, 1.5 million million tonnes of lignite or 2.8 million million tonnes of peat. These figures, finally, are equivalent to perhaps a million times the world's proven oil reserves in the late 1970s. But, while this is clearly a stupendous amount of energy, a relatively small proportion actually reaches ground-level.

With one watt equivalent to one joule per second, it is also possible to say that each square metre of the upper atmosphere receives nearly 1,400 watts (the actual figure is thought to be about 1,365 watts per square metre). In London, for example, the amount of sunshine reaching the ground on a very clear day, when the sun is at its highest point, can reach perhaps 1,000 watts per square metre; but on cloudier days most of the solar radiation is reflected or absorbed before it reaches the ground – which receives about 200 watts per square metre, or a mere 15 per cent of the solar constant.

As we have seen, when sunshine actually does reach the earth's surface, it is intermittent, diffuse and, all too often, arrives in greatest quantity where it is least needed. The problem facing solar technologists is this: in manufacturing and deploying solar energy capture devices, you often end up using more energy and sterilizing more ground than makes sense in economic terms. In selecting the appropriate technology, however, we do have an ever-increasing range of options to call upon.

## Soft Options

The energy-capture technologies discussed in the remainder of this book can initially be broken down into two main groups. First, there are those which harness direct flows of solar energy – whether in the form of *heat* (i.e. the technologies grouped on the left-hand side of Figure 2.2) or of *photons* (i.e. the direct solar technologies grouped on the right-hand side of Figure 2.2).

Heat-collection technologies, in turn, may be either 'passive' (see Chapter 7) or 'active' (see Chapter 8). Photon-capture technologies, on the other hand, may adopt one of two main routes: either they are photovoltaic, converting photons into electrical current, as with the use of photovoltaic cells (see Chapter 9), or they are photochemical, using photons to drive chemical reactions. The most significant solar technology in use at the moment involves the exploitation of the energy stored in *biomass* (see Chapter 10). This generally implies extracting stored solar energy, by whatever means, from plant materials or from micro-organisms. A traditional refinement of this biomass route involves the feeding of plants to animals, which, in effect, can be seen as solar-powered engines. In India alone, it has been estimated that it would cost at least $150 billion to replace animal power with conventional mechanical power (see Chapter 11).

The energy-capture technologies in the second main group tap into indirect flows of energy emanating from the sun. These, as the box in the top right-hand corner of Figure 2.2 shows, are hydropower, wind and wave energy. Briefly stated, solar radiation drives the climatic system, powering the ceaseless cycle of evaporation, rainfall and runoff tapped by hydropower technologies; heating up the atmosphere at different rates in different places, setting air in motion and, together with the earth's rotation, accounting for the world's wind systems; and, through the good offices of the wind, driving the waves across the world ocean. Hydropower and wave energy are both discussed in some detail in Chapter 12, and wind energy is the subject of Chapter 13.

All these technologies can then be classified as low, intermediate

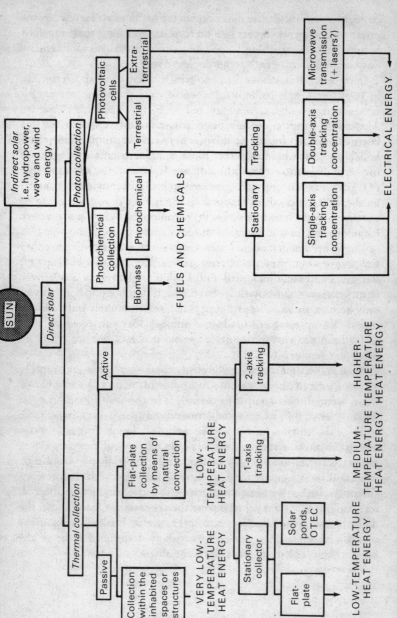

Figure 2.2: Some sun-trapping options (source: UNERG. but slightly modified).

or high, as in Table 2.1. 'Soft' technologists tend to favour low or intermediate technologies, but there is no question that any full-blooded attempt to plug a modern society into renewable energy flows would involve high technologies as well.

In the end, it all comes down to which script you happen to have in your hand. Soft technologists would take the view that photovoltaic cells are high technology, but probably acceptable. What we need to do, they would say, is to adjust our life-styles to suit the energy available to us. The solar power satellite camp, on the other hand, would tend to argue that there is little reason to change your life-style if you can plug into sufficiently large flows of renewable energy. While soft technologists see satellite power systems as ultra-hard technologies, their proponents argue that if you are going to use photovoltaic technology anyway, you might as well put it where it can operate most efficiently – in space.

These arguments and counter-arguments will be rehearsed in Chapter 9, but they do illustrate the diversity of philosophies, strategies and tactics adopted within what might appear a relatively homogeneous solar-power lobby. These differences of opinion can only become more acute at a time when solar research and development is being starved of funds in a number of countries which have so far been pioneers in this field, a trend which is discussed in more detail in Chapter 3.

As will become increasingly clear, there is a large and rapidly growing cast of energy-capture technologies, with a fair number of these technologies competing fiercely for the leading role in the 'post-oil era'. But, as Chapter 3 points out, the backers who have paid for the initial rehearsals now seem much less enthusiastic about seeing the show on the road. As oil prices fell through the early 1980s, an increasing number of government and industrial sponsors cut or cancelled their support for alternative energy research. Before considering whether we are about to see the entire production aborted, let's look at what happened during the rehearsals. One of these, the flight of the *Solar Challenger* from France to England, caught the world's imagination – but embarrassingly underlined some of the continuing problems facing solar technologists.

Table 2.1: Some available solar technologies and their applications (source: UNERG)

| Application | Thermal passive (LT) | Thermal stationary (IT) | Solar ponds (IT) | Tracking collectors 1-axis (LT/IT) | Tracking collectors 2-axis (HT) | Photovoltaics (terrestrial: HT) | Satellite power systems (HT) |
|---|---|---|---|---|---|---|---|
| Cooking | | X | | X | X | | |
| Greenhouses | X | X | X | | | | |
| Industrial process heat | | X | X | X | X | | |
| Power production | | | | | | | |
| – electricity | | | X | X | X | X | X |
| – mechanical | | | X | X | X | X | |
| Refrigeration | X | X | X | X | X | X | |
| Space cooling | X | X | X | X | X | X | |
| Space heating | X | X | X | X | | | |
| Timber and crop drying | X | X | | | | | |
| Water heating | X | X | X | X | | | |
| Water pumping | | X | X | X | X | X | |
| Water purification | | X | X | X | X | | |

Key: LT = low technology
    IT = intermediate technology
    HT = high technology

# 3 ⊙ *The Final Curtain?*

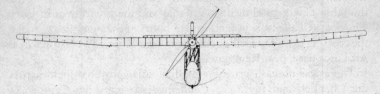

Figure 3.1: The *Solar Challenger*
(source: Du Pont de Nemours International).

Poring over their phosphorescent radar screens in the St Leonards battery, high above the white cliffs of Dover, the coastguards policing the world's busiest shipping lanes must often rub their eyes, not because of eye strain, but in sheer disbelief. Each year, the signals they transmit to shipping include reports on the increasingly bizarre attempts being made to cross the English Channel by those to whom the idea of buying a ferry ticket appears impossibly straightforward.

In a single week during 1981, for example, the Channel was crossed by two blind water-skiers, eighteen firemen in a rowing boat, seventeen swimmers and by eight men from Essex who travelled on a raft paddled by, of all things, a combine harvester. The Channel has also been wind-surfed, hang-glided, inner-tubed, solar-ballooned and walked, with the aid of ski-poles attached to floats. Yet the Channel is also probably the most dangerous waterway in the world, with innumerable supertankers passing through, vessels which have a 'blind spot' stretching up to three miles ahead of their bows and which can take five miles to stop if they do spot a problem.

A strange place, then, for one of the first attempts at long-distance solar-powered flight. A strange place, but perhaps inevitable. The first man to fly the Channel, Louis Blériot, flew from Calais to Dover in 37 minutes. His flight caused panic in Britain's War Office, which was forced to recognize that the fact that the country was an island could no longer be relied upon as the main plank in its defence strategy, but it also gave the embryonic aircraft industry a boost out of all proportion to the distance actually covered that day: 26 miles (42 kilometres).

Shortly before that combine harvester took to the waves, and some seventy-two years after Blériot's historic crossing, a single-seat aircraft piloted by Steve Ptacek, a crop-duster and flying instructor from Golden, Colorado, flew straight into the world's headlines – even though it flew a good deal slower than did the Frenchman in 1909. The *Solar Challenger*, in fact, took 5 hours and 23 minutes to make the crossing from Cormeilles-en-Vexin, near Paris, to Manston Royal Air Force base, near Ramsgate.

There was no cash prize for the first solar-powered flight across the Channel, and the *Solar Challenger*, designed by Californian physicist Dr Paul MacCready, had already displayed its air-worthiness in the skies above California's Mojave Desert and in Arizona, having first taken off on 20 November 1980 at El Mirage, California. MacCready had already won two major prizes with the *Gossamer Condor* and the *Gossamer Albatross* for the first sustained human-powered flight (worth £50,000) and for the first human-powered aerial crossing of the Channel (worth £100,000). So why did he go for a solar crossing of the Channel?

Pressed on the point, he had some difficulty in coming up with a convincing answer. 'People ask what the practical value is of flying a plane on solar power,' he mused. 'I say it's about as practical to fly a plane on solar power as it is with human power. I can't think of anything practical about it.' But, while I never consciously set out to track them down, I have seen both the *Solar Challenger* and the *Gossamer Albatross*, which Bryan Allen pedalled across the Channel, covering his 23-mile (37-kilometre) route in 2 hours and 49 minutes – and the places I came across them do, in fact, say something about their respective practical significance.

## An Embarrassing Success

The *Gossamer Albatross* was suspended from the ceiling of the National Air and Space Museum in Washington, D.C., which is part of the Smithsonian Institute. It was hanging next to the Wright Brothers' first plane and Charles Lindbergh's *Spirit of St Louis*. It seemed slightly ironic that, while Orville and Wilbur ran a bicycle shop and used their mechanical skill to build a glider powered by a 12-horsepower petrol engine, covering 40 yards (37 metres) in their first flight on 7 December 1903, MacCready went back to pedal power almost three quarters of a century later and ended up alongside the Wrights in this aerial hall of fame.

This man-powered glider flew into the Smithsonian's collection simply because it represented a world first, whereas one of the *Solar Challenger*'s first perches after its epic flight illustrated the commercial significance of its rehearsal of solar flight. When I caught up with the machine, a month or so after it touched down in England, it was hanging above the milling crowds at the Solar World Forum, in Brighton, a week-long event organized by the International Solar Energy Society to boost sales in the burgeoning solar-energy industry – and the MacCready machine occupied pride of place, a magnet for exhibitors and delegates alike.

Encrusted with some 16,000 photovoltaic cells (see Figure 3.2), which convert sunlight into electricity (as described in Chapter 9), the aircraft represented a major public-relations coup for the embry-

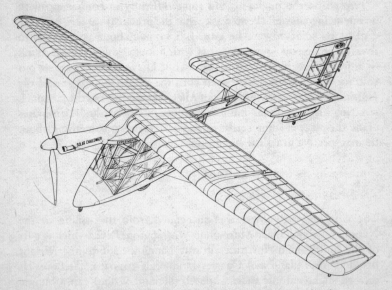

Figure 3.2: The *Solar Challenger* (source: Aerovironment, Inc.).

onic photovoltaics industry, although it remains to be seen whether Ptacek's flight will boost the industry's prospects as significantly as did Blériot's flight those of the aviation industry.

And, just as that rain-storm on South Table Mountain presaged future problems in the solar industry, so the problems experienced by Dr MacCready's team in actually getting their aircraft off the ground – and in keeping it airborne once up – illustrate some of the hurdles which the solar industry must surmount if it is to play a leading role in the transition away from oil.

Because the aircraft's photovoltaic cells all had to have their place in the sun if it were to produce enough power to stay in the air, the top surfaces of its wings and tail-plane violated both the theory and the practice of aerofoil design. They were perfectly flat, and, as one aircraft designer put it, the resulting aircraft was 'hopelessly unaerodynamic'. In developing his design, MacCready had gone back to first principles. 'Too many people,' he said, 'had been thinking of redesigning the glider.' The end result of his labours, by contrast, had a 'glide ratio' of 13.5 to 1 when the propeller was feathered, which meant that it fell one foot (or metre) for every 13.5 feet (or metres) it travelled. A strikingly poor performance by the standards of many of today's gliders, but this was just one of the sacrifices which had to be made if solar flight were to be possible at all.

One problem which this poor glide ratio entrained for MacCready and his team was that it became vitally important to ensure that the aircraft did not run into overcast conditions. There were no batteries or other forms of electrical storage aboard, although two of the three other solar planes operating at the time did carry batteries to sustain their flight if the sun went in momentarily. The upshot of all this was that, once the sun did go in, the *Solar Challenger* began to drop out of the sky – a fate which some saw befalling the solar-energy industry if the governments of the leading solar nations withdrew or cut their renewable-energy subsidies.

## A $4 Billion Industry?

By the time the Solar World Forum opened its doors in Brighton, world expenditure on solar-energy systems was estimated to be running at about $4 billion a year. Paradoxically, however, major structural changes were in train in the sun's rising industries, changes which had left Exxon, the world's largest oil company, nursing burned fingers. Earlier in 1981 it had been forced to sell its Daystar solar subsidiary. How sunny, some investors were beginning to ask, were this upstart industry's prospects likely to be?

Given their success in so many other markets, it makes sense to ask the Japanese first. By the time Exxon decided to pull out of the thermal side of solar-energy collection, Japan already had 3 million solar collectors in place on the roofs of its buildings, and was planning to equip 20 per cent of its housing stock with solar systems by 1990. A simple solar collector, suitable for putting on a roof, is shown in Figure 3.3 – although most of the pipework and the storage tank would be installed either in the loft space or in the house itself. The operation of such a flat-plate collector is described in Chapter 7.

With a proposed 25,000 factories and offices fitted with similar (if often larger) solar heating systems, Japan was calculating that it would soon be saving the equivalent of 5 million tonnes of oil a year. Sanyo, to take just one Japanese company, was already deriving one per cent of its sales from solar products, and was estimating that the solar proportion of its turnover would reach about

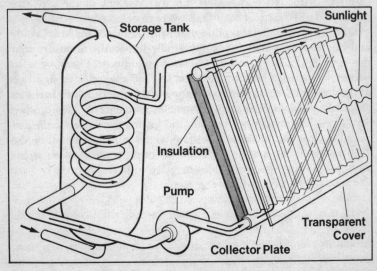

Figure 3.3: A schematic drawing of a simple flat-plate collector system (source: ATOM).

7 per cent by the mid-1980s, representing sales to the value of perhaps $450 million.

Several months after Exxon sold Daystar, Japan's Electric Power Development Company succeeded in generating 1,000 kilowatts (or 1 MW) of electricity with a new solar plant − which, in many essentials, was similar to the Soviet plant described on p. 10. This plant, located at Nio in Kagawa Prefecture, used 807 sun-tracking mirrors (or 'heliostats') to focus the sun's rays on to a central boiler, generating enough power to light 16,600 standard 60-watt light-bulbs.

'The initial cost of constructing a solar power plant is about ten times higher than the cost of a hydroelectric plant,' cautioned the man in charge of the project, Nobuyuki Kuribayashi, 'and twenty times higher than the cost of building a conventional fossil-fuel power station.' The plant also suffered from the obvious disadvantages that it could not operate at night and, once the sun bounced back over the horizon, it took two hours to build up a head of steam from a cold start. But the Japanese costings represent a very much more attractive prospect than did those from the Soviet Union (see p. 10), and the Japanese are certain that the costs of solar energy can be driven down sharply as they travel up the 'learning curve'.

On the other hand, as President Carter suggested, such plants do harness a free, renewable-energy source which generates no pollution worth mentioning (although the production and siting of their components may clearly produce some pollution and other environmental impacts) and is not subject to the vagaries of international oil politics or to oil price rises. These are both highly desirable characteristics in the eyes of the Japanese, who have to import almost all the fuel they use. If enough solar plants are built, they reason, the cost of solar energy will inevitably fall.

Solar water heating tends to be one of the first building blocks in most industrial countries' solar-energy programmes, and it has been very successful in a number of countries. There have been criticisms, however, particularly where the economics involved are marginal. In Britain, for example, the National Consumer Council warned that those who bought solar water-heating systems would be lucky to get their money back. Advising that it was 'not a good investment for most people', the Consumer Council argued that those most likely to benefit would be those already paying the full price for the electricity needed to heat water with an immersion heater − and prepared to roll up their sleeves and install their own system.

Even then, it was concluded, at a time when some 19,000 British homes had solar heating systems, 'it is likely to take longer to get your money back than the average time people live in a house before moving.'

Part of the problem, it was believed, was that consumers of solar technology were being taken in by 'cowboy' solar salesmen, who were making exaggerated claims for their products and were often failing to install them properly. Such design and installation mistakes can be tolerated with conventional heating systems, where concentrated forms of energy are used, but the low intensity of sunshine makes particular demands on the skills of the solar installer.

The more sophisticated manufacturers have been reacting by pre-assembling solar components into modules which even a careless worker would be hard pushed to install incorrectly. At the same time, too, the fledgling solar industries in a number of countries have set up solar trade associations to establish and police standards for the design, installation and performance of solar equipment. Such teething problems are to be expected, obviously, but it is important that they be properly managed – before they undermine the credibility of competent businesses.

Solar energy, however, can be harnessed in many other ways, a fair number of which, as we saw in Chapter 2, have little or nothing to do with the heating of water. Many of the more thoughtful proponents of solar energy continue to point out that solar energy is no panacea for the world's energy problems, arguing instead that it will be part of the energy mix of the future – with the significance of its role very much reflecting the price trends for other fuels and local circumstances.

At the Solar World Forum in 1981, for example, Professor David Hall of King's College, London, pointed out that solar energy was already supplying some 15 *per cent* of the world's energy, primarily in the form of biomass. Much of this energy is used in the developing countries, in the form of firewood, animal dung and waste materials. This was equivalent to about 20 million barrels of oil a day. When he opened the Solar World Forum Professor Hall, who has been a leading pioneer in the biomass energy field, was joined on the platform by solar experts representing eleven countries. To give an idea of the progress of their solar rehearsals, it may help to run through their respective activities – recognizing that the statistics given relate to the situation, at the very latest, in 1981.

Brazil, for example, was planning to spend $1.3 billion that year to produce 5 billion litres of alcohol, primarily derived from sugar-cane, to blend as a 20-per-cent mixture in its gasoline supplies. It had announced its intention to manufacture a further 250,000 cars that year designed to run on hydrated alcohol. The World Bank and the Elf oil company were both extending major loan facilities, and large programmes were also under way with the objective of pro-ducing diesel oil from vegetable sources and methanol from a range of biomass resources. A full account of these programmes may be found in Chapter 10.

Japan, some of whose activities we have already looked at, had already installed 750,000 solar collectors during 1981, bringing the total figure to 3 million, valued at $500 million. France, meanwhile, was deriving about 9 per cent of its energy from renewable sources, and was aiming to meet between 10 and 15 per cent of its (much increased) needs by the year 2000. It had, it was believed, the largest renewable-energy programme in Europe at the time, spending about $750 million on hydropower, solar-energy and biomass schemes. It was expecting to have equipped about 600,000 houses with solar systems by 1985, reaching perhaps 2 million by the end of the century. The incoming energy minister, after the election of President Mitterand, had talked of spending FF180 billion over the following ten years – or the equivalent of about $3 billion a year. The French were also excited about their 'carburol' programme, alcohol-stretched gasoline (or 'gasohol') made according to a French recipe, and about the fact that they had captured a quarter of the world market for photovoltaic cells.

In Australia, about 100,000 houses had already been fitted with solar collectors, and it was estimated that 200,000 square metres of solar collectors would be produced there during 1981. Perth was planning to host the 1983 Solar World Forum, and the country as a whole was expecting to use solar means to meet some 7 per cent of its energy requirements by the end of the century.

Canada reported that it was meeting 4 per cent of its energy needs by solar means and that it was planning to expand this three-fold over the next twenty years. The country had allocated some C$125 million for the installation of solar systems in buildings, while a 3.8 MW wind turbine was due for completion during 1983. Given that Canada was deriving some two thirds of its electricity from its hydro resources (see Chapter 12), it seemed unlikely that it had included hydropower in its calculations of its solar income.

Britain's solar industry produced about 45,000 square metres of collectors in 1980. When visible and invisible exports were wrapped into the equation, the value of Britain's solar activities amounted to £25 million (or about $45 million), and the government had published estimates suggesting that by the end of the century renewable-energy technologies would account for energy equivalent to 40 million tonnes of coal (or 12 per cent of the country's energy budget in the early 1980s). Government expenditure on the renewables amounted to £13.6 million during the year 1981–2, but the projected budget for 1982–3 was a disappointing £11–12 million, while the lack of tax or other financial incentives for the installation of solar systems made Britain the odd country out among the developed nations.

West Germany, meanwhile, with more than 30 solar manufacturers, installed some 100,000 square metres of collectors in 1980, many of these systems incorporating heat pumps. A 3 MW wind turbine was under construction on the north coast, and the government was expecting to meet between 5 and 6 per cent of the country's energy needs by solar means by the year 2000.

The European Economic Community (EEC) had stated that its member countries could obtain perhaps 8 per cent of their energy from solar technologies by the end of the century, equivalent to nearly 2 million barrels of oil a day – or the output of Britain's sector of the North Sea. The new Commissioner for Energy, Vicomte Étienne Davignon, was hoping to double the EEC's budget for research, development and demonstration projects in the renewable-energy field by 1984 – to $200 million.

Israel was conducting a wide range of research and was constructing a 5 MW solar pond (of which more in Chapter 8). It reported that it had just passed a law to ensure that all new houses included solar-energy systems. Somewhat to the south, but worlds away as far as politics were concerned, Saudi Arabia had a $40 million solar-energy programme in operation at three main centres and was also involved in the $100 million SOLERAS project, in collaboration with the United States, focusing on solar cooling, desalination and photovoltaics.

Dr Guangzhou Chen Ru-Chen, a leading authority on that country's biomass-energy programme, reported that the world's most populous country was then deriving a quarter of its energy income, equivalent to 220 million tonnes of coal, from biomass schemes – and that in the previous six years it had built over 7 million biogas digesters (see Chapter 10) for homes, agriculture and industry. Some 100,000 square metres of solar collectors were in use, and China was beginning to devote a considerable research effort to solar energy generally.

The EEC, of course, is not a country, so we are left with one more country to make up the panel of eleven at the 1981 Solar World Forum. The United States was expected to spend an estimated $1.2 billion that year, when both industry and government spenders were considered, covering a host of solar, wind and gasohol projects. The export of solar equipment had reached $30 million in 1980, while in 1981 export sales by US manufacturers had passed this figure for exports to Europe alone.

But all was not well there. Indeed, the director of the Solar Energy Research Institute was claiming that the US Department of Energy had declared 'open war on solar energy'. A series of reverses suffered by the solar-energy lobby during 1981 and 1982, in fact, represented lost battles, but there were also some who argued that solar enthusiasts had lost the war too. Given that the United States has played what is indisputably a leading role in the development of renewable-energy technology, it is worth looking at recent developments there in rather more detail.

## Solar Wars

Asked in 1980 whether he thought his position as director of the federally-funded Solar Energy Research Institute (SERI) was vulnerable in the event of a Republican victory in the forthcoming presidential elections, Denis Hayes replied that 'laboratory directorships are outside the realm of politics. I certainly wasn't appointed for political reasons and I wouldn't expect to be fired for political reasons.' He went on to say: 'I have never heard of any laboratory director ever being fired by a new President.'

No one, apparently, told Ronald Reagan. He fired Hayes along with several hundred of his staff. Many observers had expected cuts, but few had expected the solar roof to fall in on Hayes like this. To understand why the incoming Reagan administration chose to take the axe to SERI, it helps to know something about SERI and something about Denis Hayes. Surrounded by huge deposits of oil, natural gas, coal, oil shale (see Chapter 4) and uranium, SERI is based in Golden, Colorado, Steve Ptacek's home town. Golden is on the outskirts of Denver, a burgeoning city which is now second only to Houston as the nation's energy capital. The Rocky Mountain region, for example, is thought to contain something like 90 per cent of the United States' uranium reserves and, just to the west of Denver, the oil-shale formations of the Green River Basin may yet prove to be the largest concentration of hydrocarbons in the world, although it remains to be seen whether they can be extracted economically.

Unabashed, SERI had grown rapidly, from fewer than 20 employees when it started operations in 1977 to 675 in 1980 – and a figure of 850 had been projected for 1981. Its budget, channelled through the Midwest Research Institute, based in Kansas City, had been expected to be in the region of $140 million that year, 25 per cent up on the 1980 figure. Booed publicly at SERI on his appointment, because of the Department of Energy's clumsy handling of the transition from outgoing founder-director Dr Paul Rappaport, Hayes had a fight on his hands from the start. Unlike Rappaport, who was an authority on photovoltaics, Hayes seemed an unlikely choice to take over the world's leading solar-energy research facility – which in 1980 received almost as much funding as the rest of the world's solar research efforts taken together.

A Stanford graduate who had earlier spent three years hitch-hiking around the world, Hayes had not come up the recognized solar ladders. After helping to launch Earth Day in 1970, an event which marked a turning point in America's thinking on ecological issues, he had founded Environmental Action, a lobbying group, and later ran the Illinois Office of Energy for governor Dan Walker. His solar interests surfaced when he joined the UN-funded Worldwatch Institute, where he wrote *Rays of Hope: Transition to a Post-Petroleum World* (W. W. Norton, 1977) and orchestrated Sun Day in 1978.

Adopting an unusually broad definition of solar energy, Denis Hayes argued that 20 per cent of the world's energy already comes from solar resources of one kind or another. Apart from direct sunlight, which can be harnessed by thermal or photovoltaic technologies, he also wrapped in wind, water and biomass, arguing that all three are, in effect, acting as solar-energy storage batteries. By the year 2000, he was convinced, renewable-energy sources could supply some 40 per cent of the global energy budget, and he concluded that a figure of 75 per cent was on the cards for 2025.

As Hayes himself said shortly after assuming the directorship of SERI in 1979, 'probably the most important characteristic I bring to this job is a lack of bashfulness'. Not an obvious qualification, nor indeed a particularly attractive one, as far as the Department of Energy – his ultimate employer – was concerned. Some of his critics, however, argued that his undoubted enthusiasm was being used to camouflage the Department of Energy's distinct lack of enthusiasm for solar energy.

Part of the problem, in retrospect, has been that there is a very wide range of opinion on what role government should play in developing solar energy. Hayes in fact had never argued that government could lead in the development of solar-energy technologies, although he indisputably felt that its role was crucially important. 'Government will be relatively important in defining the rules of the game,' he said, 'but it's more of a referee than a captain of the team. The market place for energy has been shaped largely by oil depletion allowances and by a whole series of tax advantages given to all extractive industries, including the coal industry.' Furthermore, he pointed out, 'there have been major subsidies for nuclear power, including the ordering of a very large number of light water reactors and the federal government is running the uranium enrichment program. It is not a market place in the sense that Adam Smith talks about. It's a market place in which the government has become rather intimately involved.'

Solar enthusiasts, Hayes among them, tried to prepare the ground for a possible Reagan victory. Solar energy, he told one reporter, 'is not an ideological issue. It's not an issue about which you can say all the liberals will support us or all the conservatives will support us. You just don't win any points by coming out against us. One of the strengths of solar energy is that it potentially gives a high degree of self-determination to local communities and different regions of the country. It allows a reassertion of some frontier elements in the American mentality. It is obviously attractive to people of a fairly conservative bent.'

Not attractive enough, though. Senator Barry Goldwater was one example of a right-wing solar convert, but the basic problem is that people of a fairly conservative bent generally prefer to see research and development being carried out by private industry rather than

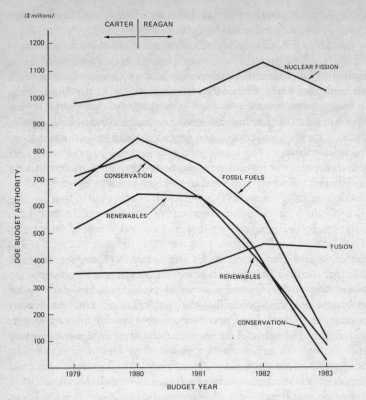

Figure 3.4: Trends in US federal energy funding (source: Subcommittee on Energy Conservation and Power, Committee on Energy and Commerce, US House of Representatives).

by the federal government. The resulting trends in federal funding once the Reagan administration took over are graphically obvious in Figure 3.4.

When I visited SERI, only days before President Reagan's cuts became public knowledge, Hayes was still confident that the government could be persuaded to see his sort of sense. Apart from working on hydrogen-producing microbes, photovoltaic cells, solar architecture and wind turbines, SERI had also focused on the vital role of energy conservation in the solar transition. Indeed, it was hoped that the so-called Sawhill Report, requested from SERI by Department of Energy deputy secretary John C. Sawhill, would put energy conservation on a more robust political footing.

Entitled *A New Prosperity: Building a Sustainable Energy Future* (Brick House, 1981), the report was seen by Hayes as an important building block in SERI's attempts to establish a bridge-head between solar energy and the energy mainstream. Like its British counterpart, *A Low Energy Strategy for the United Kingdom*, published by the International Institute for Environment and Development in 1979, the SERI report was designed to promote what Hayes dubbed 'conspicuous frugality'. But then the President swung his axe and SERI was directed away from the development of solar markets, back to long-range, laboratory-oriented research and development work.

## Eyeing the Bottom Line

Explaining the changes at SERI, a Department of Energy spokesman said that the idea was to 'pass the ball into the court of the private sector'. But is this a game that private industry will want to play without substantial government support? 'I would be the last to belittle the private sector's contribution,' Hayes had commented. 'Most of the important solar advances have been the result of private individuals and small firms having innovative ideas and developing them into commercial realities. Solar energy has begun to attract the attention of banks, insurance companies and electronics firms.'

But, he continued, 'very little of this private investment is being used to explore the solar frontiers. In part this is due to the state of the economy; high interest rates cause investors to focus on short-term horizons. In part, this is due to federal tax policies. And in rather large measure, I'm afraid, it is due to the fact that risk-taking entrepreneurs have been replaced in most corporate executive suites by unimaginative number-crunchers, who care only about next year's bottom line.'

One man who wanted to invest in solar energy was George Lucas, creator of the *Star Wars* film series. Having built up a personal fortune estimated at $100 million in just three years, Lucas set up his own venture-capital firm called the Egg Co., placing it in the hands of Charles Weber. But, although Weber put up with Lucas vetoes (for safety reasons) on a number of products vying for the *Star Wars* label, he and his staff found solar energy difficult to swallow. 'We don't want to go down the tubes with well-meaning investments,' he countered. 'It's easier just to make business decisions.'

And then there was Exxon's decision to sell its Daystar solar subsidiary. Daystar, which produced solar collectors for space and water heating, was sold to the Solar King Corporation, an infinitely smaller company than Exxon. Shortly afterwards, the Olin Corporation, another giant company, announced that it had decided to stop production of the copper plates it had previously sold to other manufacturers of solar collectors under the trade-name Solar-Bond. Two companies out of an industry estimated to comprise 360 companies in the USA hardly makes a statistical trend, but something was clearly going on.

'What is it about solar collectors,' solar commentator Barnaby Feder asked, 'that keeps the Exxons and Olins of this world from cruising in and crushing smaller competitors? Part of the answer,' he concluded, 'seems to be that they are very simple devices. Many consider solar energy as exotic and think of harnessing it as an immense technological challenge. Actually, that depends entirely on how the solar energy is captured and used. Building a satellite to capture the sun's energy in space and beam it down to earth is indeed a formidable technological problem. So is designing an inexpensive photovoltaic system that can efficiently transform solar energy into electricity.'

But, he pointed out, 'the most common collector, the flat-plate, liquid-transfer collector, is simply a shallow box with a glass or plastic top – and insulation on its bottom and sides. Inside, a plate, which is usually copper, absorbs the energy passing through the top and transfers the heat to a liquid mixture in tubes that run through or underneath the plate. The liquid, chemically related to anti-freeze, is then piped to a storage area or heat exchanger where it radiates into a house's heating or water system.' Or, to put it another way, thermal collectors of this type are well within the skills of any reasonably competent plumber.

The sort of company which thrives in this field is epitomized by Solar Economy, a small family firm which exhibited its wares at the 1981 Solar World Forum. Founded in 1975, Solar Economy in 1978 became part of the Wilmot Breedon Group, which, in turn, was taken over by yet another large American company, Rockwell Inc. Graham and Mary Holden, who had originally set up this British firm, successfully negotiated the reacquisition of their share of Solar Economy from Rockwell. Their customers, all of whom had bought solar water-heating systems, included British American Tobacco, the Dorset Area Health Authority, the John Lewis Group and Courage Breweries.

The larger companies, by contrast, have tended to concentrate in the high-technology areas, such as photovoltaic cell technology, and the oil companies have been particularly aggressive in this field. Arco Solar, which claimed to be the world's largest manufacturer of photo-voltaic cells, was a subsidiary of Atlantic Richfield, with other photo-voltaic operations being owned by companies like Mobil (see Figure 3.5), Total, Westinghouse and Pilkington Brothers – the British glass company which bought 80 per cent of Solec, a Californian firm, early in 1981. And Exxon still had solar subsidiaries after Daystar had gone, including the Solar Power Corporation, established in 1973, another photovoltaics producer.

Some analysts, like Christopher Flavin of the Worldwatch Institute, saw the Reagan axe as a major threat to future US participation in what he described as 'one of the most rapidly expanding energy sources – and one of the biggest growth industries – of the late twentieth century'. He pointed out that although US firms still have the most advanced solar cell technology, their share of the market fell from 80 per cent in 1980 to 55 per cent in 1982. The cuts in the US Federal photovoltaics budget, from $150 million in 1980 to about $50 million in 1983, would simply aggravate the trend, Flavin argued.

Britain's prime contender in the photovoltaics stakes was Lucas BP Solar Systems, a partnership between British Petroleum and solar pioneer Lucas which dated from early in 1981 – and ended in 1982, when Lucas pulled out and BP persevered with what then became BP Solar Systems. The new company had already delivered hundreds of systems to Algeria as part of one of the world's largest solar contracts. What the company called the largest-ever commercial contract, for $2.5 million worth of solar systems for radio telephones in the remoter regions of Colombia, South America, had been won by Lucas BP Solar Systems.

As Philip Wolfe, who was the company's general manager, ex-plained, 'solar electric systems are becoming cheaper all the time. They are now the most economical option for many remote electrical needs – tele-communications, navigational aids, railway crossings and so on. Recently we have seen prices fall to the level where more

# Prime mover.

Here comes the sun — shining hope of the alternative energy movement. And rightly so: it's the prime mover of most of our planet's energy.

At present, the world is largely dependent on the energy poured onto the earth by sunlight hundreds of millions of years ago — stored in fossil fuels: coal, oil and natural gas. For years, humanity has happily plundered that solar savings bank, mainly by running down the oil account.

As a result, we're entering the 1980s precariously balanced between tight oil supply and rising oil demand. We need alternatives urgently.

Coal is one. The world has plenty of it, but coal won't play a full part until it can be processed easily into liquid fuels which suit today's technology. Mobil has developed a way to convert coal-derived methanol into high-octane petrol; at present it's expensive, but we're trying to bring costs down.

Mobil is working on solar, too — with a new way to make silicon cells which convert sunlight directly into electricity. It's still a long-term project, but it looks like a pretty hot prospect for the future.

These efforts are part of a worldwide quest for viable alternative energy sources, including wind, tidal and wave power, biomass, geothermal, hydrogen and fusion. They're all still a long way from making a large-scale contribution — but hopes for the future rest on today's research.

Why should an oil company be developing alternatives to oil? Because we have unique expertise in energy; we're used to investing vast financial resources; and we're motivated: we, too, want to outlast the era of abundant oil.

We've every reason under the sun to be prime movers in alternative energy.

Last in a series on energy issues.
For a reprint of the complete series, please write to:
Energy Issues, Mobil Oil Company Ltd,
Mobil House, 54/60 Victoria Street, London SW1E 6QB

# Mobil

Figure 3.5: The oilman's view of solar energy? (Source: Mobil Oil.)

everyday uses are viable. Lights, pumps, televisions and fridges can now be used where mains power is not available.'

Having started out as components of space satellite power systems, photovoltaic cells are gradually coming down to earth, although they are still very much too expensive for most applications where they would be in direct competition with traditional forms of energy. As Arco Solar chairman Mr J. W. Yerkes explained, 'we're not competing with coal and nuclear plant so much as providing electricity to people who've never had it before.'

In fact, Paul MacCready's solar brainchild would never have got off the ground if NASA, the American space agency, had not agreed to loan the 16,000 photovoltaic cells he needed – which would otherwise have cost him $8 apiece. As it was, he had to spend some $35,000 just on wiring up and testing the cells. Freddy To, a solar aircraft designer whose *Solar One* achieved the first (if short) solar flight, has claimed that his company, Solar Powered Aircraft Developments, would have been across the Channel ahead of MacReady, if only he could have found the cells he needed without having to pay for them!

The solar market, like those for other fledgling industries such as microchip production or genetic engineering, has shown signs of developing into a muted repeat performance of the South Sea Bubble of 1720, a period of frenzied speculation prior to the collapse of the South Sea Company's over-valued stocks. Some solar investors have been busily counting their eggs before they are even fertilized, let alone hatched. Yet the next few decades will see the hatching of some highly profitable renewable-energy technologies. The industry as a whole may still be embryonic, its eventual outlines only vaguely discernible in the yolk; but its long-term future is assured.

Where, then, should venture-capital outfits like the Egg Co. invest their hard-won nest-eggs? Before turning to a close inspection of some of the latest solar technologies (see Table 3.1), however, we need to look at the non-solar competition. Despite Arco Solar's argument that it is not competing with the coal industry or the nuclear industry, no one who wants to know how long solar investments are going to take to incubate, or which of the nestlings will prove to be the long-term flyers, can afford to ignore the activities of the more established energy industries.

*Table 3.1: The development and potential utility of the new and renewable-energy technologies reviewed by UNERG (source: Earthscan)*

| Resource | Tech-nology | Eco-nomics | Potential utility North | South | Sun Traps Chapter |
|---|---|---|---|---|---|
| Heavy oil | 1 | 1 | 1 | 0 | 4 |
| Oil shale | 1 | 2 | 1 | 1 | 4 |
| Peat | 3 | 2 | 1 | 1 | 4/10 |
| Tar sand | 1 | 1 | 1 | 0 | 4 |
| Geothermal | 2 | 2 | 2 | 1 | 6 |
| Solar: | | | | | |
|   architecture | 2 | 3 | 3 | 3 | 7 |
|   water heaters | 3 | 3 | 2 | 1 | 7 |
|   cookers | 1 | 1 | 0 | 1 | 8 |
|   stills | 3 | 3 | 2 | 2 | 8 |
|   ponds | 2 | 2 | 1 | 2 | 8 |
|   pumps | 1 | 1 | 0 | 1 | 8 |
|   furnaces | 1 | 0 | 1 | 0 | 8 |
|   photovoltaics | 2 | 2 | 2 | 1 | 9 |
| Alcohol | 2 | 2 | 2 | 2 | 10 |
| Biogas | 2 | 2 | 0 | 2 | 10 |
| Fuelwood/charcoal | 3 | 3 | 1 | 3 | 10 |
| Oil-plants | 1 | 2 | 1 | 2 | 10 |
| Pyrolysis | 1 | 1 | 1 | 1 | 10 |
| Draught animals | 2 | 3 | 0 | 3 | 11 |
| Hydropower | 3 | 3 | 2 | 2 | 12 |
| Mini-hydro | 2 | 3 | 1 | 3 | 12 |
| Tidal power | 2 | 2 | 1 | 1 | 12 |
| Wave power | 0 | 1 | 0 | 1 | 12 |
| Wind power | 1 | 2 | 1 | 2 | 13 |

| Key | |
|---|---|
| *Technology:* | 0 = rudimentary; 1 = pilot stage; 2 = well developed; 3 = fully developed |
| *Economics:* | 0 = highly expensive; 1 = possibly competitive one day; 2 = potentially or sometimes competitive; 3 = competitive now |
| *Potential utility* | 0 = no likely utility in the foreseeable future; 1 = may be usable in a few countries; 2 = may be usable in many countries; 3 = of widespread use |

# Assessing
# the Competition

# 4 ☉ Buried Sunshine

'Trying to forecast oil demand, supply and price in today's market is like trying to paint the wings of an airplane in flight,' Exxon president Howard Kauffman complained as oil prices slumped in the early 1980s. 'Even if one succeeds in covering the subject, it's unlikely to be a tidy job.' The world's oil companies are likely to spend an unprecedented £1,370 billion during the 1980s on projects designed to ensure they survive in the post-oil era. This figure covers the finding and opening up of new oil-fields, pipeline projects and the development of alternative energy sources, including synthetic fuels. When all these activities are counted into the equation and the financing costs are added, the total projected cost rises to £1,749 billion, according to the Chase Manhattan Bank.

In assessing the solar prospect, it is vitally important to try and get some idea of the prospects for oil. Abundant fossil fuels have induced what one might dub the 'Butch Cassidy Syndrome' in all

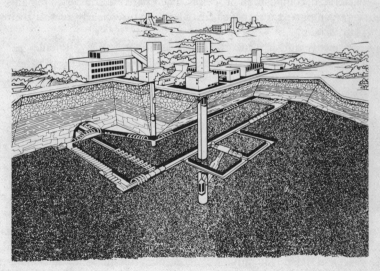

Figure 4.1: A modern coalmine (source: National Coal Board).

the developed nations – and in most developing nations too. This syndrome is perhaps best summarized by the following question: Why earn a living when you can rob the bank?

The planet's fossil fuels represent our solar deposit account. The connection is clearest if we consider the timber which fuelled the human species through the first stages of its industrial evolution. Sunlight powers the process of photosynthesis, which is covered in more detail in Chapter 10. Photosynthesis, in turn, involves the assembly of complex carbon-based organic molecules from simple raw materials such as water and carbon dioxide. When a log burns in the hearth, the heat which pours out can, in simple terms, be seen as sunshine escaping from the prison represented by the chemical bonds in those carbon-based compounds.

Coal, which increasingly replaced wood and charcoal as our main fuel, is slightly more tricky. The world's major coal seams began to form some 320 million years ago, in the wake of the evolution of the first land plants. During several hundred million years, the prevailing climate favoured the formation of vast swamps in which seed ferns and non-flowering trees flourished, capturing and storing solar energy. When these died, they slipped beneath the surface of the swamp, whose waters typically were starved of oxygen, slowing bacterial decomposition processes. Their partly decomposed remains were compacted into peat beds whose texture clearly reveals their plant origins.

Whereas timber's energy content is about 19,770 kilojoules per kilogram, peat's energy content is about 18,663. Most of the peat-beds we are exploiting today have been laid down in the last 10,000 years, forming in Europe at the rate of 20–80 cm every 1,000 years. The world's peat reserves are estimated at about 420 million hectares (1.6 million square miles), although poorly surveyed areas may well raise that figure to over 500 million hectares (1.9 million square miles).

This area of peatland is roughly equivalent to the area of the Indian subcontinent, or the whole of Europe west of the USSR, or half the area of the USA. North America, northern Europe and the USSR have the largest reserves, but peat formations are found in many parts of the world. The USSR is thought to be by far the largest peat producer, accounting for 80 million tons a year, and contributing nearly 90 per cent of world output. Finland (at 3.1 million tons a year) and Ireland (5.6 million tons) account for almost all the remaining output. Table 4.1 shows that fuel-peat production nearly doubled between 1950 and 1980.

*Table 4.1: Fuel-peat production in 1950 and 1980 (in 000s of tons at 40% moisture content; source: Earthscan)*

| Country | 1950 | 1980 |
| --- | --- | --- |
| USSR | 45,000 | 80,000 |
| Ireland | 300 | 5,600 |
| Finland | 300 | 3,100 |
| China | — | 800 |
| Sweden | 100 | — |
| Others (estimated) | 1,000 | 400 |
| Total | 46,700 | 89,900 |

A fuller account of the peat strategies of a number of countries can be found in Chapter 10. For the moment, however, our interest turns to the strange, albeit highly useful, transformation which those early peat-beds underwent – a process which considerably enhanced their energy content. As the land sank or the polar ice-caps melted, primeval seas washed in across many peat-beds, and thick sediments formed, pressing down on to the layers of peat and other material. Subjected to these pressures, and to the associated temperatures, the peat began its slow transmutation into coal.

First, it changed into lignite, which has an energy content of some 27,200 kilojoules per kilogram, representing a 45-per cent improvement on the original peat. Second, where the geological changes were such as to impose even greater pressures and temperatures, the lignite turned into various grades of bituminous coal, and in some places it underwent a further transformation into a lustrous black material, anthracite, which is nearly pure carbon – and has an energy content of some 32,560 kilojoules per kilogram, only slightly higher than bituminous coal at 32,100 kilojoules.

This change from peat into coal involves an increasing carbon content and decreasing concentrations of both moisture and volatile organic matter. Peat and lignite yield less energy partly because they contain more of such substances as cellulose and lignins, partly because they contain more water, and partly because they are less compacted than are either bituminous coal or anthracite.

Towards the end of the Carboniferous era, that period of peak solar banking on earth, which lasted for some 65 million years some 345–280 million years ago, coal 'measures' were laid down in vast quantities – a period now known as the Pennsylvanian in North America and the Westphalian in Europe. These seams of 'black gold' account for perhaps 80 per cent of the world's known coal reserves.

In what might be called the planet's 'black belt', a great band of coal was laid down in what is now central and eastern North America, Scotland south of the Highlands, England, Wales, France, the Lowlands, Germany and Poland – and thence eastwards across the USSR and China. Among later coal measures, perhaps the most important were laid down in what were to become eastern Australia, India, Antarctica and South Africa, which were all part of the same continent some 250–200 million years ago.

Even more recently, coal began to form in such widely dispersed places as the foothills of the Canadian Rockies, in New Mexico, along the Rhine Valley and in south-east Europe. These coals, however, belong to the last 50 million years and have not yet had time to form high-value coals, being found instead as lignite and brown coals. The prospects for increased coal use are discussed later on in this chapter and in Chapter 14. But, first, a word or two about the fossil fuel which toppled coal as the world's leading fuel only a few decades ago: oil.

## Four-star Rain?

One explanation for oil's formation, offered by the Dutch-born botanist Fritz Went in 1960, when he was director of the Missouri Botanical Gardens, was that the blue haze of resinous fumes given off by plants, and especially by such plants as sagebrush, conifers and eucalypts, rose high enough into the atmosphere to be altered by the action of ultra-violet light. It then, he proposed, fell back to earth as rain and accumulated in petroleum reservoirs. Nowadays Went's theory receives short shrift.

Hydrocarbons, it is generally accepted, are composed of different combinations of carbon and hydrogen, ranging from simple methane, which is a major constituent of natural gas, through heavy, viscous oils which have to be heated to flow, to complex molecular compounds – such as the kerogen found in oil shale. Whereas coal was formed from terrestrial plant material, oil was produced over millions of years by the decay of organisms which sank to the bottom of ancient seas and were buried as oil-saturated sediments under later rock formations.

Natural gas has similar origins and is often found closely associated with major oil deposits. For years, however, it was seen as a useless by-product and either vented to the atmosphere or flared. In 1973, for example, Saudi Arabia flared an estimated 14 billion cubic metres of gas, the equivalent of 12 million tonnes of oil. In fact the Middle East gas flares and the Great Wall of China were the first evidence of man sighted by at least one returning crew of astronauts.

Before turning to the prospects for oil, a brief account of the natural gas prospect is in order. Natural gas has, in fact, become a significant source of energy in many countries; indeed the USA was already obtaining nearly a third of its energy from gas at the time of the first oil crisis. The discovery in 1959 of the giant Groningen gas field in the Netherlands radically changed energy-consumption patterns there, focusing attention on the energy potential of the North Sea. Some economists argue that the flaring of Middle East gas, while it may be a resource loss, is not an economic loss, because the development of Middle East oil would have been delayed by 20 to 30 years if the oil companies had been forced to wait until they could simultaneously extract the gas. But increasing attention is now being paid to the gas prospect.

The fact that El Paso, a Houston-based pipeline company, was losing $7 million a month during 1980 – and was eventually forced to take a $365 million write-off – is an indication of the difficulties involved in using gas. The problem here was that Algeria, whose gas El Paso had been shipping to the USA in six giant liquefied-natural-gas tankers, insisted on renegotiating the price. Another long-running debate involved the proposed £2.7 billion gas-gathering pipeline for the North Sea, vetoed by Britain's Treasury. The veto came as a blow to BP, British Gas and Mobil, all of which had been closely involved in the project's planning – although BP fought on, in the hope that it could serve as an honest broker between the various organizations whose commitment was vital for the pipeline's future.

At about the same time, too, the USA was getting increasingly worried about Western Europe's plans to triple its imports of natural gas from the USSR, arguing that its allies would be forced by their energy dependence on the USSR into a process of subtle 'Finlandization'. With about a third of the world's natural-gas reserves, the Soviet Union was that rarity, a producer willing to run down its reserves in exchange for foreign currency. It also, quite clearly, had a vested interest in weaning Europe away from its high degree of dependence both on the Middle East's oil and on the USA's policies in that turbulent area.

The USA was also looking at ways in which it could increase the flow of natural gas into its homes and factories. Under the headline 'Buddy, Could You Spare $22 Billion?', the *Wall Street Journal* reported that John McMillan, chairman of Northwest Energy, a Salt Lake City-based natural-gas transmission company, was looking for a $22 billion first instalment towards the construction of a 4,800-mile gas pipeline to bring gas from Alaska south to Chicago and San Francisco. Exxon, Atlantic Richfield and Standard Oil, the oil companies which owned most of the natural gas at Prudhoe Bay, were all in favour, and so, it seemed, were the big banks. 'We're in uncharted waters,' said a top official of one of the banks. 'The scope of this is absolutely enormous and it will take quite an effort to get it done, but I think it's do-able.'

The level of expenditure being discussed for such energy projects has been such that many economists have seen it as the bright hope for an end to the economic recession, and there are a considerable number of scientists who believe that the energy prospect is itself bright – even for oil and natural gas. Some have been pursuing the implications of plate tectonics – or the theory of 'continental drift'. Research into the magnetic fields in cores drilled from beneath the so-called Western Overthrust Belt, in states like Utah and Wyoming, suggests that North America has overridden more than 4,000 miles of the Pacific floor, with ancient North American rock layers being superimposed on layers of much younger sedimentary material, forming enormous traps conducive to the formation of natural gas and oil from the remains of ancient life embedded in those layers of oceanic sediment.

Probably the strangest, but potentially the most revolutionary, theory about the origin of the planet's methane resources was that being advanced by Professor Tom Gold. If Gold proves right, as he himself has modestly put it, 'the entire fuel crisis will soon be a thing of the past' – a claim made by a not inconsiderable number of those trying to recruit investment in the energy field.

Gold, who had correctly predicted that the surface of the moon would be covered with dust, 'Gold dust' as it came to be known (although it did not, as he had expected, swallow lunar landers), had also been responsible, with Sir Hermann Bondi and Sir Fred Hoyle, for the 'steady-state' theory of cosmology, in addition to the work he had done on such diverse areas as the electroacoustical system of the inner ear, the stability of the earth's axis of rotation, and the plasma physics of solar outbursts.

He had become interested in the possibility that much of the planet's methane might have a non-biological origin. He pointed out that the earth's primitive atmosphere was largely composed of methane, which suited early life-forms very well indeed. This methane, it is thought, came up from the depths of the planet, which had itself condensed out of a hydrogen-saturated nebula. Since most of the carbon found in meteorites is in the form of complex hydrocarbons, with some chemical similarity to oil tars, it is reasonable to suppose that our planet too had a vast primordial supply of such hydrocarbons. Buried under conditions of intense pressure and heat, they may have liberated methane, which, in turn, made its way towards the surface of the planet.

Anyone who has poked a sensor down a volcano will probably have found high concentrations of carbon dioxide, and it has therefore been assumed that most of the carbon found on earth was formed from carbon dioxide, a product of volcanic action. But, Gold argues, carbon dioxide can also be produced by the oxidization of methane. If you take this together with the observation that earthquakes are often accompanied by strange booms and lights in the sky, which Gold suggests result from methane outgassing stimulated by the tremors, then the chances are that methane has been streaming up from the earth's core more or less since it was formed.

The upshot of all this, according to Gold, is that there must be gigantic reservoirs of this deep-earth methane trapped far beneath our feet. Some of it may have been enriching reservoirs of natural gas or seams of coal, but it will also be found where there are no deposits of coal, oil or natural gas. Asked where he expected this methane to be found, Gold replied that his theory suggested that it would be found 'in very convenient regions, but at considerable depths. Gas needs to be sealed by a tighter cap than oil does, and so it tends to be found deeper down, where there are more tightly packed layers.'

Very little of the earth, he points out, has been explored to a depth of 4,000 metres, where the gas is most likely to be found. 'We should begin,' he says, 'by searching where we'd most like the gas to be. New England, for example, is very short of fuel, California is a good prospect. There the oil is shallower, but no-one has looked very seriously deeper down for gas. If you want gas in a certain city, then search first in the vicinity of that city. In many areas it might turn out much like drilling for water – you build a house and drill there in the first place – except that you'll have to drill to four or five or even seven thousand metres for methane.'

But, while energy companies may finally switch to deep-earth gas as oil runs out, if it exists in the quantities which Gold is suggesting, for the moment oil is still the order of the day. Total consumption of petroleum products worldwide, but excluding the USSR, Eastern Europe and China, rose from 488 million tonnes in 1960, the year Went came up with his petroleum rain theory, to 2.34 billion tonnes by 1973 – the year the Organization of Petroleum Exporting Countries (OPEC) first broke through into the consciousness of the oil-consumer in the street.

## Oil's 'Unrepeatable Offer'

'From Maine to California', one author wrote in 1865, just a few years after Edwin Drake struck oil along the banks of Pennsylvania's Oil Creek, launching the world into the oil era, that previously ignored substance 'lights our dwellings, lubricates our machinery, and is indispensable in numerous departments of arts, manufactures and domestic life. To be deprived of it now would be setting us back a whole cycle of civilization. To doubt the increased sphere of its usefulness would be to lack faith in the progress of the world.'

Until 1973, the oil companies had achieved near-miracles in managing the supply of that vital commodity to world markets. One man who got deep inside the oil industry's skin was Anthony Sampson, whose book *The Seven Sisters* (updated Coronet edition, 1980) gave an excellent idea of the way the oil industry thinks. 'Through nationalisations in Mexico or Iran, revolution in Iraq, wars in the Middle East,' he wrote, the major oil companies (the 'seven sisters' of his title) had 'successfully maintained the steady flow of oil, increasing never too fast to make the market collapse, never too slow to make consumers go short. If anyone was expert in the subject of controlling supplies, it was not OPEC but they.'

It was easy, Sampson noted, for oilmen to feel like the Lords of Creation, in firm control of all they surveyed. Describing Exxon's headquarters in Manhattan, he spoke of fluted stone ribs soaring straight up for fifty-three storeys, behind a bubbling fountain and pool facing on to Sixth Avenue and, inside, 'the high entrance hall is hung with moons. On the twenty-fourth floor is the mechanical brain of the company, where the movements of its vast cargoes are recorded.'

A row of TV screens, visual display units linked with two giant computers, monitored the movement of 500 Exxon ships sailing between 115 loading ports and some 270 destinations, carrying 160 different kinds of Exxon oil. It was, Sampson recalled, 'an uncanny process to watch: a girl taps out a question on the keyboard, and the answer comes back in little green letters on the screen, with the names of ships, dates and destinations across the world. From the peace of the twenty-fourth floor it seems like playing God – a perfectly rational and omniscient god, surveying the world as a single market.'

Gods, however, can be toppled from their thrones. Exxon, which ranks as the world's largest oil company, was the largest single fragment to emerge from the break-up of the old Standard Oil corporation by anti-trust forces. Of all the oil companies, it is most closely associated with the Rockefeller name and it still wields power far beyond that available to most nation states. But today it surveys a very different world.

Immersed in a tide of oil wealth, people forgot – if, indeed, they ever knew – that they were spending energy capital accumulated over many millions of years, that they were exploiting Nature's literally 'unrepeatable offer'. One of the first sirens to sound came from within Shell Oil. One of the company's geologists, M. King Hubbert, was working early in 1956 on a paper to be delivered at a conference sponsored by the American Petroleum Institute. Hubbert's basic concern centred on the exponential rate of growth in the consumption of oil. He decided to go public.

At that time, America's ultimately recoverable oil resources were estimated to be some 150 billion barrels, whereas it had 'only' consumed 50 billion barrels during the first hundred years of the oil industry's existence – *ergo*, it was commonly believed, the industry still had a good deal of room to manoeuvre and over a hundred years to go before the barrel began to run dry.

Not so, said Hubbert. He showed that geological exploration and resource discovery typically follow a predictable pattern, that 'in the production of any resource of fixed magnitude, the production rate must begin at zero, and then after passing one or several maxima, it must decline again to zero'. The heart of his argument was contained in an illustration showing a production curve for petroleum plotted against a grid, with each grid square representing 25 billion barrels of oil. If the figure of 150 billion barrels were accepted, then all the country's domestic oil production could only ever cover six grid squares. By 1956, Hubbert pointed out, oil represented by two squares had been consumed. When three squares had been covered by the production curve, it followed, half of the nation's oil would be gone, and production, inevitably, would begin to decline.

Hubbert's best estimate was that the third square would be covered within ten years. Even if the recoverable oil amounted to 200 billion barrels, an increase on original estimates equivalent to the total output of eight new fields the size of the enormous Texas field, the halfway point in production would only be delayed by five years or so.

This forecast, that the USA would reach an all-time peak in its domestic oil production after which it could confidently be predicted that production would fall back to zero, burst like a bombshell in the boardroom. Shell, having read through the paper, asked Hubbert to delete the 'sensational' portion of his talk, but he refused to do so. And his voice was joined by others. Five years later, for instance, E. F. Schumacher, best-known for his book *Small is Beautiful* (Blond & Briggs, 1973), gave a lecture in Britain predicting an oil crisis and warning that world demand for coal would eventually soar. But Schumacher was then the National Coal Board's economic adviser and his warnings were discounted as coal propaganda. Neither Hubbert nor Schumacher succeeded in slowing the pace of oil consumption; but OPEC did.

## A Birth in Baghdad

No star hung in the sky over the seedy Cairo conference hall in which OPEC was conceived in 1960. 'OPEC,' one Kuwaiti explained, 'couldn't have happened without the oil cartel. We just took a leaf from the oil companies' book. The victim had learned the lesson.' But the five countries which attended that meeting would have been quite content to have squeezed a few extra cents out of the oil companies for every 35-gallon barrel of oil they sold.

By the end of the 1950s, the Seven Sisters were in trouble. The Suez fiasco, coupled with growing nationalism in the Middle East and the rise of a new class of Arab oil technocrats quite able to understand the complex workings of the oil market, compounded the pressures exerted by the rise of new independent oil companies (such as Armand Hammer's Occidental) and the export of cheap oil by the USSR. Although they still dominated the top dozen slots in the listing of the world's biggest companies, the Seven Sisters felt that the time had come to make some hard decisions.

But the oil price cuts they attempted to force through incensed the oil producers, and Iraq called on the other parties to the Cairo agreement to act. A historic conference was rapidly convened in Baghdad. Explaining Iran's decision to go to Baghdad, the ill-fated Shah of Iran said that it was not so much the price cut he minded, but the fact that, yet again, the oil companies had not consulted him before making the cuts.

The political environment in which OPEC was conceived is indicated by the fact that one of the six countries represented at the Baghdad conference, Qatar, did not become a founder member of OPEC. Venezuela, Iran, Iraq, Saudi Arabia and Kuwait all joined, but Qatar had to ask the permission of the British political agent before joining. As Frank Parra, the Venezuelan who became OPEC's secretary-general in 1968, recalled, 'the political agent generously gave it, confident that an organization that grouped Persians, Arabs and Latins wouldn't come to anything'.

OPEC's first achievement, involving a $3\frac{1}{2}$–$5\frac{1}{2}$-per-cent increase on a barrel of oil in 1965, was relatively small beer, yet, as Parra put it some years later, 'it was considered evidence of a potentially dangerous Mafia, the Cosa Nostra of the international petroleum industry'. Then, in February 1971, OPEC achieved a 35-cents-a-barrel increase, and the world's headlines brayed: 'West held to ransom!'

But the real clincher came with the overthrow of the corrupt regime of King Idris of Libya by the hitherto unknown Colonel Qadhafi. Libya had already opened up its oil resources to some of the independent oil companies which were snapping at the heels of the Seven Sisters, and Qadhafi decided to pick off the weakest companies first. Occidental (Oxy) was first to wander into his sights and, having been turned down by Esso (later Exxon) when he asked for financial support to outflank Qadhafi, Dr Armand Hammer gave in to Libyan demands. The oil companies had broken ranks and, with the Gulf States promptly demanding similar rises, the leapfrogging had begun.

When OPEC called an extraordinary meeting on 3 February 1971, it forced the hand of the oil industry once again, with a succession of oil ministers standing up and solemnly declaring that their governments would enact legislation enforcing a 35-cent price increase and embargoing those companies which failed to comply. The resulting settlement brought over a billion dollars into OPEC's coffers each year and, as one delegate put it in words which would soon echo around the world: 'We have the companies – how you say it? – over a barrel.'

The Tehran agreement was meant to last five years, but Libya had tasted blood and promptly leapfrogged again. With rising oil demand, the oil producers were in an increasingly strong position. Then, in December 1971, Libya nationalized BP's share of a joint venture with Nelson Bunker Hunt, and the ball was rolling with a vengeance. The Iraqi Petroleum Company was nationalized in 1972, and Saudi Arabia took a 25-per-cent share holding in the Aramco consortium of American oil companies, to rise eventually to 51 per cent. And little Kuwait promptly upstaged them all by winning control of 60 per cent of its own oil industry. The 1973 Arab-Israeli war, the first oil shock, the ensuing recession in the West, the Iranian revolution, the Iran–Iraq war and the oil glut are all a matter of historical record, as are the impacts of the windfall profits from oil on the OPEC economies.

By 1980, however, when OPEC celebrated its twenty-first birthday, the oil glut had raised a question-mark over its future prospects. Figures 4.2 and 3 give the demand and supply picture as seen by one major oil company, BP. In its anniversary message, OPEC reminded the world that the oil companies and their 'regime of injustice and humiliation' had led to the organization's formation. And detractors in the oil-consuming countries were reminded that, 'while some oil price adjustments had undeniably come as a shock to consumers, their purpose has been only to correct a long-standing, dangerous under-valuation of this vital resource.'

Few intelligent analysts can have had much to quarrel with in the underlying logic of OPEC's argument, although the message's gruff and unusually defensive tone hinted at the changes which had taken place in the intervening years – raising the question: would OPEC survive?

The oil producers were certainly in disarray over pricing in the face of the continuing oil glut. At one end of the spectrum were the North African 'hawks', with Qadhafi prominent among them, who had traditionally sought to exploit short-term market advantages, but had been finding it increasingly difficult to find the $41 a barrel they wanted at the time. Saudi Arabia, at the other end of the spectrum, had been maintaining its output at artificially high levels to support the West, in which the Saudis had invested heavily.

Whereas, in 'normal' times, the OPEC countries would have had a production capacity of 31 million barrels a day, they were then selling only 25 million or so, leaving a surplus – even though two producers, Iran and Iraq, were at each other's throats and their production was drastically reduced. Some economists were arguing that OPEC was losing its ability to call the energy tune, even though it had managed to boost oil prices by some 1,500 per cent since late 1973. But, as Sheikh Ali Khalifa al Sabah put it when emerging from a particularly traumatic meeting, quoting Mark Twain: 'Reports of our death are greatly exaggerated.' By early 1983, however, purchases of OPEC oil were running at only 15 million barrels a day – and the pressure to drop prices below the $30-a-barrel mark was intense.

## The Yamani Calculus

'You think that our oil is in your strategic interest,' said Sheikh Yamani to one American reporter. 'The Soviets may some day, when they become net oil importers, think that our oil is in their strategic interests. The colonial era,' he continued, 'is gone forever. We are masters of our own affairs, and we will decide what to do with our oil.'

These words, however, seemed rather more optimistic than Yamani had intended them to be in the light of a number of developments inside Saudi Arabia. On 20 November 1979, for example, while some 50,000 worshippers gathered at Mecca's Sacred Mosque to celebrate the beginning of Islam's 1,400th year, they were rudely interrupted in their dawn prayers by a group of about 350 armed men. The ensuing, fiercely fought engagement resulted in the death of the self-proclaimed *mahdi*, Muhammad ibn Abdullah al-Qahtani, in the

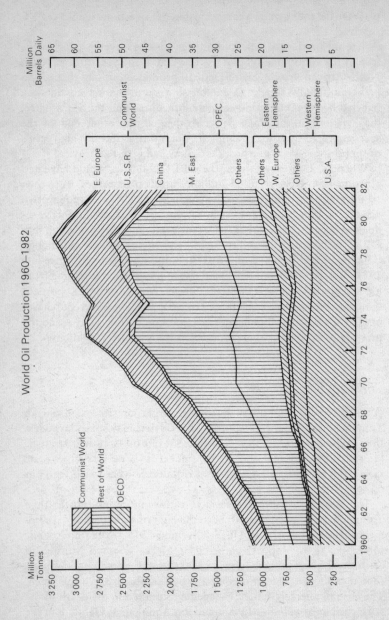

World Oil Production 1960–1982

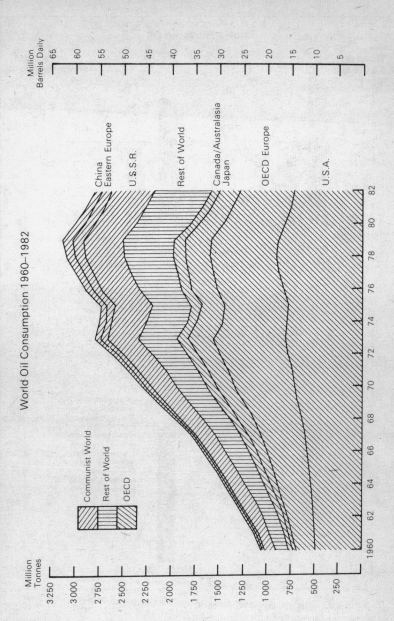

World Oil Consumption 1960–1982

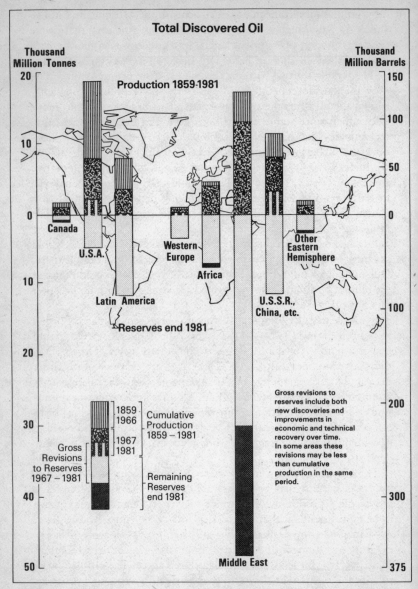

Figure 4.3: Total discovered oil, showing production 1859–1981 and reserves at the end of 1981 (source: B P).

labyrinthine subterranean passages beneath the Mosque, and it also shook the Saudi regime to its very foundations. And then there were the assassination of President Sadat, Iran's successes in its war with Iraq and the incursions of Israel into Lebanon to be contended with.

The rapidly shifting patterns thrown up – and promptly discarded – by the kaleidoscope of Middle Eastern power politics constantly caught the oil companies wrong-footed, encouraging them to move into rather more stable areas like Alaska and the North Sea, into technologies like shale-oil extraction and into completely new, non-oil areas of business like mining. As Yamani himself had said, 'if we force Western countries to invest heavily in finding alternative sources of energy, they will. This would take no more than seven to ten years and would result in reducing dependence on oil as a source of energy to a point which will jeopardize Saudi Arabia's interests.'

Or, as one oil man put it: 'If I were advising the Saudis, I would get them to push the price down as far as possible and hold it there. Our company would simply be forced to buy oil, as we couldn't invest the billions of dollars involved in alternative energy with no prospect of a pay off.'

Evidence that the Yamani calculus was beginning to pay off began to pour in during 1981 and 1982 as the oil companies started to pull out of a number of major alternative-energy projects. The implications for investment in renewable-energy sources are explored later in the book; the remainder of this chapter will review the oil industry's attempts to secure new sources of oil. This has involved new exploration efforts, often in extremely hostile environments such as the North Sea or the Beaufort Sea, and it has also involved attempts to develop new methods for extracting oil from heavy oil, tar sand and oil-shale deposits.

The significance of some of these new oil resources is indicated by the fact that it has been estimated that the heavy oil contained in a single deposit along the Orinoco River in Venezuela may prove to be more abundant than the oil deposits of the entire Middle East. As Table 4.2 shows, smaller but still significant deposits of heavy oil occur in a number of developing countries – including Colombia, Madagascar, Morocco, Peru, Senegal and Turkey. The problem with such heavy oils is that they cost a great deal to extract. Investment costs for heavy-oil extraction have been calculated at between $15,000 and $25,000 per daily barrel, compared with a figure of around

$10,000 for high-cost conventional oil operations such as those in the North Sea.

Table 4.2: World heavy oil reserves (in billion barrels; source: World Bank figures assembled by Earthscan)

| Venezuela | 2,050 |
|---|---|
| Canada | 700–1,800 |
| Iran | 50 |
| Iraq | 50 |
| USA | 29 |
| Kuwait | 15 |
| Mexico | 3.5 |
| Syria | 3 |
| Ecuador | 1–5 |
| Colombia | 1–5 |
| Ivory Coast | 1–5 |
| Oman | 2 |
| Peru | 1.5 |
| Total (approximate) | 3,500 |

While world reserves of heavy oil, which has to be heated or burned if it is to be extracted (an inefficient process, with perhaps only 10–15 per cent of the oil extracted, even with enhanced oil-recovery methods), are several times those of commercial crudes, the picture looks even brighter if tar sands and shale oil are wrapped into the equation. Tar sands are an exaggerated form of heavy oil. It is thought that tar sands, which are typically trapped in sand or sandstones, originated in normal oil deposits from which the lighter fractions evaporated over time. World tar-sand reserves are estimated to be about one and a half times those of flowing oil. Venezuela's Orinoco region may contain 150–450 billion tonnes of this sticky, asphaltic oil in tar-sand seams up to 30 metres thick; Canada has the largest known reserves – around 160 billion tonnes.

The only way to extract tar sand is to strip-mine it, with something like two tonnes of tar sand needed to produce one barrel (42 US gallons or 159 litres) of oil. The tar is removed from the sand by mixing it with hot water and steam, a process which requires at least as much water, in terms of volume, as the tar sand being processed. Further processing is then needed to produce a product which will travel through pipelines and meet the demand for low-sulphur fuels.

Apart from the problem of water availability, such operations can have a very significant impact on the environment, even if they are well managed. Subarctic ecosystems are fragile and have slow recovery rates, with water and air pollution compounding the effects of the strip-mining itself. Canada, the only country which had pushed ahead with operational, large-scale tar-sand projects, opened its first major plant in the Athabasca region of Alberta in 1967 and had been planning to produce as much as 50 million tonnes of tar-sand oil, equivalent to about half of Canada's needs, by 1990.

But then the Yamani calculus paid off. Early in 1982, Shell led the exodus of the last three of the original eight partners from the C$13 billion (£6 billion) Alsands tar-sand project. Had it gone ahead, the Alsands project would have produced about 130,000 barrels of oil a day, or 8 per cent of Canada's total oil demand – at the high cost of C$60 a barrel. A similar project at Cold Lake, Alberta, had already been postponed indefinitely by the Exxon subsidiary Imperial Oil.

The collapse of a growing number of the leading-edge synfuels (shorthand for synthetic fuels) projects forced countries such as Canada to think harder about strategies for increasing the flow of conventional oil from areas outside the Middle East. Before looking in more detail at the oil-shale industry, which is probably the clearest example of what has been going wrong with the synfuels industry, a few words about the efforts of the oil industry to find new supplies of conventional oil in non-OPEC countries.

## The Iceberg Dodgems

'This,' claimed a Texan oilman while visiting Urumqi, capital of China's Xinjiang Autonomous Region in the far west of that country, 'is going to dwarf Saudi Arabia.' He was investigating the oil resources of the Tarim Basin and indulging in the exaggeration for which Texans are well known, but China's onshore and offshore oil resources may yet prove very significant – for the Chinese, at least. The oil-fields tend to be remote from the centres of population, even in such a populous country, and suffer from a harsh climate.

All over the world people have been bumping into oilmen drilling in the most unlikely places, the first evidence most of them have had that petrol does not spontaneously leap into existence in the entrails of the pumps on the forecourt of their local filling-station. Many developing countries, whose economies have been buffeted by rising oil prices, have been expending a considerable effort on tracking down domestic supplies. India, for example, was producing about 240,000 barrels a day by OPEC's twenty-first birthday, but it was consuming far more, an estimated 675,000 barrels a day. Some such countries, including China, have been inviting the multinational companies back in to help with oil exploration and development, presumably calculating that a degree of foreign influence is preferable to energy starvation.

Few have found themselves as well endowed as Mexico, however, whose oil reserves are now believed to rank second only to those of Saudi Arabia. Most of Mexico's oil comes from the Gulf of Mexico, where the Bay of Campeche has been the world's fastest-growing oil-field. 'We have to husband our resources carefully,' said the country's industry minister. 'When the oil runs out we want to be left with the infrastructure of a modern industrial state.' Some would say that this is rather like preferring to be stranded in a Lincoln Continental rather than in a perfectly functional ox-cart. But, whatever the case, as the Shah of Iran found to his cost, this is easier

Figure 4.4: The US oil industry's view of the constraints on its domestic operations (source: Dresser Industries, Inc.).

said than done – and there has been worrying evidence that Mexico's oil income is eroding its agricultural and manufacturing industries, that its economy is, to use its own term, becoming 'petrolized'. The reverse side of the coin is that a drop in the world price can push countries like Mexico, with considerable development programmes to support, to the verge of national bankruptcy.

And the oilmen are running up against severe environmental constraints in many of their new prospecting areas (the oil industry's perspective on the problem is hinted at in Figure 4.4). In Britain's beauty spots, for example, the arguments centre around the question whether it makes sense to 'sacrifice' the Cotswolds, the Yorkshire Dales or the New Forest to onshore oil exploration and development. Shell Oil, which wanted to prospect in the New Forest, ran into problems when environmentalists learned that the oil it expected to find might only keep Britain in oil for 3–10 days, although a Shell spokesman also admitted that the company might spend £1 million and find a 'big fat zero'.

But perhaps the severest environmental constraints oilmen face come not from environmentalists, but from the environment itself, as the industry drives northwards into ever more hostile conditions,

from the turbulent North Sea to the ice-locked Beaufort Sea. Dome Petroleum, Canada's most adventurous (some would say recklessly over-extended) oil company in the early 1980s, had found gas or oil at all of the Beaufort Sea sites where it had drilled to a depth of about 6,000 feet (1,829 metres). By comparison, only one hole in five drilled in the North Sea struck hydrocarbons. The basic problem, however, is ice – and, more particularly, ice in motion.

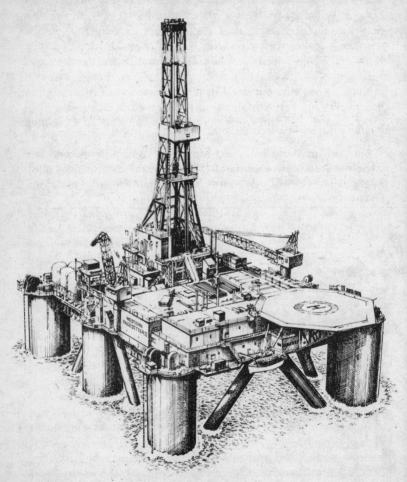

Figure 4.5: Offshore oil-rig (source: Ultramar).

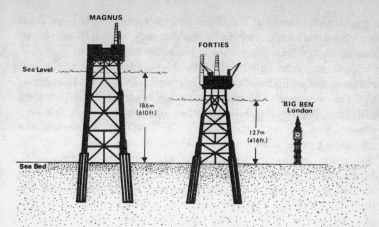

Figure 4.6: Comparison of Magnus and Forties oil platforms with London's Big Ben (source: BP).

Dome's discoveries are 50–60 miles out to sea in the so-called (and extremely treacherous) 'shear zone'. In early October, the temperature of the sea-water falls below freezing point and a sheet of ice about 6 feet (nearly 2 metres) thick starts to form along the coast and stretch northwards. At the same time, the polar ice pack builds up rapidly, expanding southwards and rotating clockwise at a speed of about 2 miles (over 3 kilometres) a day. Between these two ice-masses lies the shear zone, where ice forms in a shifting layer un-attached to either ice-mass. The polar pack grinds against the ice in this zone like the teeth of some great circular saw, driving it up into ridges as high as 35 feet (10.7 metres), with keels perhaps three times as deep.

'A piece of ice gets to be a hazard,' one oilman said laconically, 'as soon as it's as big as your ship.' The question in many minds is whether the oil-rigs will go down like a succession of *Titanics* – or whether, instead, they will spend most of their time dodging here and there, like dodgems or bumper cars, to avoid oncoming icebergs. An iceberg with an estimated weight of 8–10 million tons was sighted south of the oil-fields in 1972. And in the late 1970s Dome tracked an ice island that had probably been cruising around the Arctic for some 70 years. It measured 7 miles by 3 (11.2 by 4.8 kilometres) and stretched 120 feet (37 metres) from its peak above the water to the tip of its keel beneath. 'I don't know what kind of platform could withstand an iceberg of 8 to 10 million tons,' observed one Mobil executive, 'but I wouldn't want to be on one until I knew!'

Some companies have tried to tow smaller icebergs out of the way, although not without difficulty. 'The iceberg is a very dynamic beast,' said the president of Nordco, a research organization studying the problem. 'They tend to roll over when you tow them.' He then continued: 'You can tow icebergs up to a million tons. But there comes a breaking point when you don't know who's towing whom.' For this reason, many experts have tended to favour floating drilling platforms, which could uncouple themselves from the borehole on the sea-bed and sail out of the way of an oncoming ice mountain. But the removal of the platform would not solve the problem entirely, since the really big bergs scour the sea-bed and could well bulldoze the well-head – unless it had been buried fairly deep.

The upshot of all this, taken together with Dome's plans to build artificial islands to house clusters of production wells and to provide safe havens for tankers, is that the company was expecting to invest more than $5 billion to extract the two billion barrels of oil it believed could be got out of the Kopanoar field, its most promising discovery in the Beaufort Sea to date. This is over 60 per cent more than the cost of developing the similar-sized Forties field in the North Sea – and an indication of the premium likely to be required for oil from politically stable areas of the world. And Dome itself was soon in sore financial straits, sending shock-waves through Canada's economy.

Tar sands, oil shale and coal gasification or liquefaction were among the synfuel projects vying for funding in the late 1970s, and all were adversely affected by the slumping price of oil several years later. As a final example of the vulnerability of such projects to oil-price fluctuations, whether politically engineered or not, consider the case of the oil-shale industry.

## A Question of Shale

'That paper scared the bejesus out of everybody,' one energy expert said of a draft report circulating inside the world's largest oil company late in 1979. 'Exxon changed the game overnight.' This draft of Exxon's annual analysis of America's energy future broke new ground in several ways, casting the analytical net well into the twenty-first century and coming up with a bombshell conclusion: to meet the likely demand for liquid fuels in the early years of the next century, the USA would have to develop a synfuels industry capable of producing 15 million barrels of synthetic fuel a day.

Shale oil, Exxon chief executive Clifton Garvin once commented, 'has always mesmerized people'. In his view, at least, oil shale is 'part of the bridge between fossil fuels and renewable fuels – a bridge that could last up to 175 years. That's quite a bridge.' Or, as Oxy's Armand Hammer put it, 'you can't drill a dry hole in shale'. True, in the sense that you always hit oil. The problem, as with heavy oils and tar sands, is getting it out. Only China and the USSR currently use oil shale commercially, but Table 4.3 shows that shale deposits are found throughout the world – with North America dominating the league table.

*Table 4.3: World oil-shale reserves (in billions of tons of oil; source: UNERG)*

|  | Total known deposits | Deposits recoverable with present technology |
| --- | --- | --- |
| Africa | 14 | 1.5 |
| Asia | 15 | 3.5 |
| South America | 115 | 7 |
| South | 144 | 12 |
| Australasia* | 0.1 | — |
| Europe (incl. USSR) | 11 | 4 |
| North America | 320 | 12 |
| North | 331 | 16 |
| World total | 475 | 28 |

* According to Earthscan, recent discoveries in Australia's Rundle shale deposits suggest that this figure should be considerably higher.

Colorado shuddered when it heard of the Exxon proposals, which envisaged the construction of some 150 oil-shale plants in the state, able to produce 8 million barrels of shale oil a day within thirty years. The proposed programme would have involved exploding the local population of some 75,000 to nearer 1.5 million. 'If I'm still in the Senate, they could do that over my dead body,' growled Colorado

Senator Gary Hart, a sentiment echoed by many of his constituents. But if you ask people in Rio Blanco county for their views on the shale boom, they will probably ask, tongues firmly in cheek, 'Which one?' Colorado has been the stage for a succession of ultimately abortive shale rushes – and there are those who are convinced that this latest surge of interest will evaporate.

Oil-shale deposits are found throughout the world, and relatively small shale-oil industries have been established historically in such areas as Australia, Scotland and Spain, while others, including Brazil, China and the USSR, either have such industries or are building them up. Shale was burned in Scotland from early times, but the shale-oil industry there was started in the Lothians in the 1850s by James 'Paraffin' Young. The shale was mainly extracted by underground room-and-pillar mining, but some open-cast mining also took place. Shale extracted by either method was brought to the surface for 'retorting', or heating in a retort, a process which produced up to 45 Imperial gallons of oil per ton of shale in the early days of the industry. As the rich seams were worked out, however, this yield steadily declined.

The strange thing about shale oil, first discovered in the USA by Indians when lightning set blocks of it afire, is that it is neither a shale, in geological terms, nor does it yield much oil directly. Instead, it is a marlstone and contains kerogen, an organic substance which can be decomposed to produce shale oil. Kerogen, which appears as coloured streaks in the shale, ranging from brown to dark blue, can be extracted by a number of methods: but, first, what is it?

Some 60 million years ago, the Green River Basin was covered with a huge shallow lake teeming with microscopic life, particularly diatoms. Such lakes existed for up to 10 million years, long enough for millions of tonnes of organic material to be deposited. As the surrounding sediment hardened into rock, the organic deposits, and their buried sunshine, were converted into the rubbery substance called kerogen. This is composed of about 80 per cent carbon, 10 per cent hydrogen, 6 per cent oxygen, 3 per cent nitrogen and 1 per cent sulphur. Although it will not flow or yield to most conventional solvents, kerogen decomposes when heated above 900°F (428°C), producing shale oil, light hydrocarbon gases and a coke-like carbon residue.

To get an idea of the scale of activities which were being proposed to exploit what the Ute Indians called 'the rock that burns', I flew to Denver and then drove westwards over the Rockies towards the oil-shale country. The pioneers had found many uses for the shale, using it to light their fires, to grease their wagon wheels and to soften and preserve leather. One man used it to build a fireplace, without realizing what it was, and was stunned, when he lit his first fire, to see the entire fireplace go up in flames. By the mid-1800s, there were more than 50 companies producing oil from shale, selling their product to refineries for the manufacture of kerosene at a price equivalent to perhaps $80 a barrel in today's money – expensive stuff. But when Edwin Drake punched his drill through into Pennsylvania's oil deposits, he also punched a hole in the bottom of the oil-shale business.

Interest in shale oil revived in the 1920s with the soaring demand for gasoline which followed in the wake of Henry Ford's Model T, sold by the million. The discovery of the oil-rich Green River formation caused a mini oil-rush, with prospectors pouring into the area, setting up over 200 companies and filing something like 30,000 mining claims. But the boom ended with the discovery of liquid petroleum in east Texas. The Second World War stimulated research into shale-oil production methods, with Congress increasingly worried about America's dependence on imported oil. And then, in an often repeated pattern, the discovery of the 'super-giant' Middle East oil-fields eroded the potential market for synthetic oil.

By the time I arrived in Rifle, Colorado, however, the area was on the verge of boom conditions once again. This was the summer of 1981, and heavy trucks loaded with every conceivable type of drilling equipment and pipeline component clogged the roads. The newspapers were full of argument and counter-argument about whether Exxon's call for a 'national sacrifice area' in the region, with environmental standards being relaxed to facilitate the growth of the oil-shale industry, could be justified either economically or politically.

Exxon's partner in the Colony shale project, some 15 miles west of Rifle and 15 miles north of Parachute Creek, was Tosco – or The Oil Shale Co. Tosco had achieved the seemingly impossible, in political terms, by persuading the Reagan administration to stump up $1.1 billion in loan guarantees for the Colony project. Originally costed at $450 million in 1973, the project's estimated cost had soared to nearly $3.5 billion, a depressingly familiar pattern as far as the oilmen were concerned. Exxon had recently been involved in the scrapping of a pilot plant designed to tap Australia's oil-shale deposits at Rundle, Queensland (see Table 4.3). There the costs had tripled to an estimated A$2 billion inside a year.

The Colony tract contains a relatively thin layer of rich oil shale, so that it was being developed on the same basis as the Scottish deposits, albeit on a very much larger scale. The room-and-pillar approach involves leaving pillars of shale to support the roof of the 'room' you are excavating.

Just down the road, the Rio Blanco Oil Shale Co., a joint venture between Gulf and Standard Oil of Indiana, was trying a rather different approach, dubbed MIS – shorthand for 'modified in situ'. Rio Blanco was estimating that there were 9 billion barrels of shale oil on its tract, nearly as much oil as there is in Alaska's Prudhoe Bay fields. But the company knew that room-and-pillar methods would mean that it could extract only about 1 billion barrels of oil by the end of the site's economic life. Using the MIS approach, however, it estimated that it might extract 5 billion barrels. If, on the other hand, it went for open-cast mining, it thought it could squeeze almost all 9 billion barrels out of its tract. One Gulf executive estimated that the tract could support a 300,000-barrel-a-day output for at least 50 years.

One of the problems of bringing shale up to the surface, however, as Exxon was doing at Colony, is that you end up with nearly a ton of waste for every barrel of oil you extract. Much of this waste is in the form of a fine black silky powder that many fear could blow around and create another dustbowl. Exxon argued that it would cool and moisten the waste before dumping it into a canyon, to be covered in a layer of topsoil, which would be reseeded. But there are other problems, including the so-called 'popcorn effect'.

Every 100 tons of crushed shale leaves about 90 tons of waste after processing, but the volume of this waste is about 40 per cent greater than that of the original material entering the plant. Or, to put it another way, if you have dug 100 tons of shale out of the ground, the volume of the resulting spoil will be equivalent to at least 130 tons. A plant producing about 100,000 barrels of shale oil a day (or about half of one per cent of America's daily oil consumption) would have to get rid of about 20 million tons of waste each year. If all the shale reserves in Colorado were to be exploited, it has been estimated, the shale region would be the world's largest industrial spoil heap – by several orders of magnitude. Scotland is still dotted with the 'bings' thrown up by its relatively small shale industry, even though enormous quantities of the spoil were used in road building and other civil-engineering projects. Colorado's spoil, it is said, could raise the height of that part of the Rockies from 14,000 feet to 18,000 feet.

## The Floor's Burning!

Driving north from Rifle and then westwards from Rio Blanco, a tiny collection of makeshift buildings, you travel through the attractive, undulating and increasingly arid landscape which skirts Piceance (pronounced pea-ants) basin – where Armand Hammer's Oxy has been trying out its own MIS methods. The idea is that only 20 to 25 per cent of the shale is brought to the surface for processing, to provide access to each underground 'retort'. The retort itself is blasted out of solid rock and shale. Once the basic cavern is roughed out, a space is excavated under the shale-body and the shale collapsed into it, or 'rubbleized', by the use of explosives. The resulting heap of rubble is lit from the top and the combustion zone moves steadily downwards, its progress controlled from the surface by the injection of the air needed to keep the 'burn' going.

As you pass through Piceance Valley, oil shale is all about you, under your feet and heaped up on every side in khaki-coloured hills. The basin contains an estimated 1,800,000,000,000 (or 1.8 trillion) barrels of oil. Altogether, the Green River formation of north-western Colorado, south-western Wyoming and north-eastern Utah contains the equivalent of over 8 trillion barrels of crude shale oil, although *An Assessment of Oil Shale Technologies*, published by the US Congress Office of Technology Assessment (OTA) in 1980, estimated that only 400 billion barrels are economically recoverable with existing technology.

Looking across the scrubby piñon trees and sagebrush from the access road to Oxy's Cathedral Bluffs site in the Piceance Basin, on its C-b Tract, it was hard to fault Oxy for its handling of the project to date. Two headframes rose above the site, like windowless tower-blocks, both streaked like the shale itself with thin bands of colour, an incidental side-effect of the concrete casting method used. The larger headframe, which is taller than the Statue of Liberty, had been designed to lift 50,000 tons of rock a day up and out of the hole.

One sunny day in September 1978, the management committee of Occidental Shale Oil, Inc., went deep down into Oxy's experimental mine at Logan Wash. Directly below their feet, beneath some fifty feet of supposedly solid rock, was the sixth (and largest) retort the company's engineers had excavated, an enormous cavern measuring some 160 feet (49 metres) square and 337 feet (103 metres) deep, the size of a thirty-storey office tower. The Oxy executives had come to look at a fault in the retort, which was already well alight, burning steadily downwards and forcing the oil out of the shale. Once free of the shale, the oil flows downward by courtesy of gravity, collecting in a sump at the bottom of the retort, from which it can be pumped back up to the surface. But that was not what they had come to see.

Just before their arrival, a small hole, perhaps one foot in diameter, had opened up in the floor of the cavern in which they were now standing, revealing the inferno below. As they watched, the hole suddenly began to grow and they retreated as fast as possible. Within thirty minutes, about half the floor they had been standing on had collapsed through into the blazing retort below, damping down the vital fire.

For the next two weeks, engineers worked around the clock to save the experiment. In the end, Retort #6 produced nearly 52,000 barrels of oil – and Oxy learned some important lessons in the process. It was hoping to burn the retorts simultaneously, in clusters, once the project was running commercially. Oxy's C-b Tract contains an estimated 3 billion barrels of oil, of which approximately 1.2 billion could be recovered using the MIS method, whereas surface retorting might recover a total of 1.9 billion barrels.

The ecological constraints on the development of the shale-oil industry were proving a significant brake, however. The Office of Technology Assessment had looked at a wide range of constraints, including water availability and the fact that Nature has, somewhat whimsically, put its oil-shale deposits in the middle of some of the United States' most striking wildernesses. Apart from the waste-disposal problem, which would obviously be reduced where the MIS method is used, air and water pollution are both matters of considerable concern – although the OTA concluded that a 400,000-barrel-a-day shale-oil industry could be accommodated in the Piceance Basin area without infringing existing environmental standards.

And then, early in 1982, came the news that Oxy and Tenneco were going to slow down operations at the Cathedral Bluffs site, largely because high interest rates, soaring construction costs and slumping oil prices were threatening to undermine the economics of the exercise once again. They emphasized that they 'remain committed' to shale-oil production at the C-b Tract 'as soon as reasonably practicable'. But a far greater shock to the synfuels industry's morale came with the sinking of its flagship project, Colony. Exxon had said that it could make the Colony project pay if oil prices reached $35 a barrel, but the possibility that oil prices could fall well below the $30 mark and stay there for some time led to the announcement in May 1982 that the company was pulling out, leaving Tosco floundering.

'Synthetics have been indefinitely postponed, and may never be able to get off the ground,' commented John Lichtblau, president of the Petroleum Industry Research Foundation in New York. This forecast may prove over-pessimistic as far as the synfuels industry is concerned, but there can now be little doubt that there has been a major shift in the nature of the world's demand for energy, a shift which will have significant implications for many of the new and renewable-energy technologies, including synfuels production.

## What Future for the Petrosaurs?

'We may wax hot and cold about when we go ahead, but we will do so,' said Exxon president Howard Kauffman some months before the Colony shale project was aborted. He was talking about alternative energy, although an oilman's interpretation of 'alternative' in this respect differs from that of an advocate of soft-energy paths: he means sources of energy other than conventional oil-fields. Exxon considers that solar energy and other renewable-energy sources, such as hydropower, will only begin to be significant in the first decades of the twenty-first century, a projection which is very much at variance with those made by such solar enthusiasts as Denis Hayes.

However, it is quite possible to imagine a sequence of events in the Middle East which choked off a much larger proportion of the oil coming out of that region than did the Iran–Iraq war. It is also quite possible to imagine the various shale-oil and tar-sand projects being taken out of mothballs in response to a global energy crisis, but it is not possible to rely on such projects to cope with such crises as they occur. Often it will take between ten and twenty years to get a really large synthetic-fuel project into operation. Companies like Exxon, Oxy and Tosco may have done a lot of the groundwork already, but none of the projects is yet at a stage where it can be switched on and off like a tap.

The cost of these projects will always be a problem, whether or not conventional oil is in short supply. It costs between $3 and $4 billion to build a synfuels plant able to produce the equivalent of 50,000 barrels of oil a day – an amount which is consumed in the USA every four minutes. Britain, it is estimated, would need 33 such plants to meet its current oil needs, at a cost of around £60 billion. Indeed, the cost of building a single synfuels plant is likely to be greater than the stock-market value of Britain's largest manufacturing company, ICI.

Coal, inevitably, will become increasingly important, although the associated environmental impacts, whether in terms of local air pollution, acid rain or carbon dioxide build-up (see Chapter 14), will just as inevitably constrain the growth of the coal industry. All of the Seven Sisters had a stake in coal in the early 1980s, even Texaco – the least diversified of them all. Gulf was in pursuit of the Kemmerer Coal Co., while Exxon was sitting on coal reserves estimated at 10.5 billion tons, which some analysts assessed as the energy equivalent of all America's known oil reserves. Conoco, through Consolidated Coal, was the second largest US coal producer, while Oxy was third with its Island Creek Coal Co. subsidiary.

Texaco's vice-president, James Dunlap, was arguing that US coal reserves were sufficient to meet America's energy needs for between 200 and 300 years, with a similar time-span being suggested in Britain by the National Coal Board. Texaco and the British Gas Corporation were giving serious thought to coal gasification (Figure 4.7), while Mobil was touting its new catalysts, including ZSM-5, as *the* answer for anyone wanting to liquefy coal. General Motors, meanwhile, was unveiling a car powered by coal dust, although it warned that an enormous amount of work still needed to be done to bring the vehicle within the various air-quality standards.

The International Institute for Applied Systems Analysis (IIASA) was predicting that the world would be using 7 billion tonnes of coal a year for liquid fuels by the year 2030, with countries like Australia and the USA vying to become the Saudi Arabia of coal. Worldwide, there would appear to be enough coal to last 225 years at current rates of consumption, a figure which compares favourably with 35 years for oil, 50 for natural gas and 70 for uranium. For,

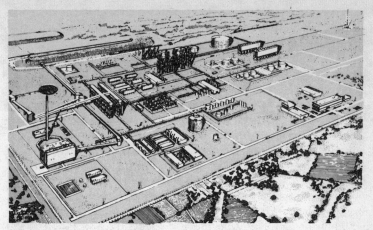

Figure 4.7: Artist's impression of a coal gasification plant
(source: British Gas Corporation).

make no mistake, oil is running out. As Hubbert showed over twenty
years ago, we can postpone the day the barrel runs dry, but, if we
continue to use oil, that day will come.

Coal has a number of other advantages which have helped make
it a prime candidate for investment by a wide range of industrial
interests (Figure 4.8). North America has 29 per cent of the economically recoverable reserves of coal, while Western Europe has 13 per
cent, India and Africa 5 per cent each, Australia 4 per cent and the
various communist countries about 40 per cent. A very different
pattern of distribution, clearly, to that for oil, where 46 per cent of
the official recognized reserves are in the Middle East or North Africa,
and only 9 per cent in North America and Western Europe combined.

But coal has so far failed to live up to expectations, a failure which
will be aggravated by slower rates of growth in oil prices – if that
is what happens. IIASA, in predicting that world consumption will
increase two and a half times from its 1980 level by the year 2000,
expects coal to meet more than 70 per cent of all additional energy
requirements in those two decades. Yet coal captured only 41 per
cent of the extra demand for energy in the non-communist world
between 1973 and 1980. By contrast, nuclear power took 25 per cent,
hydropower took 15 per cent, natural gas 11 per cent and oil 7 per
cent.

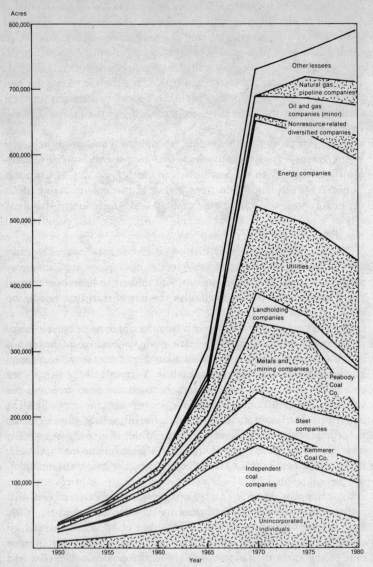

Figure 4.8: Number of federal coal acres under lease by business category 1950–80 (source: US Congress Office of Technology Assessment).

So far, at least, only three large oil companies have gained a major foothold in the international coal market: Shell, which controlled 3.3 billion tonnes of saleable coal at the time of writing; BP, which owned 2 billion tonnes; and Compagnie Française de Pétroles (Total), which was reported to have mined 5 million tonnes of coal in 1981. All three had acquired coalmines in North America, Australia and South Africa since 1973, although the profits expected from their coal operations are generally considerably lower than those deriving from oil.

South Africa, in fact, is a prime example of what can be achieved in the synfuels field if the strategic and security pressures are sufficiently intense. With the South African Coal, Oil and Gas Corporation (SASOL) planning to open a new synfuel plant during 1982, the government was forecasting that coal, of which South Africa has a relative abundance, would provide 47 per cent of the country's oil needs.

Yet, overall, the energy picture remains confused. There are clearly very considerable reserves of fossil fuels, although we are a long way from being able to extract oil from some of the less conventional sources at an economic price. With the uneasy feeling creeping up on them that oil was getting harder and more expensive to find, oil companies were far from investing every penny of their not inconsiderable windfall profits in further oil exploration. Instead some, like Exxon, threw a great deal of money into totally new areas of business, losing much of it in the process. Exxon's foray into the office systems market, with its Qyx, Qwip and Vydec products, for example, came up against unbeatable rival systems marketed by IBM and Xerox. Exxon also tried to break into the energy-conservation market, by taking over Reliance Electric, but incurred considerable losses in doing so. When big companies make mistakes, they make obvious ones, or, as one business law puts it, 'the bigger the elephant, the bigger the mess'.

Some oil companies, in fact, have been running scared. Gulf, for example, should have been sitting pretty, having started off in life with the Spindletop gusher, the 75,000-barrels-a-day column of oil which announced Texan oil on 9 January 1901 – and blew a sizeable hole in the Standard Oil monopoly which John D. Rockefeller had so ruthlessly built up. Gulf opened the world's first petrol station and bought oceans of Middle East and Venezuelan oil. But, in a move which it was long to regret, it spurned an offer to enter Saudi Arabia in the 1930s and has since had to buy West African oil, paying $40 a barrel when Saudi oil was going for $32 a barrel.

After a political payoff scandal, a bevy of lawsuits, the loss of most of its overseas oil, a devastating change of energy policy in Canada (a country where Gulf had enormous holdings) and an extraordinarily disadvantageous natural-gas sales contract, some business analysts were asking whether Gulf was on the ropes. 'I would reject that question out of hand – vociferously, vigorously, every way I could', was the way Gulf chairman Jerry McAfee reacted, but the question-mark remained.

Gulf was investing heavily in the Rio Blanco oil–shale project, of course, and in the Beaufort Sea, but its stock had plunged 35 per cent inside a year. 'It is a great temptation,' said McAfee, 'to put everything we've got into the immediate short-term, quick-payoff items.' The problem has been identifying such 'items'. Certainly none of the renewable-energy projects which the oil industry had started to fund, many of which are covered in later chapters, could conceivably be seen as quick payoff items. Indeed, Gulf had invested in another non-oil, long-term, high-risk project run by General Atomic – which was promising to reproduce the sun on earth, by developing commercial fusion reactors.

Gulf and Shell, however, had burned their fingers with two earlier nuclear projects. But the prize offered by fusion power was such that General Atomic had managed to squeeze $10 million out of Phillips Petroleum by arguing that, if the physics worked out, it could have a commercial fusion reactor by the mid-1990s. In the meantime, the nuclear industry had burned more than its fingers in its attempts to build nuclear power up as a credible alternative to oil.

# 5 ☉ Nuclear Reactions

View the world, for a moment, from the same angle as the nuclear-power industry. The vision of nuclear electricity too cheap to meter may have evaporated, but a clear majority in the industry sincerely believe that nuclear power, whether in the form of fission now or fusion (much) later, provides the only hope of the abundant energy they see as a fundamental requirement for future social stability. As oil supplies diminish, they argue, an expanding nuclear industry will help prevent the need to make forced changes in our styles of living and will provide a means for the worldwide improvement of living standards. There are risks, they accept, but these must be traded off against the potential benefits.

'It is misleading,' commented Bertram Wolfe, as vice-president and general manager of the nuclear fuel and services division of the General Electric Co., 'to gloss over difficulties in the areas of nuclear wastes, nuclear proliferation, reactor safety analysis and reactor economics on the grounds that nuclear power is needed, whatever its failings. But public discussions of such difficulties can also be misleading when they start from the philosophical presumption that nuclear power would still be unacceptable even if all its technical, social and economic problems were solved.'

What worries the industry is that many of its critics are not simply confining their attacks to such technical questions as reactor safety, which have proved difficult enough to answer convincingly, but are also questioning whether increased energy supply is, in fact, a sensible or desirable target. As an example of this argument, Wolfe quoted Amory Lovins. 'If you ask me,' Lovins once opined, 'it'd be a little short of disastrous for us to discover a source of clean, cheap, abundant energy because of what we would do with it. We ought to be looking for energy sources that are adequate for our needs, but that won't give us the excesses of concentrated energy with which we could do mischief to the earth or to each other.'

And what of the solar prospect viewed from the nuclear industry? 'There is no argument about the desirability of developing solar resources,' Wolfe concluded. 'Almost everyone, including myself and my company, General Electric, advocates solar development. But, as anyone can verify by getting an estimate from a local solar contractor, even the simplest solar technology, solar heating, is not yet here for the masses. As for other sources of energy, windmills are still losing their blades in high winds, and it is not clear whether

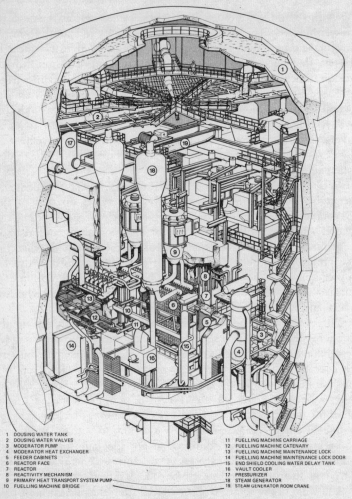

1  DOUSING WATER TANK
2  DOUSING WATER VALVES
3  MODERATOR PUMP
4  MODERATOR HEAT EXCHANGER
5  FEEDER CABINETS
6  REACTOR FACE
7  REACTOR
8  REACTIVITY MECHANISM
9  PRIMARY HEAT TRANSPORT SYSTEM PUMP
10 FUELLING MACHINE BRIDGE

11 FUELLING MACHINE CARRIAGE
12 FUELLING MACHINE CATENARY
13 FUELLING MACHINE MAINTENANCE LOCK
14 FUELLING MACHINE MAINTENANCE LOCK DOOR
15 END SHIELD COOLING WATER DELAY TANK
16 VAULT COOLER
17 PRESSURIZER
18 STEAM GENERATOR
19 STEAM GENERATOR ROOM CRANE

Figure 5.1: Cutaway diagram of the CANDU reactor (source: Atomic Energy of Canada Ltd).

large-scale biomass conversion is practical, or even a net energy producer.'

The successes and failures of individual renewable-energy technologies will be reviewed in later chapters, but the prospects of the nuclear industry are an important consideration in assessing the renewable-energy prospect. Advocates of soft-energy paths have argued that hard-energy paths tie up such a high proportion of the available capital and other resources that the two paths are mutually exclusive. This is something of an exaggeration, and there is no reason to believe that if nuclear power disappeared tomorrow the renewable technologies could even begin to fill the breach in an acceptable timescale. But General Electric's implicit assumption that the technical, social and economic problems associated with nuclear energy can be solved looks decidedly shaky in the light of recent experience in all three areas.

Installed nuclear capacity in the various member states of the Organization for Economic Co-operation and Development (OECD) grew from 17 giga-watts (1 GW = 1 thousand million watts) in 1970 to 133 GW by the end of 1981. There can be no question that this increase, representing 1 per cent of all electricity generated in 1970 and 13 per cent in 1981, was a considerable achievement, but it was less than half the growth in capacity expected by nuclear planners in the late 1960s. The OECD countries, by 1982, were forecasting a total nuclear capacity of about 215 GW by 1985 and 315 GW by 1990. And the International Energy Agency was predicting that nuclear capacity will rise to between 400 and 500 GW by the year 2000.

Optimistic predictions made in the late 1960s and early 1970s that nuclear power would provide 50 per cent of the world's electricity by the year 2000 were being revised downward, according to Dr Sigvard Eklund, director general of the International Atomic Energy Agency, so that the contribution projected in forecasts prepared in 1982 had fallen to the 20–25-per-cent range – and there are considerable uncertainties in these forecasts. Worse, as far as the nuclear industry was concerned, Dr Eklund forecast a marked drop in the rate of new reactor construction, from more than 10,000 MW a year in the early 1980s to less than 5,000 MW a year in the 1990s for countries outside the Comecon alliance, which still had an ambitious nuclear-power programme.

The previous year, Dr Eklund reported, nineteen reactors (with a rated output of 18,000 MW) had been ordered by Britain, France, West Germany, Japan, Korea and Romania, but the United States had cancelled or postponed twelve reactor projects totalling 13,000 MW. The long lead-times between the commitment to build and the commercial operation of nuclear-power stations had become a considerable obstacle to more orders appearing on the horizon.

These lead-times varied from an average of 61 months in Japan and 63 in France, to 82 months in West Germany and 121 months in the United States. Reactor-builder Bechtel produced figures to show that the Three Mile Island disaster had generated improved safety standards which would cost $20–30 million for a reactor already under construction. But this additional cost paled into insignificance when compared with the costs associated with increasing delays. During the time it takes to build an American reactor, Bechtel reported, interest and other financial charges can mount up to account for 50 per cent of the final $2–4 billion bill.

But even these figures mask the extraordinary plight of the nuclear-power industry. While Dr Ulf Lantzke, director of the Paris-based International Energy Agency, talked of a 'paralysing crisis of confidence in the future of nuclear power', many analysts had been stunned by the speed with which this new and advanced technology had been transformed into a 'lame-duck' industry. And there were some, Amory Lovins among them, who argued that the industry had developed more than a limp: 'Nuclear energy,' Lovins concluded, 'is dying.'

## Nuclear Cycles

By 1980, nearly 180 commercial nuclear reactors, each rated at over 150 MW capacity, were operating in the non-communist world, with a total gross generating capacity of over 120 GW – representing 7 per cent of the electricity generated in the non-communist world, or 3 per cent of the total energy demand. These reactors were located in 26 countries, most of them in the developed world: only about 5 GW of the total capacity figure was located outside the OECD area.

Despite the assertions made by environmentalists, and despite the very real problems encountered by the nuclear industry, it is still a very long way from death's door. One of the reasons why those responsible for electricity generation continue to buy nuclear reactors is that they are less sensitive to fluctuating fuel costs. When used for base-load power generation (with a base-load power station defined as one that runs for around 60–70 per cent of the year), the relatively high capital costs involved in building a nuclear reactor can be amortized much more quickly. The uranium costs for a reactor run in this way account for only about 20–25 per cent of the cost of power production, compared with the case of fossil-fuelled power stations where fuel costs represent 50–60 per cent of the generating cost.

The concentrated power afforded by a nuclear plant has made nuclear energy an attractive commodity in developed and developing countries alike, at least on paper. When you dig a lump of uranium out of the ground, it hardly looks like a building block for a major energy industry. Yet one tonne of uranium can produce as much energy as 10,000 tonnes of oil or 20,000 tonnes of coal. Or, taking another angle, each of the fuel pellets loaded into a pressurized water reactor, pellets which are perhaps twice as thick as a pencil and slightly more than two inches long, contains the energy equivalent of one tonne of coal or four barrels of crude oil.

The basic problem is that the isotope U–235, which splits apart spontaneously and creates heat in the process, makes up only about 0.7 per cent of any hunk of raw uranium dug out of the ground. To obtain the sort of chain reaction needed to keep a typical reactor running, the U–235 component of the ore has to be enriched to about 3 per cent. The Canadian-designed CANDU reactor (see Figure 5.2) gets along fairly well with unenriched uranium, because the fuel rods are bathed in 'heavy' water, in which the hydrogen atoms carry an extra neutron, allowing a chain reaction to take place between the relatively isolated U–235 atoms.

In a 'light' water reactor, the fuel pellets have been subjected to a good deal of processing at a uranium-enrichment facility. There the natural uranium was converted into a gas and forced by compressors into porous tubes called 'barriers'. As the gas passes through cascades of such barriers, a little of the heavier, non-fissionable isotope U–238 is left behind and a little of the lighter U–235 gets through. After something like 1,200 passages, the gas contains the required 3 per cent of the fissionable U–235 isotope – and is converted into metal fuel pellets.

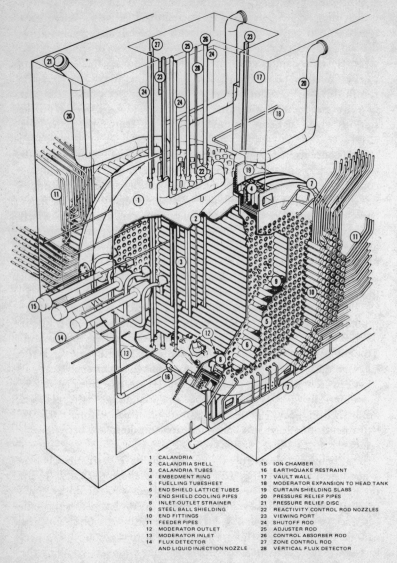

|   |   |   |   |
|---|---|---|---|
| 1 | CALANDRIA | 15 | ION CHAMBER |
| 2 | CALANDRIA SHELL | 16 | EARTHQUAKE RESTRAINT |
| 3 | CALANDRIA TUBES | 17 | VAULT WALL |
| 4 | EMBEDMENT RING | 18 | MODERATOR EXPANSION TO HEAD TANK |
| 5 | FUELLING TUBESHEET | 19 | CURTAIN SHIELDING SLABS |
| 6 | END SHIELD LATTICE TUBES | 20 | PRESSURE RELIEF PIPES |
| 7 | END SHIELD COOLING PIPES | 21 | PRESSURE RELIEF DISC |
| 8 | INLET-OUTLET STRAINER | 22 | REACTIVITY CONTROL ROD NOZZLES |
| 9 | STEEL BALL SHIELDING | 23 | VIEWING PORT |
| 10 | END FITTINGS | 24 | SHUTOFF ROD |
| 11 | FEEDER PIPES | 25 | ADJUSTER ROD |
| 12 | MODERATOR OUTLET | 26 | CONTROL ABSORBER ROD |
| 13 | MODERATOR INLET | 27 | ZONE CONTROL ROD |
| 14 | FLUX DETECTOR | 28 | VERTICAL FLUX DETECTOR |
|   | AND LIQUID INJECTION NOZZLE |   |   |

Figure 5.2: Cutaway diagram of the CANDU reactor assembly
(source: Atomic Energy of Canada Ltd).

Both heavy and light water reactors are so-called 'thermal' reactors, which represent the overwhelming majority of reactors in use today, whereas the 'fast breeder' reactor has only reached the prototype stage so far. A fast breeder, such as France's prototype 1,200 MW Superphénix power plant at Creys-Malville, has a compact core of fissionable (or fissile) plutonium mixed with highly enriched U–235 – and this core is surrounded by a blanket of U–238. Once the reactor is operating, the U–238 is converted into plutonium 239 as it is bombarded with neutrons which have escaped the core, so that fast breeders should be able to create more fissile material than they consume as fuel. If their potential is realized, they could improve the energy efficiency of the nuclear cycle by a very significant margin indeed.

By 1980, Pressurized Water Reactors (PWRs), the type which failed at Three Mile Island, represented 56 per cent of the non-communist capacity of commercial-scale reactors, while Boiling Water Reactors (BWRs) accounted for 34 per cent. Of the remainder, Magnox and Advanced Gas-cooled Reactors together accounted for 6 per cent and pressurized Heavy Water Reactors (e.g. the CANDU reactor) represented 4 per cent. The main characteristics of the various reactor types, and their respective contributions in 1980 to nuclear capacity in the non-communist world, are summarized in Tables 5.1 and 5.2.

Uranium supply has not typically been a problem, largely because the uranium-mining industry over-estimated the likely growth of the nuclear industry and invested in too much mining capacity. As a direct result, the spot market price for uranium fell from about $40 per pound in the late 1970s to less than $30 per pound by the early 1980s.

A typical modern light water reactor has been calculated to consume fuel at an annual rate equivalent to perhaps 150–165 tonnes of natural uranium per GW of capacity. On this basis, the 1980 demand for natural uranium was estimated to be about 16–20 thousand tonnes of uranium metal. With uranium production running at about 35–40 thousand tonnes a year in the early 1980s, there was clearly a significant degree of over-capacity in the uranium-mining industry, and as a result many mines were operating at a loss, some had closed and an unknown number of new mining projects had been deferred.

The performance of individual reactors varies considerably, both in terms of energy efficiency and reliability. Consider the three types of reactor operating in Britain in 1980, at a time when the proposed

*Table 5.1: Some leading fission reactors (source: BP)*

| | Country of origin | Fuel | Coolant | Moderator |
|---|---|---|---|---|
| PWR (Pressurized Water Reactor) | USA | Enriched uranium oxide | Light water | Light water |
| BWR (Boiling Water Reactor) | USA | Enriched uranium oxide | Light water | Light water |
| AGR (Advanced Gas-cooled Reactor) | UK | Enriched uranium oxide | Carbon dioxide | Graphite |
| Magnox | UK | Natural uranium metal | Carbon dioxide | Graphite |
| CANDU | Canada | Natural uranium oxide | Heavy water | Heavy water |
| SGHWR (Steam Generating Heavy Water Reactor)* | UK | Enriched uranium oxide | Light water | Heavy water |
| HTR (High Temperature Reactor)* | Europe | Enriched uranium oxide | Helium | Graphite |

* Not commercially available

*Table 5.2: Nuclear capacity by reactor type in 1980 (source: Nuclear Engineering International)*

| Type of reactor | Average annual load factor (%) | Reactors over 150 MW | Nuclear capacity (MW) |
|---|---|---|---|
| Pressurized heavy water | 72.9 | 12 | 6306 |
| Magnox | 53.2 | 26 | 8515 |
| Pressurized water | 59.3 | 88 | 70327 |
| Boiling water | 56.5 | 54 | 38683 |

PWR for Sizewell was still very much on the drawing-board. The Magnox reactor supplies something like 7,000 tonnes of oil equivalent for every pound of fuel burned, while the advanced gas-cooled reactor can supply twice that figure, at 14,000 tonnes, and the fast breeder reactor (so far only represented by the pilot reactor at Dounreay) could supply 800,000 tonnes – a hundred-fold improvement on the Magnox reactor.

Such factors clearly influence the comparative cost advantage afforded by nuclear-generated electricity, although the availability and cost of abundant fossil fuels also strongly influences the balance of advantage. According to the OECD's Nuclear Energy Agency and the International Energy Agency, electricity produced from existing nuclear plants is considerably cheaper than that produced from oil-fired plant under virtually any conditions obtaining within the OECD region. Data for France indicate that, at least as far as nuclear stations currently under construction are concerned, the relative cost ratio is 3.4 to 1 in favour of nuclear. In North America as a whole, by contrast, the cost ratio was thought to be narrower, between 1.5 to 1 and 2 to 1, both because of the higher capital costs involved in nuclear plants there (a result of the long lead-times) and because North America has access to abundant resources of oil and coal.

Because the United States leads the world in terms of installed nuclear capacity (with some 57 GW on stream in the early 1980s) and because, as Table 5.2 shows, the US-designed PWR dominates the world nuclear scene, I decided to visit PWR manufacturer Westinghouse at its headquarters in Pittsburgh, Pennsylvania. As the prime contractor for the problematic Clinch River fast breeder reactor, Westinghouse had just been singled out for special criticism in a study of the project carried out for the House of Representatives by Ernest Fitzgerald – who had earlier exposed the Lockheed cost over-runs in the early 1970s.

But the Clinch River project was only one of a cluster of problems confronting Westinghouse. It was just emerging, for example, from one of the biggest litigation exercises in corporate history, with more than sixty companies involved at one time or another, and the potential liabilities running into billions of dollars. In the 1960s and 1970s, Westinghouse had signed uranium-supply contracts with those buying its reactors without ensuring that it would have access to the uranium it would eventually need to fulfil the contracts. By 1974 it realized it had made a serious blunder. With uranium prices rising, at that time, it was in the position of having to buy very considerable quantities of uranium at prices far higher than those prevailing when it had originally undertaken the commitment to supply.

It told its customers that it could not honour its earlier agreements, pleading 'commerical impractability'. Not surprisingly, they were incensed and Westinghouse found itself facing twenty-seven utilities in seventeen separate court actions. As these actions were settled, out of court, with cash payments and new guarantees of uranium supplies, Westinghouse launched a counter-attack. Following the leak of documents from Mary Kathleen Uranium, an Australian uranium producer and part of the Rio Tinto Zinc group, Westinghouse charged twenty-nine US and foreign producers with operating a cartel. Again the actions were settled out of court, with substantial payments from companies like R T Z, Gulf Oil, Gulf Minerals Canada and Getty Oil, providing Westinghouse with something like $100 million to offset the money it had been forced to pay out to the utilities.

But things were not, in general, going Westinghouse's way. Its PWRs had already generated more than a trillion kilowatts of electrical energy, with fifty-five in operation and over a hundred either under construction or contracted for. But the rapidly shrinking market for its reactors, a trend accelerated by the Three Mile Island incident, provoked a deep sense of having been misjudged. 'The governments of France, Great Britain, Spain, Sweden, Germany, Japan and the USSR are proceeding with the application of nuclear power,' it argued, 'yet in America a relatively small number of vocal individuals demand no-risk energy alternatives. But in our complex society, there is no such thing as a risk-free technology.'

Admitted; but Westinghouse, it appeared, had not been looking out of its windows. The USSR was certainly ploughing ahead with its plans to boost its output of nuclear electricity ten-fold between 1980 and 2000, aiming to generate 14 per cent of its electrical power from fission reactors by 1985. 'There is no public resistance to nuclear power in the Soviet Union,' said Valery Pershin, director of the Atommash factory in Volgodonsk, south Russia. 'It isn't like the West,' he asserted, 'where some of the resistance comes from energy monopolies, such as oil companies.'

The absence of public resistance was simply a matter of definition, however, with nuclear dissidents treated in very much the same way as those other unwilling occupants of a prison state within a state.

But Pershin was at least right as far as *effective* protest was concerned. With about twenty-five nuclear power plants already in operation and perhaps ten under construction, the USSR had also been concentrating considerable resources on the development of fast breeder reactors and fusion power.

But the Eastern bloc's nuclear-power programmes had had their hiccoughs. East Germany's ambitious nuclear programme seemed to be having particular problems. With some 10 per cent of its electricity generated by nuclear plants, East Germany had planned to double this output by the mid-1980s, based on the assumption that eight Soviet-built 440 MW reactors would be installed at East Germany's main nuclear power station, at Lubmin on the Baltic. The Lubmin plant and a small 70 MW reactor at Rheinsberg were producing all of the country's nuclear energy. Its next five-year plan, published in 1981, showed that it was relying on its own lignite to provide most of the extra electricity it would need – with no explanation given for the change in plans. Even though it was then producing some 260 million tonnes of lignite a year, ranking as the world's largest producer, East Germany had earlier given the strong impression that lignite itself ranked a poor second to nuclear energy.

In Britain, an ambitious nuclear-power programme, which would have involved the construction of at least one new nuclear station a year in the decade from 1982, equivalent to 15,000 MW over ten years, was being cut back. As the Sizewell inquiry got under way early in 1983, the nuclear industry was talking of a programme of only about half this size, with plants ordered on a 'step-by-step' basis.

France was perhaps the most vigorous nuclear nation on earth, having recovered from its 1969 decision to scrap its own nuclear-energy technology and buy (and improve) American reactor designs. President Mitterand had promised to cut back the country's nuclear programme fiercely before coming to power, and announced the suspension of construction or planning activities at five sites, involving eighteen reactors, on assuming power. He did nothing, however, to circumscribe the operation of the twenty-nine other reactors already functioning or of the twenty-four others in an advanced stage of construction. And soon the National Assembly had backed the nuclear component of the country's energy plan by 331 votes to 67, leading one opposition spokesman to declare that 'the Ecologists have realized that you did not wait for the cock to crow three times before abandoning your fine electoral promises.'

During 1982 France also had the dubious distinction of reporting one of the first cases of nuclear terrorism, when five Soviet-made anti-tank rockets were fired across the Rhône at the Superphénix reactor, scoring four direct hits on the outer concrete shell of the $1.5 billion plant. The damage caused was only superficial, with officials assuring the local population that the three-foot-thick walls of the reactor are designed to prevent an explosion in the event of an earthquake or aeroplane crash.

Later in the same month, a series of aerial flares arced through the night sky over Illinois's largest nuclear plant, the giant Zion generating plant, and a three-minute videotape was delivered to local news organizations showing the mock attack and accompanied by a note reading: 'Zion Nuclear Power Station January 27, 1982. This was a warning. The next attack will be real.' Commonwealth Edison dismissed the incident as a 'crackpot public relations stunt', but tightened security at the Zion plant. 'We don't have the luxury of deciding that it's a prank,' commented the FBI, which was investigating the incident.

More seriously, at the end of 1982, four powerful explosions rocked South Africa's Koeberg nuclear plant, near Cape Town. Following earlier attacks on the country's SASOL oil-from-coal plants, the blasts were obviously sabotage – and a worrying signal that the optimistic assumptions adopted by nuclear planners are ill-founded.

Every so often, of course, the US nuclear industry won a victory, as when voters in the state of Maine voted three-to-two in favour of nuclear power. 'We're grateful that voters have confirmed our belief that Maine must use all of its viable energy resources in order to ensure a healthy economy and a quality environment,' said one of the owners of the state's only nuclear power plant, the 840 MW Maine Yankee.

But dreams of 1,200 reactors generating prodigious quantities of electricity by the year 2000 were fading in the United States. Indeed, many saw the US industry as itself being on the verge of a 'meltdown'. With the clean-up of the Three Mile Island plant still continuing and involving efforts to dispose of 700,000 gallons of radioactive water lying 8½ feet (2.6 metres) deep in a building next to the reactor core, public support for nuclear power was crumbling. A Harris poll found public opinion split fifty-fifty on nuclear energy, whereas an earlier poll, before the Three Mile Island accident, had shown 57 per cent in favour and only 31 per cent opposed.

But, while Metropolitan Edison was hiring teams of ratcatchers to track down the animals responsible for leaving a trail of radioactive droppings around the Three Mile Island site, news was beginning to filter through of a much more serious development as far as the US nuclear industry was concerned.

## The Whoops Mothballing

Reactor safety had relatively little to do with what, even in retrospect, was one of the nuclear industry's worst moments. The victim (or culprit, depending on your view) was the giant north-western power utility, the Washington Public Power Supply System (WWPPS) – popularly abbreviated, as I found when I visited Washington State, to 'Whoops'. The region, as anyone who has experienced its climate can readily imagine, is awash with hydropower resources, and, as Chapter 12 shows, it also has the world's largest dam, the Grand Coulee. A strange place, then, to build what soon became the world's most expensive nuclear project.

The story began in 1971, when power-supply utilities from Idaho, Montana, Oregon, Washington and Wyoming set up WWPPS and placed orders for five 1,200 MW nuclear stations. Two of these were to be built at Satsop and three near Hanford, both sites being in Washington. The original cost estimate came in at $3.8 billion, with the first power to be generated by 1978. By 1981, however, the plants were still being constructed, not a watt of electricity had been generated, and the cost estimates had gone through the roof in a way which had left the nuclear industry, together with Wall Street, which had put up much of the money, agape. Later, two of the plants were scrapped, one was mothballed, and work on a fourth was stopped.

The final estimated cost had rocketed up to an unbelievable $100 billion, representing a better than 25-fold increase on the original estimates, raising the prospect that many of the towns which signed on for the WWPPS scheme would go bankrupt. To give some sense of the amount of money involved, the space shuttle project is estimated to have cost $8 billion; the Trans-Alaska oil pipeline cost a little more, at $9 billion; and the entire interstate highway network cost the US taxpayer a total of $80 billion.

'Whichever way you calculate it,' said one Wall Street underwriting firm, 'the loans given to these people over the years add up, if you include the interest, to the biggest public debt for a single project in the entire history of mankind. In constant dollars, the Suez Canal was far cheaper.' Or, as one Seattle newspaper put it, 'If outrage could produce power, the Pacific North-West's ratepayers would be generating enough energy to light up half the country.'

Even the WWPPS fiasco, however, is unlikely to sink the nuclear industry, though the lessons learned in the process will inevitably make it harder for the US industry to raise money on the market. But Sweden, another of the countries where Westinghouse had suggested that the nuclear programme was still going well, was altogether a different kettle of fish. Its light water reactors were the only ones to have been developed without the benefit of licences from a bigger country, and they had been so successful that Sweden occupied the world's leading position as far as sustained nuclear-power output, low radiation doses, reactor safety and waste disposal were concerned. All the Swedish plants were included in the international top twenty as far as their reliability was concerned.

And yet the Swedish Parliament, after a public referendum which had shown overwhelming support for the phasing out of the country's nuclear-power programme, was seriously considering dispensing with the nuclear option – despite the fact that it has large deposits of low-grade uranium assessed as at least equivalent in energy terms to Britain's North Sea oil reserves.

Denmark, even though Niels Bohr had been among nuclear energy's most notable pioneers, was closest to turning the atomic clock back – or off. It decided in 1979 to postpone introducing nuclear power stations, despite the fact that it depended on oil for 80 per cent of its energy needs. Instead, it has been concentrating on natural gas, home-produced oil, coal and energy conservation. The International Energy Agency had praised the Danes for cutting their dependence on imported oil to under 70 per cent of their total energy consumption, or a million tonnes a year less than before the first oil crisis.

The five oil-fields discovered in Danish waters in the North Sea could yield, when all in operation, an estimated total of at least five million tonnes of oil a year over 25 years, while a possible new field on the edge of Norway's Ekofisk field was giving rise to further optimism. Denmark's natural-gas fields, expected to come on stream in the mid-1980s, were estimated to be sufficient to provide enough gas to satisfy 10 per cent of the country's total energy needs for 20 years at least. Lucky Denmark. But the Danes, in any event, would have had considerable difficulties in tracking down suitable sites for nuclear reactors in their densely populated countryside.

Elsewhere in the world, meanwhile, there were countries with an enormous amount of space lying vacant and a desperate need for energy. Libya may have been overflowing with oil, but it illustrates the difference in population densities nicely: Libya houses less than half Denmark's population of 4.9 million in more than 40 times the space. And Libya is one of the countries whose nuclear activities are causing considerable concern to those who believe that the spread of nuclear-energy technology will lead to an uncontrollable proliferation of nuclear weaponry.

## A Question of Survival?

Libya, in fact, is a prime example of what will almost certainly go wrong with nuclear power on the proliferation front. At exactly the same moment in history when the American utilities were bewailing the plight of their nuclear-power programmes, Libya was hosting a nuclear technology conference at Grado, a resort on the Italian Adriatic, designed to buy Colonel Qadhafi's regime a semblance of respectability in this field. Libya had actually signed the Nuclear Non-Proliferation Treaty, but had also been busily trying to buy atomic weapons on the open market.

In 1975, for instance, the Libyan prime minister, Major Jalloud, tried to buy an atomic bomb 'off the shelf' from the Chinese, but was told to go away and make his own. Then, in 1977, Jalloud went to New Delhi, where it is said he offered an open cheque to the Indian Atomic Energy Commission if it would build Libya the sort of fuel cycle which would give it access to weapons-grade plutonium. Later still, Colonel Qadhafi was rumoured to be pouring money into Pakistan's efforts to develop an Islamic nuclear capability.

Pakistan's nuclear scientists freely admit that proliferation is a problem, but argue that it is too late to retrieve the contents of this particular Pandora's box. 'You cannot solve the problem by limiting nuclear technology to the privileged few,' said Munir Ahmad Khan, who left the International Atomic Energy Agency in 1972 to head Pakistan's Atomic Energy Commission. 'Nuclear technology has already spread and cannot be retrieved,' he continued. 'Technical safeguards deserve our fullest support, but they themselves cannot ensure non-proliferation because the incentive towards proliferation springs from insecurity and the political climate in which we live. To strengthen the non-proliferation regime,' he suggested, 'we must also control the vertical proliferation, the stockpiling of more and more destructive nuclear weapons, which poses the most awesome threat to human survival.'

Admitting the risks involved even in the routine operation of civilian nuclear plants, Khan nonetheless insisted that Pakistan was determined to have nuclear power. 'For many developing countries,' he pointed out, 'nuclear power is simply a matter of survival. We are pursuing a nuclear-power programme not because of prestige or for political reasons. The developed nations have no conception of how the energy crisis has hit us – what it means for our future.'

To bring the point home, he quoted some statistics. 'In the United States,' he began, 'an average citizen consumes some 10,000 units of electricity per year. In Europe, this consumption is between 6,000 and 9,000 units per capita per year and even in the poorest nations of Asia the average is more than 300 units per year. In Pakistan, the average consumption of electricity is barely 160 units per person. Because of the energy crisis, we cannot meet even this amount without going nuclear. It is easy,' he told interviewer Ziauddin Sardar, 'to be against nuclear power if you are sitting in a fully lit, fully heated house in London or New York. The view is considerably different from where I am sitting.'

Meanwhile, stressing that Canada did not want to become a purveyor of nuclear systems without adequate safeguards, prime minister Pierre Trudeau warned that the country's safeguards against nuclear proliferation were costing Canada sales of its CANDU reactors. 'We are being undercut,' he said, 'by other countries who are less concerned with safeguards and less worried about nuclear proliferation.'

M. Trudeau could well have pointed his finger at his immediate neighbours. President Reagan was pledging his administration to doing 'everything in our power' to prevent proliferation, while making a 'special case exemption' to allow Brazil, which had not signed the Non-Proliferation Treaty, to purchase fuel for its first reactor, Angra 1 – built by Westinghouse under a 1972 contract and located on the Atlantic coast south of Rio de Janeiro. The original contract provided for the supply of uranium for the life of the reactor, but the 1978 Non-Proliferation Treaty barred the United States from selling uranium to countries that had not agreed to 'full-scope' safeguards for their nuclear programmes. Brazil's military government had cited security reasons for refusing full international inspection of Angra 1 or of the nine other reactors it had contracted to build. This refusal, not surprisingly, had led to speculation that the Brazilians were developing nuclear weapons.

'If we don't do something about the spread of nuclear weapons material and technology,' said Victor Gilinsky, a commissioner on the US Nuclear Regulatory Commission, 'we better tighten our safety belts because it is going to be a rough ride.' One country which did more than tighten its seat belt was Israel. Although it denied adamantly that its aircraft were involved in the bombing raid on Iraq's Isis and Osirak reactors on 30 September 1980, there was no doubt that it was Israel's fighter-bombers that knocked out the Osirak reactor on 8 June the following year.

The French nuclear industry, which has been an aggressive purveyor of nuclear technology across the world, was caught wrong-footed. 'We are in a completely new situation that was not foreseen in any international treaties,' one French spokesman piously intoned after the news came through that the reactors had been bombed. He would not be drawn on the claim that the Iraqis had earlier bought a device known as a 'hot cell' from Italy, designed to enable its technicians to handle radioactive substances from behind lead shielding. This, some said, could help the Iraqis extract weapons-grade plutonium even from irradiated uranium.

In the wake of the bombing, nuclear scientists stressed, as they did after the rocketing of the French fast breeder reactor, that reactors cannot blow up like atomic bombs, even if they themselves are bombed. Safety experts argued that even precision bombing would not normally break open a reactor. The PWR, for example, is typically housed in buildings made of reinforced concrete some 5–6 feet (1.5–1.8 metres) thick. Inside, the steel pressure vessel has walls a foot (30 cm) thick and is further protected by a concrete radiation shield.

If, however, the pressure vessel were to be ruptured, or if supplies of power or coolant to the reactor were to be disrupted for long enough, then things might turn out rather differently. A typical PWR contains hundreds of tons of water at 300°C (572°F). The pressure inside the pressure vessel ensures that the water does not boil, but if the vessel were breached, that water would flash into steam, the core would probably be destroyed and much of its radioactive material would escape. If, in the worst case, a so-called 'melt-down' occurred, in what the American anti-nuclear spokesmen have come to refer to as the 'China Syndrome', the molten fission products could burn their way through the bottom of the reactors and thence deep into the earth, resulting in considerable radioactive fallout.

But far, far worse would be the detonation of a nuclear bomb on top of a nuclear reactor; scientists who have considered this prospect conclude that a nuclear attack could turn a reactor into a devastating radiological weapon. The fallout from the bomb would initially be higher than that from the reactor. After one hour, the radioactivity released by the detonation of a one-megaton thermo-nuclear bomb would be 1,000 times greater than the radioactivity that would escape in the worst conceivable peacetime reactor accident. And if the reactor were vaporized by the bomb-burst, the resulting mushroom cloud would broadcast the radioactive materials further abroad – and they would take longer to decay than the debris from the bomb itself.

Meanwhile, however, public concern has tended to focus on the problems associated with the routine operation of commercial reactors, concern which the US nuclear industry has been particularly effective in encouraging. The industry has generally been its own worst enemy. Take the Diablo Canyon nuclear plant as an example. The so-called Abalone Alliance attempted to blockade the $2.3 billion plant in California – which had become quite as controversial as Three Mile Island and ranked as the longest-delayed nuclear plant in America.

Pacific Gas & Electricity (PG & E), the vast Californian power utility, had been forced to fight a long-drawn-out battle to get a nuclear plant into operation on the Californian coastline. Thwarted first at Bodega Bay by earthquake dangers, PG & E then tried a shoreline of dunes near Pismo Beach, and was rebuffed by ecologists. Then, in 1963, it began preparing the Diablo Canyon site. Even the Sierra Club had approved the site by 1967, although in doing so it split its membership and the more radical element span off as Friends of the Earth, a group which still inveighs against the plant.

Inveigh it might, but all the efforts of the Abalone Alliance of environmentalists had failed to stop the Nuclear Regulatory Commission from giving PG & E permission to start testing its plant. So, with the blockade fading and the plant about to start low-power operation, what happened? What happened was that mighty PG & E was forced to announce that it had discovered construction errors in the plant which necessitated an indefinite shut-down. The plant's environmental opponents had always challenged its location a mere 2½ miles (4 km) from an active earthquake fault. And then, while engineers were examining reinforcements designed to protect the reactor's workings against this seismic threat, they realized to their horror that they were checking one set of cooling water pipe supports against a plan showing their mirror-image. Someone had installed them back to front.

The plant was originally meant to have two reactors, and it appeared that the construction engineers had used the diagram for reactor Number 2 when they installed reactor Number 1. A PG & E spokesman pointed out that the mix-up could mean that some pipes were even stronger than they needed to be, but others would be much weaker. Come an earthquake, and some of the supports would almost certainly have collapsed, rupturing some of the plant's cooling water supply pipes.

As though that were not enough, several days later the Nuclear Regulatory Commission announced that the errors extended to the plant's power supply, with closer inspection having shown that the cable supports, metal trays that each hold up to a hundred electrical conduits, had been put together incorrectly. The Commission said that it regarded the cable support problem with 'the same level of concern as the pipe supports'. The Commission's chief of reactor construction in the San Francisco area explained that 'the cables could break loose and lose the ability to carry the required electrical current'. A reactor's cooling circuits and power supply, as we have seen, are its two most important Achilles heels – and at Diablo Canyon both had proved to be suspect.

Later the same month, Consolidated Edison was forced to admit that part of its Indian Point reactor, which the previous year had sat in three metres of water from the Hudson River for an unknown time, was corroding far faster than had been expected. But, since sixteen other reactors around the country also appeared to be affected by the same corrosion problems, the fact that the Hudson had been allowed to flow around the reactor's entrails seems to have had less to do with the problem than did basic design flaws.

A study carried out for the Nuclear Regulatory Commission by Sandia National Laboratories, and leaked late in 1982, concluded that the worst-case death toll if a US reactor failed could exceed 100,000. Assuming severe core damage, the melting of uranium fuel, a failure of safety systems and a major breach of the reactor's containment, the study calculated that the worst death toll would occur if such a worst-case accident happened at Salem, New Jersey, where a nuclear power plant sits alongside the Delaware River. The greatest property damage would occur if such an accident happened at the Indian Point 3 reactor, north of New York City – which could result in $314 billion worth of damage. The study estimated that such an accident could happen once in 100,000 reactor years, giving a 2-per-cent chance that it will happen in the USA by the end of the century.

All reactors are, in effect, prototypes – and tend to behave as such, frequently developing serious, unexpected faults. All but two of the reactors affected by these corrosion problems were built by Westinghouse between 1968 and 1976. The basic problem was located in the primary cooling loop, which circulates water around the reactor core. The pipes bearing this water, which is heated to 600°F (316°C), are themselves cooled by the secondary loop, which discharges direct to the environment. If the primary loop corrodes, radioactive water could well pass from the primary loop to the secondary loop, and thence into the outside world. The outside world, understandably, was getting somewhat nervous.

'On the information available today,' said Dr Thomas Murley, director of safety technology for the NRC, 'I would say we'd get very nervous after another year or so.' He was talking to the press shortly after the discovery of the reactor rusting problem, but he was concerned about a completely new problem which had emerged in the intervening weeks. Each reactor core is surrounded by an eight-inch-thick steel shell, which, it transpired, was becoming brittle far faster than had been expected. Normally this shell is heated to a temperature of 550°F (288°C) and is designed to withstand a working pressure of 2,200 lbs per square inch (155 kg/cm²) for the reactor's life-time.

The NRC called urgently for further information from the operators of the forty-six reactors potentially at risk, concerned that the containment vessels could rupture if, in an emergency, they were abruptly cooled. If the problem turned out to be a real one, the reactor owners knew they were sunk. The containment vessels are an integral part of nuclear plants, so that their replacement would involve rebuilding the plants in their entirety. Faced with such a choice, some believed, the owners of PWRs could well be forced to abandon them altogether.

By early 1982, NRC staff were calculating that nineteen nuclear plants then under construction would be cancelled, wiping out billions of dollars in investment. A spokesman for the Atomic Industrial Forum commented that 'we've had a recession for several years and the growth rate for electricity is down.' In fact, he continued, power demand increased by only 0.3 per cent during 1981, 'and we could save just about that much by turning off refrigerator light-bulbs.'

A retiring member of the NRC, Peter Bradford, took the opportunity to comment that new nuclear orders 'are not likely without a substantial period of accident-free operation, a general drop in capital costs, a larger rate of growth in electricity demand, viable assurance against the clean-up and perhaps replacement power costs of major accidents, renewed investor confidence, and a public willingness to have plants sited in some communities.' The French have encouraged some communities to accept nuclear power plants by providing them with cheaper power, but even if that method were adopted elsewhere, this long list of requirements is a tall order indeed.

With a shrinking market, the nuclear industry in the West has been forced to engage in increasingly cut-throat competition. A study by the Rockefeller Foundation and Britain's Royal Institute of International Affairs estimated that the capacity of the West's nuclear industry for building new reactors was between 49 and 58 units a year by the early 1980s, compared with a forecast demand ranging between a low figure of 14 and a high estimate of 25 a year during the 1980s. Competing furiously for this work are four giant American companies, three in Japan and one each in France, Germany, Sweden, Canada and Britain. Paradoxically, the US reactor manufacturers, who had been without a new domestic order for some years, were keeping themselves afloat on redesign work and the supply of components to meet the new NRC standards enforced in the wake of such highly publicized accidents as Three Mile Island.

## Mini-reactors and Fusion

Faced with such constraints, the nuclear industry has adopted a number of strategies. First, it has tried to export more reactors and related products and services. One target has been Mexico, which announced a 10–20-reactor programme valued at up to $50 billion and designed to double energy production in the country within twenty years. The companies bidding for the work included Westinghouse Electric, Combustion Engineering and General Electric of the United States, France's Framatome, Atomic Energy of Canada, Sweden's Asea-Atom and Kraftwerk Union of West Germany. And then Mexico, like a number of other countries, announced that it would postpone any further orders, because of the oil glut and its huge and increasingly troublesome foreign debt.

*Table 5.3: Nuclear fission capacity by non-communist location*
*(source: Nuclear Engineering International)*

| Country | Reactors over 150 MW | 1981 nuclear capacity/MW |
|---|---|---|
| USA | 69 | 56,615 |
| Canada | 10 | 5,820 |
| Europe total | 76 | 45,173 |
| UK | 23 | 8,220 |
| France | 20 | 15,292 |
| West Germany | 10 | 8,949 |
| Rest of Europe | 23 | 12,712 |
| Japan | 23 | 15,676 |

Mexico's proven hydrocarbon reserves were estimated at the time to be sufficient to meet current needs for at least sixty years. By contrast, Japan has little oil of its own and, as Table 5.3 shows, has pushed itself into the front ranks of the nuclear nations. Although no Japanese reactor manufacturer had gained an export order for a nuclear reactor by 1981, modest quantities of components had been exported and the country's Ministry of International Trade and Industry (MITI) was backing the development of new 'mini-reactors', designed with export markets, particularly in the Third World, very much in mind.

Small reactors with a 200,000 kW capacity are in demand in many parts of the developing world where electricity generating needs are too small to justify the installation of larger reactors. They also have potential, MITI believes, in supplying power to energy-hungry industries such as paper and chemicals manufacturing and metal processing. The attraction of such mini-reactors for a country like Japan is that they could be mass-produced, using prefabricated modular designs. Such reactors would probably be marginally more expensive (per kWn produced) to operate than larger reactors, but the feeling has been that the margin between nuclear and oil-fired plant is so great that such a marginal increase in the cost of the nuclear option is unlikely to be significant.

Fusion power, which has been the great white hope of the nuclear industry, has looked more attractive as fission has hit one problem after another – but no one yet knows whether it can be made to work on a commercial basis within the foreseeable future. Sometimes described as a renewable source of energy, fusion's most promising fuel currently seems to be a mixture of the heavy hydrogen isotopes deuterium and tritium – supplies of which are derived from lithium ores, which are not by any means unlimited.

Given sufficient advances in fusion technology, it should eventually be possible to use deuterium, which can be obtained from water, as the sole fuel. Jules Verne, yet again, may have got it right: in *The Mysterious Island* he suggested that 'water may be the coal of the future'. A more accurate description of fusion power, however, would therefore be 'virtually inexhaustible'. But, this qualification aside, *if* the fusion option can be made to work, there is every prospect that its contribution to global energy supplies could vastly exceed that available from all the other renewable-energy resources put together.

Another striking advantage of fusion power is that it may well sidestep the radioactive waste problems which are proving such a headache with nuclear fission. Even if all the reactor operation problems were sorted out permanently tomorrow, the disposal of nuclear wastes will remain a major brake on the fission option until someone comes up with a safe way of disposing of materials with very, very long half-lives. None of the existing disposal options is satisfactory. Dumping the waste into the ocean will not be tolerated indefinitely, and the glassification route, involving the solidification of nuclear wastes in blocks of glass, is not yet proven.

After a three-year study in Britain, a country which was still dumping considerable quantities of radioactive waste in the sea, despite strenuous protests from groups such as Greenpeace, the official view has been that the problem of waste management is manageable. The nuclear industry, it was reported, had only produced enough high-level radioactive waste to fill two small houses and, by the year 2000, it would 'only' fill two swimming pools. 'The problem of radioactive waste management is resolving itself into one of manageable proportions,' one civil servant summarized the research findings. 'We've not flushed out any problems at the front end of the science, no big unknowns. It's very largely a morass of practical problems.'

There has been no shortage of ideas about how we might dispose of high-level wastes, from the Americans who have suggested shooting it into deep space or dropping it into subduction zones on the ocean floor, through the West Germans who store such wastes down a salt mine near Gorleben, to Professor Ted Ringwood of the Australian National University who argues that his 'Synroc' formula is the answer. This, a synthetic rock, consists of a mixture of titanium minerals which, Ringwood hopes, could encapsulate and safely immobilize high-level radioactive wastes for millions of years.

But what, meanwhile, of the much greater volumes of low-level waste? Companies like Westinghouse admit that one of their most worrying Achilles heels is their inability, even after decades of operating nuclear plants, to offer any permanent, commercially acceptable solution to the waste-disposal problem. Not so the Russians. 'Our scientists are working on this,' Atommash director Valery Pershin reassured the world. 'Some of it can be recycled. And we have a big country with plenty of room to store used fuel.' As the inhabitants of Kyshtym in the southern Urals know only too well – or, at least, those who survive.

According to Zhores Medvedev, who studied the environmental effects of an explosion there in 1957, nuclear wastes had been dumped in the area and, for some reason, went critical. A mass evacuation had to be mounted, vegetation and milk had to be destroyed, and hundreds of people are reported to have died a slow, agonizing death from radiation poisoning. The area is still largely uninhabited, and women living nearby are advised to have abortions should they have the misfortune to become pregnant.

A fusion reactor, by contrast, would produce less radioactive waste, and it is thought that the wastes would decay relatively rapidly – but it would bring its own unique problems. In broad terms, it would produce a net release of energy from the fusion of the nuclei of fuel atoms, which would be super-heated to overcome the repelling forces which separate them. The fuel nuclei have to be concentrated, by magnetic or inertial confinement in a vacuum, at a temperature of about 100 million degrees centigrade for a minimum period of about one second. Once 'lit', the fusion reaction would reproduce the conditions prevailing inside our massive solar reactor. To show what this means, consider the NOVA fusion reactor which is being built at the Lawrence Livermore National Laboratories, forty miles east of San Francisco.

A single-bar electric fire rated at 1 kW emits one kilojoule of heat during one second of operation. NOVA, in attempting to trigger a fusion reaction, will have to compress 500 kilojoules into 10 pico-seconds (a few tenths of a billionth of a second) – or some 25 trillion watts while the pulse is on. As the 'lead' agency in fusion research in the United States, Lawrence Livermore hosts two major fusion experiments: the magnetic mirror fusion experiment and SHIVA. The first of these will use superconducting magnets to contain the white-hot vapour-cloud of plasma inside a large cylindrical reaction chamber. The second, SHIVA, involves the focusing of twenty laser beams down a many-armed reaction chamber on to a tiny fusion target, a glass bead containing the deuterium-tritium fuel, which is about the size of a grain of sand.

The most popular fusion-reactor design, however, is still the Tokamak, pioneered by the USSR. Here the plasma is confined in a toroidal, or doughnut-shaped, chamber by a strong magnetic field produced by coils wrapped around the doughnut. One of the leading US Tokamak research teams, at Princeton University, used radio-frequency heating to generate an estimated 60-watts-worth of nuclear fusion reaction, enough – if it were all to be converted into electricity – to power a single light-bulb. The excitement, however, was not about the fact that the reactions could have powered a light-bulb, but about the fact that the team had demonstrated that radio-frequency heating could generate plasma temperatures of around 800 million degrees centigrade. This form of heating is five times more energy-efficient than the rival neutral beam heating, and radiowaves can be delivered through smaller tubes than neutral beams.

The main problem with fusion research, apart from sheer expense, is that the pay-off is so far in the future. Even fusion's optimists, like Princeton's Harold Furth, find it hard to imagine a commercial fusion reactor before the year 2020. In contrast to the space programme launched by NASA, which brought one milestone after another, and all of them seen on television, fusion research has a good deal less to offer the politician in the short term. But, just as the Sputnik success was a shot in the arm for the US space programme, the US fusion programme really took off after the announcement from the USSR in 1969 that the Tokamaks T–3 and TM–3 had achieved very much hotter, denser and longer-lived plasmas than previous experiments. The Princeton Tokamak's most advanced rival is JET, the Joint European Torus, which is expected to produce more energy than is fed into it some time in the late 1980s – although even at full power JET will not be a working fusion reactor.

Despite fusion's long-term promise, however, there are those who feel it represents something of a technological blind alley, and even among proponents there are those who argue that today's large-scale programmes are in danger of repeating the mistakes which have bedevilled nuclear fission. 'Fusion is a clever way to do something that we don't really want to do,' Amory Lovins has commented: 'to find yet another capital-intensive, complex, centralized source of large blocks of base-load electricity.' And, over at PG & E, company president Clint Ashworth has argued that America 'needs . . . to orient its fusion program more toward turning fusion into a real energy option and not just another nuclear reactor. What we don't need,' he stressed, in the wake of the Diablo Canyon fiasco, 'is a huge, complicated (fusion) plant with many of the same problems as the nuclear plants we already have.'

Some observers have been even more trenchant in their criticism of existing fusion programmes. Over at Dow Chemical, for example, William Sauber had been tracking fusion, to assess how it might help the chemical industry with its energy problems. He was not entirely reassured by what he saw. 'There seems to be a Doomsday disorder that afflicts all government programs where you have an elitist group spending oceans of money and figuring on fifty years to develop a commercial reactor,' he reported. 'The entrepreneur is thwarted because the government has sucked up all the capital from the private sector. If allowed to remain with the entrepreneurs, a commercial reactor would be developed much sooner.'

Many people would put that down to Dow's own hard-nosed business philosophy and its readiness to stick out its political neck in the cause of free enterprise. But down in the ravines of Torrey

Pines Mesa, near San Diego, California, Dr Tihiro Ohkawa of the General Atomic Corporation was living something of a schizophrenic working life – and doing so in high hopes of demonstrating the applicability of E. F. Schumacher's dictum *Small is Beautiful* in the fusion field.

General Atomic, owned by Gulf Oil and Royal Dutch Shell, has been working on the world's largest privately built Tokamak fusion reactor, Doublet III. Gulf and Shell had already burned their fingers, having invested hundreds of millions of dollars in two ill-fated nuclear projects; one was an advanced gas-cooled fission reactor which ploughed into the commercial sand, and General Atomic also built the Barnwell nuclear-fuel-reprocessing plant, in South Carolina, which ended up unused because of President Carter's concern about nuclear proliferation. But, with help from Phillips Petroleum, Dr Ohkawa was off on a fusion tangent which he hoped would lead to a fusion reactor which could be mass-produced by 1990, which would be about a tenth the size of machines like Doublet III (his daytime work) and could be plugged in and out of existing power plants with all the convenience of a light-bulb.

Like the Tokamak design, Dr Ohkawa's miniaturized fusion reactor is a toroidal or doughnut-shaped machine, within which ionized gas is produced by extremely high temperatures. And, like the Tokamaks, this design – dubbed OHTE, for Ohmically Heated Toroidal Experiment – confines the plasma within powerful magnetic fields. The difference between the OHTE reactor and the Tokamaks, however, is that it bypasses the need for the complex, expensive equipment used to boost the ohmic heating capacity of the Tokamaks – and its use of magnetic fields is so elegant that it should work out much cheaper than the larger magnetic-field reactors.

According to Ken Partain, the engineer who directed the construction of OHTE, General Atomic could have a fusion reactor in mass production by 1992, probably about 2 metres in radius and producing 100–500 MW of electricity at a cost of $100 million. As Dr Ohkawa explained, 'the idea up until now has been to make fusion engineering harder and the physics easier, so that we could study the fundamentals of the physics involved. But now is the time in fusion when we must make the job harder for the physicist and easier for the engineer, so that we can create power plants that are simple enough to build commercially. From an engineering standpoint, OHTE is almost like a dream.'

Allowing for a degree of hyperbole, the view that the future lies with throwaway Tokamaks, with the cores lasting for only a few months before they needed to be recycled or thrown away, has won increasing support in fusion circles. One advantage is that there would be very much less of a radiation problem than there would be with a thirty-year-old large fusion reactor, and new developments in what will inevitably be a fast moving field could readily be incorporated during the change-over. Just down the road from General Atomic, in La Jolla, International Nuclear Energy Systems Company Inc. (INESCO) has also been developing a small fusion-reactor design, called the Riggatron, which would work rather like a supercharged engine – with gas fed in once initial ignition had been achieved, in a process dubbed 'pop-gas fueling'.

Riggatrons would also burn out rapidly, but, as INESCO president Dr Robert Bussard pointed out, 'the gadget costs almost nothing. You could lease them like Xerox machines. If you decided to charge them off against taxes, you could throw them away.' But one problem such reactors will not have to cope with is the pulsed explosions which have imposed such strains on the physical fabric of existing Tokamaks, because they could operate in the 'steady-state' mode. INESCO has been negotiating with the Israelis, who want to build a fusion reactor near Tel Aviv.

The promises that have been made on fusion's behalf look extraordinary if listed on a piece of paper. Dow Chemical, for example, suggests that the chemical industry would experience a 'total rebirth' if small-scale fusion becomes a reality, using the plasma to produce complex molecular structures without having to go through hydrocarbon processing – avoiding pollution and resulting in very much purer chemicals at the end of the process.

If General Atomic, INESCO or any of the other fusion researchers succeeds in bringing the sun to earth, then the prospect for the various genuinely renewable-energy technologies harnessing energy flows deriving ultimately from the sun will be significantly affected. But the technological and commercial obstacles which remain will take a great deal of effort, money and skill to surmount. We shall achieve fusion power on a continuous basis, instead of the explosive release of fusion energy afforded by an H-bomb, but it remains an open question whether we shall be able to convert the resulting technology into a commercially attractive power generation option before the middle decades of the twenty-first century.

In the meantime, around the world, the oil companies have joined the ranks of those who have been attempting to harness a very different type of nuclear reactor, turning from the stars to the ground beneath their feet. Before we consider the solar technologies proper (and turn to the single lunar energy technology, tidal power, in Chapter 12), Chapter 6 briefly reviews the geothermal prospect.

# 6 ⊙ *Inner Fires*

Huge, blood-red worms loomed out of the dark to greet the small band of geologists who went diving deep into the sunless world of the Galapagos Rift in 1977. Eyeless, mouthless and gutless, the worms had no right to be there, according to the laws of marine ecology, let alone flourish. Anchored in seething clusters and measuring up to 2.5 metres long, the worms were found some 2.5 kilometres (1½ miles) beneath the surface of the eastern Pacific in what amounted to sunless oases.

The Galapagos Rift, the deep-diving scientists knew, forms the boundary between two of the earth's massive crustal plates, some of which support entire continents. The two plates, the Cocos Plate and the Nazca Plate, are moving steadily apart, while molten magma surges up from the earth's mantle to fill the resulting gap. What no one had realized before the 1977 expedition was that warm-water vents, which occur in many places along the Mid-Oceanic Ridge, could support such a bewildering profusion of life. The vents, or 'black smokers' as they were soon dubbed, are believed to result when sea-water seeps down through porous rocks into the planet's super-heated mantle. Picking up minerals along the way, the water is blasted back into the sea through the chimney-like vents.

Billowing up like smoke from some sea-bed steel works, the plumes power an ecosystem which has few, if any, direct links with the sun which circles some 150 million kilometres overhead. One of the first things the ecologists did was to lower temperature sensors vertically down into the vents, where they recorded 350°C and promptly melted. As these boiling, mineral-saturated plumes hit the surrounding water, which is almost 350°C cooler, they produce a heavy metal fall-out, coating rock and organism alike with an armour of iron, manganese and zinc sulphides. A strange place indeed for life to take root.

Closer inspection, however, revealed that life had found ways of softening even this harsh environment. The entire ecosystem may be driven by chemical synthesis, rather than by solar-powered photo-synthesis, but its basic mechanics are similar to those of thousands of other systems studied by ecologists. They convert hydrogen sulphide,

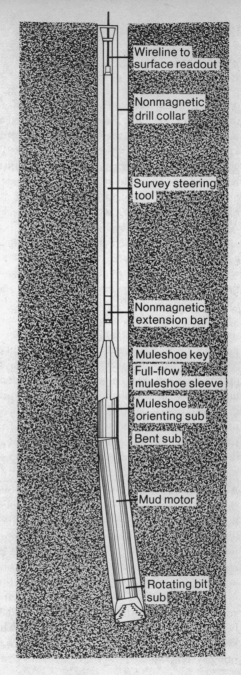

Figure 6.1: Drill used in the U K geothermal programme (source: Camborne School of Mines).

carbon dioxide and oxygen into fatter bacteria. Indeed, the bacteria-count near the vents can run as high as one million per cubic centimetre – or, to put it another way, four million bacteria in a teaspoon of water. They were, in fact, very similar to the bacteria found on the flanks of Mount St Helens as that blasted volcano slowly returned to life. When the volcano blew up, obliterating hundreds of square kilometres of forest, it also swept geologist David Johnston and his entire mobile laboratory, Coldwater II, off the ridge where it had been parked – out into space over Coldwater Creek. A brave man, Dr Johnston, for he had known only too well the risks he faced, having barely escaped with his life several years earlier from an Alaskan volcano, Mount St Augustin.

Whatever possessed him to risk life and limb on the flanks of a geological time-bomb? Strangely, there is a link with those black smokers on the floor of the eastern Pacific – and it is not the fact that chemosynthetic bacteria were found to be thriving both around the warm-water vents and on the flanks of Mount St Helens. Both volcanoes and vents, in fact, represent windows through which scientists can see something of the inner workings of our planet. Far beneath the earth's surface, great convection currents stir the red-hot rock of the planet's inner mantle, providing the driving force which moves the continental plates inexorably across the globe. Scientists, however, are at odds about the pattern, depth, and indeed the cause of those currents.

Some are convinced that the heat which drives the currents is simply a relic of the planet's fiery creation, while others maintain that the decay of radioactive elements deep within the planet's core fuels what might be described as a planetary nuclear reactor. Faced with problems in getting other energy technologies to operate as the accountants would like, some power utilities and sundry energy prospectors have been trying to harness the reactor which powers those submarine oases.

## Going Underground

Miners working and sweating deep in the bowels of the earth have long known that the deeper you go the warmer you get. Rock temperatures, in fact, can rise surprisingly quickly, and excess heat has been one of the principal problems barring the way to ever-deeper mines. It is almost as if microscopic miners were digging slowly down through the successive layers of shielding around the core of a nuclear reactor, extracting minerals from the shield-wall as they go.

One of the deepest mines in the world, if not the deepest, may be found in the Western Deep Levels in South Africa. It descends 4.5 kilometres into the planet, and needs a massive refrigeration system to cool the workings. But miners also know that temperatures do not rise uniformly as you move down different mine-shafts only a few miles distant from one another. Generally speaking, the closer you are to the edge of one of the tectonic plates which make up the planet's crust, the more likely you are to have ready access to geothermal heat – or, if you are a miner, the more likely you are to need to construct yourself an underground refrigerator.

Some hot spots are easy to get at; others, like those at the bottom of the Galapagos Rift, are economically out of the question. New Zealand, which sits astride the Pacific and Australian plates, is, in one sense at least, luckier. The Wairakei steam fields are found in an area showing a very steep temperature gradient. High-temperature zones can be reached at comparatively shallow drilling depths, say 200 metres, which makes geothermal energy that much more attractive.

Life on the leading (or receding) edge of a continental plate has always had its drawbacks – and Iceland is no exception to the rule. On 23 January 1973, the year of the first oil crisis, Iceland's most important fishing port, Heimaey, was showered with ash and rock by the volcano Helgafell. In a sense, the planetary reactor was undergoing a minor 'melt-down'. During the space of a few hours, one metre of ash accumulated in some parts of the town. One third of Heimaey and 400 homes were burned or buried. Nearly 5,000 people had to be evacuated, but, by a stroke of great good fortune, the lava flows actually improved the town's harbour, by providing an extended breakwater.

Heimaey was a mere skirmish, however, in comparison with earlier Icelandic eruptions. When the Laki fissure erupted in 1783, for example, basalt lavas poured out over several months, inundating tens of square kilometres and filling the Skaftar and Hverfisfljot river valleys to a depth of over 100 metres. Few people were actually caught in the advancing lavas, but some 10,000 (or 20 per cent of Iceland's population at the time) died of starvation. The ash-fall carpeted grazing lands, with disastrous effects on Iceland's livestock economy. According to one estimate, some 190,000 sheep, 28,000 horses and

11,500 cattle died – at a time when Iceland had almost no trade with the outside world.

Given that they were condemned to live astride a nuclear reactor which was guaranteed to undergo periodic and disastrous melt-downs, the people of Iceland decided that they might as well try to extract energy from it. By the time I went round the country's geothermal power stations, in the summer of 1977, Iceland – having no oil, gas or coal reserves of its own – was meeting about one third of its energy needs by means of geothermal heat or power. About 70 per cent of Iceland's homes were geothermally heated, with heating bills typically about one fifth of those for houses heated by oil. Each year, it was estimated, geothermal energy was saving some two tons of oil for each member of Iceland's population.

Iceland's first hot-water borehole was drilled as long ago as 1928, at Thottalaugar, a hot spring traditionally used by the people of Reykjavík for doing their laundry – though it is a good hour's walk from the town. The extracted water was piped three kilometres and used to heat two schools, seventy houses and a swimming pool. The success of this first scheme led to others, until eventually geothermal fields were discovered under Reykjavík itself. Because of their higher temperature (103–128°C), the useful heat extracted is more than three times as great per volume of water as that from earlier fields. Reykjavík's own fields were supplying some 75 per cent of the city's geothermal heat by the time Sniöbjorn Bjarnason of the Hitaveita (or municipal district heating service) showed me around the system.

A major environmental problem associated with some geothermal fields is the accumulation of by-products such as sulphides. The Larderello steam field west of Florence, Italy, was originally tapped for its boric acid content. Tuscany's geothermal power stations are unattractive places, wreathed in steam and hydrogen sulphide – used in schoolboy stink bombs. Indeed, long before it was harnessed for electricity generation, Larderello was considered a thoroughly un-wholesome place. With its seething, steaming pools, it is reputed to have inspired Dante's vision of Hell in the *Inferno*.

Someone else who believed he had discovered the gates of Hell was William Elliott, an explorer-cum-surveyor at the time of the Californian gold rush. He happened upon a canyon full of erupting steam vents while tracking a wounded bear. That canyon was later harnessed by the Geysers power plant, built in 1960, which displaced Larderello as the world's largest geothermal plant in 1973.

## Geothermal Pipe-dreams

Driving ninety miles north of San Francisco, up into the rugged and parched Mayacamas Mountains, I saw no grizzly bears. But, after several hours twisting and turning through a sweltering summer afternoon, I found myself at the Geysers. In 1967, the pioneering Magma and Thermal power companies had merged their holdings in the Geysers with those of the Union Oil Company of California, resulting in a pooling of resources and boosting exploration and development work. Finding the various geothermal plants (Figure 6.2) was fairly

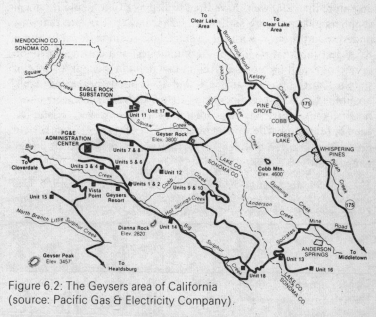

Figure 6.2: The Geysers area of California
(source: Pacific Gas & Electricity Company).

easy, even if they were hidden by trees: they were generally at the base of a column of steam with that characteristic rotten-egg odour of hydrogen sulphide. Dotted around the landscape are some of the older plants, now inactive and rusting, while later plants, such as those run by the Hughes Aircraft subsidiary Thermogenics, Inc., and Aminoil USA, Inc., a subsidiary of P. J. Reynolds Industries, were surrounded by fairly tight security.

Each 110,000 kilowatts of generating capacity at the Geysers means that PG & E can buy one million barrels of oil less a year, and the company, which was already generating more than one million kilo-watts of electricity, believes that it will reach two million by 1990. Even its existing generating capacity of about 1.2 million kilowatts provides enough power to satisfy the needs of a city of approximately one million people, while the higher figure represents something like 10 per cent of the total capacity of the PG & E system.

Early attempts, in the 1920s, to harness geothermal power in the Geysers foundered because of the corrosiveness of the steam, which destroyed pipes and turbines, and hydroelectricity was easy to come by. By the mid-1950s, however, stainless-steel alloys were available, and more than 200 wells have been drilled as PG & E and its steam suppliers plugged more and more generating capacity into that vast underground reactor, with the average hole running down to about 8,500 feet (about 1.6 miles or 2.6 kilometres) and costing, in round terms, one million dollars. About two million pounds of steam, supplied to the turbine at 335°F and 100 pounds per square inch, are needed each hour to operate a 110,000 kilowatt generating unit.

Of all the countries using geothermal energy, however, Iceland has been by far the most dependent on this source of energy (Table 6.1). In

Table 6.1: *Installed low-temperature geothermal capacity in 1980 (over 15°C). Nearly 100% of the bathing capacity is in Japan, Hungary, Iceland and Italy, and 97% of total capacity is installed in these four countries plus China and the USSR (source: UNERG, adapted by Earthscan)*

|  | For bathing | | For other purposes | | Total | |
|---|---|---|---|---|---|---|
|  | MW | % | MW | % | MW | % |
| Japan | 4,394 | 82 | 81 | 3 | 4,475 | 56 |
| Hungary | 547 | 10 | 619 | 23½ | 1,166 | 15 |
| Iceland | 209 | 4 | 932 | 35 | 1,141 | 14 |
| USSR | 0 | 0 | 555 | 21 | 555 | 7 |
| Italy | 192 | 4 | 73 | 3 | 265 | 3 |
| China | 7 | 0 | 144 | 5½ | 151 | 2 |
| USA | 4 | 0 | 111 | 4 | 115 | 1 |
| France | 0 | 0 | 56 | 2 | 56 | 1 |
| Czechoslovakia | 8 | 0 | 35 | 1½ | 43 | 1 |
| Romania | 0 | 0 | 30 | 1½ | 36 | 0 |
| Austria | 3 | 0 | 2 | 0 | 5 | 0 |
| Total | 5,364 | 100 | 2,644 | 100 | 8,008 | 100 |

1979, for example, it met 33 per cent of its total energy needs with geothermal heat or power, compared with 37 per cent coming from imported oil and 30 per cent from the country's many hydropower stations. El Salvador, on the other hand, qualifies as the world's largest producer of geothermal *electricity*, supplying 37 per cent of her total electricity needs geothermally in the late 1970s, against 44 per cent from hydropower and a surprisingly small 19 per cent from imported fossil fuels.

Nicaragua, El Salvador's much larger next-door neighbour, has steered well clear of nuclear energy. 'What use is nuclear energy to us?' asks Fernando Cuevas, planning director of Nicaragua's Department of Energy. 'It would only make us dependent upon the import of the technology and the uranium and would severely constrain our political independence. We have enough resources from our land, the sun and the rain to meet all our needs and the development of these is the best way for the future of our people.'

After the Sandinista guerrillas took over the country in 1979, the United States had cut off all aid to the country anyway, so Nicaragua was forbidden territory for US reactor manufacturers. And meanwhile the Nicaraguans were beginning to exploit their country's twenty natural nuclear power stations, its volcanoes. They were drilling for super-heated steam at the base of Momotombo volcano, about forty kilometres north-west of Managua, and were planning further drilling programmes in the Cordillera los Maribios – the country's chain of volcanic mountains. They were also thinking of tapping an even larger source of geothermal energy, a region lying between the three towns of Masaya, Diriamba and Granada, although engineers estimated that they would need to drill to a depth there of over 2 kilometres, rather than the 600 metres needed in the Cordillera los Maribios.

The most rapid geothermal developer, however, has probably been the Philippines, and with good reason. With little in the way of fossil fuel reserves of their own, the Filipinos have been alarmed at the way their bill for imported oil has rocketed over the years since 1973. In 1979, for example, the country paid $1.4 billion, and was expecting the 1980 figure to be double that. Not surprisingly, they have put a great deal of effort into energy prospecting, but they have drawn a blank in many areas and, overall, have come up with a much weaker hand than have countries like Australia, Britain, the USA or the USSR. However, the Philippines also happen to be located in the so-called Pacific 'fire-belt', a zone of intense seismic and volcanic activity. Indeed, one of the concerns of the anti-nuclear lobby has been that at least one of the country's nuclear power stations has been located, like the Diablo Canyon plant, in an area which is a strong candidate for an earthquake. In energy terms, the Philippines turn out to be sitting on something of a gold-mine, although it is by no means clear that the Filipinos will have the political will and technical expertise to exploit it. The Asian Development Bank came up with estimates of the country's geothermal resources which suggest a very considerable untapped potential, and a number of geothermal plants are already in operation. Two plants were producing geothermal electricity on the northern island of Luzon when the Asian Development Bank published its calculations, and a third had been installed on Leyte Island. Between them, they were supplying 257.5 MW – or about 5 per cent of the Philippines' needs at the time.

And the value of those geothermal resources? The Asian Development Bank was understandably wary of attaching any really concrete figures to them, but their significance can perhaps be judged by comparing the country's then current installed capacity of over 4,000 MW with an estimated rating of its geothermal resources of 38,000 MW. No one doubts that the Philippines will be a very long time in harnessing even a small fraction of these resources, but its energy planners now have a distinctly geothermal gleam in their eyes.


## An Electrifying Prospect?

Strangely, geothermal energy tends to come near the bottom of any listing of alternative energy resources. But there are a number of good reasons for this low ranking. The Workshop on Alternative Energy Strategies, sponsored by the Massachusetts Institute of Technology (MIT), published its report *Energy: Global Prospects 1985–2000* as I was poring over Reykjavík's geothermal heating system, concluding that the generation of electricity from geothermal sources will still be in its infancy by the year 2000.

Yet the first light-bulb was lit by geothermal electricity as long ago as 1904. Why is the development of this aspect of geothermal energy proceeding so slowly? The basic problem seems to be that, while electricity is a much more attractive way in which to receive your energy than is hot water straight from the ground, since hot water does not travel as well as electricity and has a relatively limited number of applications, electricity generation is only possible if a geothermal field meets a number of demanding requirements – and many signally fail to do so.

Simply stated, a viable geothermal field, in the eyes of an electrical engineer, should be something like a kettle. There should be water, and it should come in the right quantities. There needs to be a 'vessel', formed by a layer of impermeable rock, permitting a good head of steam to be built up. And there should be a reliable source of heat. The rate at which heat can be extracted from a geothermal field depends on the rate at which the rock itself can conduct heat. In an attempt to sidestep this problem, the United States has been experimenting with what it calls 'hydrofracturing' of igneous rock. Hot rock is first shattered, deep under the ground, creating a larger surface area for heat exchange. The kettle, in short, is enlarged.

Water is then injected into the resulting cavity, steam is generated and turbines are turned, generating electricity (Figure 6.3). But the layers of rock surrounding the cavity often prove to be too permeable, especially in naturally dry fields, to allow a usable head of steam to form. The generation of electricity tends, therefore, to be the last step in the development of geothermal resources – although the Geysers field clearly contradicts this general rule. Table 6.2 (p. 135) shows the electrical generating capacity for a number of countries in 1980, and gives estimates for the year 2000.

While you concentrate on low-temperature fields and use the resulting heat for space heating or drying produce like seaweed, very little heat is wasted: in short, the cycle is highly efficient in energy terms. But once switch to electricity generation, and your conversion efficiencies plummet. The overall efficiency in Iceland dropped from 90 per cent in 1960 to something like 45 per cent in 1980, with the difference largely accounted for by the poorer conversion efficiencies involved in going for geothermal electricity.

That said, however, country after country is taking up the geo-thermal torch. China, which was one of the earliest countries to recognize the therapeutic benefits of bathing in hot springs, an activity recorded over 2,000 years ago, has been a relatively late starter but now has survey teams out drilling in many areas – and has located over 2,000 likely sites for geothermal development.

In Europe, meanwhile, only Greece, Italy and Turkey (as their

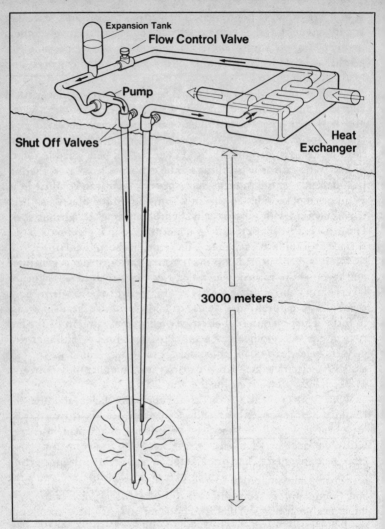

Figure 6.3: The Los Alamos 'hot dry rock' geothermal experiment (source: ATOM).

*Table 6.2: Geothermal electrical generating capacity, 1980 and 2000 (estimated). Some percentages have been rounded; less than 1% is shown as zero; a plus indicates a minimum figure (source: UNERG, adapted by Earthscan)*

| | 1980 | | 2000 | |
| | MW | % of world total | MW | % of world total |
| --- | --- | --- | --- | --- |
| USA | 923 | 38 | 5,824 | 33 |
| Japan | 168 | 7 | 3,668+ | 21 |
| Italy | 440 | 18 | 800 | 5 |
| New Zealand | 202 | 8 | 382+ | 2 |
| USSR | 5 | 0 | 310 | 1 |
| Turkey | 0.5 | 0 | 150 | 1 |
| Iceland | 32 | 1 | 68+ | 0 |
| France | 0 | 0 | 15+ | 0 |
| Total north | 1,771 | 72 | 11,217 | 64 |
| Mexico | 150 | 6 | 4,000 | 23 |
| Philippines | 446 | 18 | 1,225+ | 7 |
| El Salvador | 95 | 4 | 535 | 3 |
| Costa Rica | 0 | 0 | 380+ | 2 |
| Nicaragua | 0 | 0 | 100 | 1 |
| Indonesia | 0.25 | 0 | 92+ | 0 |
| Ethiopia | 0 | 0 | 50 | 0 |
| Kenya | 0 | 0 | 30+ | 0 |
| Chile | 0 | 0 | 15+ | 0 |
| Total south | 691 | 28 | 6,427 | 36 |
| World total | 2,462 | 100 | 17,644 | 100 |

earthquake record might suggest) sit astride high-temperature fields. Elsewhere there are either low-temperature aquifers, as in the Paris and Southampton sedimentary basins, or 'hot spots' created by impermeable granites. Total, the oil company, has been trying out the temperature of the waters underlying the Paris region. France has, in fact, adopted a particularly aggressive policy on the geothermal front, as with nuclear power and, indeed, solar energy. It is aiming for 500,000 geothermally heated homes by 1990.

But Total was not particularly successful with its first experimental scheme, at Villeneuve. 'We were just unlucky,' said Jean-Claude Soulie, project manager for Total. The company found that it had drilled into something of a geological anomaly for the area. The water it was extracting was not all it had been cracked up to be. Instead of the 90 cubic metres an hour which Total had been expecting, and that at a temperature of 65°C, it found it was getting 50 cubic metres at 52°C. A chilling experience as far as the economics of that particular project were concerned, but Total was keen to try again. One reason for its enthusiasm was its experience in drilling, which it believes gives it (and other oil companies, like Union Oil in California) something of a head-start in the geothermal field.

And what about the granite? Back in Britain, the Department of Energy had announced a £6 million project in 1980 designed to explore the feasibility of exploiting Cornwall's hot rock. The basic idea sounds simple: what one is trying to do is to create artificial geysers. But the mechanics of the exercise, as we have seen, can be tricky. The project has been undertaken by the Camborne School of Mines, which has estimated that the heat stored in Cornwall's granites is equivalent to some 6 billion tonnes of coal. Some of this heat will have come up from the planet's molten core, but at least half of it is thought to derive from natural nuclear reactions in the granite itself.

As Tony Batchelor of the Camborne School of Mines put it, Cornwall's granites represent 'a very weak natural reactor that has been switched on for 250 million years.' Dr Batchelor recognized that his team was lucky in that this natural reactor is overlain by an insulating blanket of other, thermally non-conductive rock, so that the temperatures are pushed even higher. At depths of $1\frac{1}{4}$ miles (2 kilometres), rock temperatures reach more than 80°C. By pumping in cold water, through a fine network of fissures blasted deep underground, heated water can be extracted. The problem is ensuring that the blasting creates sufficient fissures to link up with the boreholes, without fusing the rock and sealing off the boreholes in the process.

'Once we have got over the fissure blasting,' said Dr Batchelor, 'we are laughing.' Despite this optimism, however, there are a fair number of hurdles which still have to be surmounted. For one thing, although the existing wells (see Figure 6.4) represent a considerable drilling achievement, wells more than $3\frac{3}{4}$ miles (6 kilometres) deep would have to be drilled to tap into water at the pressures and temperature (over 200°C) needed to drive power-generating turbines. But present turbine technology is only 10-per-cent efficient at this sort of temperature, which means either that the technology has got

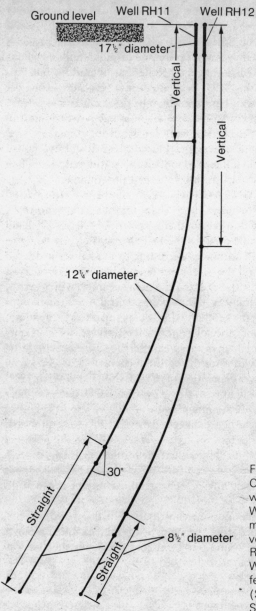

Ground level
Well RH11
Well RH12
17½″ diameter
Vertical
Vertical
12¼″ diameter
30°
Straight
Straight
8½″ diameter

Figure 6.4:
Camborne's two trial
wells in Cornwall.
Well depth: 2,000
metres (1¼ miles); true
vertical depths: Well
R H11 6,683 feet;
Well R H12 6,745
feet.
(Source: Camborne
School of Mines.)

to be improved or that very large quantities of warm water are going to go to waste.

Fruit growers had been beating a path to the Camborne project's front door to see how they might exploit the surplus 5 million gallons of hot water generated during the geothermal operation; but estimates produced during 1982 suggested that geothermal power produced from Cornwall's granite would be three times as expensive as conventionally generated power. 'Geothermal power is not an alternative to coal or nuclear power,' Dr Batchelor commented. 'It is an additional source of energy.' Indeed the British government announced in 1983 that it intended to spend an additional £11 million over three years on the Cornish geothermal programme.

However, with UNERG expecting geothermal electricity-generating capacity to grow more than six-fold in the northern countries and nine-fold in the southern countries between 1980 and the year 2000 (see Table 6.2), geothermal energy is clearly going to be of growing local importance. According to the figures produced at UNERG, Japan and the United States look like being the biggest users of geothermal electricity at the end of the century, with Mexico, the Philippines and a number of the smaller central American nations expected to be among the geothermal-power pace-setters in the south.

But the overall significance of geothermal electricity, which is only one type of geothermal-energy use, can perhaps best be shown by comparing the 1980 figures for the northern countries (1.8 GW) with those for nuclear power generation in the OECD (133 GW) in 1981. If we are to believe the figures produced by the OECD, nuclear power capacity will grow to a minimum figure of 400 GW by the end of the century, whereas the figure suggested by UNERG for geothermal electricity by the same date was just over 11 GW for the northern countries and 6.4 GW for the southern hemisphere. Clearly, our use of our planetary reactor has a considerable way to go before it stands any chance of matching the power streaming out of the world's nuclear power plants.

And a much more important contribution to the world's energy supplies already comes from the energy-capture technologies which tap the radiation streaming out through space from the sun, our largest local fusion reactor.

# The Renewable Cast

# 7 ⊙ Building Tomorrow

'Solar energy': mention these two words to the man or woman in the street, and the image conjured up in his or her mind will almost certainly be that of a solar roof. As we have seen, the solar flat-plate collector, typically installed on a building's roof, has made significant inroads in countries like Israel and Japan, but its total annual contribution to world energy supplies in the early 1980s was, as reported in Chapter 1, equivalent to a mere 400,000 tonnes of oil or about 0.01 per cent of the world's annual oil consumption.

Flat-plate collectors, however, are only part of the story. The use of solar energy by architects and builders has a long, long history. Few deaths have been stranger than that of the Greek tragic poet and playwright Aeschylus, who was almost seventy when he died in 456 B.C., reportedly because an eagle, mistaking the old man's bald pate for a rock which would comfortably crack a tortoise's shell, promptly dropped a tortoise on it. More importantly, for our present purposes, the prodigious output of the father of Greek tragedy gives a number of interesting clues about the extent to which the ancient Greeks had embraced solar energy.

A south-facing orientation, it seems, was a normal feature of Greek homes. This feature, Aeschylus argued, was a clear sign of a modern, civilized home, in stark contrast to the dwellings of more primitive

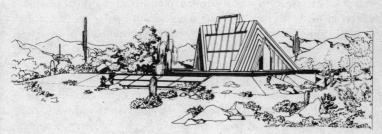

Figure 7.1: The Ahwatukee house (source: Frank Lloyd Wright Foundation).

peoples, who, 'though they had eyes to see, they saw to no avail; they had ears, but understood not. But like shapes in dreams, through-out their time, without purpose they wrought all things in confusion. They lacked knowledge of houses turned to face the sun, dwelling beneath the ground like swarming ants in sunless caves.'

Aeschylus, one suspects, was being rather hard on his barbarian neighbours, but solar architecture certainly seems to have been brought to a fine pitch by the Greeks, who recognized that the design of buildings could do a great deal to exploit free energy from the sun. When modern archaeologists uncovered part of the city of Olynthus, one of the leading settlements of northern Greece during Hellenic times, they found clear evidence that it had been one of the world's earliest solar communities. Built in the fifth century B.C., North Olynthus was a city of about 2,500 people and its streets ran north–south and east–west, so that all the houses had equal access to sunlight, which was regarded as a political right.

Recognizing that the sun travels in a low arc across the southern sky during the winter, and high overhead in summer, the Greeks built their homes in such a way that winter sunshine could penetrate direct into a south-facing portico. The average house in the city covered about 300 square metres (or 3,200 square feet) of floor space. The north walls were 1.5 metres (5 feet) thick, with few windows, to keep out the cold north winds in winter. These thick adobe walls and earth floors absorbed heat on hot days, releasing it into the house when temperatures dropped at night.

One of the most impressive books on solar-energy technologies published in recent years is *A Golden Thread* (Cheshire Books, 1980), subtitled '2,500 years of solar architecture and technology'. Written by Ken Butti and John Perlin, it marshals impressive evidence to show that solar architecture was developed to an enviable level of sophisti-cation in many ancient civilizations. American solar architects, for example, might think themselves to be the pioneers and pace-setters in a new energy revolution, but today's solar architects still have a good deal to learn from traditional designs. Since solar architecture scores such a high ranking in the 'Potential utility' columns of Table 3.1 (see p. 56), it is worth looking back at some of these designs.

When the first pioneers moved into the American South-west, they found the ruins of many solar communities, although they were not immediately recognized as such. The Pueblo Indians, some of whose settlements I visited during the summer of 1973, were particularly skilful in this respect. During the eleventh and twelfth centuries A.D., the Anasazi Indians built a number of large community structures which rank alongside those of the ancient Greeks in solar sophistication. Some of these were south-facing cliff dwellings, like the mis-named 'Montezuma's Castle' (he never went near the place), built by the Sinagua Indians, while others stood out on open plateaux.

The 'sky city' of Acoma Pueblo is one of the most sophisticated of these communities. 'Built atop a plateau as was the Greek city of Olynthus,' Butti and Perlin note, 'Acoma has three long rows of dwelling units running east to west. Each dwelling unit has two or three tiers placed so as to allow every residence full exposure to the winter sun. Most doors and windows open to the south, and the walls are built of adobe. The sun strikes these heat-absorbing south walls much more directly in the winter than in the summer. By contrast, the horizontal roofs of each tier are built of straw and adobe layered over pine timbers and branches to insulate the interior rooms from the high, hot summer sun.' Indeed, a study carried out by Professor Ralph Knowles of the University of Southern California proved just how well suited these buildings were to their environment. In winter, over one third of the sun's heat reaches their living spaces, while in summer only a quarter does so. And, as in Olynthus, the town plan guaranteed that all residents had full, equal access to the sun's heat.

Later on, the Spanish colonial architecture in the American South-west was often designed with solar heating (and over-heating) in mind, as were the New England 'saltbox' houses – which were built facing the sun, with their backs turned to the cold prevailing winds. Many of these saltbox houses also had a lattice-work overhang called a 'pergola' which jutted out from the building's southern façade, above the ground-floor doors and windows. Deciduous vines were often grown up and over these pergolas, affording shade in the summer and, when their leaves had fallen in the winter, letting the sun shine through uninterrupted into the living spaces.

By the late nineteenth century, however, solar architecture had become something of a lost art. It enjoyed a revival during the Weimar Republic in Germany, after the First World War, and it did so for several reasons. One reason was the new mood of experiment which infused many areas of art and science as the old Prussian culture died in the wake of Versailles. Architects began to design buildings which were functional, rather than simply pleasing to the eye, exploiting the properties of window glass to achieve a degree of 'solar gain' – which later became a considerable problem in buildings whose outer skins were entirely composed of glass.

Another important reason for this resurgence of solar architecture was the fact that the victorious Allies had occupied the Ruhr, the source of most of Germany's coal. Vast housing estates were built, although the estates designed according to the *Zeilenbau* plan, which involved long, narrow apartment blocks laid out along a north–south axis, often proved less than satisfactory. One scientist who studied them concluded ruefully that the streets collected more sunshine than did the dwellings. For various reasons, a switch back to smaller-scale residential buildings began, a trend which was accelerated by the Nazi aversion to large-scale worker community developments, which were held to be 'communistic'. The Nazis, instead, pushed for small-scale, country-cottage-style homes, which it was believed would make it harder for the workers to organize themselves against the architects of the Third Reich.

The same basic architectural principles found at Olynthus and in some Weimar building are beginning to emerge again, however, as in a recent design prepared for Italy's AGIP by Dominic Michaelis Associates of London. South-facing windows are large, while on northern walls there are fewer windows – and they are very much smaller (Figure 7.2). A basic problem facing anyone wanting to study pre-war solar buildings in Germany, however, is that many were destroyed during the Second World War. The buildings which remain, whether in Germany or elsewhere, typically reflect the declining real cost of energy as oil became an energy staple.

Figure 7.2: A modern solar estate, designed for Italy's AGIP (source: Dominic Michaelis Associates).

Many of the buildings which remain represent a considerable headache for those responsible for maintaining them – and, indeed, living in them. Energy consultants have had a hard time dealing with a significant proportion of these structures, especially where there has been a façade which had to be conserved for historic reasons. 'There's no magic wand that we can offer, especially for historic homes,' said a consultant working for an energy-conservation programme financed by Connecticut's seven largest power utilities. 'If you don't have a wall cavity,' he continued, 'you have to go either outside or inside and add insulation. Typically, we are at a loss to recommend anything if we want to maintain the building's character.'

## What Is Acceptable?

Part of the problem, of course, stems from the fact that today's 'acceptable' levels of internal temperature and climate control are very much higher than those prevailing when most houses were first put up. But the architectural styles of the last fifty years have displayed an increasing negligence about their energy-consumption implications. As Denis Hayes, in his pre-SERI days, pointed out in *Rays of Hope* (W. W. Norton, 1977), the energy required per square foot of new office space in New York doubled in the twenty years from 1950 to 1970 – and these new styles have been widely exported.

Throughout the world, modern buildings 'resemble one another; moreover, they are nearly identical on all four sides, seeming to ignore entirely the existence of the sun,' as Hayes put it. 'Only in their entrails, in the relative sizes of furnaces and air conditioners, is the external world taken into account at all.' Worst of all, he suggested, were the buildings where 'all the incoming air is super-chilled and then partially reheated as necessary – a technique known as "terminal reheating".' If this approach were to be adopted worldwide, Hayes implied, it could well prove terminal for civilization as we know it.

Yet wherever one goes in the Third World, particularly in the Arab countries, traditional architectural styles and traditional building materials such as brick, adobe, mud, plaster and grass thatch, all of which can be most effective in trapping and storing solar energy, have been replaced by western styles of building using concrete, glass and steel. By the early 1980s, the heating, cooling and lighting of the world's buildings consumed nearly a quarter of its annual energy budget, with approximately two thirds of this demand met directly or indirectly by the burning of oil or natural gas. There have been some signs, however, that a reaction is beginning to set in, albeit patchily. In 1980, for example, Professor Hasan Fathy of Egypt received a special Aga Khan award for his lifelong championship of traditional Arabic architecture, with its use of mud-bricks in arches and vaults.

Meanwhile, in the United States, Christopher Flavin of the Worldwatch Institute was arguing, in *Energy and Architecture: the Solar and Conservation Potential* (Worldwatch Institute, 1980), that the amount of energy used in the world's building could be cut by 25 per cent by the end of the century, even assuming substantial growth in the housing stock. Although there were fewer than 20,000 passive solar homes in the United States in 1980, Flavin was arguing that a 'reasonable goal' would be to have five million 'climate-sensitive' structures in place by 1990 – and to have such buildings dominate the market during the 1990s. If such a new building programme were to be combined with an extensive solar and energy-conservation retrofit programme, he argued, it could save the United States the equivalent of five million barrels of oil a day – considerably more, he pointed out, than would initially be produced by the national synthetic fuels programme (see Chapter 4).

'Until recently,' Flavin commented, 'little heed was paid to the energy efficiency of lifetime fuel costs of buildings as they went up. During the sixties and early seventies, energy use in this sector increased at a 5 per cent annual rate. As a result, the heating, cooling and lighting of buildings now consumes nearly one quarter of global energy supplies. Today, the world's cities are full of structures that will simply be too expensive in 20 years' time.'

A well-designed solar or other low-energy building almost always has a lower life-cycle cost than a comparable conventional building does. 'In the short run,' as Flavin concluded, 'the most important government programs will be those that encourage energy efficiency improvements in existing buildings. Since 80 per cent of the buildings in use today will still be around in the year 2000, it is essential that they be improved in response to the altered energy situation. Each community needs a "home doctor" who can go door-to-door recommending energy-related improvements and doing on-the-spot retrofits. And for many people, particularly low income families without large financial resources for energy investments, public help in weatherizing their homes will be essential.'

Essential, perhaps, but not at the top of President Reagan's list of priorities, nor uppermost in the minds of many of the other governments which espoused monetarism in the late 1970s and early 1980s. Many solar and energy-conservation projects were downgraded or cancelled outright, in the belief that the market would provide the required incentives without the need for much help from central government.

But, while most solar lobbyists resisted the cuts in government spending in their favoured areas of research and development, there was some evidence that builders were beginning to get the message. 'Passive solar buildings have long been thought of as unconventional and costly,' Flavin noted, 'a major deterrent to professional developers. But much of the initial resistance to solar design reflected builders' perceptions of market demand, and the industry is now beginning to respond as home buyers pay more attention to the energy characteristics of houses.'

Most home buyers, however, would still have been baffled by the inevitable sales-talk about the 'passive' and the 'active' features of their prospective homes. So it is worth briefly reviewing the different approaches adopted in designing these live-in solar collectors.

## The Shape of Homes to Come

By far the simplest method of harnessing solar energy for use in buildings is the burning of wood or fossil fuels, but passive solar heat-collection systems are hardly more complicated once their operation is thoroughly understood. The buildings in Olynthus, Acoma Pueblo or the 'saltbox' communities of New England are all representatives of the passive approach to solar energy. More recently, solar dwellings have exploited the greenhouse effect afforded by glass, whether as large south-facing windows or attached 'sunspace' or greenhouse extensions – some of which have been used as a source of heat for the main house.

The heat-storage properties of adobe walls have been further developed by solar pioneers like Felix Trombe and Jacques Michel of France. Solar houses incorporating a so-called 'Trombe wall' have a south-facing glass wall, behind which a dark concrete wall acts as a solar collector. Openings near the top and bottom of the concrete wall permit a natural circulation cycle to operate, with hot air rising and being conducted into the living space while cooler air is drawn back beneath the wall, to be heated on its way back towards the uppermost vents. In a canny variant of this approach, Steve Baer used 91 metal barrels to collect solar energy for his New Mexico home, with a glass wall to prevent undue heat loss from the 4,800 gallons of water in the system. Additionally, he built an outer wall of lightweight insulation material which could be raised or lowered to control the house's heat intake.

Another approach, in suitably dry climates, may be used for both heating and cooling, particularly for single-storey houses. The roof is designed to contain a heat-storage medium, often water in bags, which is exposed to the sun during the day and insulated at night by movable shutters, so that the heat is forced down into the living space. Alternatively, in hot weather, the roof can be opened at night to take advantage of the cooling effect of the evening sky. During the heat of the day, the heat-storage medium would be insulated by the same shutters.

Passive collection is generally the simplest approach to solar heating, and therefore also tends to be the most cost-effective approach. The techniques have typically been used for centuries, are well understood and in good designs the solar contribution generally falls within the range 30–60 per cent of the space-heating load. It is rather more difficult to apply such techniques to existing structures, however, although the use of night shutters can help improve the balance between solar gains and unwanted heat losses.

Active heat-collection systems, by contrast, are more readily adapted to existing structures and represent an identifiable 'product' for industry to develop and sell. Active solar thermal systems use a liquid or gas to transfer heat from where it is absorbed by the collector to the point of use. There are three main types of collector: flat-plate collectors, evacuated tubes and tracking collectors. The tracking variety will be covered in Chapter 8; the overwhelming majority of systems installed to date have been of the flat-plate variety.

In essence, a flat-plate collector consists of the following elements, working in from the sunward side: a transparent glass or plastic cover (or covers); an absorber; a heat-transfer medium; insulation to reduce heat loss from the system; and an enclosure, at its simplest a shallow box, to house the other components. Solar radiation passes through the transparent glazing, heating the absorber, which promptly transfers the heat to the working fluid – be it water, air or some proprietary fluid.

Flat-plate collectors, which harness direct, diffuse and reflected solar radiation, are typically mounted on the roof of a building, using water to transfer the heat collected to a large water tank, from which it can be drawn off for use in radiators or other domestic applications. Although such systems are relatively simple, in theory at least, they have to be very carefully designed and installed – as we saw in Chapter 3. They have to be resistant to continual expansion and contraction as the sun goes in and out, or as night follows day, and the glass panels must not craze or become opaque in the prolonged exposure to the sun which is their lot. They also need to be kept clean, so that their efficiency can be maintained at a relatively high level.

Typically such systems capture between 40 and 60 per cent of the energy falling on them, heating water to between 40° and 80°C (104–176°F). With the use of special absorbent coating and double or triple glazing, it is possible to reach temperatures of 100° to 150°C (212–300°F), but this approach tends to be prohibitively expensive. Flat-plate systems are used economically and extensively in countries such as Australia, Israel and Japan. Half of Israel's households were using solar hot water in 1980, and it was estimated that some 7 million square metres (or 75 million square feet) of such collectors were then in operation. Their average cost, it was calculated, was about $500 per square metre ($46 per square foot) when the storage tank and associated plumbing were counted into the equation.

Evacuated-tube collectors are rather more sophisticated (Figures 7.3 and 4). Whereas a flat-plate collector can be as simple as a

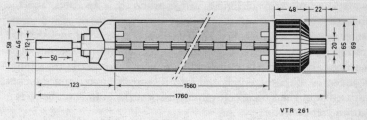

Figure 7.3: Evacuated-tube collector (source: Philips).

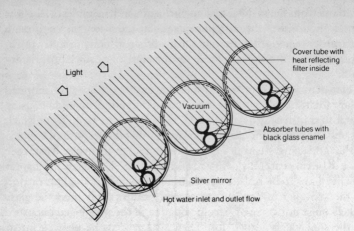

Figure 7.4: Pattern of absorption in evacuated solar collector (source: Philips).

domestic radiator painted black, evacuated tubes use a vacuum to insulate the heat collector, cutting down on heat losses. Companies like Philips and Philco Italiana have thrown their weight behind this technology, which exploited their background in street lighting and other related technologies. Each evacuated-tube collector looks like a long fluorescent light, although its outer skin is transparent, and it contains a long black collector, inserted into the tube rather like a knife blade in a long, thin bottle.

The blade-shaped collector, which is sealed inside the evacuated tube, is coated with a special, highly selective layer which converts a large proportion of the incoming radiation into heat and, at the same time, suppresses radiant heat losses. The heat is transferred to a small quantity of liquid, which promptly evaporates, and the resulting vapour rises to the upper end of the tube, which is plugged into an array of such tubes, angled in such a way that they capture as much solar radiation as possible. At the top of the heat pipe there is a condenser, which is cooled by the user's circuit. As the vapour condenses, the heat is released into the user's circuit and the condensed liquid falls, thanks to gravity, back to the bottom of the system for the repeat cycle.

Such evacuated tubes are highly efficient in collecting direct (and, with some designs, diffuse) sunlight, and can heat the working fluid to 150°C (300°F). But at lower temperatures their efficiency can be markedly poorer than that of a flat-plate collector, despite the fact that such tubes cost several times as much.

Wherever you travel in the world these days, you are probably not far from an experimental solar house (Figure 7.5). Some of their

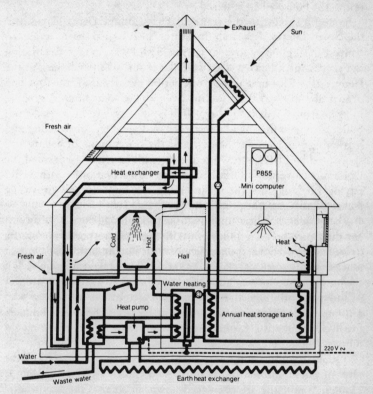

Figure 7.5: The Philips solar house (source: Philips).

builders have the courage of their convictions and live in their creations, although many are still 'inhabited' by computers. At the Solar Village developed by Colorado State University, near Fort Collins, Colorado, for example, a computer simulates the activities of a normal family by periodically dumping hot water into its drains. This cluster of solar buildings, some active and one passive, means that careful comparisons can be made of the performance of solar systems built into standard timber-frame houses. Solar House II differs from the others in that it uses air as its heat-transfer medium and, at least when I visited it in the summer of 1981, stores heat in a rock bin. This wooden bin contains about 26 tonnes of small rocks which absorb heat from the circulating air, and then release it into the house when required.

Some fifty miles to the south of Fort Collins, Denis Hayes and the Solar Energy Research Institute (SERI) had been trying to convert local builders to solar energy. SERI was, in fact, celebrating the success of its recent 'Passive Solar Tour' of solar homes in the Denver area. During a three-week period in early 1981, the tour had drawn about 100,000 visitors to twelve new solar houses, ranging in price from $56,000 to $199,000. The idea was to help residential builders to gain first-hand experience in designing, constructing and marketing passive solar homes, and the programme of events was sponsored by SERI, the Western Solar Utilization Network and the Colorado Governor's Office of Energy Conservation – with SERI paying for solar designers chosen by the builders and providing technical advice as the programme proceeded.

The builders had been unanimous in proclaiming the tour 'a success for the entire building industry'. Although this response involved a degree of hyperbole, the tremendous turnout indicated something more than idle curiosity. For an initial $150,000 investment by SERI, the builders were presented with over 100,000 prospective customers – and promptly signed thirty-one sales contracts valued at $2.5 million. Based on reservations made at the time, the twelve builders involved projected a further eighty-seven sales in the following six months, for a total value of $6.3 million.

'Other Colorado and out-of-state builders were impressed by the level of public interest in the tour,' said Chuck Ochsner of Unique Homes, 'and many are convinced now that solar is the way to go.' Or, as SERI architect Sears Barrett put it, 'the program achieved several other goals, too. We wanted to show the buying public that solar doesn't have to be the expensive privilege of an elite few. And we wanted to show the builders that solar design doesn't have to be complicated or outlandish.'

Jim Ferguson, former head of the Denver Home Builders' Association and a participant in the tour, summed up the feelings of many builders when he said that 'the home-buying public is concerned about rising utility bills, and is extremely well-informed about solar energy. Any local builder who fails to offer at least some sort of solar housing in the near future just won't be able to compete with the rest of us.'

Back in Europe, meanwhile, solar architecture was also making progress, although the politicians there, like President Reagan and his advisers, were far from convinced of the inevitability of the solar contribution. Speaking at the Third International Solar Forum in Hamburg, during 1980, the West German federal minister for research and technology, Volker Hauff, told 1,000 delegates from thirty-five countries that his country could have as many as 30,000 solar-heated homes within a year or two, but that even if this target were to be reached, their contribution to the total energy picture would inevitably be small – given that each house would 'only' contribute the equivalent of some 800 litres of fuel oil each year. Even if there were fifty times as many solar homes in West Germany, Herr Hauff said, the country's bill for imported oil would only be one per cent lower.

The following year, at the Homeworld 81 exhibition held in Milton Keynes, England, the idea was to show the house-buying public the 'shape of houses to come' – and several of the thirty-six purpose-built houses were solar or partially solar in design. One of these, the larger of two built by Autarkic Potentials, may not have included any flat-plate collectors, but a substantial contribution to its heating budget was provided by a full-height conservatory attached to its south and west sides.

Windows opening on to the conservatory permitted warm air to circulate through the house, and a further development was the provision of hollow, translucent glass walls between the conservatory and the living space. These walls consisted of hollow glass blocks filled with a derivative of Glauber's salt (crystalline sodium sulphate), developed by Calor Alternative Technology, which can store a substantial amount of heat by undergoing a phase change.

For all domestic heating and many industrial applications, where the required temperatures are below 70°C (158°F), it is possible to use either sensible or latent heat storage. Systems which use water or rocks are storing sensible heat, whereas the use of salt hydrates to store latent heat is based on a principle which affords much greater heat storage – at a price. The physical basis for the high heat-storage capacity of such chemicals involves a process very much like that involved in the melting of ice. As a salt hydrate melts, it absorbs a very considerable amount of energy, typically in the range of 40–60 calories per gram, compared to 1 calorie needed to raise the temperature of 1 gram of water by 1°C. This 'stored' energy can, in principle at least, be recouped when the salt hydrates recrystallize as they cool beneath their melting temperature.

Other features included in this house were a high standard of insulation, including floor insulation, double glazing on the north and east façades, controlled mechanical ventilation and a 'skin' some six times more airtight than that of most houses. All these features were estimated to repay their cost in seven to ten years at the then prevailing fuel prices.

A second house, and probably the most publicized at the Homeworld 81 exhibition, was 'Futurehome 2000', sponsored by the BBC2 *Money Programme*. This was claimed to cut domestic fuel bills for a normal family by 60 per cent and boasted such features as another south-facing conservatory, electronic controls and the Fiat 'Totem' combined heat and power package, based on a Fiat 127 car engine. This could provide heat and power for up to ten average homes, and was adapted to run on either natural or liquid gas.

Futurehome 2000 was also heavily insulated, and the external doors were magnetically draught-sealed. Inside, there were various appliances designed to use as little energy as possible, including energy-efficient kitchen appliances and gas-filled light-bulbs which fit standard light fittings but use only a quarter of the electricity used by standard bulbs. There was also an electrically operated garage door, which, because it was always closed unless being used, prevented the heat loss often associated with an integral garage.

The conservatory on Futurehome 2000's south side provided as much as 2,000 kWh of useful heat a year, representing about 25 per cent of the house's space-heating demand. Small fans assisted the flow of heat into the house. Among the controls tested in the house was the Honeywell-developed microprocessor-based unit which enabled the home-owner to switch off any electrical equipment in the house from a single point, without additional wiring. This was because the mains wiring was used to carry the signals to each appliance, which would include a receiver to decode them.

But perhaps the most adventurous of the solar houses was the Ideal Home Solar House – an unconventional-looking three-storey house designed by Dominic Michaelis. This also had a two-storey conservatory, indeed the entire south façade of the house was covered with glass, so that the main rooms opened out into the solar conservatory. The house also had conventional flat-plate collectors connected to a Calor 31 energy-storage unit on the ground floor – with a thermal capacity of 60 kWh. The heating was by warm air, and solar energy was expected to provide between 50 and 60 per cent of the house's heating load.

The heat-storage unit was about the size of a conventional refrigerator, but weighed about three quarters of a tonne. Calor had mixed in a stabilizing fluid which kept the salt hydrates in permanent suspension. The complete active solar-heating system cost about £3,000. By contrast, the Solar World Forum held in Brighton in the same year produced estimates suggesting that £1,000, or about a 4-per-cent increase in the cost of a conventional new home in Britain, would buy a reasonable solar system.

The basic principles of passive building design are well understood. As Dr Douglas Balcombe, of the Los Alamos Laboratory, told the Brighton conference, 'the successful designs are a bit like Russian dolls – a sort of house within a house within a house. But,' he added, 'they provide very high-quality living conditions and impose few constraints on occupants.' The question with active systems, however, is how to tease out the heat collected during sunny periods for use when the sun is not working. In one experimental house in Virginia, a Professor Yuan was convinced that the answer lies in the soil.

## Something of a Hot Potato

Applying what he called the 'principle of the baked potato', Shao Yuan, engineering professor at George Washington University, was trying out a solar heat-storage method which he had developed and patented. From April to November, Professor Yuan was collecting the sun's heat in an array of water-filled collectors connected to an underground system of coiled plastic piping that heated the surrounding earth. By the beginning of November, the temperature of the ground surrounding the coils had risen to 77–82°C (170–180°F), creating an underground reservoir of heat – with the normal winter minimum underground temperature varying between 13° and 18°C

(55–65°F). This reservoir stayed hot enough through the winter, said Professor Yuan, to heat the water in the plastic piping, and thence the water in the domestic supply system, until the spring.

'The ground,' he explained, 'will hold heat longer than water will. It's something like the difference between a cup of coffee and a baked potato. When you go out to dinner, order a coffee and a baked potato with your meal and then set them aside. At the end of the meal, the potato will still be hot, but the coffee will be lukewarm. The ground under the house is like the baked potato, storing the heat all winter.'

Recalling his boyhood in China, Professor Yuan pointed out that 'in the old days, you cut ice from the river in the winter and stored it in the cellar, and it would stay cold all summer. When you have a watermelon, you want it to be cold, so you stick it in a well over-night, and when you take it out in the morning, it is ice-cold. The earth is one of the best insulators. It is also,' he observed, 'one of the cheapest.'

The system, he had calculated, would cost $18,000 at 1981 prices to heat a house with 1,500 square feet (139 square metres) of floor space. However, he predicted, the annual cost of heating such a house over a twenty-year payback period would be one third that of electric heating and two thirds that of conventional solar heating. It is fair to point out, though, that he based these figures on a yearly inflation rate for the prices of other fuels of 12 per cent, on a $2,000 tax credit for the installation of the underground system and on a twenty-year amortization of the capital at 9 per cent interest – figures which look rather optimistic at the time of writing.

But there is heat to be captured beneath the ground even if you have not put it there yourself. The earth beneath our feet is, after all, a giant solar-energy collector in its own right and the soil provides a fairly effective insulating layer, keeping underground water (or 'groundwater') at, say, the 50-foot (15-metre) level at a fairly constant temperature throughout the year. Wells as shallow as 15 metres will produce groundwater at temperatures of about 25°C (77°F) in Florida and about 4°C (40°F) at the Canadian border. By using heat pumps, a growing number of Americans are striking a blow for energy independence by drilling between their feet in their own backyards.

Even water which is cold to the touch contains heat and can be made to give up that heat by means of a heat pump. Heat pumps work on the principle that heat moves from a warmer body to a cooler body, and encourage it to do so by exploiting the physical properties of a refrigerant such as freon. Developed by Du Pont, the same company which sponsored the flight of the *Solar Challenger*, freon is a gas which liquefies when put under pressure. Liquid freon boils at extremely low temperatures. At normal atmospheric pressure, it boils at *minus* 41°F ( − 40°C).

Using groundwater, a heat-pump system can heat a building three to five times as efficiently as a fossil-fuel system, in terms of heat output per unit of energy put in. Such systems can be much more efficient than conventional solar energy systems but, as the business magazine *Fortune* put it so succinctly, 'energy from water has no billion-dollar, federally funded scheme behind it. It is a grass roots movement, cultivated by private contractors, heat-pump manufacturers and well-drillers.'

One such cultivator has been Jay Lehr, a hydrologist and president of the US National Water Well Association, based in Columbus, Ohio. As he saw it, 'heat-pump installations will start to snowball because all the rises in fossil fuel prices are in our favour. We really don't have to do anything but sit back and let it happen.' He also predicted that the twelve million Americans with existing water wells would provide the first major market opportunity. Indeed, he expected some 600,000 homes a year to switch to heat pumps, with those having existing hot-air central heating or air-conditioning plant in the vanguard.

When *Fortune* investigated the growing use of groundwater in the United States, it found that a number of manufacturers, including Westinghouse, were already producing heat pumps for the larger users – such as industrial plants, office and commercial buildings, and apartment blocks. The St Paul Town Square office and shopping complex in St Paul, Minnesota, illustrates what can be done with new buildings. Cooled and heated by a groundwater heat-pump system, the complex was saving an estimated $300,000 to $400,000 a year in fuel costs in the early 1980s. The Campbell Soup Company was also investigating the groundwater option. The company had carried out a study which suggested that if it were to use groundwater power at its frozen-food plant in Salisbury, Maryland, it could cut its fuel bill of over $450,000 a year by some 60 per cent.

Some users, however, were less ambitious. In Harrogate, Tennessee, the Lincoln Memorial University was saving nearly $2,000 a year by simply extracting heat from a nearby stream to heat a dormitory

– an approach adopted many years earlier in London, England, where the Royal Festival Hall extracts heat from the River Thames. At the time of writing, research is continuing in Britain. The Institute of Geological Sciences, for example, is experimenting with the use of groundwater-derived heat in warming greenhouses in Cambridge-shire (Figure 7.6). There the groundwater at 15 metres averages

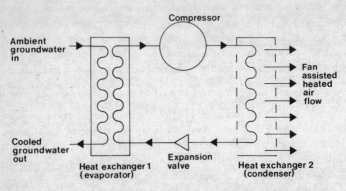

Figure 7.6: The principle of the Institute of Geological Sciences' American heat pumps (source: IGS).

between 11° and 13°C. Experiments have shown that each 3 kW machine can heat a 21-square-metre (226-square-foot) greenhouse to 65°F (18.3°C), even in very cold weather.

The quantities of groundwater needed to heat an average-sized house with a heat pump are relatively modest. A heat output equivalent to 10 kW or 10 single-bar electric fires, for instance, can be obtained from about 280 gallons (1.3 cubic metres) an hour. In the IGS experiments, the groundwater is being used in a water-to-air heat pump, providing warm air at about 30°C (86°F).

The attraction of owning your own energy source is obvious. As *Fortune* put it, 'so far, no one has formed an Organization of Water Producing Countries.' But there has been a striking difference in the lengths to which people have been prepared to go in achieving a degree of energy self-sufficiency. The IGS scientists, for example, experiment with their greenhouses and then return home to their standard-issue homes. Elsewhere, however, some have chosen to live in their greenhouses.

## Tomorrow as a Permanent Address

'As electricity, fuel, fertilizer, food, storage and transport costs rise and their petroleum bases dwindle,' wrote John Todd in the late 1970s, 'nations requiring substantial energy will have to reduce their standards of living, which is precisely what is happening at the present.' On the other hand, Todd and his colleagues at the New Alchemy Institute argued, 'they have the option of taking a bolder step and redesigning themselves to accomplish much more with less.'

The Institute itself had taken this bolder step, in collaboration with Solsearch Architects, by building two 'Arks', one on Cape Cod, Massachusetts, and a second on Prince Edward Island in the Gulf of St Lawrence. The genesis of the Ark concept can be dated back to the first 'bioshelter' built by Todd and his colleagues in 1971. This consisted of an 18-foot (5.5-metre) geodesic dome containing a fish tank adapted from a children's swimming pool, and a few salad plants growing around the edge of the pool.

By the time the Cape Cod and Prince Edward Island Arks were operational, however, the Institute was well up the learning curve. Both Arks were defined by the New Alchemists as 'autonomous structures, in that they have had no reliance on an outside energy source like fossil fuels, but regulate their own internal climates through the collection and storage of solar energy.' The Cape Cod Ark is used for food production in all seasons, while the Prince Edward Ark also contains living quarters.

Self-sufficiency in food was never an objective as far as these latter-day arkwrights were concerned, although the Arks have produced considerable volumes of fish and vegetables for the New Alchemy tables. The architecture of the Arks was explicitly solar, both buildings facing south and presenting an upper wall of flat-plate collectors to the sun. But the New Alchemists took things a step further by incorporating a fish farm (see Figures 7.7 and 8). The first stage in the Prince Edward Island fish culture cycle starts with two rows of forty translucent tanks – which contain dense 'blooms' of algae. The algae provide food for the fish, but they also act as an efficient solar-energy collection surface, while the tanks serve as heat-storage units.

The New Alchemists decided to locate their second Ark on this exposed headland overlooking the St Lawrence, which freezes each winter, reckoning that if the concept worked there it would work

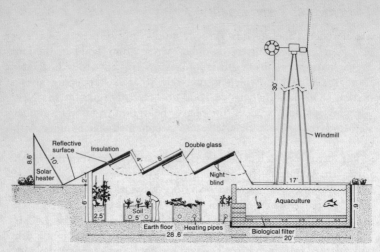

Figure 7.7: Solar aquaculture and greenhouse complex
(source: New Alchemy Institute).

anywhere. When the temperature drops in the Ark, the fish tanks
re-radiate the stored heat into the greenhouse area and thence into
the living space behind the greenhouse. Indeed, during one three-day
blackout caused by a violent late-November storm, the solar-algae-
pond complex was the only operational heating system. While outside
temperatures dropped below 0°C (32°F), and the wind speeds were
in excess of 50 kilometres per hour (31 miles per hour), the crops
within the Ark survived.

When the sunlight fails, an advanced *Hydrowind* windmill is used
to provide electricity for heating and for the laboratory sensors and
other equipment. The fish tanks have achieved unprecedented levels
of biological productivity, yielding the highest recorded fish production per unit volume of water for a standing water body.

So what is it like living in a twentieth-century ark? It is, according
to Todd, 'an extraordinary experience. Living and working in a structure where the sun, the wind, architecture and ecosystems are operating in concert has affected most of us. It seems to foretell what the
future could bring. Each of us involved in the project would like
to one day live in an Ark-inspired bioshelter.' The Ark's inhabitants,
Todd suggested, had come to feel a sense of wholeness, of ecological
integrity. 'Working with vegetable crops, flowers or trees, or tending

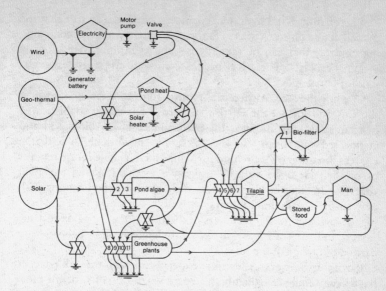

Figure 7.8: Energy-flow diagram for the complex shown in Figure 7.7. Key: 1 = Circulation of fish-pond water through biological filter. 2 = Increased growing temperature for algae. 3 = Nutrient cycling from fish wastes. 4 = Terrestrial plants to *Tilapia*. 5 = Increased temperature for *Tilapia*. 6 = Removal of growth inhibitors. 7 = Fish husbandry. 8 = Earth heat warming the pit-greenhouse. 9 = Night warming of greenhouse. 10 = Irrigation by nutrient/rich water. 11 = Vegetable gardening. (Source: New Alchemy Institute.)

the fish while a howling blizzard rages outside, is exciting. Watching the sensors in the laboratory read out the Ark's various functions and monitor its health while the cold wind blows connects one consciously to the forces sustaining all life.'

As the New Alchemists themselves recognized, 'possibly the most serious criticism of bioshelters is that they are too complex. Being engineered ecosystems, containing high levels of information, they are esoteric, beyond the ability of the average person to operate and maintain. It is true that the Ark is the product of a synthesis created by biological designers, materials experts, agriculturalists, a soil specialist, an integrated pest control scientist, algologists, fishery experts and fish culturalists, architects, solar energy scientists, electronic and computer designers, a systems ecologist, a philosopher, and aeronautical and hydraulic engineers; but it is also true that the overall design objective was to fabricate a system with its accompanying controls that can be taught to – and even improved upon by – non-specialists. There has been a conscious effort to design the Ark for lay people.'

So while the New Alchemists (motto: 'to restore the land, protect the seas and inform the Earth's stewards') have used sophisticated instrumentation to monitor the performance of the biological and engineered components of the Arks, they have done so with the express intention of 'searching for signposts to enable future tenders of bioshelters to do without expensive mechanical and electrical controls.' In fact, the New Alchemists have been experimenting with new forms of community living as well as with new forms of ecological engineering. All members of the Institute were paid the same salary, and the staff was 'diluted' with non-scientific people, who carried out much of the research.

Inevitably, however, these first experiments with the Ark concept have been small-scale (Figure 7.9), perhaps too small-scale for most tastes. Indeed, one of the pioneering efforts in this general area in Britain involved the conversion of an old Welsh farmhouse, Eithin-y-Gaer, into BRAD (Biotechnic Research and Development) – and clearly demonstrated the problems associated with what have been called 'intentional communities'. When I worked there for a brief period in the spring of 1974, the small community was already under severe strain.

Robin Clarke, whose idea BRAD was, had characterized the new sciences and technologies being pioneered by the New Alchemists and others as seeking 'to put men before machines, people before governments, practice before theory, student before teacher, the country before the city, smallness before bigness, wholeness before reductionism, organic materials before synthetic ones, plants before animals, craftsmanship before expertise and quality before quantity.' The new breed of communard, as Clarke saw it, would be a 'techno-peasant'. Having worked as editor of the *Science Journal*, until its demise in 1971, Clarke had clear ideas as to what he wanted to achieve, ideas which were not necessarily shared to the hilt by all the other BRAD intentional communards.

The four main objectives behind the BRAD experiment, briefly stated, were to ensure that science and technology were ridden rather than riding roughshod over real human needs; to slow and eventually

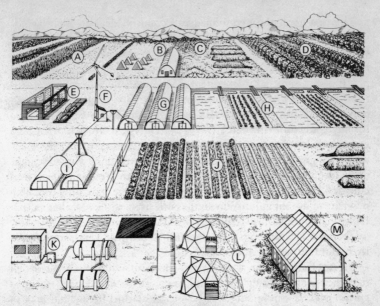

Figure 7.9: Blueprint for a polyculture farm. Key: A = Grains, green manure and forage crops. B = Solar grain-drying structures. C = Windrow compost piles on fallow section. D = Diverse, multi-storied orchards with undergrowth of refuge plants and green manure crops. E = Fish-food stocks; aquaculture insectary and worm cultures. F = Wind generator. G = Solar-heated Quonsets for rearing warm-water fishes and crustaceans. H = Outdoor fish ponds and row-crop fields. I = Agriculture insectary for rearing beneficial insects. J = Experimental vegetable/herb/flower/weed beds for investigating diverse cropping systems. K = Poultry shelter with methane digesters, sludge ponds and gas storage tanks. L = Dome-greenhouses. M = Solar-heated laboratory/homesite. (Source: New Alchemy Institute.)

halt the flight from the country to the city by setting up rival centres – or, more accurately, networks – of attraction; to ensure real, sustainable development for the Third World, with experiments like BRAD showing the developing nations that some people in the industrial nations were sufficiently convinced by the potential of alternative or intermediate technologies to base their own lives around them; and, finally, to resolve the looming ecological crisis, predicted by such studies as the MIT Limits to Growth project, by reintegrating mankind with natural systems.

This new Utopia was envisaged as 'a countryside dotted with windmills and solar houses, studded with intensively but organically worked plots of land; food production systems dependent on the integration of many different species, with timber, fish, animals and plants playing mutually dependent roles, with wilderness areas plentifully available where perhaps even our vicious distinction between hunting and domestication was partially broken down; a life style for men and women which involves hard physical work, but not over excessively long hours or in a tediously repetitive way; an architecture which sought to free men from external services and which brought them into contact with each other, rather than separated them into cubicles where the goggle box and bed were the only possible diversions; a political system so decentralised and small that individuals – all individuals – could play more than a formal, once-every-five-years role.' And so on: all eminently worthy and attractive objectives, but the vehicle proved unequal to the task.

BRAD foundered in the end partly because, while everyone agreed that they were looking for – and prepared to help in setting up – an intentional community, they all came with different ideas as to just what that community would look like. Some saw it as a home-grown version of the New Alchemy Institute; others wanted little more than a country club with solar panels on the roof. And, while Clarke, Todd and others pursued their visions of Utopia, based on an increasing level of ecological and social sophistication, there were others who were aiming for electro-mechanical sophistication. This trend has attracted funding in a way that the 'small is beautiful' approach has not, and is perhaps best illustrated by recent developments in the country where energy profligacy had been developed almost into an art form: the United States.

## A Leaning Tower of Power

If a house built by the Frank Lloyd Wright Foundation in the community of Ahwatukee, just down the road from Phoenix, Arizona, is anything to go by, the house of the future will not only keep the family's accounts up to date but will also ring the police in the event of an attempted burglary and the fire department or hospital in the event of a fire or accident.

Rising out of the Arizona desert like some vast copper tent (see

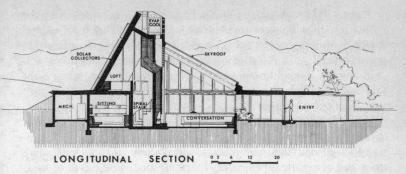

LONGITUDINAL SECTION

Figure 7.10: Plan of the Ahwatukee house
(source: Frank Lloyd Wright Foundation).

Figures 7.1 (p. 141) and 7.10), the copper-clad 'shining house of dreams' is striking not only for its visual qualities but also for its dependence both on solar energy and on computers. The Ahwatukee house, in contrast to 'Montezuma's Castle', the various buildings designed by Paolo Soleri for his Cosanti Foundation (in Scottsdale) or his fledgling 'arcology' Arcosanti (some seventy miles north of Phoenix), is aggressively active in its pursuit of solar energy.

Having visited Arcosanti in the midst of the first oil crisis, I had been impressed by the way in which Soleri's great apses and domes achieved the same passive solar effect as was achieved by the Sinagua Indians with 'Montezuma's Castle' and the Anasazi Indians with Acoma Pueblo. Arizona communities appear to have almost negligible roots in the landscape. To the European eye, they seem to squat on that arid earth, awaiting the order to fly. It is no coincidence, one feels, that the road is bordered by a glittering succession of mobile-home parks. Soleri's first landing ground after he split away from Frank Lloyd Wright's tutelage was on the outskirts of sprawling, anonymous Scottsdale. The general impression at the Cosanti Foundation was one of a crop of concrete mushrooms breaking through the earth's crust. In soaring temperatures, it spoke volumes that we were more comfortable there than in nearby Phoenix, for all that city's air-conditioning plant.

But, once again, Soleri and his ilk operate for the most part on the margins of society, where money is always a constraint. The Ahwatukee house, by contrast, suggests that money was no object as far as the Frank Lloyd Wright Foundation was concerned. The house responds to its environment by means of a highly sophisticated five-unit multi-computer network which controls everything from the stereo system to the security locks. It opens and shuts doors and windows to control internal temperatures, and 'knows' when night has fallen, switching on lights for approaching visitors or, if they try to get in by an unorthodox route, calling the local police.

The Ahwatukee house can be heated in three different ways: apart from the heating afforded by the solar collectors and by several carefully designed skylights, there is also a heat pump (adapted for cooling too) and conventional resistive electric heating. In the eyes of most alternative technologists, this house suffers from technological over-kill but, with the investment world operating in the way it does, the Ahwatukee house is just as likely to serve as a model for the American house of the future as are the New Alchemy Arks. Or, even stranger, perhaps entire houses will track the sun – as in the 'astronaut's house', designed for American astronaut James Irwin and developed into the 'Astro-unit' by Dutch architect Dirk Vorhaar (Figure 7.11), which is mounted on a column so that it can follow the sun in its course across the sky.

Figure 7.11: The 'Astro-unit'
(source: Architektenbureau Bouwhuis Vorhaar).

Against all expectations, too, some architects have been trying to convert high-rise buildings to solar energy. Take the inverted wedge shape of the Georgia Power Company's new headquarters building in Atlanta, Georgia. Said to be the most energy-efficient high-rise building in the United States at the time of its opening, in 1981, it uses some 65 per cent less energy than comparable post-war structures – the sort of buildings Denis Hayes was complaining about. The twenty-four-storey building has a stepped south face, to afford shading in the summer and allow the sun to shine in during the winter. The top of the south face of the 345-foot (105-metre) building protrudes 23 feet (7 metres) beyond the base, making it look like the sort of wedge used, in earlier times, to split logs for the fire – and accounting for its nickname, the 'leaning tower of power'.

The building, which has a 764,000-square-foot (70,978-square-metre) floor area, has a 24,000-square-foot (7,315-square-metre) array of parabolic-trough solar collectors (of which more in Chapter 8). This was believed to be the largest commercial application of this type of collector to date – and meets 15 per cent of the building's peak energy demand. The building's lean and the solar collectors, however, are only the visible tip of an energy-conservation iceberg, which is hinted at by the fact that 75 per cent of the tower's exterior walls are insulated to a standard equivalent to that used for refrigerated rooms, and there are no windows at all in the north and east façades. Lift and mechanical shafts are grouped against the outside walls to provide additional insulation and 'round-the-clock' functions are clustered in such a way that the entire building does not need continuous lighting and air-conditioning.

Meanwhile, in downtown Calgary, Canada, the new Gulf Canada Square complex dispenses with solar collectors, using instead solar gain (the heat deriving from sunshine coming in through the building's glass curtain walls) and the heat from people, lights and equipment to provide all the heat its occupants need. The twenty-storey building can readily achieve internal temperatures of 70°F (21°C) even when external temperatures drop to −40°F (−40°C).

But the building which pulls together more advanced energy ideas than any other comparable building is the Ohbayashi-Gumi Research Institute, on Tokyo's northern outskirts. Described as a 'super energy-conservation building' by its builders, architects and engineers Ohbayashi-Gumi (one of Japan's largest construction companies), the gleaming office block incorporates ninety-eight energy-saving ideas and is seen as a shop-window by Ohbayashi-Gumi, demonstrating energy-saving technologies to potential clients as well as saving the company millions of yen a year. Solar energy is used to provide hot water, space heating and air-conditioning. The building also uses underground heat storage reminiscent of Professor Yuan's system described above.

Another feature of the building is a double skin of coated glass on its south side, with an additional wall sloping out over the conventional windows, providing an air pocket. This provides a trap for heated air, which can be extracted for use in other parts of the building by fans and ducts. In summer, when the heat would be an embarrassment, the hot air is vented out through openings at the top of the sloping window. The building is only three stories high, with a basement beneath, and its architects have tried another solar technique which has a long history, this one harking back to the New England 'saltboxes'. A line of trees has been planted on the south side of the building, providing shade in summer and, when their leaves fall in winter, letting the sun through.

Like the Ahwatukee house, too, this building has a fair number of advanced electronic features contributing to energy efficiency, like the light-switch in the conference room. Instead of a switch, there is a plastic key, which employees have to return after using the room, ensuring that the lights are switched off. With the whole system integrated through a computer, the building uses 60 per cent less energy than a conventional building of the same size, although the initial costs were 20 per cent higher. According to Ohbayashi-Gumi, however, these costs will be recouped in 8.7 years, which is good by the standard of many solar installations.

But those who design buildings from scratch to incorporate solar technologies can still run into problems. When Citibank's architects, Hugh Stubbins and Associates, designed a Citibank skyscraper headquarters in midtown Manhattan, the towering building was built with a steeply sloping, south-facing roof to take solar panels – when the appropriate technologies caught up with the architect's solar ingenuity. That had not happened at the time of writing, although Citibank were on the verge of beginning a small experiment with 5,000 photovoltaic cells (of which more in Chapter 9) on that sloping roof. It is perhaps indicative of the state of this end of the solar art that the experiment was not designed to do much more than power a small exhibition downstairs – an exhibition, predictably, on solar energy.

Meanwhile, despite Aeschylus's diatribe against those who lived beneath the ground in 'sunless caves', a growing number of people and companies are choosing to build their houses, offices and warehouses underground – largely for energy reasons. In some places, as in Kansas City, existing underground chambers are being put to new uses. An 18-million-square-foot 'underground industrial park' has been developed by a subsidiary of Beatrice Foods in a disused underground limestone-mine. Among the activities which have located there are a trout farm and various manufacturing activities, although warehousing is the main use. Energy bills for a simple warehouse are reckoned to be 90 per cent less if you go underground, while a refrigerated underground warehouse costs about 40 per cent less to maintain. Altogether, some 180 million square feet of mined-out space have been developed in the area. The fastest-growing operator has been the Great Midwest Corp., which calls itself a 'subterropolis'.

But, short of a catastrophe, the bulk of our living and working space will continue to be above ground for the foreseeable future, and, as energy prices rise, whether they do so slowly and steadily or periodically and precipitately, architects and builders will become more sensitive to the contribution which solar energy can make to their energy budgets. But the technology will have to be developed considerably if it is to enjoy widespread use in countries which have not got Arizona's climate. And before people turn to solar technology, the chances are that they will start off with energy conservation – a field which has also been badly hit by the cuts in government spending in most countries.

In a country like Britain, the return from energy-conservation expenditure is likely to be more attractive for some time to come than that from investment in even simple solar technology, such as flat-plate collectors. Extra insulation and careful draughtproofing can cut the energy consumption of existing houses very significantly, with a considerable contribution of heat coming through solar gain and from electrical appliances and the bodies of the occupants of the house. Researchers at the Electricity Council estimate that over half of the energy needed for space heating in a well-insulated house can come from such sources. There are snags, however, including the build-up of trace gases from gas cookers, cleaning fluids, cigarettes and other activities which are normally insignificant in this respect. Another problem is that a well-insulated house can rapidly over-heat if its solar gain is unusually high or if there are a considerable number of people in it; so research is being carried out on ways of making heating systems much more sensitive to temperature changes – with the advent of microelectronics coming at just the right time. It is reckoned that, whereas existing houses need about 12–20 kW to maintain comfort, the 5 kW house is now very much on the cards.

The vital importance of energy conservation is illustrated by the fact that some 70 per cent of Britain's houses, according to BP estimates, need to be 'retrofitted' with energy-saving equipment. Dr Paul Freund, who is responsible for BP's own low-energy housing project, comments that 'the UK housing stock is being augmented at less than one per cent a year, so existing buildings are going to continue to dominate the market for energy conservation for many years to come.' Given that these houses were not typically built with the sun's orientation in mind, it is also more likely that energy conservation will be suitable than it is that there will be roof-space correctly orientated for a solar panel.

Meanwhile, however, others have been working on solar technologies designed to achieve very different objectives, including very much higher temperatures than those reached by flat-plate collectors or even by evacuated tubes. Indeed, while some alternative technologists may blanch when they hear about the Ahwatukee house and similar high-technology ventures, some of the things that are being done in the name of solar energy could almost be classified as 'hard-path' energy technologies. Chapter 8, which looks at point- and line-focus solar collectors, covers some systems which would fall into this category, as does Chapter 9, which zeroes in on photovoltaic technology.

# 8 ⊙ *Focal Points*

'We have here what the U.S. Department of Energy says we can't possibly have until 1986,' said Robert Charlton of Solectro-Thermo, Inc. (STI), in 1980, 'and we've had it since 1975.' As vice-president responsible for marketing the company's new hybrid solar collector, a system which simultaneously provided both heat and electricity, Charlton was beginning to understand his employer's persecution complex.

Interviewed by *Mother Jones* magazine, Arthur Manelas, who invented the hybrid system and owned the small solar company producing it in an old textile mill in Dracut, Massachusetts, argued that the oil companies and the Department of Energy were conspiring to corner the solar market for the multinationals and to squeeze out the small independents like STI. The interview was conducted by Ray Reece and the theme was not light-years removed from that pursued in his own book *The Sun Betrayed*, published in the previous year.

Corporate America, Reece suggested, was following a five-point strategy in relation to solar energy – a strategy which, while he confessed it had never been published or admitted by the alleged conspirators, would have exactly the effect bemoaned by Manelas, of squeezing out the small independent entrepreneurs. The sun, according to Reece, had been betrayed at a series of high-level meetings in Washington, D.C., between 1971 and 1974.

The first principle of this 'strategy', which Reece and others alleged had been hammered out between big business and the federal government, has been to control the pace at which solar power becomes a viable alternative in the energy market and to allow the oil companies to maximize profits on the remaining oil and to consolidate an expanded electrical power grid based on coal and nuclear energy – into which they had been buying heavily, as we saw in Chapters 4 and 5.

The second principle, Reece contended, emphasized those applications of solar energy that 'are most compatible with the present system of capital-intensive, centralized power facilities. This means, primarily, promoting solar-electric technologies such as the "power

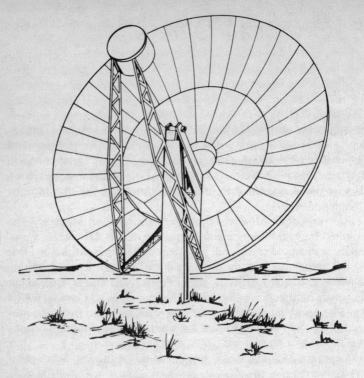

Figure 8.1: Boeing faceted thin-film concentrator. Some heliostat manufacturers have studied the application of heliostat technology to the distributed receiver concept. Although no system has been fully designed, several of the components that would be used in such a system are operating as part of the heliostat technology for central receivers (source: Jet Propulsion Laboratory).

tower", photovoltaic cells, ocean thermal generating plants and giant, expensive wind turbines' (all of which are covered in the following pages).

The third plank in this strategy involved minimizing corporate risk in the evolution of solar technologies and markets by soliciting heavy government subsidies and allowing small companies to shoulder as many of the early risks as possible, while – and this was the gist of the fourth principle underpinning the conspiracy – meshing the burgeoning solar market into the larger corporate power structure by absorbing either the small successful firms or, preferably, their ideas.

Fifth, and herein lies a political accusation which has increasingly been levelled at big industry, corporate America had sought to 'deter the public from identifying solar (energy) as a possible means of altering the present economic and geopolitical structure of the United States. Small,' Reece concluded, 'is not beautiful in corporate eyes. Neither is the prospect of local communities declaring independence from utilities and energy corporations once they have developed their own renewable energy resources.' Just as different people brought different visions of Utopia to BRAD, then, different interests are slotting the renewable-energy technologies into radically different views of the future.

## Solar Iscariots?

Is this a perceptive analysis of the underlying business strategies adopted by the large corporations, or is it evidence of solar paranoia? Reece himself said that 'Manelas does not look like a revolutionary, nor his factory a hotbed of subversive intent.' But Reece's argument was that men like Manelas are indeed subversive in so far as they challenge the increasing concentration of the energy industry.

The final stakes involved, such critics believe, are not simply a question of industry cheating its customers out of an opportunity to lower their fuel costs by the development of local, inexpensive and renewable energy systems. 'The rapid deployment of renewable energy technologies – controlled by people and institutions at the local level – could,' or so Reece believed, 'trigger a peaceful revolution. The 80-year trend towards concentration of wealth and power in the hands of the corporations could begin to reverse. The drift toward coal and nuclear power as replacements for oil and natural gas could be halted. The inability of the corporate state to provide its people with steady employment and small business opportunities could be transformed into a blossoming of work for those who need it. The environment could be pampered instead of being brutalized, the sprawling metropolises gradually broken into smaller communities capable of producing their own food and energy supplies.

'A revolution emphasizing local self-reliance and social equity instead of servitude, waste and mega-profits would, of course, undermine the corporations and financial institutions that presently dominate American life. The corporations,' Reece suggested, 'understandably, do not intend to let this happen.'

The Department of Energy's Solar Division, it has been alleged, had been filled with executives from companies like General Electric, Rockwell International, Texas Instruments and Westinghouse, all former contractors for the nuclear and space industries. Most of the relatively modest federal solar budget, its critics argued, had been directed towards such complicated, high-cost and centralized technologies as power towers, solar power satellites and multi-megawatt windmills. It is fair to say, however, that photovoltaics and synthetic fuels have been the most favoured 'alternative' energy investments for the major oil companies.

The Reagan administration's cuts in the US solar budget, described in Chapter 3, were welcomed by many people in these large corporations – because they hit hardest at what they saw as the 'creeping solar socialism' espoused, in their eyes at least, by such organizations as SERI under the direction of Denis Hayes. These industrialists, like the officials they work with in the federal government, tend to believe that the solar industry will eventually be dominated by three or four enormous corporations, just as is the US car industry.

The whole debate, in the end, resolves into a single question: has the 'free' market system delivered the goods in the past, and, even if it has, is it likely to do so with solar energy? The General Motors and Fords of this world will point to the incomparable mobility of today's Americans or Europeans and suggest that our solar needs can be satisfied with nothing more than a continuation of the 'business as usual' strategy. The more radical solar exponents, by contrast, point to the annihilation of mass transit, the destruction of city centres, the surging eczema of suburban sprawl and all the other ills associated with the motor car: evidence, they will say, of the social and ecological devastation which follows in the wake of the development and deployment of new technologies by those whose sole interest is in profit.

Clearly, the level of investment in solar energy by the big corporations must mean that they will continue to exert a controlling – and, sometimes, suffocating – interest in the development of many of the renewable-energy technologies. But would the radical technologists have developed these technologies in any case? Photovoltaic cells, for example, would never have got off the ground – nor would they have lifted the *Solar Challenger* – if the resources of big industry had not been harnessed to the task. And, it is worth pointing out, the American oil companies, big though they undoubtedly are, are not alone in the solar or renewable-energy fields.

Big oil certainly now dominates the photovoltaics industry, yet some centres of excellence have so far escaped the clutch of oil money and oil politics, including the R CA laboratories in Princeton, New Jersey. David Cohen, the man who was heading R CA's efforts in the solar field at the time when President Reagan was assaulting the federal solar budget, was indisputably uneasy about the situation, but saw a counterbalancing factor to the dominance of companies like Exxon, Chevron (Standard Oil of California), Arco or Shell in the emergence of an aggressively competitive Japanese solar industry.

Sanyo, Dr Cohen pointed out, was already building a $50 million plant to produce 100 MW of solar cells each year, cells which were expected to convert solar energy to electricity with an efficiency of about 7 per cent and at a cost of 80 cents per peak watt. If this target is achieved, and there is no reason to doubt that it will be, then Japan is already moving ahead of the US target of 80 cents per peak watt by 1986 – and Sanyo was also believed to be designing its follow-up plant, able to turn out 1,000 MW of cells at a cost of 25 cents per peak watt. And, as we shall see in Chapter 9, other Japanese companies (like Sharp and Matsushita) are busy in the solar field.

So, whether or not the radical technologists like the fact that others want to take the high technology road while they opt for the low, and whether or not the US oil industry wants to keep solar energy under wraps until it has milked the last few cents of profit from its reserves of oil, gas, coal and uranium, the chances are that it will be outflanked – just as it is being outmanoeuvred in the microchip market. The Japanese, it should be remembered, have no vast fossil-fuel reserves to rely on, and, even if they are not planning an immediate transition to solar energy, their 'Project Sunshine' has given them a distinct edge in this new market. They know, too, that solar technologies are just the sort of technologies they will have to trade in order to buy increasingly expensive oil on the world market.

## Cooking the Cook

The world, in short, is unlikely to go willingly or passively down the route mapped out for it in the 1960s and 1970s by the radical, alternative or intermediate technologists. Even the solar systems developed by the New Alchemists have an active component, and it will be increasingly hard to play the solar purist. Indeed, when it comes right down to it, while passive and moderately active solar capture systems may be perfectly acceptable and cost-effective for residential applications such as space and water heating, most industrial applications require higher temperatures and, in direct consequence, more sophisticated solar technologies, which may be either thermal or photovoltaic, harnessing either solar heat or photons.

In the previous chapter we looked at a number of moderately active solar collection systems, including flat-plate collectors and evacuated tubes. If higher temperatures than those afforded by such capture systems are needed, however, the collectors must either track the sun or focus its radiation – or, typically, some combination of both.

At their simplest, such technologies may be illustrated by looking at solar cookers. Many of the world's development agencies have endorsed such cookers, which are typically made up of a parabolic reflective dish some 1–2 metres (3–7 feet) in diameter, with the cooking vessel placed at the dish's focal point and the food, theoretically at least, cooked by sunlight.

'Ever thought of using a solar cooker to make tea or coffee in your office? Sounds impossible,' claimed the United Nations Environment Programme in 1980. Well, no, I hadn't considered using a solar cooker in the office; but, then again, it did not seem impossible even in London, given the expertise, equipment and finance. The Chinese, however, appeared to have found an elegant, cheap solution, using local materials like bamboo and small, simple mirrors. According to Dr Reynaldo Lesaca, deputy director of UNEP's regional office in Bangkok, one such cooker which he saw at a school in Chengchow, capital of Hunan Province, consisted of a collapsible wooden box which could be unfolded on an adjustable stand. Inside each half of the unfolded box were 396 mirrors stuck on to a parabolic surface, and temperatures of 600°C could apparently be reached at the cooker's focal point – perfectly adequate for cooking bread, noodles or vegetables.

With a total reflective area of about one square metre, the Chinese solar cooker was rated as equivalent to a 1 kW electric oven. The whole device weighed only 15 kilograms (33 pounds) and its construction cost was estimated to be less than $20. The Chinese authorities claimed that 100 units had already been produced and several villages were already using them.

Typically, however, solar cookers have proved a considerable disappointment. The cooking process tends to be slow and cannot easily be controlled; and the 'active' component of the system involves the cook constantly reorienting the parabolic dish to track the sun around the sky. Solar cookers have proved awkward to use, blowing over in the wind, and sometimes severely burning the cook when the cooking vessel is put in place or removed.

The real problem, however, is that solar cookers only cook on sunny days, in the middle of the day and away from the shade. Third World cooks, by contrast, tend to prefer cooking in the evening and, if they have to do so during the day, prefer to stay in the shade. Until some simple, cheap method of collecting solar energy when it is available and storing it until it is needed is developed, solar cookers are unlikely to take the world by storm.

Solar stills have also been used for over a century to desalinate drinking water, with solar-powered distillation units in operation in the Greek Aegean islands, the USA and USSR. At its simplest, solar water distillation involves shallow trays filled with salt or brackish water. Their bottoms are blackened and a sloping sheet of glass is superimposed on each tray, trapping the sun's heat in the evaporator and allowing the evaporated water to condense on the glass – down which it promptly runs, to be collected in a trough. The salt remains in the tray, while the evaporated and condensed water is fresh and drinkable. According to Earthscan, each square metre of still can produce 3–5 litres a day, or $\frac{1}{2}$–1 UK gallons per square yard, of desalinated water. The costs are high, ranging from $20 to $30 per thousand litres ($90–140 per thousand gallons). Even at this price, however, solar stills may be cheaper than flash distillation or reverse osmosis for small desalination plants.

Solar desalination has been a major plank in the solar-energy programmes of a number of Arab countries, including Saudi Arabia and Jordan. One experimental solar desalination plant, however, failed to live up to expectations. The Aqaba plant, which had fifteen solar panels affording a 375-square-metre (448-square-foot) collection surface, from which a refrigerant carried the heat to an evaporation unit. According to the designers, Dornier System of West Germany and the Jordanian Royal Scientific Society, the plant should have produced 1,875 litres, but in fact it delivered only 750 litres a day during the summer and a mere 375 litres in the winter. The Jordanians, who had originally hoped to market the system throughout the Middle East, were forced to give up the hope, but decided to continue with the plant's testing.

It has been estimated, however, that over 3 billion MW of solar radiation fall on the Arab countries each year, the energy equivalent of three million large oil-fired or nuclear power stations, and they are increasingly thinking about ways in which they can harness a proportion of this giant resource. At Kuwait's Institute for Scientific Research, for example, solar energy is seen as one of the Institute's most important programmes – and KISR is aiming to achieve a commercially viable solar cooling system by the mid-1980s. A test solar house uses a lithium-bromide absorption cooling system to produce chilled water, used to cool air which is then used to air-condition the living space. Water is heated by solar means, with a thermal rock storage system used to tide the system over between periods of sunshine.

Saudi Arabia has also been boosting its solar funding. In October 1977, for example, Saudi Arabia and the United States signed a project agreement involving co-operation in the solar-energy field – dubbed SOLERAS. The initial five-year, $100 million joint programme has focused on solar water desalination and pumping, with cheap desalination techniques needed in both countries. In Saudi Arabia, water is needed principally for municipal and agricultural purposes. In the United States, on the other hand, it is mainly required to control river salinity and to provide drinkable water to selected communities with critical water-quality problems.

The SOLERAS programme, which has been administered by SERI, has involved many of the large corporations whose activities so worried Ray Reece – including Boeing, General Electric, Honeywell, Martin Marietta Aerospace and Mobil Tyco. When I visited Boeing, for instance, the company was developing designs for a solar water-desalination system that would transform brackish well water into drinkable water for such communities as Rankin and McCamey, in south-western Texas – a region with widespread water-quality problems. Boeing, however, was planning to use reverse osmosis, with the entire electrical energy requirement for the 1.8 million cubic metres a year (an average of 1.6 million gallons a day) coming from a solar thermal generating plant. Elsewhere, though, some solar scientists were trying to increase the concentration of salt in water in order to squeeze more power out of the sun.

## The Dead Sea Enrolled

Very few news stories filed from Sodom reach the world's headlines. One eye-catching item, however, did appear in the columns of at least one major international newspaper on 18 December 1979. Its first line read as follows: 'Israel, giving itself a Hannukah present from the sun, last night flooded the shores of the Dead Sea with lights powered by solar energy'.

A dramatic beginning to a very brief news item, but it did whet the appetite for more information. Israel is almost totally dependent on imported oil for its energy needs. Of the 10 million tons of oil imported in 1979, 6 million had had to be purchased on the precarious and expensive spot market. Worse, most of the world's oil was in the hands of the very Arab governments which were sworn to see the State of Israel committed unceremoniously to the dustbin of History. The fall of the Shah's regime in Iran was a body-blow to Israel, which had been receiving some 2 million tons of oil a year from that direction. The Ayatollah Khomeini turned that tap off before the dust of revolution had even begun to settle.

The Israelis had been very late in setting up an energy ministry, doing so finally in 1977. Once set up, it spent a great deal of its time and resources fighting off the rival claims of a number of other ministries with overlapping responsibilities and interests. However, it did find time to check how Israel was using its energy. Some 35 per cent was going into power generation plants, while transport accounted for 21 per cent, and industry and the domestic and service sectors took another 30 per cent. The production of chemical feedstocks and refinery losses accounted for the balance.

Israel's parliament, the Knesset, placed a growing emphasis on the need to switch away from oil to coal and other energy sources. By 1990, some 70 per cent of Israel's electricity may be generated by a series of coal-fired power stations, although these were still on the drawing-board in the early 1980s. Meanwhile, a range of alternative energy sources and technologies had been proposed by Israeli scientists.

One proposal was to build a power station on the path of a new aqueduct carrying water, mostly underground, from the Mediterranean to the Dead Sea (see Chapter 12). However, the costs of the project continued to escalate, while environmentalists were worried about the possible ecological effects of introducing massive quantities of Mediterranean water into this most salty of saline environments.

Plans to build a peat-fuelled generating station near the Sea of Galilee had also come under fire. Environmentalists and other pressure groups argued that the extraction of the peat would jeopardize the role played by the Sea of Galilee as a source of another of Israel's perilously scarce resources – fresh water. The Israelis have also claimed that they could readily extract uranium from their phosphate reserves, although the country's enthusiasm for nuclear power cooled slightly when planning permission was refused for a proposed reactor on the coast.

So, like the Arabs about them, the Israelis have been turning their eyes to the sun. One multinational team, involving the Dutch company Solmecs and US and British money, has been working on an idea developed by an Israeli, Professor Herman Branover. The idea, which addresses a target which others have failed to hit before, centres around a solar generator with no moving parts. Based on magneto-hydrodynamics, it involves a molten fluid (typically an ionized gas) being passed through a magnetic field and generating a direct current in the process. In the designs which are being pursued by the United States and the USSR, the two leaders in this field in recent years, fossil fuels have been seen as the main energy source for ionizing the gas, but Professor Branover, who has chosen to use molten metal (mercury in the first trial) as his working fluid, sees solar energy or waste heat from industrial processes as possible candidates for the external heat source needed to power the process.

More conventionally, one in three Israeli homes was equipped with a solar water heater by the early 1980s, although these systems were only contributing one per cent of Israel's total energy supplies at the time. The Knesset hoped to develop this option rapidly, however, doubling the number of solar water heaters by 1985 and investing an increasing amount of money in solar research generally.

Two scientists who benefited from this new emphasis were previously dismissed as cranks – and, more importantly, their applications for research funds had been regularly turned down. Nonetheless, Rudi Bloch and Harry Tabor of the Hebrew University of Jerusalem persevered with their attempts to mimic the formation of heat layers in salty water. Their goal was solar pond power. Their ideas, once again, will have ecological implications for the Dead Sea environment, but that is very unlikely to impede them. Israel's energy planners have been fired with enthusiasm for the basic concept, which would involve turning a major section of the Dead Sea into a patchwork of near-boiling solar ponds.

The basic phenomena harnessed in such solar ponds has been known since the early years of the century, although it has only been seriously researched during the last twenty years. One of the most impressive natural solar ponds is Medve Lake in Hungary, which reaches temperatures of 71°C (160°F) at a depth of 1.2 metres (4 feet) in late summer. Others are located near Oroville, Washington State; near Eilat, Israel; in the Venezuelan Antilles; and, of all places, in the Antarctic, under permanent ice cover.

Taking the Dead Sea as an example of the phenomenon, solar radiation penetrates the clear upper layers of water and is retained in the much saltier, denser layers at the bottom of the Sea. The few naturally occurring salt ponds can produce water close to boiling point in their bottom layers. Indeed, scientists at the University of New Mexico demonstrated this with their experimental solar pond by boiling eggs in the water. After 5 minutes at 109°C, they were perfectly done.

In an engineered solar pond, it can take a considerable time to set up the required layering. The densest layer must be formed first and successive layers then require a progressively weaker solution. The salinity gradient works in this way: heat losses by means of convection currents are minimized, provided the layers can be stabilized, and the clear water on top provides an effective insulating layer. The heat trapped in the denser bottom layers is extracted from the pond by means of a network of pipes filled with the familiar refrigerant, usually a freon, which has a very low boiling point and can be evaporated to drive a turbine, generating electricity in the process.

The cost of constructing a solar pond is very roughly 10 per cent that of constructing a flat-plate collector, per unit area, so the lowered collection efficiencies (typically about 20 per cent) found in such ponds are more than offset by the substantial reduction in the capital costs involved. Small ponds are uneconomical, because of heat loss from their relatively large surface area and edge-zone, and fairly robust materials must be used to line the pond, given the aggressive nature of the salts used.

In their tests of solar-pond technology, the University of New Mexico found that even if the sun were overcast for a week, there would be little change in the temperature of the underlying storage layer of salty water – which lost heat at a rate of 0.4°C a day even when, as in the winter of 1976, the pond was covered by ice for two weeks. The New Mexico team, led by Professor Howard Bryant, used a pond with a surface diameter of 15 metres (49 feet), with sides sloped at 34° to the horizontal, and 2.5 metres (8 feet) deep in its deepest zone.

A one-kilometre-square (247-acre) solar pond can gather energy equivalent to 43,000 tonnes of oil a year and requires about 3 million cubic metres (1,660 million gallons) of fresh or salt water each year for surface flushing. But it needs only two people to maintain it, since the plumbing is extremely simple.

Australia's first large-scale solar pond for power generation was opened at Alice Springs, in the Northern Territory, late in 1981. With an area of 2,000 square metres (21,528 square feet) and a depth of 2 metres (6½ feet), the pond powers a 20 kW turbine generator. The electricity thus produced runs a restaurant, vineyard and winery complex. Built by David Frederiksen and Robert Collins of Australian Solar Ponds, it was expected to produce some 60,000 kWh a year of electricity, costing about 26 Australian cents a kWh. The pond cost A$120,000 (US$136,000) to build, much of this sum going on the 660 tonnes of salt needed for the storage layer – mined from a dry salt lake some 240 kilometres away.

Meanwhile, in the United States, the Jet Propulsion Laboratory of the Californian Institute of Technology was scouring twenty-five states for suitable sites for large-scale solar-pond schemes. Generally, these states were in the south-east, mid-continent and the south-west, and the leading contender was the Salton Sea, a 360-square-mile (932-square-kilometre) salt lake in southern California. The Salton Sea (see Figure 8.2) was formed between 1905 and 1907 when flood-waters from the Colorado River (now held to be threatened by oil-shale development – see Chapter 4) were accidentally diverted into the Salton Basin.

The Jet Propulsion Laboratory was already working on a pre-liminary design for a 5 MW solar-pond plant there, with help from Ormat Turbines (established by Yehudah Bronicki, an Israeli who

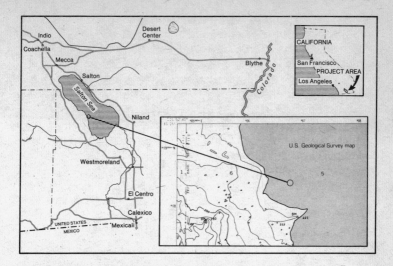

Figure 8.2: Site of the Salton Sea project
(source: Jet Propulsion Laboratory).

had also helped Bloch and Tabor with their Dead Sea schemes) and Southern California Edison. The project was being funded by a wide range of bodies: the Department of Energy, the Department of Defense, Southern California Edison, the State of California and Ormat itself.

The proposed 5 MW plant (see Figures 8.3 and 4) was to be one square kilometre in area, contained by dykes rising about 3 metres (10 feet) above the surface of the pond itself. If the 5 MW plant proved to be satisfactory, there were plans to scale it up through a 50 MW version to a 600 MW plant – sufficient to power a city of 350,000 people. It has been estimated that 120 square kilometres (46 square miles) of the Salton Sea would be needed for the 600 MW plant, or about 13 per cent of the Sea's surface area.

Interestingly, the ecological studies carried out as part of an environmental impact statement completed for the 5 MW scheme suggested that the solar pond would bring ecological benefits. The only real problem appeared to be the possibility that diving birds might boil themselves alive, although it was felt that the absence of food species in the ponds would help dissuade them from embarking on the exercise.

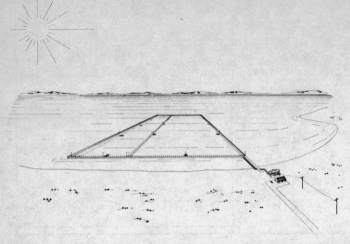

Figure 8.3: Artist's impression of the 5 MW plant at the Salton Sea (source: Jet Propulsion Laboratory).

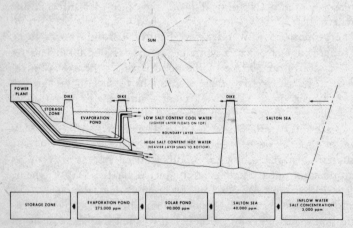

Figure 8.4: The Salton Sea solar-pond concept (source: Jet propulsion Laboratory).

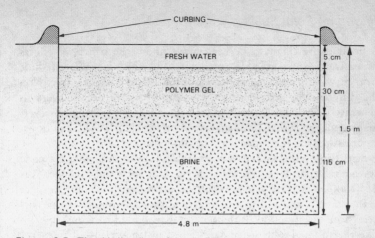

Figure 8.5: The University of New Mexico gel pond. Two hundred materials were screened as potential gel materials, with the final candidate needing to be transparent to solar radiation but unaffected by solar ultra-violet light, stable at the operating temperatures, less dense than brine, denser than fresh water and non-toxic (source: Jet Propulsion Laboratory).

A good deal of work needs to be done on the concept before it takes firm root, although Professor Bryant and others are working on new methods by which solar ponds can be made to layer themselves. One study which Bryant carried out with Ian Colbeck of Queen Mary College, London, suggested that a solar pond about the size of the University of New Mexico's pond at Albuquerque, and costing perhaps $1,000 to build, could heat a house in London with a floor area of 186 square metres (2,000 square feet), at a price per kilowatt-hour which would be competitive with gas heating. The problem, of course, would be to find somewhere to put such a pond in a densely built-up metropolitan area. The New Mexico team has also been experimenting with gel ponds (see Figure 8.5), with a gel floating on top of a saturated brine – the gel helping to prevent convection in the pond.

For those who were concerned about the land-take of such schemes, or about the cost involved in shipping in large volumes of salt to ensure that the water in their solar pond was three times as salty as ocean water, there was another option – involving using the world ocean itself as something of a solar pond in reverse.

## Plumbing Solar Seas

A great many claims have been made about the beneficial effects of sea-water, some credible, some not. One which was dismissed for over fifty years emerged in France in the 1920s. The idea: to exploit the difference in temperature between successive ocean layers to generate electricity. In the wake of the 1973-4 oil crisis, however, many concepts which had languished on the shelf were taken down and brushed off. This idea was one of them.

Scientists in the United States realized that technology had made considerable strides in a number of relevant areas since the idea was first mooted. Given that most of the earth's solar income is spent in the planet's seas and oceans, any project which promised to harness even a minute fraction of that energy was bound to win support – like the ill-fated kelp scheme described in Chapter 10. The energy stored in the thermal gradients in the major oceans is estimated to be many hundred times that consumed by our industrial societies each year, and it is constantly renewed. Clearly, only a very small proportion of that energy could ever be economically recovered, but scientists were impressed by the relatively simple engineering likely to be involved.

Unlike most advanced renewable-energy technologies, ocean thermal energy conversion (OTEC) generators are really little more than large-scale plumbing stuck out in the ocean to exploit the different temperatures of the ocean's surface and deep waters. It is difficult to dismiss the technology's inherent advantages: the fuel, for one thing, is free; the system is intrinsically safe, unlike nuclear power; and it generates no pollution – indeed, although it will exert a local chilling effect on the marine environment, it would be likely to get a clean bill of environmental health were it ever to need one.

The French have been involved in OTEC technology longer than anyone else, largely because it was a Frenchman, Arsène d'Arsonval, who first came up with the idea. France has been looking to the Ivory Coast and French Polynesia as possible OTEC markets, while the Dutch and the Swedes are also working in the area with an eye to the potential export opportunities. The Japanese are hot on the trail, and OTEC also received a considerable boost in the United States during 1980, with the passage of the Ocean Thermal Energy Conversion Research and Development Act. An OTEC Demonstration

Fund was set up under the terms of the Act, backed by $2 billion in loan guarantees.

President Reagan was soon trying to cut back OTEC funding, however, partly because OTEC enthusiasts had oversold the technology to the point where the Republican administration appeared to believe that it was ready for commercialization with no further federal help. OTEC is, nonetheless, probably the most attractive of the renewable-energy technologies as far as the powers-that-be in the United States are concerned, for geographical, institutional and political reasons. The Gulf of Mexico could provide suitable sites for OTEC plants, which could supply base-load electricity around the clock – a strong point in the technology's favour as far as the US Department of Energy and high-technology companies such as Lockheed and TRW are concerned, because it makes OTEC seem the only serious renewable contender challenging nuclear power.

In an attempt to discover whether the idea will work in practice, a pilot scheme was carried out off the coast of Hawaii. The technology may be relatively simple, but there was nothing simple about the companies involved in the exercise. The project, dubbed 'Mini-OTEC', was funded by the State of Hawaii, the Lockheed Missiles and Space Company and the Dillingham Corporation. Lockheed designed the system and built it in fifteen months, for the most part using off-the-shelf components. Alfa-Laval of Sweden made two of the most vital components, the titanium heat exchangers.

The experiment, which was mounted on a converted US Navy barge (Figure 8.6), operated by the University of Hawaii's Natural Energy Laboratory, which, interestingly, had started tinkering with OTEC technology in 1972, a year before the first OPEC oil shock. Most of the problems faced by the OTEC engineers do not involve radical developments in design or construction, requiring instead a stretching of current engineering practice. OTEC, said William Whitmore of Lockheed, is 'nothing more than sophisticated plumbing'.

Although OTEC plants might be operated from land-based sites near a sharply sloping sea-bed, and the world's first land-based OTEC plant opened on the Japanese island of Nauru in 1981 (built by Shimizu Construction, Toshiba and Tokyo Electric Power Services), the majority of sites will be at sea. The minimum temperature difference needed is 15°C (59°F), and significant quantities of power have been generated in ocean areas where the temperatures

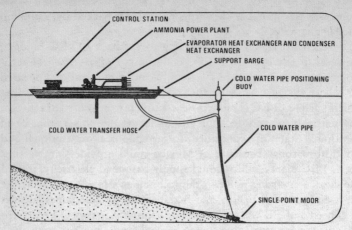

Figure 8.6: Mini-OTEC scheme off Hawaii
(source: Lockheed Missiles and Space Company).

range from between 25°C and 30°C (77° − 86°F) at the surface to between 4° and 7°C (39° − 45°F) in deeper water. In the basic solar sea thermal power plant, warm water is drawn into a broad-mouthed tube at the top of the system, where it produces steam under low pressure in the boiler, and is then cooled in the condenser by the intake of cold water from the deep sea (about 750 metres or 2,460 feet down). The system is perhaps 2–3-per-cent efficient, low by the standards of heat engines using conventional fuels − but, then, the fuel *is* free.

European designs propose a 100 MW station and require either a 210,000 tonne semi-submerged concrete caisson or a 100,000 tonne semi-submersible steel vessel. Either of these would be comparable with a North Sea oil platform, which explains the interest of some British companies in the technology. A number of major problems face such companies in their efforts to break into the OTEC field, including the fact that there will be no domestic market for the technology, because European offshore waters do not provide the required range of temperatures. Instead, the platforms would have to be towed to their eventual locations, generally in tropical waters (see Figures 8.7 and 8). The Dunlin A platform was towed several hundred kilometres across the North Sea, but this would be an altogether more complicated feat, at least equivalent to crossing the Atlantic.

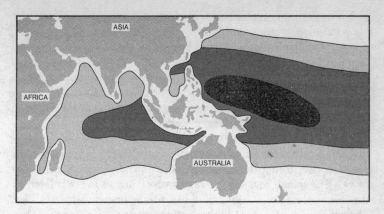

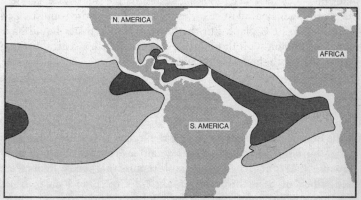

Figures 8.7 and 8: Suitable areas for OTEC operations. OTEC is an option where there is a temperature difference of at least 18°C (32°F) between the surface and the water at 1,000 metres down – or more (light shading). Seas with a temperature difference of over 22°C (40°F) are found in tropical regions (dark shading), with the most promising areas of all found in the West Pacific (shown in black). (Source: Earthscan.)

On the other hand, as the Marine Resources Project at the University of Manchester has pointed out, there could be an important market for the ancillary equipment likely to be required, including turbines, pumps and heat exchangers. Even more attractive is the idea of breaking into the more specialized market for monitoring and control systems, communications equipment, safety apparatus and so on. Britain's technical sophistication in these fields would give it a particular advantage.

Huge volumes of water would have to be processed, however, to achieve the required power outputs. A 250 MW Lockheed design for a floating OTEC station involves pumping cold water up from a depth of 1,000 metres (3,280 feet) in a 30-metre (98-foot) diameter pipe. The flow of water would be comparable to that of the Missouri River: about 1,500 cubic metres a second.

If OTEC schemes were to be coupled with marine aquaculture, this huge upwelling of nutrient-rich water might be put to some practical use, tilting the economic equation rather more in favour of OTEC. Some solar engineers, however, are so overwhelmed by the sheer volume of working fluid likely to be involved in an OTEC plant that they have been looking at alternative solar systems. Here the plumbing may need to be orders of magnitude more sophisticated than in an OTEC plant, but the flows of heat-transfer liquid have more in common with those inside an office block's central-heating system than with the Missouri River.

## Some Like It Very Hot

While no one now seems to believe the legend that had Archimedes using 'burning mirrors' to destroy an invading Roman fleet at Syracuse in 212 B.C., there are reliable reports that such mirrors were used, albeit on a smaller scale, in ancient Greece, in Roman times and, indeed, in China. They were used for lighting sacred flames in temples. According to Plutarch, the Greek philosopher, when the barbarians sacked the temple of the Vestal Virgins at Delphi, extinguishing the sacred flame, it had to be relit with 'pure and unpolluted flame from the sun'. Concave vessels of brass, held by the holy women, ignited 'light and dry matter'. And, according to the *Chou Li*, a book describing ancient ceremonies and rituals and written about twenty years after those strange events in Bethlehem, 'the Directors of Sun Fire have the duty of receiving, with a concave mirror, brilliant fire from the sun in order to prepare brilliant torches for sacrifices'.

The capacity of the parabolic mirror to concentrate the sun's rays to useful effect has been known for thousands of years, although the limitations of technology have meant that the applications of this knowledge have also been constrained. Every so often, interest would flare up, as when the Franciscan monk Roger Bacon read a book by the eleventh-century Arab scholar Ibn Al-Haitham. Bacon spotted a clue in the elaborate mathematical formulae in Al-Haitham's writings to a means of building a medieval doomsday weapon, a weapon which could perhaps be turned against the Crusaders who at that very moment were waging war on the Saracens in the Holy Land. 'This mirror,' Bacon argued, 'would burn fiercely everything on which it could be focused. We are to believe that the Anti-Christ will use these mirrors to burn up cities, camps and weapons.'

Bacon's arguments, in fact, contain more than an echo of those

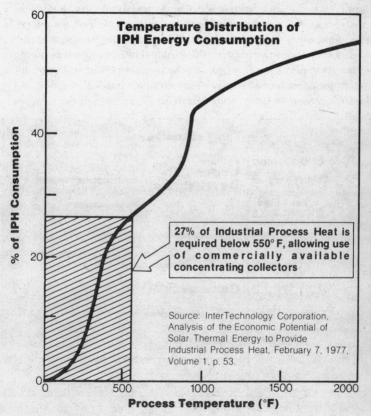

**Temperature Distribution of IPH Energy Consumption**

% of IPH Consumption

Process Temperature (°F)

27% of Industrial Process Heat is required below 550° F, allowing use of commercially available concentrating collectors

Source: InterTechnology Corporation, Analysis of the Economic Potential of Solar Thermal Energy to Provide Industrial Process Heat, February 7, 1977, Volume 1, p. 53.

Figure 8.9: Potential contribution of commercially available solar collectors to industrial process heat needs (source: SERI).

used by today's arms peddlers to convince the governments of the day that their rivals have access to the ultimate super-weapon – and that they should be funded to catch up or overtake the Anti-Christ of the moment. However that may be, he failed to convince the authorities that his proposed parabolic weapon could sweep the Holy Land clear for Christianity. Indeed, Bacon was eventually confined to a dungeon as a heretic – and interest in such burning mirrors suffered something of a setback.

By the sixteenth century, however, no less a scientist than Leonardo da Vinci was in hot pursuit of burning-mirror technology, proposing a giant parabolic mirror 6.4 kilometres (4 miles) across that could 'supply heat for any boiler in a dyeing factory, and with this a pool can be warmed up, because there will always be boiling water'. It is interesting that, while Leonardo appears to have got rather carried away with the prospects for solar power, he focused on the industrial applications it might find. By the early 1980s, industry was the largest consumer of energy in an advanced industrial nation like the United States – accounting for about 37 per cent of the nation's

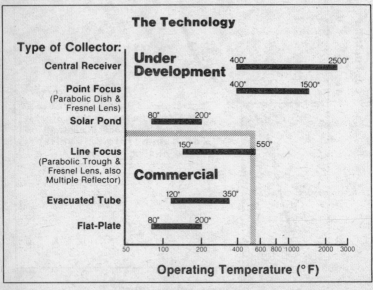

Figure 8.10: Suitability of a range of different solar collection technologies for industrial applications, in terms of operating temperature (source: SERI).

gross energy consumption of some 77 quads annually (a quad equals $10^{15}$ British thermal units), 50–70 per cent of this demand being for industrial process heat.

As Figure 8.9 shows, about a quarter of the industrial process heat used by US industry during the 1970s was used at a temperature of less than 288°C (550°F). And, as Figure 8.10 suggests, flat-plate collectors, evacuated-tube collectors and 'line-focus' parabolic trough

*Table 8.1: Some industrial process heat trials undertaken by public and private sector research teams in the United States (source: SERI)*

| Location | Process | Collectors | Owner | Status (1981) |
|---|---|---|---|---|
| **Hot water (140°–212°F)** | | | | |
| Sacramento, Calif. | can washing | flat-plate and parabolic | Campbell Soup Co. | operational (April 1978)) |
| Harrisburg, Pa. | concrete block curing | multiple reflector | York Building Products | operational (Sept. 1978) |
| LaFrance, S.C. | textile dyeing | evacuated tube | Reigel Textile Corp. | operational (June 1978) |
| **Hot air (140°–212°F)** | | | | |
| Fresno, Calif. | fruit drying | flat-plate | Lamanuzzi & Pantaleo Foods | operational (May 1978) |
| Canton, Miss. | kiln drying of lumber | flat-plate | LaCour Kiln Services, Inc. | operational (Nov. 1977) |
| Decatur, Ala. | soybean drying | flat-plate | Gold Kist, Inc. | operational (May 1978) |
| Gilroy, Calif. | onion drying | evacuated tube | Gilroy Foods, Inc. | operational (Sept. 1979) |
| **Low-temperature steam (212°–350°F)** | | | | |
| Fairfax, Ala. | fabric drying | parabolic trough | WestPoint Pepperell | operational (Sept. 1978) |
| Sherman, Tex. | gauze bleaching | parabolic trough | Johnson & Johnson | operational (Jan. 1980) |
| Pasadena, Calif. | laundry | parabolic trough | Home Cleaning & Laundry | construction |
| Bradenton, Fla. | orange juice pasteurization | evacuated tube | Tropicana Products, Inc. | construction |

| Location | Process | Collectors | Owner | Status (1981) |
|----------|---------|------------|-------|---------------|
| **Intermediate-temperature steam (350°–550°F)** | | | | |
| Mobile, Ala. | oil heating | parabolic trough | Ergon, Inc. | design |
| Dalton, Ga. | latex production | multiple reflector | Dow Chemical | construction |
| Newberry Springs, Calif. | hectorite processing | parabolic trough | National Lead Industries | design |
| Hobbs, N. Mex. | oil refinery | parabolic trough | Southern Union Co. | construction |
| San Antonio, Tex. | brewery | parabolic trough | Lone Star Brewing Co. | construction |
| Henderson, Nev. | chlorine manufacturing | parabolic trough | Stauffer Chemical Co. | design |
| Ontario, Ore. | potato processing | parabolic trough | Ore-Ida Co. | construction |
| **Privately funded industrial process heat applications** | | | | |
| Youngstown, Ohio | aluminium anodizing | fixed half-parabolic | General Extrusions, Inc. | operational (Sept. 1977) |
| Jacksonville, Fla. | beer pasteurization | evacuated tube | Anheuser-Busch, Inc. | operational (Feb. 1978) |

collectors all fall within this range. Table 8.1 shows some of the field tests which were being undertaken by various organizations during the late 1970s.

It is now recognized that it is extremely difficult to obtain fluid temperatures higher than 150°C (302°F) with the use of even the most sophisticated flat-plate collectors. To achieve higher temperatures, it is necessary to climb up the spectrum of solar technologies to those which concentrate or focus solar radiation. Since such approaches inevitably mean that the system loses all or most of the diffuse radiation available to it, concentrating only the direct radiation, it is obviously vital that the concentrating device should track the sun across the sky.

## Mirror, Mirrors...

Such concentration devices can be classified into two main types: linear-focusing concentrators and point-focusing concentrators. The former are typically equipped with a single-axis tracking system and the latter with a two-axis system. To get some idea of what a line-focus system looks like, one could do worse than climb up on to the roof of Honeywell's headquarters building in Minneapolis. This company supplied the switch-off-any-appliance-from-anywhere unit in Futurehome 2000 (described in Chapter 7), but its interest in solar energy has taken it very much further down the road than that unit on its own might suggest.

The target Honeywell set itself in designing its new headquarters building was that solar energy should provide all the energy needed to drive the air-conditioning system in high summer. This was a tall order, given that the eight-storey building had a floor area of 100,000 square feet (9,290 square metres), accommodating 500 heat-producing people. The required 200-ton air-conditioning plant is powered by solar energy, as is the building's hot-water system and, in winter, part of its space-heating system.

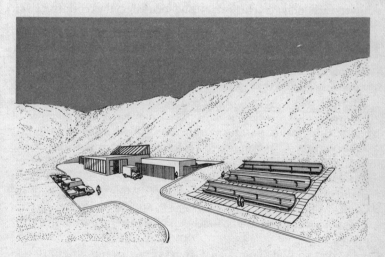

Figure 8.11: An array of parabolic-trough collectors at the proposed SERAPH facility (source: SERI).

The solar collectors, each of which is a long silvered trough, focus the sun on to a pipe which runs the length of each collector, occupying the focal line. A heat-transfer fluid runs through the pipe as the collector tracks the sun. A sensor notes the position of the sun, operating an array of electric motors which keep the reflectors correctly aligned. If the sun is not shining, the collectors are turned upside-down, like so many overturned horse-troughs atop all that sophisticated tracking and rotation equipment, to ensure that the grit and grime of Minneapolis does not collect on their brilliant surfaces. Figure 8.11 is an artist's impression of an array of parabolic-trough collectors at a pilot plant planned by the Solar Energy Research Institute, while Figure 8.12 is a schematic diagram of a 150 kW solar-powered water pump for irrigation.

The technical viability of line-focus systems has been demonstrated by a wide range of projects, some of which are listed in Table 8.1 above. But while commercial line-focus systems are now very much in prospect, point-focus systems, especially those of the central receiver system (CRS) configuration, are still at the R & D stage. A CRS consists of two main elements: a tower which holds the receiver and heat-transfer system, and a field of heliostats (computer-controlled mirrors) which are distributed around the base of the tower, each individual heliostat being focused on the central receiver. Figure 8.13 shows a typical CRS configuration.

But such 'distributed-focus' systems, based on a field of heliostats and a single central receiver mounted on a 'power tower', are not the only type of point-focus technology. Some parabolic-dish concentrators are also on the market, although their widespread use is likely to be delayed by the complex operating and maintenance procedures required. Their development has been pioneered by a number of highly enterprising scientists, from Hero of Alexander in the first century of the Christian era to Professor Augustin Mouchot in the mid-1800s (he exhibited an enormous solar motor at the 1878 Universal Exposition in Paris) and the American engineer John Ericsson – who designed the ironclad battleship *The Monitor* which sank the Confederate ironclad *The Merrimack* off the Virginia coast on 9 March 1862, a year after Mouchot patented his first primitive solar pump.

'A great portion of our planet enjoys perpetual sunshine,' Ericsson wrote enthusiastically in 1868. 'The field therefore awaiting the application of the solar engine is almost beyond computation, while

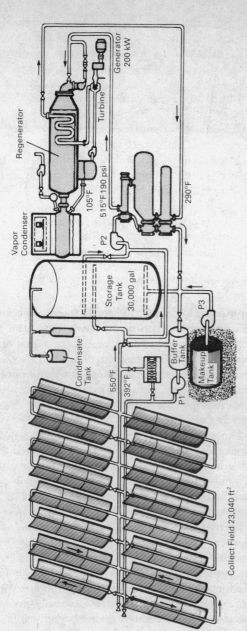

Figure 8.12: A flow diagram of a 150 kW solar-powered irrigation plant (source: SERI).

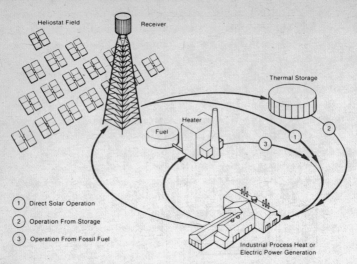

Figure 8.13: A typical central receiver system (source: SERI).

the source of its power is boundless. Who can foresee,' he asked, 'what influence an inexhaustible motive power will exercise on civilization and the capability of the earth to supply the wants of our race?' The problem, he soon found, once he decided to devote the rest of his life to solar energy, was that 'although the heat is obtained for nothing, so extensive, costly and complex is the concentrating apparatus' that solar engines were actually more expensive than the equivalent coal-powered motors.

Mouchot, who had returned to his mathematical studies in 1880 (the year Abel Pifre's solar-powered printing press, exhibited at the Garden of the Tuileries, printed 500 copies of the *Journal Soleil*), had astonished onlookers with his own solar engine, which he exhibited at Tours in 1874. This comprised a huge cone-shaped mirror, 8¼ feet (2.6 metres) wide at its mouth and affording 56 square feet (5 square metres) of reflective surface. It generated enough steam to drive a half-horsepower engine at 80 strokes per minute.

This solar engine, however, occupied an area of 37 square metres (400 square feet) and produced only half a horsepower. Two hundred such engines would thus be needed to drive a typical 100-horsepower industrial motor. If, Mouchot calculated, 200 such solar engines were to be arrayed in four lines, with enough space between the lines to prevent them casting shadows across one another, they would cover a total of 9,290 square metres (100,000 square feet). Such arrays, Mouchot realized, would be out of the question in built-up areas – just like solar ponds.

A number of companies, however, are pursuing research on parabolic concentrators. Figures 8.1 (p. 172) and 8.14–16 show a faceted, thin-film concentrator designed by the Boeing Engineering and Construction Company, based in Seattle; two designs developed by Acurex Corporation, based in California; and a stretched, thin-film concentrator devised by A AI Corporation of Baltimore, Maryland. Both the Boeing (Figure 8.1) and the AAI (Figure 8.16) designs are attempts to use new materials to reduce the cost of parabolic-dish concentrators. The Boeing system uses an aluminized polyester film bonded on to formed steel plating with an adhesive, while the AAI reflecting surface consists of a metal-coated thin membrane which is stretched into its parabolic shape by a partial vacuum between

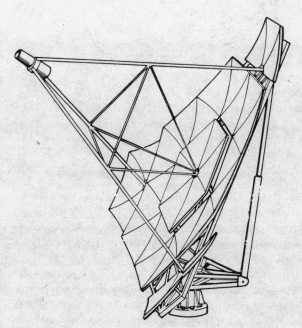

Figure 8.14: Acurex's alternative low-cost concentrator design (source: Acurex).

Figure 8.15: Acurex advanced parabolic concentrator (source: Acurex).

the membrane and the back shell of the supporting structure.

The first significant CRS plant was built in 1965 by the University of Genoa, Italy, and consisted of 121 small mirrors producing super-heated steam at temperatures above 450°C (840°F). Four years later, the French opened a 1 MW experimental power tower in the Pyrenees which reaches temperatures of 3,300°C (6,000°F). This, the solar furnace at Odeillo, near the ski-resort of Font-Romeu, has sixty-three large heliostats spread over 0.4 square kilometres (10 acres). These reflect radiation on to a parabolic mirrored wall which, in turn, reflects it back on to the solar furnace atop a tower.

In 1979, France abandoned a second solar power plant, called

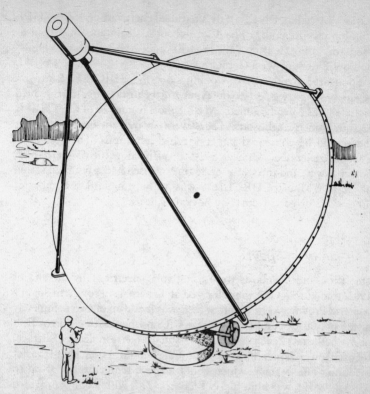

Figure 8.16: A A I stretched, thin-film concentrator
(source: A A I Corporation).

Themis, which was to have produced 2 MW of electricity for the
national grid – and had been intended to give France a clear lead
in the solar field. The main problem was that the site had been poorly
chosen, so that snow and adverse weather conditions hampered
construction work and the resulting cost escalation made the project
uneconomic.

By that time, however, France was also involved in the 1 MW
EURELIOS CRS plant at Adrano, Sicily. When completed, in
December of 1980, EURELIOS became the world's first large-scale
(megawatt-range) experimental solar power plant to produce electricity and feed it into a national grid. The plant was designed and
built by an impressive consortium of European industrial organ-

izations: Ansaldo, ENEL (Italy's national energy utility), CETHEL (combining Renault, Five-Cail-Babcock, Saintgobain, Pont-à-Mousson and Heurtey, all French) and MBB (Messerschmitt-Bölkow-Blohm of West Germany).

Sponsored by the EEC Commission, the EURELIOS project began testing two different types of heliostat: its mirror field included 112 23-square-metre MBB heliostats and 70 of CETHEL's 52-square-metre heliostats. These were arrayed in such a way that they could be compared under varying conditions. The system as a whole generated steam at 512°C (954°F) atop the 55-metre-high power tower, and the steam-cycle turbine used had a nominal rating of 1.2 MW. But if EURELIOS was in the vanguard, a number of other CRS projects were soon hot on its heels.

## Sun-struck in Spain

One thousand Spaniards were using solar electricity by the end of 1981, thanks to a CRS plant located at Tabernas, in southern Spain's Almeria Province. The plant, in fact, was made up of two completely different 500 kW units. One was a CRS proper, with a mirror field of 93 heliostats (each having a 39-square-metre reflective surface) focused on a boiler filled with liquid sodium as its heat-transfer medium. This system, which could achieve temperatures of up to 530°C (986°F), was built by INTERATOM, with a boiler provided by Sulzer of Switzerland and heliostats by the US company Martin Marietta.

The second system was a distributed collector system, with over 5,000 square metres (53,820 square feet) of parabolic-trough collectors driving a second 500 kW turbine. Acurex and the West German company MAN supplied these collectors, while Sweden's Stal-Laval supplied the turbines. Electricity from the two systems was being fed to consumers through the grid of Sevilliana de la Electricidad, and the project as a whole was largely funded by West Germany – which provided 37 per cent of the $30.4 million cost, with the remainder coming from Austria, Belgium, Greece, Italy, Spain, Sweden, Switzerland and the United States, by way of the International Energy Agency.

Just down the road, the 1.2 MW CESA–1 (Central Electrica Solar de Almeria) project, initiated in early 1979, was also nearing completion. Here the power tower was 80 metres (262 feet) high and the mirror field was made up of some 300 heliostats, each of which had a surface of 36–40 square metres, resulting in a total reflective surface of 11,400 square metres (122,708 square feet). The system was projected to have an overall efficiency of 90 per cent and to reach temperatures in the range of 520°C (968°F).

CESA–1 was also to be hooked into the national grid, but its engineers would not be drawn on the economics of the exercise. 'Although these plants are officially part of the high voltage system,' said Antonio Munoz Torralbo of the Centre for Energy Studies, 'they are essentially research projects. Come back in the year 2000 and we'll talk about competitive electricity costs.'

If the Almeria CRS plant performed to specification, INTER-ATOM (which, to reveal it in its true colours, stands for Internationale Atomreaktorbau) planned to build a much more ambitious 20 MW gas-cooled solar power tower scheme – dubbed GAST. This plant, which would be forty times larger than the CRS system at Almeria, might be built at Badajoz in south-western Spain, an area which enjoys 3,000 sun-hours a year. GAST, which would almost certainly be the biggest plant of its type when commissioned, had been on the drawing-board since 1978. It should cover an area of 0.5 square kilometres (124 acres), with a field of over 3,000 heliostats, each having a 40-square-metre surface, and it is hoped that it will heat air to 800°C (1,472°F) in a receiver atop a 200-metre (656-foot) tower.

Figure 8.17 gives some idea of the various components of the system, which would be a joint effort with MAN, MBB and Dornier System – who were involved in the ill-fated Aqaba desalination plant described earlier. Heated air would be used in the GAST plant to drive a gas turbine, and a fossil-fuel-fired back-up boiler would be provided to take over generation in low or zero sunlight conditions.

At about the same time, the Japanese 1 MW solar thermal power plants at Nio, Kagawa Prefecture (see Chapter 3), were warming up for their trial runs. Nio was chosen for its solar characteristics, although it is interesting to note that it only records 850 sunshine-hours a year, compared with the 3,000 reported for Badajoz. Again, one CRS and one distributed-collector system were being tested, built as part of the Ministry of International Trade and Industry's 'Sunshine Project'. Mitsubishi Heavy Industries designed and built the CRS, while Hitachi was responsible for the distributed-collector plant.

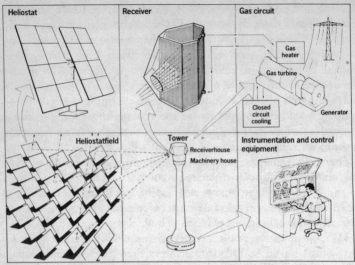

Figure 8.17: INTERATOM's 20 MW gas-cooled solar power tower plant (source: INTERATOM).

The Nio CRS incorporates a 69-metre (226-foot) tower sur-rounded by 807 heliostats, each with a 16-square-metre (172-square-foot) reflective surface and made of a 5-millimetre-thick white glass able to reflect 94 per cent of incoming sunshine up to the central receiver. The plant is controlled by twenty-seven satellite micro-processors, all of which feed information into a central computer. Steam is produced at about 250°C (480°F) and drawn off to drive a turbine.

The distributed-collector system is different in that it uses 124 parabolic-trough collectors, each measuring 3.6 by 3.8 metres (12 by 12.5 feet). Whereas the Almeria system used oil-filled pipes to extract heat from the collectors' focal lines, the Nio system uses water – which is converted into steam. Solar radiation is reflected into these parabolic-trough collectors by 2,480 flat-plane mirrors or heliostats, each with a 4.5-square-metre (48-square-foot) reflective surface. The heat-storage system uses a mixture of potassium chloride and lithium chloride, with a 352°C (666°F) melting point. Both systems had a maximum storage capacity of three hours.

West Germany's Ministry for Research and Technology, which provided that country's funding for the Almeria plants, was also involved in the construction of a 'solar chimney' at Manzanares, in Spain's Ciudad Real Province. The scheme consisted of a 200-metre (642-foot) chimney made of corrugated steel sheet and supported by steel rods. This chimney stands in the middle of an area whose diameter is 250 metres (820 feet) and which is covered by a plastic sheet or membrane, pitched 2 metres off the ground at its periphery and rising to a height of 8 metres above the ground beneath the chimney itself. The membrane collects solar energy, heating the air beneath it – which promptly shoots up the chimney, driving a turbine in the base of the chimney.

The same technology, it has been estimated, could be used to produce 1,000 MW solar chimneys, some 900 metres (2,953 feet) high and using seven turbines. Large solar chimneys for desert or semi-arid areas, which would be 10 kilometres (over 6 miles) in diameter, are already on the drawing-board.

The cost of such a plant, according to the West Germans, could be about $2,100 per installed kW. The various CRS and distributed-collector plants described so far, however, have been pilot plants, and their costs have tended to be in the range $20,000–30,000 per installed kW. Their designers are convinced that these costs can be brought down to between $2,000 and $4,000 per installed kW, a capital cost which is perhaps twice as high as for a fossil-fuelled plant.

Such plants are not popular with radical technologists, who argue that solar furnaces and similar schemes are little more than an attempt to centralize an energy resource which is naturally decentralized. But industrialists and government agencies continue to build their Temples of the Sun, such as the 'Solar One' facility, twelve miles from Barstow in California's Mojave Desert – where the *Solar Challenger* first flew. This desert site has more than 300 cloudless days a year, and the 1,818 heliostats, designed to rotate 270° on their vertical axis and 95° on their horizontal axis, are expected to produce 10 MW of electricity at nearly ten times the cost of power derived from oil-, coal- or nuclear-powered plants.

The question in some people's minds, however, is whether 'Solar One' and similar facilities will prove to be milestones on the road to new, renewable-energy sources – or whether they will merely rust away as monuments to an abandoned technology. A great deal will inevitably depend on how far and how quickly manufacturers can pull down the costs associated with the various components of such systems. At Barstow, each heliostat of twelve panels cost $15,000

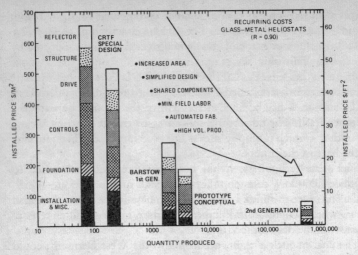

Figure 8.18: Projected fall in CRS costs (in 1978 dollars; source: US Department of Energy).

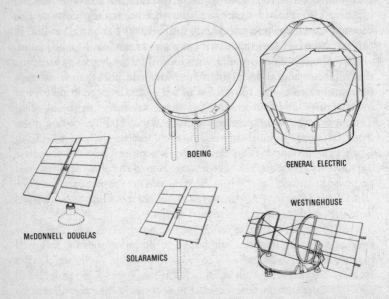

Figure 8.19: Second-generation heliostats (source: US Department of Energy).

at 1981 prices, and it was then estimated that the power utilities would have to order at least 100,000 of the mirror assemblies – enough to build five or six plants ten times the size of Solar One – to affect that price significantly.

Variously described as 'a white elephant', 'a gold-plated turkey' and 'science fiction solar', Solar One cost $142 million to build – and confounded its critics by working to specification. Its operators, Southern California Edison, are so impressed that they are planning to build a plant ten times the size, without government funding. 'The technical success makes everyone a lot more comfortable,' said Gerald Braun, as director of the US Department of Energy's solar thermal technology division. 'The prevailing opinion among policy makers has been that this and other solar technologies couldn't make any significant energy contribution until after the year 2000. But now we've built a solar project on time, without big budget overruns, and found that it's either commercially viable today or at least tantalizingly close. We've shown that solar energy is not pie-in-the-sky. It's here.'

Companies like Boeing have produced diagrams like Figure 8.18, which was published by the US Department of Energy showing the way they expect the cost of heliostats to fall as the quantity produced increases. Boeing and McDonnell Douglas are among the companies which are working on new designs such as the second-generation heliostats shown in Figure 8.19. But tumbling oil prices upset some of the assumptions on which those calculations were based and, while the long-term trend in oil prices must be up, there are those who believe that the cost of photovoltaic cells will fall far faster than that of heliostats and other CRS components, giving the photovoltaics industry a decisive edge by the end of the century. So what are photovoltaic cells – and how do they work?

# 9 ⊙ Cell Mates

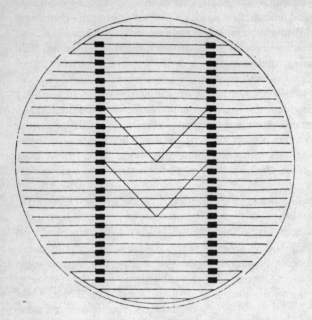

Figure 9.1: Typical solar cell with front electrode grid pattern
(source: Lucas B P Solar Systems – now B P Solar Systems).

Compared with solar building or the use of focusing mirrors, the photovoltaics industry is something of a parvenu. The 'photovoltaic effect' has been known since the middle of the nineteenth century, but the industry has only really begun to take off since our species began its move out into space. The word photovoltaic (derived from the Greek *photo*, meaning 'light', and 'voltaic', which stems from the name of Alessandro Volta, the inventor of the electric battery cell) refers to the production of direct electrical current from light.

The photoelectric properties of selenium were discovered in 1873 by George May at Valentia, Ireland, and in 1888 Rudolf Hertz constructed the first selenium photoelectric cell. The first public demonstration of such a cell was given by Westinghouse, of whom more in a moment, in October 1925, and the first commercial installation may well have been that at Wilcox's Pier Restaurant, six years later.

Practical solar cells were first developed in the 1950s by the Bell Telephone Company, although the cost of those early cells was very high indeed – at several thousands of dollars per *watt* produced. Nonetheless, there were some places where users were prepared to pay even that sort of premium, particularly in space. When the US satellite *Vanguard* went into orbit in 1958, seventy years after Hertz came up with that first selenium cell, it carried a small array of photo-voltaic cells to power its radio transmitter. Since that date, thousands of satellites have been rocketed into earth orbit or into deep space with photovoltaic arrays to power their vital processes. Today, however, selenium is not the material of choice, having largely been replaced by silicon. Cells are being made from single crystals of high-purity silicon, from polycrystalline or amorphous silicon, and, more

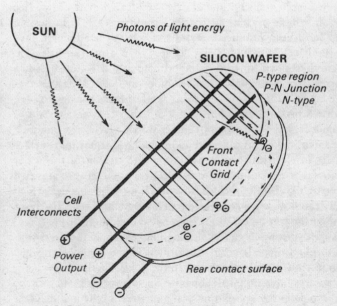

Figure 9.2: Principles of solar cell operation
(source: Lucas B P Solar Systems – now B P Solar Systems).

speculatively, from cadmium sulphide, copper sulphide and gallium arsenide.

The photovoltaic effect occurs in minute quantities at the junction of any two different materials of the right type: the problem lies in identifying materials which convert a high proportion of the sunlight falling upon them into electricity. Most solar cells are made from semiconducting materials, composed of two layers, one or both of which is 'doped' – or impregnated – with a photo-active chemical (Figure 9.2). A solar cell is typically small: a cell 10 centimetres (4 inches) in diameter will produce about 1 peak watt of electric current at 0.5 volts. The efficiency of such cells varies from 5 to 15 per cent, with some laboratory experiments reaching 25–30 per cent.

To give an idea of what this means, if you took 8 square feet (0.74 square metres) of a cell material with a 12-per-cent conversion efficiency, you could produce enough electricity to power one 100-watt light-bulb, provided the sun was shining.

The standard method of producing single crystals of silicon for solar cells is the Czochralski technique, in which a 'seed crystal' is dipped into molten silicon and slowly withdrawn as it grows (see Figure 9.3). Single crystals of over 12 centimetres (4.7 inches) in diameter have been produced, crystals which at their longest have been several feet (although generally less than a metre) in length. These are then sawn up with diamond blades into wafers 0.2–0.35 millimetres thick – or perhaps one should say 0.2–0.35 millimetres *thin*. Up to half the silicon is lost as 'kerf' in the slicing process, although US producers are hoping for a 50-per-cent better yield of cells from a crystal by producing thinner wafers with better saws.

Once sawn, the cell is polished and doped to form a thin surface layer with an electrical conductivity opposite to that of the wafer itself. Now that the cell is a battery, electrical contacts are attached to the top and bottom of the cell, to provide a circuit through which electricity can flow when connected to a load. An anti-reflective layer is added to the top layer, to maximize its absorption of light, and the cells are then interconnected in a module, which, in turn, is encapsulated in glass or plastic for protection. These modules are then made up into an 'array' appropriate to the power requirement.

Such an array must typically operate for four years in an average climate to recoup the energy that was expended in the manufacture of its silicon components. But the system's life should be of the order of twenty years.

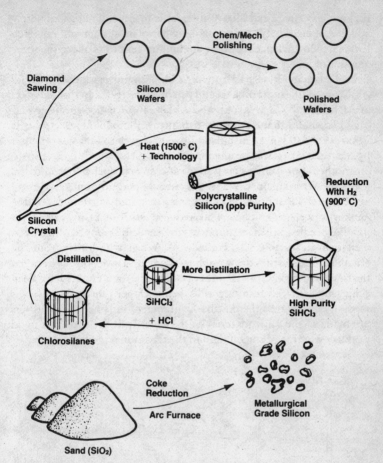

Figure 9.3: Steps in the production of photovoltaic cells by means of the Czochralski technique (source: SERI).

There is fierce competition to produce cheaper cells, cheaper modules and cheaper arrays. Companies like Martin Marietta are also working on ways of boosting the performance of their cells by concentrating the sunlight falling on them. Martin Marietta and E-Systems, Inc., are among the companies experimenting with the use of Fresnel lenses, which intensify the light received by a single cell by over thirty times. A Martin Marietta concentrating array using

Fresnel lenses required 50,000 solar cells to generate approximately 500 kW of electricity. A photovoltaic flat-plate system without such lenses would have needed some 1.6 million cells to produce the same amount of power.

One plant built as part of the SOLERAS programme in Saudi Arabia used this technology – and provides electricity to three villages at Al Jubaiylah, Al Uyaynah and Al Hajrah. It is not cheap power: SERI estimates that the cost of producing photovoltaic electricity is in excess of $10,000 an installed kilowatt, and the Saudi system, built by Martin Marietta, is producing 350 kilowatts.

Another approach has been to try and find cheaper cell production methods. Westinghouse, whose Advanced Energy Systems Division I visited near Pittsburgh, Pennsylvania, patented what it called the 'dendritic web technique'. This reduced kerf losses by using two parallel needle-like silicon filaments (or dendrites) dipped into silicon melted in a crucible (see Figure 9.4). When withdrawn from the crucible, the dendrites draw up the silicon like a soap bubble between the tines of a fork. Growth rates of 6 centimetres a minute have been achieved, with the resulting cells being 15-per-cent efficient. This method ensures that there is low contamination (since the dendrites are made of the same material as the cells) and that there is a good deal less wastage of silicon than in the traditional methods.

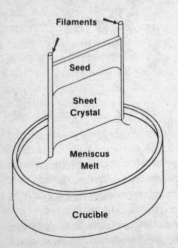

Figure 9.4: The edge-supported pulling process (source: SERI).

There is also a very good chance that this sort of approach can be automated. When I was in Pittsburgh, Westinghouse had achieved a production rate of 27 centimetres a minute for cell widths up to 4.7 centimetres, and estimated that if an output of 25 centimetres per minute could be maintained continuously the 1986 US goal for solar panels of 70 cents per peak watt of power output could be achieved with this technology. It was also quick to point out that the fact that the web was rectangular meant that, once cut down by a laser and converted into rectangular cells, it produced a very high packing density in the module – producing higher module efficiencies.

A third technique is called edge-defined film growth (EFG) or capillary action shaping technique (CAST), developed by Mobil Tyco and other companies. Here a die is used to present only a very thin edge of molten silicon to the seed crystal.

Other manufacturers, such as West Germany's AEG-Telefunken, are looking at polycrystalline silicon, in the hope that a favourable trade-off can be achieved between lower cell efficiencies and cheaper materials, both being features of polycrystalline silicon. The problem is that the boundaries between the various crystals in such materials tend to inhibit the flow of electric current. When I visited SERI, its photovoltaics division was looking at two ways of making these boundaries 'invisible' to the electrons kicked out of the cell by sunlight. The first involved exposing the polycrystalline material to a hydrogen plasma, so that the hydrogen permeated the grain boundaries, easing the flow of electrons across the boundaries. The second approach revolves around the belief that in large-grain polycrystalline cast material these impediments to electron flow are reduced.

With the ultimate goal of finding photovoltaic materials which can simply be sprayed on to a plastic sheet and rolled up at the end of the production line, SERI was also looking at a range of thin-film materials. By accident, it had been discovered that amorphous silicon (produced from silane), in which there is no visible crystalline structure, performed rather more like single-crystal silicon. It was eventually discovered that the films contained hydrogen, which was uprating the amorphous silicon's performance – such that RCA had reported producing silicon cells with a 6.1-per-cent efficiency.

Among the advantages of amorphous silicon is its ability to capture 90 per cent of the solar radiation falling on it when only 1 micrometer thick. It can also be produced at low temperature, requiring less energy, and deposited on low-cost materials such as glass, steel or even plastic. It should be cost-effective if its efficiency can be boosted to 8 per cent. Early in 1983, Matsushita of Japan announced that it had found a way of printing a cadmium sulphide paste through a screen on to a glass base. After drying and sintering at high temperature in a nitrogen atmosphere, another layer of cadmium and tellurium is sintered on – and then a top layer of carbon is added. Silver electrodes are overlaid in another printing stage, and the resulting material is sold in sheets up to 30 centimetres square. Energy conversion is reported to be 13 per cent and the capital cost per watt is under £3.00, compared with about £7.00 for conventional silicon cells.

Among other technologies which are being pursued are electrochemical cells, multi-junction concentration cells and cells using so-called III–V compounds, such as gallium arsenide and indium phosphide. But I also came across another very elegant technology while visiting Bayer, the West German chemical company. This involves the use of 'luminescent' concentrators.

By selecting a chemical dye which fluoresces when illuminated, it is possible to impregnate a glass or plastic sheet with it such that sunshine is captured and refracted back and forth between the inner and outer surfaces of the sheet. When it reaches the edge of the sheet, it is a simple matter to conduct it to photovoltaic cells, which thus receive an intense, tightly focused beam of light. The sheet, in fact, is acting as a lens, though a much cheaper lens than a custom-made Fresnel lens.

Shell had also announced dye-based cells which, while they were perhaps fifty times less efficient than those used in space, held out the prospect of extremely cheap materials. By carefully choosing the dyes, it is hoped, it should be possible to trap a higher proportion of the solar spectrum. Moreover, there is the prospect that the great areas of glass favoured by modern architects in their skyscraper blocks might be harnessed to provide power for the buildings they enclose.

## A Switch for the Poor?

'Users do not want a clean, safe, reliable and silent source of power,' as Philip Wolfe of Lucas BP Solar Systems (now BP Solar Systems) put it, 'unless it is also economical.' Wolfe went on to run Solapak, a small company set up to design solar systems – the total world market for which he estimated was about $100 million (£70 million) by 1983. Solapak had worked in such countries as Abu Dhabi, Botswana, Guinea, Libya and Oman, supplying power systems for the cathodic protection of pipelines, unmanned radio beacons, telemetry equipment and microwave repeater stations. It had also been supplying systems for rural electrification and for holiday homes. All of which adds up to a meal ticket for a small company like Solapak – but this is still a highly fragmented and, ultimately, small market as far as the really big companies are concerned.

A fair number of photovoltaics experts have nonetheless been happy to predict that photovoltaics will be providing, say, 30 per cent of the United States' electricity by the year 2025. This fascinating technology, however, has a considerable way to go before its promise is brought down to earth – and it enjoys widespread terrestrial applications.

The *Solar Challenger* illustrated not only the fact that photovoltaics are gradually finding their way down from earth orbit, but equally the fact that MacCready had to beg and borrow the 16,000 cells which took his solar aircraft aloft showed that the economics are a long way from being attractive for such applications. If he had not been so dead-set on flying by the sun, he could have crossed the Channel at a fraction of the cost, perhaps by ripping an engine out of a scrapped Volkswagen. The interesting thing, though, is that some users are now junking petrol- and diesel-driven engines in favour of solar arrays or windmills.

Based on the gloomy, if realistic, assumption that when the sun is not shining the wind must be blowing, Britain's Independent Broadcasting Authority launched a new television transmitting station powered by the sun and wind. Admittedly, the station was only beaming TV signals to the 300 people living within a two-mile radius of the North Cornwall village of Bosiney, but this sort of experiment is vital in determining the practicality of using solar energy. The system, which comprised a 150-watt windmill and twenty-four solar panels supplied by the French company LGT, was expected to fail only in the unlikely event of a persistent, still fog setting in.

Such installations only make sense, at present, in remote locations: for offshore oil platforms and navigation buoys, or for remote radio-telephone installations such as that installed on the island of Soay, off the isle of Skye's south-west coast, which has no electricity, no roads, no shop and no church. In 1978, the Post Office engineers had had enough of their periodic trips out to the island to service the fuel-powered generator which ran three private telephones and a public telephone call-box. They went solar, as did the Saudi Arabians, Australians and Jordanians – in some places. The Australians, for example, opened a 370-mile (595-kilometre) telephone repeater system based in Alice Springs.

Companies like Solarex, set up in 1973 by solar pioneer Dr Joseph Lindermayer (who was responsible for a number of developments in photovoltaic technology) and Dr Peter Varadi, concentrated from the start on terrestrial applications of such technology. Some of its products, like its solar flashlights and executive toys such as the 'Solar Cube' (which used a solar cell to drive a propeller inside a clear plastic box containing few visible working parts), seemed to have more to do with consumer education than with mass marketing. 'Take a close look at the Solar Cube in your hands,' said Solarex. 'It's the power source of the future.' Solarex, in fact, was planning the world's first 'solar breeder', a plant at Frederick, Maryland, which will use a 200-kilowatt array of photovoltaic cells to supply power for the production of more solar cells.

Gimmicks aside, such companies were competing fiercely for such serious domestic or export orders as did arise. The more practical side of photovoltaic technology has been demonstrated by the growing number of solar villages around the world. The first of these was almost certainly Schuchuli (pronounced, for anyone reading aloud, Schtew-chewlik), a Papago Indian village located some 120 miles (192 kilometres) west of Tucson, Arizona, in the Gunsight Hills area at the western edge of the 3-million-acre (12,140-square-kilometre) Papago reservation.

The 3.5 kW solar electric power system installed there in 1978 by NASA and the US Department of Energy provided the ninety-six villagers with sufficient electricity to run fifteen refrigerators, a washing machine, a sewing machine, a two-horsepower water pump (producing 5,000 gallons or about 19 cubic metres of water a day) for the community well, and forty-seven fluorescent lights for the village's fifteen homes, church, feast house and new domestic services building. Until then, the people of Schuchuli had relied on kerosene lamps for lighting; washing had been done by hand or taken 20 miles

(32 kilometres) to the nearest laundry; and perishable foods or medicines could not be stored.

'There are more than 3 million villages without electrical power in the world today,' commented Dr Louis Rosenblum of NASA's Solar and Electrochemistry Division, 'mainly in the less developed countries. The success of the solar cell power system here at Schuchuli could influence the direction taken by developing countries to satisfy the pressing energy needs of their large rural populations.'

Cynics might say that NASA and the Department of Energy could not afford to run demonstration projects in each of these 3 million communities, but NASA was claiming that, even at current costs, the needs of rural communities requiring less than 5,000 kWh of electricity a year could be met more cheaply with photovoltaic arrays than by other power-generation methods. The problem, so far as Solarex and other photovoltaic manufacturers are concerned, is that the Third World currently has little use for electricity because of the high cost of the electrical appliances they would need to cook their meals, light their homes, pump their water or grind their grain.

The Department of Energy's goal of 70 cents per peak watt within the 1980s had been seen as optimistic, particularly when compared with figures around $10 per peak watt in the early 1980s, but a number of recent announcements have made this target seem rather more credible. Speaking at the 1981 Solar World Forum, for example, a spokesman for Energy Conversion Devices, which has backing from Standard Oil of Ohio (Sohio), claimed that ECD was on the verge of producing solar cells at $1 per peak watt. 'If that's true,' one delegate said, 'the rest of us can go home.'

Basing its approach on the use of fluorinated amorphous silicon, ECD predicted that it would soon be producing electricity over the twenty-year life of a photovoltaic module at a cost of 5–9 cents per kW, compared with the 5–8 cents charged by US power utilities at the time. Given that a conversion efficiency of 7–10 per cent would be needed to achieve this sort of result, companies like RCA and Sanyo dismissed the news as mere fabrication. Stanford Ovshinsky, ECD's founder, was unabashed, however. The ECD cells, he said, would have a conversion efficiency of 8.2 per cent, and, he announced, his company had built a machine capable of producing solar cells at a rate of 3 MW a year. Under a phased deal with ECD, Sohio had already invested $11 million in ECD's photovoltaics programme, and it was understood that a further $65 million could be forthcoming to build a production plant able to turn out 100–200 MW of cells a year. In fact, the first plant to mass-produce amorphous silicon cells started operation at Shinjo, Japan, in 1983 – and represented a joint venture between ECD and Sharp, the Japanese calculator manufacturer. The automated production machine will produce cells with a generating capacity of 3 MW each year. It turns out cells on sheets a foot wide at the rate of one foot a minute. Within five years, ECD hopes to have a machine able to produce a four-foot-wide sheet at the rate of ten feet a minute.

Another oil company, Atlantic Richfield, through its subsidiary Arco Solar, was also pursuing its photovoltaic targets steadily. Early in 1982, for example, it announced that it would build the world's largest photovoltaic electricity generating plant near Hesperia, California, to supply power to Southern California Edison – which was also involved in the 10 MW Barstow plant described in Chapter 8. The 1 MW plant, which was expected to produce enough electricity to supply the needs of 400 families, was billed as nearly three times larger than the largest existing solar-electric plant, in Saudi Arabia. Interestingly, Southern California Edison, which serves more than 3.2 million power consumers, had decided to make the cells track the sun – all the 100 separate photovoltaic panels will be mounted on sun-tracking systems.

Photovoltaic technology, even the pessimists were prepared to admit, was on its way back to earth. Among the more grandiose (or imaginative, depending on how you looked at them) plans for exploiting solar cells has been the proposal advanced by AEG-Telefunken for 'solar hydrogen plantations', discussed in Chapter 14. But there were some solar scientists who were still arguing that solar cells were far better used where *Vanguard* first took them: in earth orbit.

## Leaving the Weather Behind

'My timetable has never varied,' said Dr Peter Glaser, inventor of the solar power satellite concept, some thirteen years after his ideas were first published in *Science*. 'Once people stop smiling about the concept, it will take us twenty years. And that twenty years,' he assured an interviewer from *Omni* during 1981, 'ain't gonna change.

If we had started in 1970, let's say, we would be pretty far along. If we started up in 1981, we could have it by the year 2001.'

But even Dr Glaser, a vice-president with Arthur D. Little, Inc., the Boston-based engineering consultancy firm, recognized the basic problem. Asked what sort of reaction his original article had triggered, he replied that it 'set off a terrible storm. Here was a respected publication like *Science* obviously publishing science fiction. There were a lot of people who felt I was absolutely out of my gourd, that somewhere I had a screw loose.' And, it is fair to say, there still are.

'As I became more deeply involved in the space program,' he reflected, 'I grew aware of the opportunities space presents and realized that the solar-energy problems I'd faced on Earth could be reduced, or perhaps even solved, by moving the solar-conversion hardware into orbit where sunshine is continually available.'

As Professor Gerard O'Neill, author of *The High Frontier* (Bantam Books, 1978) and *2081* (Simon and Schuster, 1981), explained in the second book: 'because of interruptions by night-time and clouds and lower illumination near sunrise and sunset, a solar cell at the Earth's surface puts out power, averaged over the year, that is only a sixth as much as its output at high noon on a clear day. By contrast, a solar cell in synchronous orbit receives constantly an intensity of sunlight that's about 30 per cent higher than we ever experience on the ground, giving it an overall advantage of a factor of eight over the ground-based cell.'

This conclusion took into account the fact that the ground-based energy reception facility, or 'rectenna', would be about 90-per-cent efficient in converting the incoming energy into power for the electricity grid – and that this facility would take about one thirty-sixth of the land area needed if the solar energy collection was undertaken at ground-level by 15-per-cent-efficient solar cells.

Dr Glaser patented his idea in 1973, as US Patent 3,781,647 for a 'Method and Apparatus for Converting Solar Radiation to Electrical Power'. Describing the concept in his 1968 article, Dr Glaser had said that the solar power satellite could supply the world with 'an abundance of power that could forever free man from his dependence on fire'.

Despite the unthinkable price-tag attached to the SPS concept, well over one million million dollars over fifty years, this promise was too enticing to ignore, although it took Glaser a further four years to persuade the US government to undertake a three-year study of the technical, economic, environmental and social issues likely to be associated with the SPS concept. After the $16 million study was completed, in June 1980, NASA and the Department of Energy announced that they had found no 'show-stoppers' in the way of plans to deploy a fleet of sixty solar power satellites – except for finance.

The basic idea was relatively simple, once you had thought of it: put your photovoltaic cells above the weather, in geosynchronous orbit around the earth (at 35,890 kilometres above the equator, you orbit the planet in exactly 24 hours), and beam the energy you have gathered back down to the surface of the planet for use. But it is worth recalling the gargantuan scale of the technology Dr Glaser proposed. The NASA/DOE study based its evaluation on a 'reference system' consisting of a 50-square-kilometre (19-square-mile) array of 10,000 million photovoltaic cells – each satellite being, very roughly, equivalent to 625,000 *Solar Challengers* strung out in orbit – mounted on a thermoplastic structure reinforced with carbon-fibre.

Despite these lightweight materials, each satellite would weigh upwards of 10,000 tonnes, supplying 5 billion watts (or 5 gigawatts) apiece. The direct current produced by the cells would be converted by an array of some 100,000 klystron tubes into microwave radiation, which would be beamed down to the rectenna on the ground. This would 'rectify' the microwave radiation, converting it back into electrical current.

In this reference design, each satellite had its own rectenna, a mesh structure supported some distance off the ground and allowing sunlight and rain to pass through. Each rectenna had 2.5 million sub-array panels and covered, in total, 78 square kilometres (30 square miles). Each rectenna, it was estimated, would need 170,000 tonnes of aluminium, 1.4 million tonnes of steel and 11 million tonnes of aggregates. To transport all this material, within the 25-month construction schedule assumed, would require 2,400 lorries a day and a 2,500-man construction crew – for a total cost per rectenna of $1.1 billion in 1977 dollars.

Later calculations suggested that some sixty satellites would be needed for the United States, while Western Europe would need perhaps forty. One difference would be that the European rectennas, located at latitudes above 50°, would need to be about 20 kilometres (12.4 miles) longer in their north–south axis. They would thus cover a total of 6,400 square kilometres (2,470 square miles), supplying perhaps 20 per cent of Western Europe's electricity demand by the year 2030.

Among the problems likely to be encountered in the technical sphere, should a demonstration system ever be attempted, would be the temperature changes of perhaps 200°C (392°F) imposed on an SPS during an eclipse. It would also be necessary to shield the hundreds or even thousands of construction workers from all the ionizing radiation which, as we saw at the beginning of Chapter 2, streams out constantly from the sun.

Eventually, it may be possible to win materials from the Moon to build such solar power satellites, an attractive proposition since it takes twenty times more energy to haul materials up through earth's gravity field; but, to start with, considerable tonnages would need to be transported up from this planet. Given the difficulties encountered by the Space Shuttle, many space engineers are understandably nervous about the idea of hauling 100,000 tonnes a year up to earth orbit – although this quantity would only be needed continuously if NASA went for the full 300 gigawatt array. The Space Shuttle, which carries some 30 tonnes, would have to be replaced by 'space freighters' carrying at least 400 tonnes – and the full programme would involve at least one such launch a day for thirty years.

One concern voiced by some critics has been that the satellites would eclipse the sun as far as the earth below was concerned. However, it has been estimated that 17,700 SPS satellites would fit into geosynchronous orbit fairly happily – rather more than are currently being proposed. Assuming a surface area of 50 square kilometres for each satellite array, the total array would be some 885,000 square kilometres in area if all 17,700 satellites were airborne. Only 855 of these would be between the earth and the sun at any given moment, however, with a total area of 42,750 square kilometres. The sunlit area of the earth has been calculated to be about 129,223,075 square kilometres in extent, so that the shaded area would be only 0.0331 per cent of that.

And what about the heat energy interrupted by the SPS units? Well, here the calculations suggest that we have even less to worry about. If the earth receives $2.46288 \times 10^{18}$ (246288 followed by thirteen zeros) calories a minute and the heat energy falling on the

SPS units would be $7.68 \times 10^7$ calories a minute, then we are talking about interrupting 0.00000000003118 per cent of the available heat. Clearly the eclipsing effect would be much higher under the equatorial orbit occupied by the satellites, but these calculations assume the full 17,700-satellite fleet is deployed, rather than the 120 or so maximum currently being considered.

The National Academy of Sciences reported on its review of the SPS concept during 1981, arguing that NASA and the Department of Energy had underestimated the likely cost. Three trillion dollars, rather than the $1 trillion suggested in the earlier study, would be closer to the mark over the fifty years. Concluding that solar satellites 'could become an interesting option at some time in the 21st century', the NAS nonetheless went on to recommend that $30 million should be spent on research and development over the next five years.

Glaser and his supporters dismissed the NAS figure as a 'figment of their imagination', pointing to recent developments such as Boeing's thin-film technology to support their contention that their own cost assumptions had been unduly pessimistic. 'In the technical area, I'm very comfortable,' said Glaser. 'Not a single show-stopper has been uncovered, and a lot of people have been looking for one. In the environmental area, I believe we need more R & D. I don't believe that the biological effects of low-level microwaves are going to be a major factor, but we don't have the necessary data yet. As for accidentally burning up cities or frying ducks, I'm not worried. The low density of the microwave beam makes this impossible.'

Such assurances left many question-marks in the minds of environmentalists, however, and optical and radio astronomers were worried that the flashing satellites or stray radiation would make their task impossible. As usual, the SPS proponents had a ready answer: ship the astronomers to the dark side of the Moon, where they would be shielded from anything the SPS engineers might get up to.

The astronomers, needless to say, were not over the Moon about the idea – and there the matter rested. Various European countries were also investigating the prospects for SPS technologies: Britain, for example, had been looking at the area since the late 1970s. Companies such as British Aerospace had been involved in feasibility studies with the Royal Aircraft Establishment, Marconi Space and Defence Systems, General Technology Systems and ERA Technology. The General Technology Systems study, commissioned by the Department of Industry, had estimated that the potential component-manufacturing market could be worth over £10 billion ($22 billion at the then prevailing exchange rates).

British Aerospace had also been involved in producing the 356-square-foot (33-square-metre) array of solar cells needed to power the Space Telescope, due for launch in 1985. The problems facing today's array designers are very much more complex than they were when *Vanguard* went into orbit. As Reg Fox, project manager for the Space Telescope, put it, 'in the 1960s, we were able to stick the solar cells around the Ariel, Intelstat and Comstar satellites. We could carry the cells around the building without trouble and just stick them on to the satellite. Now we are involved in a solar array of 356 square feet with 48,760 solar cells. At one G, it would fall apart and we have had to design a sophisticated water bed to support the arrays for testing.'

British Aerospace was using 4 × 2 centimetre solar cells and expecting the array to have an initial power output of 5 kW. Solar radiation and occasional collisions with micro-meteorites, however, were expected to reduce that output to 3.7 kW by the end of the cells' design life. So the solar panels have been designed in such a way that astronauts can unbolt them after five years – to be returned in the space shuttle to earth, where the hope is that they would be refurbished at British Aerospace's Filton works.

Meanwhile, the Space Shuttle is due to lift a huge solar 'wing' into orbit in 1984. The 175-kilogram solar array should consist of 84 hinged panels which expand, like a concertina, from 10 centimetres to an astounding 35 metres across. Each wing will support 130,000 solar cells, to be shipped in a 10-centimetre-by-4-metre package, and should supply 12.5 kW. Eight such wings could power a twelve-man space station. The initial tests will involve only 900 cells, given that the full complement of 130,000 cells would cost some $10 million.

The European Space Agency, encouraged by the pace at which the relevant technologies were moving forward, was beginning to think about going it alone on SPS technology, arguing that the 'geographical, environmental and societal conditions are sufficiently different (in Europe) to imply that many conclusions reached in the American studies are probably not valid'. The Agency concluded that solar satellites could provide as much energy during the twenty-first century as fast-breeder or fusion reactors.

No one will really know how the equation will work out until a great deal more work has been carried out on the feasibility aspects of the SPS concept. Expect some sort of answer in the late 1980s or, more likely, in the 1990s; but do not be surprised if, in the meantime, some solar scientists suggest that there are better photon-capture systems already in operation. Plants, for instance, worked out how to exploit solar radiation aeons before Dr Glaser visited the Patent Office. Their tried and tested approach, which some estimates suggest already contributes 15 per cent of the energy the world uses each year, equivalent to perhaps 20 million barrels of oil a day, may yet prove a more politically acceptable solar option than the solar power satellite. The increasingly wide spectrum of biomass technologies is the subject of Chapter 10.

1. (*above*) The Ideal Home version of solar living (source: Dominic Michaelis Associates).

2. (*top right*) Solar houses in Milton Keynes, England, each of which has approximately 20 square metres of solar collectors (source: Laing Research & Development).

3. (*bottom right*) Artist's impression of a solar housing estate in West Germany (source: INTERATOM).

4. (*left*) Artist's impression of a solar skyscraper for Citibank in New York, with a photovoltaic array on its roof (source: Westinghouse Electric Corporation).

5. (*right*) At Sandia's central receiver test facility near Albuquerque, New Mexico, 222 automatically focused heliostats can be trained on the 61-metre-high test tower, collecting and concentrating more than 5 million watts of thermal solar energy (source: Boeing Engineering and Construction).

6. (*top*) An array of evacuated-tube collectors manufactured by Philips; see Figures 7.3 and 4 (source: Philips).

7. (*left*) Artist's impression of a central receiver plant using Boeing's 'second-generation' collectors, which are encapsulated in plastic bubbles to protect their lightweight reflectors from dust abrasion and wind damage (source: Boeing Engineering and Construction).

8. (*right*) Design for a central receiver facility (source: I N T E R A T O M).

9. (*top*) Tapping heat from natural reactions deep within the planet, the world's largest geothermal generating plant is Unit 13 in the Geysers, California, operated by Pacific Gas & Electricity (source: Pacific Gas & Electricity Company).

10. (*middle*) Among the safer and more reliable fission reactor designs is the C A N D U reactor, shown here at the Pickering atomic power plant in Canada (source: Atomic Energy of Canada Ltd).

11. (*left*) Toroidal field coils of the Culham Laboratory's H B T X 1 A fusion experiment, England, built to study the confinement of high-temperature plasma in a magnetic field (source: U K Atomic Energy Authority).

12. (*top*) Inside the Dinorwic pumped storage plant in Wales (source: Central Electricity Generating Board).

13. (*middle*) The disued tide mill at Carew, South Wales (source: John Elkington).

14. (*right*) Artist's impression of wave energy generators moored at sea, based on Cockerell's Raft (source: Atomic Energy Research Establishment, Harwell).

15. (*top*) Vertical-axis aerogenerator designed by Peter Musgrove (source: Dr Peter Musgrove).

16. (*bottom left*) One of the 2.5 MW aerogenerators at the Goldendale site, Washington State (source: Boeing Engineering and Construction).

17. (*bottom right*) Small, Danish-built windmill installed by the Scottish Hydroelectric Board to provide power for a 630-acre farm on South Ronaldsay in the Orkneys (source: Scottish Hydroelectric Board).

18. (*top*) The *Solar Challenger* hangs over the Solar World Forum
(source: John Elkington).

19. (*bottom*) Artist's impression of a solar power satellite in orbit,
during assembly (source: Boeing Aerospace).

20. (*top left*) A hydrogen-powered car. Hydrogen may prove to be an attractive long-term fuel for many applications, although there are a considerable number of technological and economic hurdles which have to be crossed first (source: Billings Energy Corporation).

21. (*top right*) A more likely approach to oil shortages in the short term will involve the redesign of fuel-consuming equipment to reduce its consumption. Here the Pirelli petrol-saving tyre is shown on the Volvo Concept Car, itself designed with energy efficiency very much in mind (source: Pirelli).

22. (*bottom*) Meanwhile, however, many developing countries continue to depend on animal power, like the camel train in Niger, seen transporting firewood – another renewable energy source, but under increasing pressure throughout the world (source: Mark Edwards/Earthscan).

# 10 ⊙ Power Plants

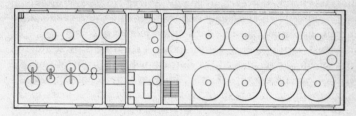

Figure 10.1: Conventional batch process for ethanol fermentation (source: Alcon Biotechnology).

Following up claims by a Kidderminster man that he had run a small electric motor for five months on the power produced by a single lemon, scientists working for the Chloride Group accepted the basic principle. 'The lemon is a perfectly well-known power source,' said John Jones of Chloride, which has carried out pioneering work with batteries and electric vehicles, 'and has long been used to demonstrate the principle of the battery to school-children. Place one copper and one zinc wire in a half lemon, place your tongue across them, and the acid in the fruit will produce a very small shock.'

But the Chloride scientists did not stop at their estimate that a single lemon, under laboratory conditions, might power a digital watch. They went further, calculating that it would take 10 million lemons to power a single television set – and 5 billion to power a small electric vehicle, which, as they pointed out, would be hard pressed to carry even a small fraction of these fruit. A further calculation, presumably on the back of the proverbial envelope, suggested that to operate a fleet of three electric vehicles you would need to use Israel's entire annual citrus production.

The problem faced by lemon-power proponents, then, was very much like that faced by Chloride itself: how to pack enough power into a battery to run a reasonable-size vehicle without making it impossibly heavy in the process. Chloride delivered the coup de grâce to the lemon idea by working out that the 43,223 tonnes of lemons imported into Britain that year would have been enough to power forty standard light-bulbs or four electric fires, at a cost of £10.5 million. Lemons failed to pass the acid test of energy economics, as did the tangerines used by Japanese scientists at Mie University. They ran a 500 c.c. car and two motorcycles on tangerine oil, although they had to squeeze 11,000 tangerines to extract a single litre of oil.

Biomass energy, however, or energy derived from plant or animal matter, is already an extremely important energy source, with some estimates suggesting that its contribution might be as high as 15 per cent of total world energy consumption – equivalent to 20 million barrels of oil a day. Indeed, as Earthscan pointed out during the UNERG conference, 'for about 2.25 billion people, half the world's population, living mainly in the rural Third World, biomass in the form of fuelwood is overwhelmingly the most important source of energy'.

Like the photovoltaic cell, plants harness the photons in the sun's

*Table 10.1: Annual productivity and photosynthetic efficiencies of various agricultural crops (source: Earthscan)*

|  | Yield (*in tons per hectare per year*) | Photosynthetic efficiency (%) |
| --- | --- | --- |
| *Temperate* | | |
| Ryegrass (UK) | 23 | 1.3 |
| Potato (Netherlands) | 22 | 1.0 |
| Sugar-beet (Washington, USA) | 32 | 1.1 |
| Wheat (Washington, USA) | 30 (grain) | 0.1 |
| Maize (Ottawa, Canada) | 19 | 0.7 |
| *Subtropical* | | |
| Alfalfa (California, USA) | 33 | 1.0 |
| Wheat (Mexico) | 18 | 0.5 |
| Bermuda grass (Georgia, USA) | 27 | 0.8 |
| Maize (Egypt) | 29 | 0.6 |
| *Tropical* | | |
| Oil palm (Malaysia) | 40 | 1.4 |
| Cassava (Tanzania) | 31 | 0.8 |
| Rice (Peru) | 22 | 0.7 |
| Sugar-cane (Hawaii) | 64 | 1.8 |

radiation, but they do so very much less efficiently in absolute terms. Plants can only use about half the wavelength spectrum of sunlight, and the maximum proportion of the solar energy falling on a crop which can be converted into biomass is about 5 to 6 per cent. In practice, however, observed photosynthetic conversion efficiencies tend to cluster around the range 0.5–1.3 per cent in temperate regions, and between 0.5 and 2.5 per cent for most subtropical crops (see Table 10.1 for some illustrative photosynthetic efficiencies).

But, unlike photovoltaic-cell technology, photosynthesis is a natural process which has proved reliable for several billion years in capturing and storing solar energy. It is not surprising, therefore, that biomass energy has increasingly been identified as a potentially significant energy resource, not simply for the Third World but for the developed nations of the world as well. 'We now consider biomass the most significant contributor of all the solar energy sources,' said one US Department of Energy spokesman. 'It already supplies over 3 per cent of our energy needs [i.e., in the USA], and it could easily and renewably rise to over 10 per cent.'

One of the scientists I talked to at the Solar Energy Research Institute, Dr Paul Weaver, points out that photosynthesis is responsible for all the energy stored in fossil fuels and produces about 300 quads (1 quad $= 10^{15}$ Btu) of stored energy as biomass each year – or about ten times the amount our species currently consumes. The problem involved in harnessing all that energy has essentially been two-fold: first, you have the problem of extracting energy from your biomass without spending more energy than you get back from your efforts, and, second, there is the question of environmental impact. Both of these subjects will be dealt with in detail later.

## The Other Energy Crisis

At its simplest, biomass energy means burning wood for heat, with the officially recorded production of firewood (or fuelwood, as it was described at UNERG) and charcoal supplying some 20 per cent of the developing world's current energy consumption. If you look at the figures for the world as a whole, they are less impressive: wood and charcoal supply only 5 per cent of the total global energy budget (Table 10.2). But the average figure for the Third World is 21 per cent, and in the least developed countries of Africa and Asia wood

*Table 10.2: Consumption of fuelwood and charcoal (but not crop residues etc.; source: UNERG)*

| | Population (millions) | Fuelwood and charcoal consumption per capita (cubic metres of wood) | Energy equivalent of fuelwood (millions of giga-joules) | Fuelwood as percentage of total energy use |
|---|---|---|---|---|
| *North* | | | | |
| Market economies | 775 | 0.07 | 508 | 0.3 |
| Centrally planned economies | 372 | 0.24 | 855 | 1.4 |
| Total | 1,147 | 0.13 | 1,363 | 0.7 |
| | | | | |
| *Africa* | | | | |
| Least developed countries | 138 | 1.18 | 1,532 | 85.7 |
| Total | 415 | 0.85 | 3,318 | 57.9 |
| | | | | |
| *Asia* | | | | |
| Least developed countries | 130 | 0.26 | 319 | 63.9 |
| Centrally planned economies | 1,010 | 0.22 | 2,068 | 7.9 |
| Total | 2,347 | 0.34 | 2,387 | 16.6 |
| | | | | |
| *Latin America* | | | | |
| Total | 349 | 0.78 | 2,557 | 18.4 |
| South total | 3,111 | 0.46 | 13,353 | 20.6 |
| World total | 4,258 | 0.37 | 14,720 | 5.4 |

represents 86 per cent – and charcoal 64 per cent – of total energy consumption.

The advantages offered by charcoal over wood are illustrated by Sri Lanka's recent experiences. The country's foresters have been clearing the vast Mahaveli forest to create new irrigated farmland, with much of the funding coming from the World Bank. As a result, the Sri Lankans have a great deal of wood, in the form of felled wira trees, on their hands. Along with kerosene, wood is Sri Lanka's staple energy source, but the 25 million tonnes of wood which the Mahaveli forest was expected to supply during the early 1980s was a long way from towns and villages, and was too expensive to transport over any distance. It was estimated, for example, that the wood became prohibitively expensive to transport over 80 kilometres, so most of it had been burned or left to rot.

But a new company, Charlanka, was set up to exploit this biomass windfall by converting it into charcoal. The company has been helped by Enterprise Development, Inc., of Washington, D.C., by Intermediate Technology Industrial Services of the UK and by the Sri Lanka State Timber Corporation. Using new portable steel kilns, manufactured by Shirley Aldred Engineering, a British company, Charlanka expressed the belief that it could persuade the Sri Lanka Cement Corporation to substitute charcoal for some of the 300,000 tonnes of coal it imports each year – and, in addition, produce a further 15,000 tonnes of charcoal a year for export.

Of more immediate benefit to the people of Sri Lanka, however, is the fact that the charcoal is a much lighter and more efficient fuel than was the original wood, so that it can be transported economically up to 200 kilometres – making it available to an estimated 200,000 people. Charcoal stoves are almost twice as efficient as the most widely-used three-stone fires and traditional earth stoves, which achieve a theoretical energy-conversion efficiency, at the very best, of about 10 per cent.

The problem with charcoal, however, is that, although it may burn more efficiently, it only captures about 20 per cent of the energy contained in the original wood. That said, most people in the Third World would probably be happy to use charcoal, provided they could get it at a reasonable price. In the meantime, they continue to rely on wood, consuming an average 0.5–1 cubic metre per person per year to meet their cooking and water-heating needs. If heating is included, the annual domestic energy requirement of people living in cold, mountainous regions can easily reach 2.5–3 cubic metres per person.

And the problem here is that there is an increasing shortage of accessible fuelwood. It is estimated that more than 100 million people are now unable to obtain enough fuelwood to meet even their basic needs, while another 1,000 million are affected by lesser shortages. If present trends continue, it is estimated, over 2,500 million people will need alternative cooking fuels to replace wood by the year 2000.

Meanwhile, the cutting of trees and other vegetation is proceeding at such a rate that massive deforestation is taking place in many areas of the world.

A clear example of the vicious cycle in which deforestation leads to soil erosion, siltation of rivers and widespread flooding – threatening food production on what the UN Food and Agriculture Organization calls 'an alarming scale' – is Nepal, sandwiched between India and Tibet. Wood supplies some 85 per cent of Nepal's energy, with each Nepalese consuming an average of 600 kilograms (1,322 pounds) a year. But the country's forests grow at a rate of only about 80 kilograms per person per year, so that its forest cover is being consumed over seven times faster than it is being replaced. And the Nepalese also use wood for building, because it is a great deal cheaper than importing cement overland.

As the forest area shrinks, Nepalese villagers are being forced to move after it or to spend a growing proportion of their time finding fuelwood and transporting it back to their homes. In an economy which is already often close to the breadline, such additional burdens could well spell ultimate disaster. At the same time, too, the accelerated erosion from the bare hillsides intensifies the siltation problems which are already plaguing the major rivers of the Indian subcontinent.

Meanwhile, on the island of East Lambok, next door to the Indonesian island of Bali, the government's subsidy on kerosene (or paraffin) has been the only factor holding back the same sort of catastrophic deforestation which has already hit the Andes, the Himalayas and much of Africa. According to William Knowland, at the time a Fellow of the US Institute of Current World Affairs, the price of fuelwood had been rocketing up at a rate in excess of 30 per cent a year on East Lambok.

Between 1978 and 1979, the fuelwood costs of the island's brick and tile factories went up by 39 per cent, equal to the total price rise over the previous four years. Fuelwood prices had risen so fast, in fact, that the tobacco industry – which had been the largest industrial consumer of fuelwood – had almost ceased using it. The government, however, had had a hand in the process, weaning the industry away from wood by subsidizing the price of kerosene, derived from Indonesia's own oil-fields. The tobacco producers were fairly happy, because the price of kerosene had remained stable and because its heat can be more easily controlled, resulting in a higher-quality product which commands a higher price on the market.

The Indonesian government clearly takes the fuelwood crisis seriously, but the question remains whether other governments, without access to their own oil-fields or other sources of fossil energy, can readily follow the approach adopted on East Lambok.

The UNERG conference identified six major needs as far as fuel-wood is concerned. First, existing resources need to be better managed, which may mean allocating fuelwood a higher national priority and educating local people in elementary silviculture. Second, new forest resources must be created, including large-scale plantations, community woodlands and individual plantings. Third, fuel-wood distribution and storage systems will have to be significantly upgraded. Fourth, there is room for considerable improvement in charcoal conversion technologies, which currently waste about 80 per cent of the energy contained in their feedstock. Fifth, fossil fuels such as coal and kerosene will have to be substituted for wood, as on East Lambok, although price will be the major inhibiting factor.

The sixth, and probably most vital, point is that land-tenure patterns have got to change. For one thing, much fuelwood gathering takes place on common lands, where there is no incentive to husband resources or to replant. Why do so when someone else will almost certainly enjoy the fruits of your labour? 'Ultimately,' UNERG concluded, 'proper wood management may require reconstruction of the entire basis of land ownership and control.' A tall order.

## Sweden Takes to the Trees

More than half of Sweden's land area, or 23 million hectares, is covered by forests – how are the Swedes doing in harnessing biomass energy? With a population of over 8 million, substantially less than the populations of either Nepal or Sri Lanka (both of which have populations in the region of 14 million), Sweden has been taking biomass energy rather more seriously than most other developed countries, investing in a wide range of research projects and technologies.

Shortly before the first oil shock, Sweden was the world's largest per capita consumer of oil, and imported oil still meets something like 70 per cent of the country's annual consumption of 35 million tons of oil equivalent. The average Swede, in fact, uses nearly 50 times as much oil as does the average Chinese – and 75 times as much as the average Indian. The long-term goal of Sweden's energy policy is to develop an energy supply system based on sustainable, preferably renewable and domestic energy sources producing minimal environmental impact. Again, a tall order, and one made more difficult by the restrictions which have been placed on both nuclear energy (which supplied 5 per cent of Sweden's energy in the early 1980s) and hydropower (which supplied 15 per cent).

Among Sweden's short-term goals has been an increase in the use of biomass resources such as forest wastes and peat, while in the longer term it is hoped that custom-made 'energy plantations' will produce a continuous supply of raw-energy materials. Experiments with solar water heating have so far proved disappointing, but the biomass option makes a good deal of sense for such a heavily afforested country. Sweden, in fact, harvests over 70 million cubic metres of timber each year, using it mainly for pulp and paper production. Following such industrial harvesting, over 45 million cubic metres of material such as roots, deciduous trees and other residues are left on the felling sites. The energy content of these wastes is estimated to be approximately 8 million tonnes of oil equivalent – or more than 20 per cent of the country's annual energy budget.

The Swedish Oil Substitution Commission stresses that suitable harvesting machines still need to be developed, as do more efficient methods for harvesting, storing, drying and converting the wood into usable fuels. Perhaps most important all, however, it argues that in order for forest wastes to become a viable fuel alternative for district heating schemes and other large-scale applications, wood fuels must become established commercial commodities, with clear channels for marketing and distribution – one of the six major objectives highlighted by UNERG.

The emphasis is being placed on new methods of 'whole-tree' harvesting, with the first generation of the new harvesting technology planned for 1987. Research is being carried out on conversion methods which will produce easily transportable fuels (such as wood chips or pellets) for all-year-round use. If these efforts are successful, and sufficient demand for wood can be established, it is estimated that in the long term as much as 23 million cubic metres of forest wastes could be harvested and used for energy purposes in Sweden, representing a total fuel value of 5 million tons of oil equivalent.

Energy plantations are very much a longer-term prospect, but it is calculated that they might displace as much as a quarter of Sweden's oil demand. Results currently to hand suggest that short rotations, lasting about two or three years, of *Salix* plantations would be the best technique for most of the available land in central and southern Sweden. To gain practical experience with the concept, two 100-hectare pilot farms have been started on selected marshland and on abandoned agricultural land. The ecological impacts likely to be associated with such schemes are being intensively studied, as is the role of potential pest problems – including, apparently, moose.

Marshland, in fact, makes up between 10 and 15 per cent of Sweden's land area, or approximately 5 million hectares (19,305 square miles, against a total land area of 173, 732 square miles). The exact amount of extractable peat in those areas is not fully known, but the total energy content has been estimated to be equivalent to 3 *billion* tonnes of oil. Theoretically speaking, then, Sweden's total supply of peat is sufficient to replace its total oil consumption, at current rates, for nearly a century. More realistically, given the various ecological constraints and the fact that it takes energy to extract the peat, it has been calculated that Sweden's peat could provide up to 900,000 tonnes of oil equivalent by 1990.

During the Second World War, the Swedish peat industry extracted as much as 1.3 million tons annually, although peat today is used almost exclusively as a soil improver. One pump and paper company in northern Sweden, however, recently rebuilt its existing oil burners to permit the combustion of pulverized peat – which is imported from Finland. The company was developing plans to set up its own full-scale peat-harvesting operation, but Sweden, in this respect at least, is lagging rather behind the lead countries in the peat field.

## Invest for Peat's Sake

Peat showed up reasonably well among the new and renewable-energy sources evaluated in Table 3.1 (see p. 56). Once the peatlands of the tropics have been fully surveyed, the International Peat Society calculates, the global area of peatland could be of the order of 500 million hectares – or 17 times the area of the British Isles. Worldwide, peat is believed to be accumulating at an average rate of 0.7 millimetres a year, equivalent to some 210 million tonnes of fixed carbon. Or, to put it another way, the world's peatlands may contain

$150 \times 10^{15}$ grams of carbon and are accreting at a rate of about $0.21 \times 10^{15}$ grams a year.

Canada and the USSR account for more than three quarters of these peatlands, reporting 150 million hectares (36 per cent of the world total) and 170 million hectares (40 per cent) respectively. In fact, the Canadians estimate that there is more energy potential in their peat deposits than in their forests. The National Energy Board puts Canada's peat reserves at 89 billion tonnes, equivalent to about 17 billion cubic metres of natural gas – compared with the country's known reserves of 2.4 billion cubic metres.

The peat reserves of the United States are thought to be about 13 billion tonnes. One former administrator at the US Department of Energy has been promoting a scheme for converting peat into methanol (methyl alcohol – of which more later). 'Mr Methanol', as Robert Fri is sometimes known, had set up the Energy Transition Corporation (ETCO) with a number of other refugees from government service and had been working on a number of pioneering schemes.

One of these, based on a discovery by Texan inventor Leonard Keller, involved the transport of coal by pipeline. Instead of using coal-water slurries, however, which tend to settle out unless constantly agitated, ETCO was thinking of slurries of 65 per cent coal mixed with methanol to form a stable suspension – dubbed 'methacoal'. Better still, the pipeline could well prove to be a long, thin reactor in its own right, converting the coal into liquid hydrocarbons as it is transported. By penetrating the coal particles, the methanol can partially dissolve them, converting perhaps 20 per cent of the coal dust into clear liquid hydrocarbons in the course of a few days.

The first peat scheme, meanwhile, is being built around a gasifier which can gasify any form of carbon, it is said, 'from peat to diamonds', at atmospheric pressures. Among the attractions of the peat-gasification project for ETCO are the facts, first, that one of Fri's partners, First Colony Farms, owns 105,000 acres (42,492 hectares) of peat in Northern Carolina, estimated to contain 120 million tonnes of peat – and second, even better, that the North Carolina peat, once dried below the 30-per-cent moisture level, will not readily pick up water again and can therefore be stockpiled in the open.

First Colony Farms was also planning to use an interesting harvesting technique, involving the removal of the top inch of peat. Once the next inch-thick layer is exposed, it begins to dry out in the sun and, once its moisture content has fallen from about 90 per cent to less than 30 per cent, it is skimmed off and stacked, leaving the next layer prepared for solar drying. Dewatering can be a considerable problem elsewhere, however. Swedish peat production has often been limited to a two-month season, while it can take seven years to drain an Irish peat bog before harvesting can start.

Once the peat has been extracted, the question remains as to just what can be done with the exhausted workings. Bord na Mona, Ireland's Peat Development Board, has found that some bogs can be reclaimed for agriculture after peat extraction. At its Derry-greenagh production site, some 50 miles (80 kilometres) west of Dublin, wheat and cows are prospering on one such site. But an alternative idea is to use worked-out peat bogs for energy plantations.


## Trees in the Fast Lane

With something like 17 per cent of Ireland's land surface covered with peat bogs, the question of what to do with them is an important one, particularly since Bord na Mona expects the country's peat to be exhausted by the year 2020. In one experiment designed to develop profitable after-uses, Bord na Mona planted one 1,000-acre (404-hectare) site with fast-growing trees, dividing the trial plantations between conifers, which would have to be replanted after each harvesting, and hardwood trees – which can be 'coppiced', or mown almost like grass, at intervals.

Frank Lunny, one of the Bord's consultants, had expressed doubts about the conifer biomass programme, favouring the coppice approach instead. 'You can cut these stumps again after four years and then new sprouts will come,' he explained. 'It is thought that you can go on doing that for 30 years – or seven crops – before the roots lose their vigour and you have to replant.' As for the output expected, he said that 'it appears that it is not over-optimistic to hope for a yield of 8 tonnes of dry matter for each acre a year. That figure corresponds to about 3 tonnes of oil.'

In England, meanwhile, planting had started on three trial sites, using such species as *Populus* (poplar), *Salix* (willow), *Alnus* (alder), *Nothofagus* (southern beech) and *Eucalyptus* (gum). Coppicing has been practised in the British Isles for many centuries, and the new trials were designed to compare the yields afforded by different species growing in similar conditions – and similar species growing in different conditions. With harvesting every 7 to 16 years, it was known that root-stocks had lasted up to 100 years, and in some cases longer. The Forestry Commission's experiments involve harvesting the root-stock much more frequently – every two, three or five years – to see how harvesting frequency affects the yields and life of the root-stocks.

Only 5 per cent of Ireland is forested, compared to an EEC average of 20 per cent. In fact, as Frank Lunny put it, 'we are the least forested country in the EEC'. He argued that large tracts of poor agricultural land in counties Clare, Kerry, Leitrim and Mayo would be 'ideal' for reafforestation, with bogland being replanted as it became available. He also estimated that a peat bog produces four times as much energy as the same-sized area of land devoted to fast-growing trees, but he noted that the peat can, to all intents and purposes, only be used once – whereas the trees are, in theory, almost indefinitely renewable.

One of the Bord's senior engineers estimated that if just 2.5 per cent of Ireland's land surface were to be devoted to biomass production, it would be enough to supply 10 per cent of the country's needs. 'I think that if we play our cards right,' said Mr Lunny, 'we could be the lead country in biomass production.' Much, of course, will depend on the selection of appropriate species for cropping, and here some of the developing countries have been moving up fast, whether with crops like sugar-cane (as in the case of Brazil) or with fast-growing trees (as in the Philippines).

One tree which may yet provide part of the answer to the Third World's energy problems is the giant ipilipil (*Leucaena leucocophala*), which matures in eight years, grows to 20 metres (65 feet), responds well to coppicing and produces wood which burns well. It has all the persistence of a weed, producing a long tap root which enables it to survive through protracted periods of drought; but this very resilience is seen as an advantage as far as its use as an energy crop is concerned.

In the Philippines, where over 12,000 hectares (30,000 acres) have been planted with the tree, it produces the energy equivalent of a million barrels of oil every year, and stands have been cropped for sixty years without apparent depletion of the root-stocks. Experience shows that the tree produces more wood than any other yet tested, and it produces good charcoal which burns at about 70 per cent of the efficiency of fuel oil. A one-acre (0.4-hectare) plantation can easily produce 14 cubic metres (500 cubic feet) of fuelwood a year.

An evergreen native of central America, the tree comes in all shapes and sizes, although there are three major types – ranging from a squat bush to the 20-metre tree, and over a hundred varieties are now known to be grown. Such genetic diversity is seen as a considerable attraction, in that it provides the basis for selective breeding to enhance the best characteristics. Interestingly, too, whereas most energy plantations will mine nutrients from the soils on which they are planted, *Leucaena* is a member of the legume family and, because it can fix nitrogen from the air, is able to increase soil fertility.

The tree's ability to thrive in semi-arid conditions, and on some fairly marginal soils, suggests a useful role in land-reclamation and erosion-control projects, too. It does have a number of shortcomings, though, including the fact that it typically grows rather poorly on the acidic and aluminous soils found widely in the tropics. On the other hand, in suitable soils, the bush variety can get out of hand, a problem experienced in Tanzania, where the trees has turned into a choking weed – and, more seriously, into a favoured breeding ground of the tsetse fly.

Foliage from the tree provides nutritious fodder for animals, while the seed-pods can be eaten by humans. It is usually fed to cattle, however, because of one rather strange side-effect: it can cause hair loss in people, sheep and goats. Those who see an opportunity in every problem argue that it can be used to produce self-shearing sheep; but we are probably some way from making the world's sheep-shearers redundant.

There is no shortage, meanwhile, of space for planting fast-growing trees, especially where they promise to improve soil fertility, but some biomass schemes are already running into a number of serious problems. One problem is that some of the sites chosen for biomass plantations are also suitable for other uses, particularly food production, or unsuitable for any sustained economic use. The fate of Daniel K. Ludwig's 25-year, $1 billion attempt to create a major commercial forestry industry in Brazil's Amazon jungle should give food for thought to those planning grandiose biomass plantations. Just as Henry Ford lost a large fortune in the 1930s trying to grow rubber on 2.5 million acres of land by the river Tapajos, so the enormous Jari paper and pulp operation has eroded Ludwig's fortune, forcing him to sell out to the Brazilian government.

Ludwig had got it right with supertankers, making a fortune when the Suez Canal closed, and with floating factories, two of which were towed around the world from Japan to Jari. He also seems to have been right in picking fuelwood as the major source of energy for the Jari site; but in buying up 4 million acres of Brazilian rain-forest, an area the size of Belgium, he over-reached himself. He failed to wait for proper soil surveys and persisted with the theoretically fast-growing *Gmelina arborea* tree, even after it had showed relatively poor growth on the sandy soils which made up a large portion of his land-holdings.

After a hunt lasting many years, the tree had been brought to Ludwig's attention because it grew one foot a month in its natural habitat in India and Burma. It had been exploited by the British colonial service in Nigeria, to provide pit-props for gold-mines, and Ludwig decided that this was the 'miracle' tree he had been waiting for. 'That's all he ever talked about,' one US paper company president recalls. 'He thought it could do anything. He was the only one in the industry who did.'

Ludwig landed himself in an ecological trap. He had planned a highly mechanized harvesting operation; much of the land was cleared with bulldozers, and the resulting felled timber was burned off in huge conflagrations which triggered thunderstorms – the last thing Ludwig needed, as the site already received something like 100 inches of rain a year – which washed out roads and eroded deep gullies in the cleared hillsides. Many of the *Gmelina* seedlings died as soon as they were put in the ground. The tropical rain-forest soils are precariously thin, with most of the nutrients being locked up in the standing biomass which Ludwig's felling-teams had cleared and burned. The heavy machinery he had used compacted the fragile soil so badly that even weeds found it hard to grow.

Eventually, the foresters went back to saws and axes, and 2,000 seasonal labourers had to be shipped in, throwing the project's cost estimates even further out of joint. But perhaps the ultimate irony is that the Jari plant was soon forced to use many of the native species which had been so profligately cleared and burned in the early days of the operation. They were being used both in the pulping operations, making up 20 per cent by volume of the Jari pulp, and for energy purposes too.

To keep the situation from worsening still further, the project managers uprooted many of the original plantations, replacing them with another inadequately tested tree, a tropical eucalyptus. 'We're really pushing it in a big way,' said the director of the project's seedling nursery, though he admitted that 'we may be making the same mistake as with *Gmelina*.'

The Jari fiasco should temper our enthusiasm when we hear the latest set of predictions about how much energy we could produce if we planted such-and-such an area with a particular species. Such calculations abound, however. University of Pennsylvania scientists, for example, estimate that four-year rotations of poplar trees could provide 5–12 tons of dry wood per acre each year (12–30 tonnes per hectare) with potential yields of 117 gallons (443 litres) of 192 proof ethanol per ton, at a price ranging between 10 and 15 per cent of that of corn-derived ethanol. A poplar plantation covering 31 million acres (12.5 million hectares), they estimate, could produce 19.6 billion gallons (74 billion litres) of ethanol, almost 20 per cent of the US consumption of gasoline.

To achieve this target, they say, all that would be needed would be to plant an area the size of Pennsylvania with poplar trees – or, to be accurate, an area slightly larger than that of Pennsylvania. But then, we should remember, not all of Pennsylvania would be suitable for growing poplar trees, because of environmental constraints, so presumably we are talking about a rather larger area when these figures are transferred into the real world. Yet anyone who doubts that large-scale energy plantations will ever materialize ought to visit Brazil.

## Fuel of the Future?

'Within a few years the state of Sao Paolo will be just one enormous sugar-cane plantation, straddled by fly-overs,' said one former Brazilian minister. Like most of the developing countries, Brazil was hit much harder than the industrialized world by the oil price rises which followed the first oil shock. The declining purchasing power of a range of non-oil commodities exported by developing countries is discussed in Chapter 1, and Brazil was hit by exactly the same problem. Unlike many other developing countries, however, Brazil has a very considerable surface area, much of which is, in the land economist's mind at least, under-exploited or unexploited.

This fact persuaded the Brazilians to pursue the biomass option and, in particular, alcohol fuels. 'Alcohol,' explained Colonel Sergio Ferolla, director of the fuel alcohol programme at Brazil's Centre for Aerospace Technology, near Sao Paolo, 'is bottled solar energy. A fleet of alcohol-powered cars is the purest form of solar transport yet devised.'

Henry Ford was no solar enthusiast, but he too had dubbed alcohol the 'fuel of the future', although he wisely neglected to say when that future might arrive. In fact, before the vast oil-fields of the Middle East became the world's major source of fuel in the 1950s, cars ran on a variety of fuels, including highly carcinogenic benzene (derived from coal), 'producer' gas and alcohols – either in blends with petrol or as fuels in their own right. In the early years of the twentieth century, most engine manufacturers were able to offer engines which could readily run on alcohol fuels.

Until the late 1920s, most cars were fitted with low-compression engines, to avoid the severe 'knocking' problems caused by low-octane fuels. Then two alternatives emerged, tetra-ethyl lead additives and alcohol blending. In the light of the widespread opposition to lead in petrol by environmentalists, it is ironic to note that Standard Oil, which effectively controlled the fuel market at the time (see Chapter 4), pushed through lead additives – in spite of the fact that there had been a spate of fatal lead poisonings of workers in the motor and motor-fuels industries. After some twenty deaths, during which the victims became violently insane, tetra-ethyl lead additives were banned for a year, but they were reintroduced when it was found that lead in the fumes emitted by the average car exhaust did not appear to have the same effect.

To be fair, analytical techniques were in the Stone Age at the time, when compared with the parts-per-billion accuracy achievable today, and there were many fewer cars on the road. But, as Bill Kovarik, who has extensively researched the use of alcohol fuels, points out, 'Standard Oil claimed there was absolutely no alternative to lead octane boosters. In fact, Standard was actually testing an alcohol blend in Baltimore at the time.'

And, during the 1930s, Standard Oil itself marketed alcohol-blended fuels – such as Cleveland Discol (see Figure 10.2), which was well known in Britain. By 1936, at a time when Standard Oil was attacking alcohol fuels in the States, it was advertising Cleveland Discol in Britain as having greater power and less knock than normal

Figure 10.2: Advertisement for UK alcohol-petrol blend,
Cleveland Discol, in the Magazine *Speed* (source: Earthscan).

unadulterated petrol, and saying that it offered freedom from the very same starting and phase-separation problems which it was using in the United States to justify its opposition to alcohol fuels. Such an advanced state of corporate schizophrenia must raise question-marks over some of the assertions made today about the renewable-energy technologies by Standard Oil's corporate heirs.

Two types of alcohol have been commonly used as fuel, either neat or blended with petrol: methanol ($CH_3OH$), the simplest alcohol which corresponds to methane, the simplest hydrocarbon; and ethanol ($CH_3CH_2OH$), or ethyl alcohol, which corresponds to ethane – the second simplest hydrocarbon. The 'gasohol' sold in the USA is a blend of 10 per cent ethanol with 90 per cent petrol (or gasoline, as it is called there).

Alcohols are hydrocarbons with one hydrogen atom replaced by the hydroxyl (OH) group and, like the hydrocarbons, the alcohols form a series: ethanol, for example, is a two-carbon molecule, propanol is a three-carbon molecule (corresponding to propane), and butanol a four-carbon molecule (corresponding to butane).

Methanol, or 'wood alcohol', can be made in two ways. The first involves the destructive distillation – or pyrolysis – of wood, the process taking place in the absence of air, and the resulting liquids and tars being distilled to yield methanol. This is, in effect, an indirectly solar and renewable-energy technology. The second approach, involving the production of methanol from natural gas, is not. Among the renewable ethanol sources used or proposed are wet biomass (e.g. sewage, algae, seaweed or animal dung) and dry biomass (e.g. wood, crop residues and urban wastes).

The second route to methanol has been favoured ever since the process was first discovered, and, Bill Kovarik predicts, natural gas is likely to be the favoured methanol feedstock for the remainder of the century. 'Despite the rising cost of oil,' he argues, 'natural gas is still so cheap at many remote oil-fields that some six trillion cubic feet (170 billion cubic metres) are flared into the sky every year.' Saudi Arabia and the Soviet Union are, in fact, building methanol-producing facilities to exploit some of the gas they currently waste.

Ethanol, by contrast, is already being produced commercially from biomass. It can be derived from three main biomass sources: sugar (e.g. from cane, molasses or sweet sorghum); starches (e.g. cassava, corn or potatoes); and celluloses (e.g. wood and agricultural wastes). The basic process has three main steps. The first involves the reduction of the material to water-soluble sugars, a step which is clearly unnecessary for sugar-bearing plants. The second step is the fermentation of the sugars to produce alcohol. And the third step involves the distillation, by boiling, of the resulting liquor, to separate the alcohol (ethanol, for example, boils at 178°F/81°C) from the water (boiling point 212°F/100°C).

*Table 10.3: Ethanol yields for a selection of crops (based on average yields in Brazil, except for corn, which is based on US yields. Two crops a year are possible in some areas, and it is calculated that cassava yields, for example, could be boosted to 3,600 litres per hectare per year by improved cultivation methods; source: Earthscan)*

|  | Litres of ethanol per tonne of crop | Litres of ethanol per hectare per year |
|---|---|---|
| Sugar-cane | 69 | 3,500 |
| Cassava | 177 | 2,160 |
| Sweet sorghum | 85 | 3,010 |
| Sweet potato | 123 | 1,875 |
| Corn (maize) | 364 | 2,220 |
| Wood | 157 | 3,200 |

For the current state of the various technologies, Table 10.3 shows the ethanol yields achieved for a number of energy crops. It is interesting to see that while sugar-cane produces fewer litres of ethanol per ton of crop fermented, it is the best performer – because of its productivity per area planted – in terms of litres of ethanol per hectare per year.

Both methanol and ethanol mix readily with any amount of water, whereas higher alcohols do so less readily. Butanol, for example, accepts only 7 per cent of water. If an alcohol contains no water, it is called 'anhydrous'; such alcohols are used to prevent 'phase separation' in blended fuels. If a blend of 10 per cent alcohol and 90 per cent petrol is exposed to as little as 0.25 per cent extra water, it can cause the blended fuel to separate in the fuel tank into two unmixed layers. The addition of small quantities of the higher alcohols as blending agents can help reduce these problems to an acceptable level.

Among the other problems advanced as reasons for the oil industry's lack of enthusiasm for alcohol fuels have been 'vapour lock', where bubbles of evaporating alcohol block fuel lines and pumps;

starting problems; corrosion of fuel tanks and carburettors; and the lower heat content of a given volume of alcohol when compared with petrol, producing lower mileage. None of these problems, in fact, has proved intractable. In fact a test carried out with 45 cars driven over 2 million miles in Nebraska showed no vapour lock, no corrosion problems, no phase separation, 5.3 per cent better mileage, better winter starting, and cleaner emissions.

In Europe, meanwhile, a test by the West German government, Shell and Volkswagen had shown that a blend of 15 per cent methanol with petrol could be an attractive fuel. 'Anticipated problems either failed to materialize or proved relatively easy to solve,' said the VW report on the study. The test vehicles achieved better mileage, and phase-separation problems were solved by the addition of higher-alcohol blending agents.

Methanol is also being promoted for use in aircraft, with ex-astronaut Gordon Cooper and his partner Bill Paynter among its most devoted supporters. The main drawback of methanol is that its energy content is lower than that of kerosene, with methanol rated at 18,000 kilojoules per litre and kerosene or gasoline at 28,000 kilojoules. On paper, then, you would need something like 65 per cent more methanol to fly a given distance. But methanol enthusiasts are convinced that this calculation is wrong, and Cooper for one had plans to fly a twin-engine aircraft for 3,000 hours, with one engine fuelled with methanol and the other with kerosene, to test out his theories.

'There won't be a dissenter alive,' said Paynter colourfully; 'there won't be one that can say anything, because we'll have so much documented evidence that we'll bury them.' But, while methanol does appear to be kinder on engines, it seems very much more likely that it will be most commonly used as a chemical feedstock rather than as a motor fuel – although the Bank of America in San Francisco has apparently converted its entire fleet of 1,800 cars to methanol made from natural gas, and plans are afoot to begin production from eucalyptus. But the prospects for such alternative fuels very much depend on the sort of political decisions that Brazil took in launching its 'Proalcool' programme.

## Brazil's Alcoholic Hiccups

When the Iran–Iraq war began in late 1980, it cut off almost half of Brazil's oil imports, although emergency shipments from Saudi Arabia, the Soviet Union and Venezuela made up some of the gap. But Brazil's car manufacturers found themselves overwhelmed with orders for alcohol-powered vehicles; indeed at one time the production of alcohol cars accounted for 60 per cent of all cars made in Brazil. In some showrooms, there were eight alcohol cars for every petrol-driven model, at a time when petrol was not available from Friday night through to Monday morning.

In fact, the odds were heavily stacked in favour of alcohol cars at the time. The road licence for an alcohol car was also half that for its petrol-driven twin, and the hire-purchase payback period was longer for the alcohol-propelled driver. Even better, early in 1981, while petrol was retailing at 87 US cents a litre, alcohol cost only 38 US cents a litre. But, the world being the sort of place it is, the bubble had to burst – and burst it soon did.

Brazil was by no means the only country exploring the alcohol option. In Malawi, for example, the Ethanol Corporation was building a plant to produce 1.3 million US gallons of alcohol from by-product molasses. The country is landlocked, with no oil supplies of its own, and supplies from the coast have tended to be erratic. But Brazil's Proalcool programme was launched on an unparalleled scale – and its successes and failures have been in the world's headlines ever since.

It all began, in a political sense at least, when President Ernesto Giesel visited the Centre for Aerospace Technology, in 1975, and was impressed by what he saw. He ordered a massive campaign designed to replace imported oil with home-grown alcohol. Having harvested sugar-cane for four hundred years, the Brazilians' attitude was summed up by one official: 'Why send dollars (which we haven't got) to the Arabs, when we can send cruzeiros (which we have got) to the farmers of Brazil?'

At the time, 151 distilleries were producing about 900 million litres (240 million US gallons) of industrial-grade ethanol from sugar-cane each year. Most of the distilleries, in fact, were using molasses, a by-product from sugar production, obtaining 12 litres (3 US gallons) per ton of cane. The original target was to blend 20 per cent of ethanol in all petrol by 1980, and to bring alcohol production up to 5.8 billion litres (1.5 billion US gallons) by 1985. But, in 1977, as Brazil's trade deficit continued to worsen, a new 1985 goal of 10.7 billion litres (2.8 billion US gallons) was set. The 1982 actual production figure was 4.2 billion litres, 13 per cent up on the 1981 figure of 3.7 billion litres.

According to the Proalcool planners, a level of 20.5 billion litres (5.4 billion US gallons) was to be achieved by 1990, or earlier if possible, achieving cumulative savings estimated at $11 billion in foreign exchange – for a total investment of $8 billion. To achieve these substantially higher targets, new distilleries were being financed which were switching from molasses to the sugar itself, and producing about 70 litres (18 US gallons) of alcohol for each ton of cane processed.

'The alcohol car idea,' said one Ford official, 'caught on like wild-fire.' The problem was that the sheer number of alcohol cars on the road, coupled with Proalcool's success in marketing alcohol overseas – the United States took 480 million litres in 1980 – and some production snags, led to shortages on the domestic market. In an attempt to bring demand in line with supply, the Brazilian government cut the price differential between alcohol and petrol, so that, when the fact that alcohol cars burn more fuel was taken into account, the real saving to alcohol-car owners fell to 15 per cent. Whereas in late 1980 eight out of ten car buyers plumped for alcohol, the figure fell to less than 15 per cent of all cars sold one year later.

Brazil's dream of seeing one million all-alcohol cars on the road by 1982 remained just that, with the country's total fleet having reached perhaps half that number by the end of 1981. By early 1982, some 4 billion litres (1.1 billion US gallons) of alcohol a year were being produced, about 500–600 million litres down on earlier estimates. At the time, about 2.5 million hectares (6.1 million acres) of cane were under cultivation, covering about 5 per cent of Brazil's total arable area of 48 million hectares (120 million acres). Projects amounting to a total annual production of 8.5 billion litres (2.2 billion US gallons) were in the pipeline, implying that at least another 2 million hectares (4.9 million acres) of sugar-cane would need to be brought into production.

It has been estimated that 4.4 million hectares (or about 9 per cent of Brazil's land surface) could produce 16 billion litres (4.2 billion gallons) by 1987, according to trade minister Camilo Pena. A great deal will depend on the world energy climate, of course, and on the political direction of Brazil's development.

In the United States, meanwhile, the initiative had been seized by farmers, small businessmen, inventors and academics. To start with, government agencies and spokesmen tended to dismiss 'gasohol', Deputy Secretary of Energy John O'Leary calling it 'the new laetrile'. Since laetrile was seen by many as a phoney anti-cancer drug, but got immense publicity, the implication of Secretary O'Leary's comments was not well received by gasohol proponents.

President Carter, however, set a goal of 1.9 billion litres (500 million US gallons) of ethanol a year by 1981. But his successor, President Reagan, had other ideas; for example, the Reagan administration opposed the 4 cents a gallon exemption from federal gasoline taxes which had been approved in 1978.

Despite the initially slow reaction from the federal government, however, gasohol took off impressively from a small base. From the time it was first offered to motorists at several dozen mid-western service stations during the summer of 1978, the public response was good, and the number of gasohol pumps soared. By the following year, the year Secretary O'Leary launched his attack, a thousand service stations were offering gasohol, and by 1981 over 9,000 stations, in forty-five out of the fifty states, were selling it. In addition, the Treasury Department had received something like 6,000 applications for permits to produce alcohol.

Some saw it as rather ironic that a vast effort had been expended over the years, before, during and after Prohibition, to track down and destroy illegal 'white lightning' stills in areas like Tennessee, and now here were some of the people queuing for licences to run essentially the same processes – but legally, this time, and with their product (or most of it) picked up as on a milk-collection route.

Anyone reading through the various studies which have been produced by government agencies, universities and consultants on the prospects for the US gasohol industry cannot help but be struck by the extraordinary divergence in the forecast production and sales figures. The Department of Energy, for example, had estimated that by the year 2000 all biomass renewable-energy sources could produce 205 billion litres (54 billion US gallons) of ethanol *and* 586 billion litres (154.7 billion US gallons) of methanol. The National Alcohol Fuels Commission, on the other hand, put maximum production very much lower – at *either* 66 billion litres (17.3 billion US gallons) of ethanol *or* 72 billion litres (19 billion US gallons) of methanol.

The difference between the two sets of figures is largely explained, however, by the fact that the Department of Energy was talking about the total resource base, while the Commission was focusing on the economically usable resource base.

France was also stepping up its activities in the fuel-alcohol field, with one slogan reading 'Put a topinambour in your tank'. The topinambour, or Jerusalem artichoke, had become the symbol of the anti-nuclear lobby's response to the energy crisis, although France's energy plans also foresaw the production of alcohol from such materials as sugar-beet, maize, lucerne, alfalfa, straw and forest undergrowth, all of which were seen as contributing to the production of petrol substitutes – or 'carburols'. The aim had been to provide 25–50 per cent of the country's vehicle fuel needs by 1990, although the target is now much less ambitious. In the initial phase, with the addition of up to 10 per cent carburol to four-star petrol, existing engines and distribution networks would not need to be changed; but both will need to be redesigned if carburol levels are to be pushed very much higher. France has also been working on the methanol option, gambling on a process known as 'acétonobutylique', developed by the National Oil Industry Research Centre.

The interesting thing about Brazil, France and the United States is that all three produce an agricultural surplus while running an energy deficit (see Figure 10.3), so that it makes sense to convert some of that surplus into fuel alcohol, in the hope of reducing these energy deficits. Among the other countries in the top left quadrant, a fair number now have biomass energy programmes – as do many countries which are not included. The tiny central American republic of Costa Rica, for example, ought to be somewhere in there. Its oil bill shot up from $11 million in 1972 to $230 million, but it has a large untapped agricultural potential. Each year, for instance, it throws away some 220,000 tonnes of bananas, because they are unfit for export or domestic consumption – and it is now considering using some of them as an ethanol feedstock.

Kenya does appear, however, and its fuel-alcohol programme illustrates a number of the problems which developing countries have been encountering in pursuing ideologically 'acceptable' renewable-energy technologies. Kenya's Kisumu plant was designed to turn molasses from the sugar factories of the Nyanza region into alcohol – and several other useful products. Initially, at least, the target was 20 million litres a year of fuel alcohol, to be blended in the ratio of 15 per cent to 85 per cent petrol; 3,000 tonnes of citric acid for the soft-drinks industry; 1,800 tonnes of baker's yeast; and 2,160

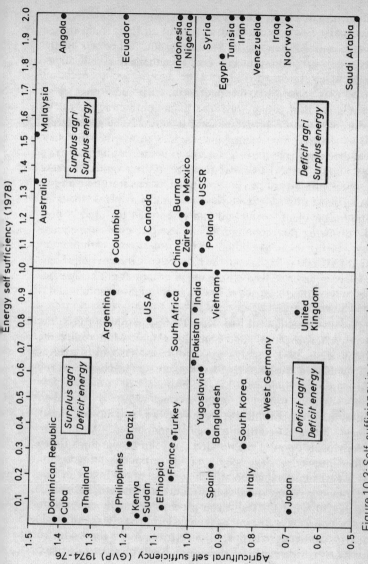

Figure 10.3: Self-sufficiency in energy and agriculture for a range of countries. The countries in the top left quadrant (e.g. Brazil, Kenya and the USA) are best placed to exploit alcohol fuels, having an energy deficit and an agricultural surplus. (Source: Dr Norman Rask, via Earthscan.)

tonnes of vinegar. It was also expected to produce sulphuric acid, gypsum and carbon dioxide. And, on top of all that, sophisticated waste treatment was envisaged, accounting for 10 per cent of the plant's capital cost and producing enough methane to supply 50 per cent of the plant's fuel requirement.

With all that going for it, one might say, what could possibly go wrong? A good deal, apparently. The main contractor, the Kenya Chemical and Food Corporation, went bankrupt. The government delayed its share of the funding, uncertain as to whether the plant would be economic, and the original cost estimates doubled. Kenya's electrical supply authorities failed to agree to the required increase in the capacity of the grid, so that the plant had to start up using its own diesel generators. Methane was not initially available from the waste-treatment plant, so fuel oil had to be used for process heat as well, throwing the economics of the exercise even further into disarray. Having spent £4 million on the project, and with only an estimated £350,000 still to spend, the Kenyan government pulled out, the Israeli contractor walked off the site in protest at not being paid, and the Swiss plant designer, Process Engineering, went into liquidation.

But the news was not all bad. Kenya's first gasohol project, the little-known Agrochemical Food Company plant in Muhoroni, came on stream late in 1982, supplying ethanol-based gasohol to garages in the Nairobi area. Molasses feed-stocks were supplied by the nearby East African Sugar Industries Ltd, and about 1,200 tonnes a year of baker's yeast was produced as a by-product.

As in so many other fields, the technology was still moving ahead, with new products constantly being announced. Alcon Bio-technology, which pooled the resources of John Brown Engineering and Allied Breweries, developed a rapid continuous fermentation process for ethanol production affording a five- to ten-fold reduction in the fermenter volume needed to produce a given ethanol output (see Figures 10.4 and 5). The Alcon process, originally designed to produce beer, proved a disaster as far as saleable beer was concerned – but it also turned out to be a highly attractive process for producing ethanol from a wide range of sucrose and hydrolysed starch feed-stocks.

Meanwhile, in Sweden, Alfa-Laval's Biostil process, another continuous fermentation process, was being operated at a 800-litres-a-day pilot plant, and a larger 20,000-litres-a-day demonstration plant

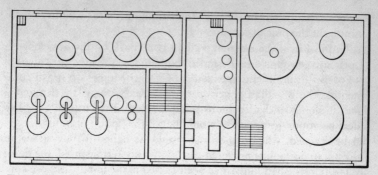

Figure 10.4: Alcon Biotechnology's continuous ethanol fermentation process. Compare with the batch process in Figure 10.1 (p. 225). (Source: Alcon Biotechnology.)

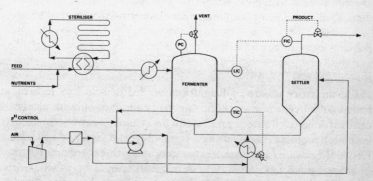

Figure 10.5: Flow diagram of the Alcon continuous fermentation process (source: Alcon Biotechnology).

based on wheat feedstocks was planned with joint funding from the Swedish Farmers' Cooperative. A 12,000-litres-a-day plant has been operating in Queensland, Australia, since early in 1981 and has consistently produced higher alcohol yields than a neighbouring batch distillery. The first commercial-scale Biostil plant in Brazil came on stream late in 1982 – and achieved 95 per cent of the theoretical alcohol yield, compared with 86 per cent for a conventional batch process plant run in parallel. Considerable progress had been made in side-stepping one of the major problems involved in continuous fermentations, bacterial infection. The Alcon process, for example, had been successfully run continuously for well over three months at the time of writing.

And in Brazil the car makers had gone back on the attack, with a propaganda campaign designed to put across the message 'Alcohol is Forever'. But, as the president of General Motors do Brasil commented, the Brazilian government had tried to legislate demand – and, in doing so, had demonstrated just how hard it is to do. 'The ideal position,' he advised, 'would be for the "point of indifference" to be reached, when a motorist would be happy to buy either an alcohol or a gasoline powered car.' But, it soon transpired, the point of indifference had long since been passed in the minds of those concerned about the impact of the Proalcool programme on the environment and on food supply. Early in 1983, for example, Brazil's Bodaquena project, which was to have been the country's largest sugar-based alcohol complex when it came on stream in 1985, was cancelled – because of local fears about its potential ecological effects.

## Put Hunger in Your Tank

Fact: an area the size of Belgium is needed in Brazil to replace a mere 20 per cent of the country's petrol consumption with alcohol. Fact: if America wanted to replace 10 per cent of its current fossil-fuel use with biomass energy, using a suitable species such as *Euphorbia*, it would need to commandeer an area the size of Arizona for the purpose. Final fact: Shell, whose forecasts should be viewed with a certain amount of caution, has estimated that if the world's entire crop of maize, sugar-cane, cassava and sweet sorghum were to be converted into alcohol, it would meet a mere 6–7 per cent of the world's energy needs. The energy yields of a number of crops are shown in Table 10.4.

The underlying argument, however, is clear. The use of increasing areas of land to grow alcohol crops may well fuel inflation in world food prices and narrow the already precariously thin margin of survival of those in the Third World. Or, as Lester Brown, director of the Worldwatch Institute, put it: 'The demand by motorists for fuel from energy crops represents a major new variable in the food-population equation. The potential demand is virtually limitless: even converting the entire world grain crop to alcohol would not provide enough fuel to operate the current world automobile fleet.'

Table 10.4: A comparison of a number of potential energy crops in terms of crop maturation time, seasonal availability, yield and calorific power (source: Industrial Biotechnology)

| | Years | Crop (months) | Yield (ton/ha) | Calorific power (KCal/kg) | Calorific power (KCal/litre) | Specific gravity | Octane number |
|---|---|---|---|---|---|---|---|
| Cotton | 1 | 3 | 0,11 0,20 | 8.300 | 7.600 | 0,92 | 44 |
| Peanut | 1 | 3 | 0,57 0,76 | 8.950 | — | — | — |
| Babassu nut | 7 | 12 | 0,1  0,3 | 8.430 | 7.700 | 0,92 | 45 |
| Coconut | 7 | 12 | 1,3  1,9 | 8.680 | — | — | — |
| Palm | 8 | 12 | 3,0  5,0 | 9.230 | — | — | — |
| Sunflower | 1 | 3 | 0,54 1,92 | 9.100 | — | — | — |
| Castor | 1 | 3 | 0,53 0,88 | 8.300 | — | — | — |
| Soybean | 1 | 3 | 0,24 0,36 | 8.800 | 8.100 | 0,92 | 35 |

*Table 10.5: Comparison of the grain and land requirements for dietary and fuel alcohol purposes (source: Worldwatch Institute)*

|  | Grain (pounds) | Cropland (acres) |
|---|---|---|
| Subsistence diet | 400 | 0.2 |
| Affluent diet | 1,600 | 0.9 |
| Typical European car (7,000 miles per year at 25 miles per gallon) | 6,200 | 3.3 |
| Typical US car (10,000 miles per year at 15 miles per gallon) | 14,600 | 7.8 |

Energy crops, he was convinced, 'will intensify pressures on the earth's limited cropland – pressures that are already excessive in many parts of the world and have led to extensive erosion and soil deterioration.' His argument is summarized in Table 10.5.

These figures suggest that to run an average American car for a year on alcohol fuels derived from purpose-grown energy crops would demand the output from land which could (theoretically) provide a subsistence diet for 39 people. But the National Alcohol Fuels Commission disputes these figures, pointing out that 80 per cent of the estimated 5.3 billion litres (1.4 billion US gallons) of alcohol likely to be produced in 1985 will be made from corn (maize), as shown in a 1981 estimate (Figure 10.6). And corn, the Commission has argued, is typically fed to animals rather than providing subsistence diets.

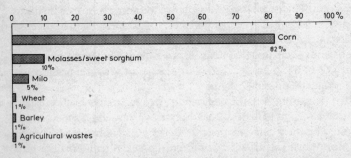

Figure 10.6: The United States' estimated 1985 ethanol capacity of 5.3 billion litres a year is seen as coming overwhelmingly from corn (source: National Alcohol Fuels Commission).

Lester Brown retorts that 'two billion gallons of ethanol (or 2 per cent of US gasoline consumption) would require 20 million tons of corn or its equivalent – one fifth of the currently exportable grain surplus of the United States'. Not so, protested some Congressmen and industrialists, pointing out that only the starch is converted, leaving the protein for use in cattle-feed. But, it is widely accepted, the Third World does not suffer so much from a protein deficiency as from a lack of food generally.

While some analysts expected the influence of the ethanol industry on the corn market to be relatively small, Brown disagreed vehemently. 'For the world's affluent,' he said, the resulting price rises 'may lead to belt tightening, but for the several hundred million who are already spending most of their meagre incomes on food, the expected price increases will further narrow the thin margin of survival.'

And there have been other critics of these early attempts to wean the world from fossil fuels to fuel alcohol. One area of controversy has centred on the question: does a litre of ethanol deliver more energy than was used in its production? Most authorities now agree that it can do so, though it has often been, as the Duke of Wellington said of the Battle of Waterloo, 'a damned nice thing – the nearest run thing you ever saw in your life'.

An interesting turn-about came with a study carried out by the American Petroleum Institute in 1978, which concluded that a positive energy balance was possible with sugar-cane ethanol and with wood methanol, but that grain ethanol was at best a break-even proposition. Then a 1979 study by the Solar Energy Research Institute reported a favourable energy balance for a small diesel-powered distillery in Springfield, Colorado, showing that to distil 2.8 gallons of ethanol from grain used the energy in one gallon of ethanol – an energy balance of 1:2.8, thanks to heavy insulation of the fermenting vats, distillation columns and piping.

But if bagasse (the pulp remaining after sugar has been crushed from the cane) is used as a fuel, or sorghum wastes, with process steam generated by their combustion, the energy balance turns out a good deal more positively. This calculation, however, fails to take into account the energy used in producing and applying the chemical fertilizers and pesticides used in growing energy crops, and in harvesting them. Energy-intensive farming accounts for 30 per cent of the energy in a gallon of ethanol, according to the US Office of Technology Assessment.

A great deal remains to be done in carefully designing bio-energy systems and in producing more efficient micro-organisms for use in fermentation processes – some of which may be able to convert cellulose readily into alcohols, while others may operate at such high temperatures that fermentation and distillation can take place together or, at least, with no intermediate cooling stage, saving further energy. Work is also under way, including a project at the Mitsui Shipbuilding Company, to develop yeast strains which can tolerate higher levels of alcohol, so that instead of their dying when the brew reaches 10–12 per cent alcohol, they continue to be active until there is perhaps 17 per cent alcohol.

And Proalcool has had its environmental critics, too. Agricultural engineer José Lutzenberger, who founded the environmental group AGAPAN, has called Proalcool 'a calamity'. He has argued that the programme 'will be in the hands of the international petroleum, automobile and chemical companies'. It will, he believes, encourage further centralization of power in the hands of small minorities. And, while alcohol fuels may burn more cleanly than petrol, Lutzenberger is not alone in viewing the clearance of tropical rain-forest to make way for energy-crop plantations as a potential ecological time-bomb.

'The most complex and wonderful of biomes,' he says, 'is being burned, knocked down by dragging great chains between huge tractors, defoliated with Agent Orange ... Entire communities of plants and animals are being irrevocably lost ... In their place are being planted vast monocultures, which are inherently unstable. Most don't last five years, and require massive doses of biocides and fertilizers that pollute rivers and lakes and kill wildlife.' With many indigenous tribespeople being dislodged or killed in the process, Lutzenberger asks: 'Who is the real barbarian?'

The International Institute for Applied Systems Analysis (IIASA), meanwhile, was arguing that 'the use of renewable resources presents a large potential [for] ecological disturbance: to consider relying on them to provide a substantial fraction of our energy supplies is to contemplate undertaking active ecological management on an awesome scale'. IIASA estimated that replacing all oil by biomass energy by the year 2010 would need 30 million square kilometres (12 million square miles) of forest, compared with perhaps 13 million square kilometres (5 million square miles) at the moment. This, IIASA suggested, would mean 'operating a worldwide herbarium'. And, in many areas of the world, it would involve converting what some see as the last vestiges of the Garden of Eden into a world-wide Garden of Ethanol.

## A Cry for Kelp

'They were talking about yields for these plants higher than any yields ever recorded,' sniped one critic, commenting on General Electric's plans to grow kelp plantations in the ocean as a source of renewable energy. Indeed, if the public has tended to get the idea that only big conventional power schemes are mismanaged and run foul of Murphy's Law, the kelp controversy, which was raging at about the same time as the GPU staff were flushing out the Three Mile Island reactor, showed that renewable technologies sometimes have feet of clay.

If you fail, try, try and try again appears to have been the motto of the kelp researchers. The basic idea here was to grow kelp, for conversion to methane, on millions of acres of floating platforms out on the deep ocean. Early efforts, directed by the US Navy and with funding from the National Science Foundation, the Energy Research and Development Administration (ERDA) and the American Gas Association (AGA), had not been notable successes. By 1975, a couple of years after the first oil shock, two attempts had been made to grow kelp on tailor-made ocean facilities – and both times the plants died.

Despite these early failures, kelp enthusiasts pressed on. Howard Wilcox, a nuclear physicist based at the Naval Underseas Laboratory, and Ab Flowers, a metallurgical engineer with AGA, proposed that the idea be tested at sea on what they called a 'quarter-acre module' or QAM. This was a wire and rope lattice, suspended from a buoy, on which the plants were suspended. The idea had soon been further developed to include the pumping up of nutrient-rich water from the deep-sea, to fertilize the kelp beds.

From the start, the project had its critics. One, Roscoe Ward, then branch chief of the Department of Energy's Fuels from Biomass Program, wrote a memo early in 1978 arguing that: 'the staff of the Fuels from Biomass branch does not feel that the AGA quarter-acre module should be supported. However, we do feel strongly that we need additional data on kelp growth and nutrient requirements. This data cannot be obtained by the quarter-acre module experiment. We believe that growth under well-controlled conditions can be performed readily on land-based aquatic test sites.'

Another critic, Wheeler North of CalTech, had expressed misgivings about other aspects of the kelp project. 'There is not 100 per cent control over the dispersal of the upwelled water,' he said in a letter to Wilcox, so that there was no way in which one could predict how much of a particular nutrient each plant would receive. He was also concerned about the possible effects of the upwelled water itself on the kelp and about the physical vulnerability of the test farm. 'Protection against current is extremely important,' he warned. 'We need a curtain around the entire farm. The curtain should remain in place at all current velocities.' He also suggested that 'one-way valves are needed in the exhaust hoses of the upwelling system to prevent flow reversals when one or two pumps shut down. Flow reversals,' he pointed out, 'have happened and nearby plants have been sucked into the ports, seriously damaging them.'

The fact that both these factors had contributed to the complete destruction of the trial kelp crop within two months, however, probably annoyed the project's critics rather less than the inflated yield projections put out by General Electric, which had replaced the Navy in the programme. While GE was estimating yields of 25–100 tons of dry, ash-free biomass per acre per year, the marine biologists consulted by the Department of Energy had advised that the maximum theoretical yields would lie in the range 30–50 tons. One, based at the Woods Hole Oceanographic Institution, was particularly concerned about these 'extravagant claims', and had written to Roscoe Ward saying that 'with the certainty and conviction that comes from complete and utter ignorance, the kelp farm proponents have stipulated and projected yields and other characteristics of their proposed operation that are wholly unrealistic and unreasonable'.

Other scientists were incensed by the quality of GE's final report, and by the fact that there were no progress reports, as required by the original contract. The final report, according to Ward, was a 'series of disorganized items hastily thrown together'. There were, he complained, 'no data, discussion of results, conclusions or recommendations on how to solve the problems'. And an outside reviewer reported: 'I found the information to be identical to that received from General Electric in March of 1978 (before the experiment began). There does not appear to be any new information in the document.'

Roscoe Ward, who had tried to point out the weaknesses in the concept from the beginning, soon fell victim to a series of bureaucratic backhanders. A subsequent official inquiry found that he had been put under considerable pressure, some would call it harassment, by his superiors, who justified their actions by saying that, though Ward 'knew his business and was competent from a professional standpoint', he 'lacked sufficient political judgement'. Ward was transferred to the United Nations, where, presumably, it was felt that his critical faculties would do less damage.

None of this, apparently, threw the DOE off its tracks. Despite the fact that its initial $1.2 million grant to GE had been for a 'discrete one-time effort', with GE responsible for all cost-overruns, a further $4 million was offered as another 'one-time' grant, with the money to be used in making the very modifications to the platform which North had argued would be indispensable several years earlier.

## Where There's a Weed

'I believe', said one of Roscoe Ward's erstwhile superiors, 'that aquatic biomass has the potential of being a real winner in the long run. There's the potential for high yields; there's the potential for specialized products; and there's the potential for growing biomass in facilities that do not compete with farmland in the US.' But this last argument could equally well be used in support of energy crops grown on marginal land and has, indeed, been used to justify an increasing number of biomass projects – some of which are likely to be associated with significant environmental impacts.

Cassava, which is probably the most likely ethanol crop in the Third World, is seen as particularly attractive because, besides being one of the most efficient photosynthetic converters, it flourishes on marginal land which is no good for traditional farming. The water hyacinth is another plant which is seen as a prime contender because of its ability to exploit marginal resources. Long seen as a major headache because of the way it infests waterways and lakes, doubling in size in eight days and producing one kilogram of biomass per square metre of water per day (3.3 ounces per square foot per day), water hyacinth also thrives in relatively polluted water, offering a cheap method for 'polishing' urban waste-water.

And, at the University of Minnesota, scientists were looking at another 'weed', cattail. In the huge marsh which makes up the body of the Agassiz National Wildlife Refuge, the cylindrical brown heads and long, slender leaves of the dense stands of cattail riffle in the breeze, much as they must have done when the Indians came to cut them for food, bedding and basket-weaving materials.

The cattail stands, which produce an average of 5 tons of biomass per acre each year (12 tonnes per hectare), are periodically cut down to maintain the desirable 50:50 ratio of open water to reed-swamp – to encourage the area's waterfowl. According to the head of the university's botany department, Douglas Pratt, the gleanings from this periodic harvesting suggested a considerable energy future for cattail. Although the plant burns far too rapidly to be used as it comes, it can be compressed into fuel pellets or fermented to produce fuel alcohol.

Pilot projects to produce gas from Minnesota's vast acreage of peat were already in the pipeline, but Douglas Pratt pointed out that once the peat has been extracted it takes something like 3,000 years to regenerate completely. Instead, cattails could be grown on a residue of peat, he says, ensuring a continuous supply of energy – as in the Bord na Mona's proposed schemes. The researchers estimated that Minnesota has 10 million acres (40,467 square kilometres) where cattails would grow, enough, they say, to meet the state's entire energy needs. But conservationists would certainly resist any idea that a significant proportion of the state's wetlands should be transformed into energy plantations – even if it is using a plant which they see as acceptable in many existing wetlands.

'With cattails, we're starting way ahead of the game,' said one University of Minnesota ecologist, 'and we haven't even looked yet for the best genetic strains.' This point is important, of course, because more productive energy-crop plants will use less land to produce whatever fuel alcohol we decide we need. Genetic engineering methods are already being used to produce more productive strains of existing energy-crop plants – and to turn novel plants into significant biomass resources.

Research is still proceeding into the ways in which the so-called

C4 plants, such as maize, sugar-cane and sorghum, have sidestepped the 'physiological Catch 22', as one scientist dubbed it, which has hampered the spread of their C3 competitors in tropical regions. C3 plants must sacrifice water in the transpiration process while they take in carbon dioxide, a penalty which can have serious implications in hot, dry climates. C4 plants reduce these losses by fixing carbon temporarily, then releasing it and promptly refixing it, enabling them to conserve water and grow extremely quickly in hot climates. The possibilities for producing new C4 plants are considerable, but many other plants are also being experimented with.

At Battelle's Columbus laboratories, for example, they are focusing on milkweed, seeing it as a potentially important source of biomass for conversion to synthetic fuels and chemical feedstocks, as well as a source of fat, protein, rubber, oil and fibre. Dr George Kidd and Suzanne Groet suggest that it may be possible to double the total hydrocarbon and biomass content of milkweed, not by using conventional plant-breeding techniques, but by exploiting the new techniques offered by tissue culture. This involves taking a piece of plant tissue, whether from the root, shoot or leaf, and placing it on a growth-promoting medium containing mineral salts, sugars, vitamins and a combination of plant hormones.

The minerals, sugars and vitamins nourish the cells, while the hormones stimulate cell division. 'A small piece of proliferating tissue grows as an undifferentiated mass called a callus', the Battelle researchers explain. 'Callus can be used to start new cultures, so that the tissue culture can be maintained indefinitely. When a callus sample is removed from a solid medium and placed in an agitated liquid medium, the cells break away from one another and form a suspension of single cells – or small clumps of cells – that continue to grow'.

By regenerating whole plants from single cells, it is possible, in theory at least, to produce whole generations of plants which show particular desirable characteristics displayed by their cell parents – such as resistance to a problem disease or to a pesticide used to suppress some problem, or higher yields of some desirable product.

Another plant in the biomass sweepstakes is the gopher plant, *Euphorbia lathyris* whose promoters include Professor Melvin Calvin, whose work on photosynthesis, the most important biochemical process in the world, won him the Nobel Prize in 1961. Shortly after the United States set up its Synfuels Corporation, to promote synthetic fuels such as those derived from oil shale (see Chapter 4), Calvin argued that if the Corporation had been given a brief to tackle biomass as well, the country could have been getting 10 per cent of its oil requirements from green plants by the end of the 1980s.

## Diesel Sap on Tap

Struck by the fact that the rubber tree, *Hevea brasiliensis*, produces hydrocarbons from atmospheric carbon dioxide, Professor Calvin decided to look for other plants which might help meet our energy needs, developing his 'green-factory' concept along the way. The idea is to use marginal land to grow oil-plants, although it is worth pointing out that marginal soils are not able to produce high yields of anything indefinitely – which is why they are marginal. Nonetheless, Calvin and his wife soon found suitable plants of the *Euphorbiaceae* family on their own ranch in northern California, including the gopher plant, which contains latex very much like that in *Hevea* plants.

According to Calvin's calculations, something like 1,000 tonnes of dry plant material can be treated with solvents to extract 80 tonnes of hydrocarbons and 260 tonnes of sugar, which can be converted to about 100 tonnes of ethanol. After the bagasse has been used to supply energy for solvent recovery, Calvin believes that nearly 200 tonnes would still be available for use as fuel.

Both the plants which Calvin has studied most intensively, *Euphorbia lathyris* and *tirucalli*, grow in semi-arid conditions and can be mechanically harvested. Using wild plants, oil yields of about 10 barrels per acre (2,471 barrels per square kilometre) have been achieved, although Calvin argues that selective breeding – or, presumably, tissue-culture propagation methods – could easily double this figure. 'Some of these varieties of plants not only grow in semi-arid regions, which is why we picked them,' Calvin told Martin Sherwood of *Chemistry and Industry*, 'but are also resistant to brackish and saline water. If we can develop those, a much larger area of culture land becomes accessible for them, which isn't used for anything else.'

Calvin is convinced that the pressure for 'green factories' will come from outside the United States. The effective lobby, as far as he is concerned, 'is going to be the developing countries' governments: many of the African countries can grow their own oil and they don't have any coal, so that's where it is going to come'. He knows the workings of capitalism well enough, however, to predict that once private companies see someone else growing oil-plants on a large scale – and thereby taking the first risk – they will be much more interested in breaking into the market. One company, Diamond Shamrock, has already invested significant sums in trial plantations in the USA, while Japanese companies have apparently been growing *Euphorbia tirucalli* on 5–10-acre plots for several years.

'We've got to have plantations producing oil before the next Middle East war cuts us off from foreign oil completely', Calvin has argued. Interestingly, he has also targeted milkweed as a possible energy-crop plant. Farmers in the south-western United States, he points out, have been producing something like a ton of steer per square mile of land each year. Milkweed is proving a considerable problem, destroying pasture and proving resistant to herbicides. Calvin suggests that the problem could be turned into an opportunity, with farmers in areas like Montana and Nevada growing tons of milkweed, producing oil worth considerably more than the beef they currently harvest.

Calvin has also thrown his weight behind the leguminous Copaiba tree. Its sap is tapped by Brazilian natives who drill a two-inch hole in the tree's trunk, cork it up and then leave it for six months. When they return, they uncork the hole and stand back while it discharges three or four gallons of diesel-like oil. They do not, however, have diesel cars, using the oil instead to soften their skins. But researchers have found that a hole drilled in the tree can yield 20–30 litres (4–7 gallons) of oil in 2–3 hours. Toyota trucks have been run on oil poured direct from the tree into their fuel tanks.

Rudolf Diesel would not be particularly surprised, as Professor David Hall of King's College, London, has pointed out, by the resurgence of interest in alternative fuels for his engine. As long ago as 1911 Diesel wrote that 'the diesel engine can be fed with vegetable oils and would help considerably in the development of the agriculture of the countries which will use it. This may appear a futuristic dream, but I can predict with great conviction that this use of the diesel engine may in the future be of great importance'.

Were Diesel still alive, he would be interested in the work under way at the Perkins Engines plant in Peterborough, England. 'For our experiments we often just pop down to Sainsbury's and buy gallon cans of vegetable oil,' explained David Bacon, combustion and performance research engineer at the Peterborough plant, 'and pour it straight into the engine without further refinement. It works very well. It smokes a bit more than diesel, but the difference is hardly measurable.' According to the company's calculations, enough oil can be obtained from the sunflower crop of one field to fuel a tractor while it ploughs ten fields of similar size.

Brazil, which announced plans to meet 16 per cent of its diesel fuel needs with vegetable oils by 1985, has been testing oils extracted from soybean, sunflower, peanut, rapeseed, dende palm and castor feedstocks, among others. South African engineers, with obvious reasons for being interested in alternative fuels, found that the injection nozzles of diesel engines fuelled with a high proportion of sunflower oil became clogged, particularly when the engines were not run at full speed. They overcame the problem, however, by installing different fuel filters, by retuning the engines and by further processing (esterifying) the oil, to improve its combustion characteristics.

Trials with sunflowers and soya beans in South Africa, according to David Hall, 'show that yields can be 1 tonne of oil per hectare with unsophisticated processes for extracting oil (something like 40 to 50 per cent by weight of the harvested crop is oil) while yields as high as 2 tonnes per hectare are not uncommon, and claims of up to 5 tonnes per hectare have been reported.' Another contender, the oil palm, can produce average oil yields of nearly 4 tonnes per hectare each year, and top yield of 5.6 tonnes per hectare, and Uni-

*Table 10.6: World average yields of oilseeds (source: Unilever)*

|  | Tonnes/ha seed | Oil % | T/ha oil |  |
|---|---|---|---|---|
| Soya | 1.4 | 20 | 0.28 | ⎫ |
| Groundnut | 0.9 (in shell) | 20 | 0.18 | ⎪ |
| Cottonseed | 1.1 | 20 | 0.22 | ⎬ World averages |
| Sunflower | 1.1 | 40 | 0.44 | ⎪ |
| Rapeseed | 0.8 | 40 | 0.32 | ⎪ |
| Sesame | 0.3 | 50 | 0.15 | ⎭ |
| Coconut | 1.1 | 64 | 0.70 | ⎫ |
| Oil palm | 12.0 (bunch) | 25 | 3.0 | ⎬ Malaysian Estates |
| kernel |  |  | 0.7 | ⎭ |

Table 10.7: *Best average yields of oilseeds (source: Unilever)*

|            | Tonnes/ha seed | % Oil | T/ha oil |                 |
|------------|----------------|-------|----------|-----------------|
| Soya       | 2.5            | 20    | 0.5      |                 |
| Groundnut  | 4.5 (in shell) | 20    | 0.9      |                 |
| Cottonseed | 2.5            | 20    | 0.5      |                 |
| Sunflower  | 2.0            | 40    | 0.8      |                 |
| Rapeseed   | 2.5            | 40    | 1.0      |                 |
| Sesame     | 1.0            | 50    | 0.5      |                 |
| Coconut    | 4.0 (copra)    | 65    | 2.6      | New hybrids     |
| Oil palm   | 20.0 (bunch)   | 28    | 5.6      | Best Malaysian  |

lever has been working on tissue-culture propagation to boost yields still further (see Tables 10.6 and 7). Meanwhile, around the world, scientists were showing how sophisticated photosynthesis is by their own faltering attempts to imitate it artificially.

## Reinventing the Leaf

Calvin's goal was the construction of artificial photosynthetic systems, able to convert solar energy into chemically-bound energy. His belief has been that they will initially be developed by the chemical industry for use in the production of specialized, high-value chemicals, giving hydrogen as a by-product. 'As the demand for hydrogen increases,' he predicted, 'we will soon outrun the chemical production capability to produce hydrogen as a by-product. We'll have to produce it as a main product and throw away oxygen. But that will take ten years or more; liquid fuel from plants,' he said, harking back to his oil-plants, 'will come a lot sooner.'

Someone else working on a similar idea was Sir George Porter of Britain's Royal Institution, and a 1967 Nobel Prize winner for his work on ultra-fast chemical reactions. His idea was to produce an artificial leaf, but on a very much vaster scale. By picking a cheap, stable material analogous to chlorophyll, Sir George foresaw energy plantations which would look rather like an inch-high greenhouse several square miles in extent.

Although he pointed out that 'it is most important to say that this process has not been demonstrated, it does not yet work,' he was convinced that it would. The fact that more solar energy falls on the planet during a single week than is stored in all the coal, oil and gas ever stored here, was itself a sufficient reason to pursue the idea as far as Sir George was concerned. He assumed a conversion efficiency of 10 per cent, arguing that this was pessimistic, so that if 100 watts of solar energy were available in one square metre, only 10 watts would be harnessed. Given that the world uses something approaching 10,000 billion watts of energy each year and that an average figure of 200 watts per square metre represents a world average, Sir George estimated that that would imply that 500 billion square metres would need to be covered with the synthetic leaf – or about a thirtieth of the world's currently cultivated land.

But there were a number of different ways of reinventing the leaf. The discovery, in the mid-1970s, that light could split water into hydrogen and oxygen, involved the use of membranes containing chlorophyll – with enzymes added to the water as catalysts. It also gave a considerable boost to those who foresaw biological routes to hydrogen, although in the early days the process would generate hydrogen for only a matter of minutes before its biological component failed. In recent years, however, research has extended the life of such processes considerably, so that they continue producing hydrogen for ten hours or more, while their rate of hydrogen production has improved too.

'It isn't difficult to turn water into hydrogen and oxygen,' comments Professor David Hall. 'An electric current applied to water through electrodes also splits water. This is the well-known process of electrolysis. However, electrolysis is not a way to make a storable energy source because valuable electricity – itself usually derived from stored energy, coal, oil and gas – is used, and there are heavy energy losses in converting fossil fuels into electricity and then hydrogen.'

It makes little sense to convert solar energy photovoltaically into electricity, and then to convert the electrical current into hydrogen, but Hall and others are convinced that the direct use of solar energy may do the trick. The process, photolysis, has a number of major advantages which, as Hall points out, 'are unmatched by any other known energy system: the substrate (water) is abundant; the energy source (sunlight) is effectively unlimited; the product (hydrogen) can be stored and is non-polluting; and the process is completely renewable because when the hydrogen is "consumed" the substrate, water, is regenerated.'

There are two distinct routes to solar water splitting: one is that pursued by Calvin and Porter and by Michael Grätzel of Switzerland, involving photochemical hydrogen-production processes, while the other involves photobiology. While photochemical reactions take place in a mixture of a number of chemicals, photobiological reactions typically take place within membranes.

While Calvin has attempted to mimic photosynthesis, Grätzel and Porter have focused on the properties of transition metal catalysts such as platinum. Catalytic methods, such as those developed by Grätzel, tend to use several catalytic components, and the chemistry has proved highly complex. The energy produced by the process, for example, can be wasted in back-reactions, or, if the concentration of catalysts becomes too high, the process can de-activate itself. A possible solution is that worked out by David Cole-Hamilton and Rodney Jones of Liverpool University's Department of Inorganic, Physical and Industrial Chemistry. Using a platinum-phosphorus catalyst, they set up a process which converted dilute sulphuric acid into hydrogen and persulphuric acid. The process may produce less hydrogen than Grätzel's process, but its single catalyst could well bypass some of the problems which the Swiss researcher has faced.

Photobiological methods are proving just as difficult. 'The problems in constructing a stable biochemical system that will function for years rather than hours', says Professor Hall, 'are enormous and may never be solved. However', he adds, 'if we could understand how the biological processes work, and then possibly mimic them by constructing a completely synthetic system, we might eventually be able to harness the solar energy that is available in temperate and hot climates. Such systems', he points out, 'would use light at all intensities and temperatures, an attribute they would share with electricity-generating photovoltaic cells. Only the intensity of the light would determine the rate of hydrogen production.'

# 11 ⊙ Drafting Animals

By the late 1970s, despite all the attempts to mechanize Third World agriculture, there were still 80 working draught animals for every tractor. Estimates were published at the UNERG conference suggesting that the total number of large animals domesticated worldwide for both food and draught purposes is about 1.5 billion, of which perhaps 400 million are Third World draught animals. Of these, between 280 million and 300 million are estimated to be working animals, the rest being too old or too young to work. Assuming that 215 million of these animals work in agriculture, either directly on the land or in related transport activities, they represent an extraordinarily significant resource – especially when compared with the Third World's 2.7 million tractors.

To get some idea of the scale of their contribution to the world energy picture, consider the amount of energy available from a single human being. When Bryan Allen pedalled Dr Paul MacCready's *Gossamer Albatross* into aviation history by becoming the first man to power an aircraft across the English Channel, he generated an estimated 0.3 horsepower during the two hours and 49 minutes of the crossing. He covered 22.5 miles, or the equivalent of 35 miles in still air, and maintained a cruising speed of 12 to 14 miles (19–22 kilometres) per hour.

Interviewed after the flight, Dr MacCready explained that the flight had been 'a great challenge and fun. With limited energy supplies, the ability to do jobs with low power or even human power is important.' Pedalling at something like 80–90 revolutions a minute, Allen worked far harder than most slaves could on a sustained output basis, but his epic flight gives us a yardstick for measuring the energy flows through social systems, whether they be based on slave power, animal power or on the use of fossil fuels.

Switching on your calculator, you might like to feed in the following items of information. First, Allen's efforts were rated at 0.3 horsepower. Second, one horsepower is equal to 745.7 watts or 0.7457 kW. Run these two figures together and you find that this output of energy can be expressed as equivalent to 0.2237 kW an hour, sustained over nearly three hours. Assuming that Allen's output was unusually high, it seems reasonable to assume that the output of a human slave working hard for a full working day would be equivalent, very roughly, to 1 kilowatt-hour (kWh) or 1.34 horsepower.

Using this yardstick, we find that the average daily output of one of those beautiful traditional windmills which still grace parts of the Dutch landscape (see Chapter 13) was about 240 kWh – or the equivalent of some 240 of our energy slaves working for a full day. By 1850, the output of US windmills was rated at a staggering 1.4 billion horsepower, equivalent to the annual exertions of over one billion of our slaves.

Pursuing this analogy, consider the energy content of two ships: the first was the sadly misnamed *Amistad* (or *Friendship*), sailing from West Africa to Cuba with a load of slaves during the sixteenth century, and the second the *Amoco Cadiz*, which ground ashore off the coast of Brittany on 16 March 1978. The Spanish frigate was loaded with 733 captives in West Africa and disembarked a mere 188 some fifty-two days later when it arrived in Havana, all the rest having perished during the voyage. By contrast, the 220,000 tons of oil which belched from the holds of the *Amoco Cadiz* could have provided nearly ten thousand times as much power as the 733 slaves originally loaded aboard the Spanish slaver could have provided over a full 365-day year – and nearly forty thousand times the potential maximum annual power output of those wretched survivors, who would have needed feeding into the bargain.

A single ton of oil can generate something like 4,000 kWh, so that the stranded supertanker's cargo could have generated something like 880 million kWh. This is theoretically equivalent to the output of something like 880 million slaves working flat out for a day or, to look at it through the eyes of a slave-owner, the output of some 2,411,289 slaves working a full 365-day year. Basil Davidson, whose book *Black Mother* (Pelican Books, 1980) documents the history of the Atlantic slave-trade, estimated that a total of eleven million slaves (or half the present-day population of Canada) were landed alive between 1451 and 1870, at least a further 1.5 million (or more than the present-day population of the Congo) having died aboard the slave ships.

On these figures, it looks rather as though the *Amoco Cadiz* could have provided as much energy in five trips from the Gulf oil ports as the entire population of slaves shipped across the Atlantic could have provided when working flat out for a 365-day year. That said, however, man-power has achieved some prodigious feats. One of Robert Stephenson's assistant engineers during the construction of the London and Birmingham railway, which was completed in 1838, carried out some calculations which show how extraordinary even this single railway construction project was in terms of the energy expended by its navvy builders.

According to Lieutenant Peter Lecount's estimates, the labour expended in building the Great Pyramid was equivalent to lifting 15,733,000,000 cubic feet of stone one foot into the air. This, according to Diodorus Siculus, was accomplished by 300,000 men (or 100,000, if you believe Herodotus) and took nearly twenty years. But to build this single railway, Lecount concluded, 25,000,000,000 cubic feet of material was lifted the equivalent of one foot – or some 9.267 million cubic feet more than for the Pyramid, all this being accomplished by 20,000 men in less than five years. Dismissing the Great Wall of China in a similar fashion, he pointed out that if the circumference of the earth were taken in round figures as 130 million feet, then the 400 million cubic feet of earth moved by 'his' navvies during those five years would, if spread in a continuous mound one foot high by one foot wide, encircle the equator more than three times.

From Spartacus on, however, these human engines were prone to disrupt the social equilibrium of the communities whose life-styles they underpinned with their exertions. Most industrialists, in fact, welcomed the energy slaves afforded by machines powered by fossil fuels with open arms. Indeed, many of the slave-based plantation economies were already experiencing a crisis in profitability which only mechanization, coupled with cheap and abundant fossil fuels, could solve.

Admittedly, the British railway engineers initially fought shy of that new-fangled American invention, the steam-powered mechanical excavator, which could be made to excavate 1,500 cubic yards of earth in twelve hours for a cost of twelve shillings' worth of fuel – but there were good reasons why they were able to do so. The problem, as far as Britain's engineers were concerned, was the capital outlay of £1,500 involved, at a time when men and spades were available in droves. In Canada and the United States, by contrast, the mechanical excavator caught on to such an extent that the word 'navvy' came to mean a steam shovel, rather than a man with pick and shovel.

One steam navvy could fill 240 wagons, containing nearly 1,000 cubic yards, in a ten-hour day. If a contractor had excavated at the same rate using human navvies, he would have needed a hundred of them. Given that only thirty men were needed to work with the mechanical excavator, it can be said that it performed the work of seventy men. With rapid technological innovation running hand in hand with the development of cheap new energy sources, the days of human slavery were effectively numbered in most industrial countries. Human labour and animal power were replaced with mechanical slaves, like the steam navvy, which consumed energy (e.g. fossilized sunshine) rather than food, largely derived from the planet's solar income via the food-web.

## 192 Billion Enslaved

By the early 1970s, indeed, it was calculated that the average American citizen was consuming 87 million kilocalories of energy a year, compared with the basic human requirement of about one million kilocalories – which satisfies the physiological needs associated with breathing, drinking and eating. Switch on the calculator again.

One kilowatt-hour equals 859,845 calories or 859.845 kilocalories. Divide that figure of 87 million kilocalories by 859.845 and you get a figure of 101,181.0268 kilowatt-hours for the typical American's energy consumption in 1970. So he or she was consuming energy each year which was equivalent to the energy output of some 277 of our energy slaves working flat out for a full 365-day year.

Americans, of course, have been a great deal more profligate with their energy resources than have most of their neighbours on planet Earth. In 1975, according to the International Institute for Applied Systems Analysis (IIASA), based at Laxenburg, Austria, the average rate of energy consumption in the world was approximately two kilowatt-years per person per year – or, in simpler terms, two kilowatts of continuous power per person.

This represents a staggeringly large population of our invisible 1 kWh per day slaves. Given that our energy consumption is rated at two kilowatts of *continuous* power, demanded every hour of a

24-hour day, the world's four billion inhabitants are effectively being supported by 192 billion energy slaves working every day of the year at a rate which no self-respecting modern trade union would condone for an instant. But, while the average American actually used 11 kilowatt-years a year, Europeans 'only' used 5 kilowatt-hours, and the average inhabitant in the Third World consumed less than 1 kilowatt-hour. So the American was supported by the equivalent of over 260 of our energy slaves, or, to put it another way, a typical family of four was being supported in the lap of relative luxury by the exertions of over one thousand energy slaves. The average European was supported by roughly 120 energy slaves and the average Third Worlder by fewer than 25.

Various research institutes around the world have been looking into ways of making more of those twenty-odd slaves available to the average inhabitant in the Third World. Using the technology which powered the *Gossamer Albatross* across the English Channel, for example, the Tropical Products Institute in London came up with a pedal-powered grain mill intended to speed the conversion of grain into the Third World's daily bread. The mill consists of a bicycle mounted on blocks, with the grain being ground into flour by a grinder attached to the rear wheel.

However, much of the Third World's energy is in fact supplied by draught animals. An ox, one might say, is an ox is an ox, but in the eye of today's energy technologist an ox is a 'renewable-energy, appropriate-technology, solar-powered engine', with the solar power coming in by the same route as it did with the slaves – through their mouths, in the form of plant and animal foods.

There are those who see animal power, particularly horse power, enjoying a revival in the developed world as fossil fuels become increasingly expensive and are reserved for chemical feedstocks. 'There is nothing sentimental about the revival of the horse as a tool of modern farming,' says Charles Pinney of the Cart Horse Company, based near Winchcombe, Gloucestershire. 'Tractors have their place, of course,' he admits, but he believes that 'the shire horse is far more economical as a utility investment round the farm. More important, it can be used in all weathers – unlike the tractor which damages pasture irreparably in rainy conditions.'

Pinney observes that the initial investment needed for a fully-trained horse would be between £500 and £1,500, compared with between £6,000 and £15,000 for a tractor. The horse lasts perhaps twenty years and breeds its own replacements. Its shoes, moreover, cost £10 a set, compared with a tractor tyre at something like £200. Importing horse-powered machinery from Poland, where there are still more than two million working horses, Pinney was developing improved horse-drawn tools with a neighbouring engineering company, using modern engineering techniques and lighter, tougher alloys.

Faced with the argument that a pair of horses can only plough an acre a day, compared with ten acres when a tractor is used, Pinney retorted that a horse can go out in any weather and do some sort of work, so that at the end of the year it could well have done as much work as the tractor. He did not talk about the serious drawback that horses need forage, and that a considerable quantity of land in horse-drawn economies was always tied up for this purpose. But he capped his argument, casting sentiment to the winds, by using a series of statistics calculated to chill the marrow of animal lovers. 'When the shire horse comes to the end of its working life,' he pointed out, 'it is still worth £500 for the table – you'd not get that much for a twenty-year-old tractor.'

Horses, however, are outnumbered by cattle, yaks and buffaloes in the Third World. Of those 400 million draught animals, 246 million (61 per cent) are cattle or yaks, while 60 million (15 per cent) are buffaloes. Twenty per cent are equine, with 40 million donkeys (10 per cent), 27 million horses (7 per cent) and 10 million mules (3 per cent). There are also estimated to be 16 million camels (4 per cent), plus something like 1 million llamas and perhaps 20,000 working elephants used in logging operations.

The power output of all these animals obviously varies considerably, but a conservative estimate of an average of half a horsepower apiece emerged from the UNERG conference, suggesting a total energy output for the world's draught animals of around 150 million horsepower. It was also estimated that it would cost at least $150 billion to replace just India's animals with mechanical power, with a further $1 billion needed each year for fuel.

Speaking at the UNERG conference, Mrs Indira Gandhi claimed that India's animals provide some 30,000 MW of power, more than the 29,000 MW provided by electricity. The number of bullock carts in the country has doubled since it won independence in 1947, and bullocks are also used for ploughing, turning water-wheels, working crushers and threshers. According to Dr N. S. Ramaswamy, director of the Indian Institute of Management at Bangalore, as much money ($5 billion) is invested in the country's animal-drawn carts as in its railways, and much more than in its public transport system ($3 billion). Dismissing the widespread assumption that the use of animal power is a passing phase in human history, Dr Ramaswamy argues that it will be a long time before solar or biogas systems are affordable by the poor majority in countries such as India. Animals, he says, represent the only 'alternative' source of energy available to them, so that 'the problem before us is not how to get rid of the bullock cart but how to make it more efficient'.

Only about 7 per cent of all those carts are of a reasonably efficient design. The traditional bullock cart can travel only 8–16 kilometres (5–10 miles) a day, carrying perhaps 750 kilograms (1,650 pounds). Its wooden wheels have high-friction bearings, while the hardwood yoke can bear down on an animal's neck with a force of 100 kilograms (220 pounds) even when the cart is only carrying 60 kilograms (132 pounds). Improved suspension, better-designed yokes and the replacement of wooden wheels with pneumatic tyres would all help considerably. The latter can increase a cart's carrying capacity from 750 to 2,500 kilograms (5,500 pounds); and Dr Ramaswamy has called for research designed to produce improved suspension for bullock carts – a development he believes could add a year to each animal's nine-year working life, saving India $250 million a year.

As an additional bonus, meanwhile, India's animals produce prodigious quantities of dung, much of which is used as a household fuel. Indeed, some studies have suggested that this dung represents a further input of 10,000 MW a year to the Indian economy. The attempts being made to improve the conversion of this resource into usable energy illustrate the growing importance of biotechnology in the energy field and, more particularly, of micro-organisms.

## Tailing the Sacred Cow

'When the lights flicker for an instant and then brighten in the pig houses on their Suffolk farm, brothers Peter and John Downing are happy men,' reported one British agricultural correspondent recently. 'It signals that their electricity bill – rather than the supply – is going to be cut. For the system is switching automatically from the electricity board's costly product to a source generated from the waste produced by their large pig herd.' Their farm, which at the time had 350 sows and raised 6,000 bacon pigs a year, had found itself with a problem on its hands. Each pig can generate as much as a gallon of waste a day, and the farm was being threatened with prosecution because it was polluting a nearby stream. By installing an anaerobic digester, which, in the absence of air, can convert 18 tonnes of slurry a day into methane, the brothers used a Ford Cortina engine to drive their generator and turn the methane into electricity. Waste heat from the engine is used to pre-heat the slurry before it is fed into the digester, and the process leaves a residue which can be used as a fertilizer.

Smaller units are in use throughout the world. Remember the deforestation problem in Nepal? Several hundred biogas plants fuelled by cow dung had been brought into operation in an attempt to cut down the use of fuelwood. In a country where cattle are not killed, for religious reasons, there are almost half as many cows as there are people. But the experience of the Indian sub-continent with biogas plants, also known as gobar gas plants, has not been entirely a happy one.

The problem has been that the methane-producing process involves a series of bacteria, the first of which decompose the organic materials and the latter of which synthesize methane. These biochemical reactions, however, are extremely sensitive to shocks, such as rapid fluctuations in temperature, acidity or in the rate at which the system is fed with new material – making it very difficult to obtain a steady supply of biogas from the digester. Sometimes, most of the energy produced by the digester has been needed simply to keep it warm enough for the digestion to continue.

In India, cow dung is used, being mixed into a slurry and poured into a tank at a temperature of about 35°C (95°F). By keeping the tank underground and insulating the uppermost parts, the process can be made rather more efficient. But of the 100,000-odd biogas plants built in India's one million villages, most are believed to be no longer fully functional. Indeed Earthscan has argued that, 'where gobar gas has been used, there is some reason to believe that it may have worsened the energy problems of the Indian poor, since it is only the relatively rich farmers of the village who can afford to put up a plant. The poor, who used to collect cow dung from the fields and burn it for cooking, find that even this inefficient, smelly and smoky resource is no longer available'.

China, by contrast, uses digesters which can convert animal, crop and human wastes into methane, and reported to the UNERG conference that it had over 7 million such digesters in operation, nearly all of them in its central Sichuan Province. They apparently supply methane to some 30 million people, and in addition there are 150 methane-fired power stations in operation.

Whereas the Indian digesters tend to be fitted with costly steel caps, the Chinese variety rely on cheap cement, with water pressure helping to keep the gas inside. And, while the Indians have had difficulty in persuading villagers to bring in their cow dung to the digesters, China's well-organized commune system overcame this problem. The peasants are paid for the dung, although China does admit that it too has had problems. Indeed, it has ordered a slow-down in the construction of new digesters, while the earlier models are restructured.

Part of the problem in India, and in other countries, has been the taboo about human excreta. This has not been a major difficulty with the Anglian Water Authority, however, which is responsible for treating sewage in a wide area of the east of England. At many larger sewage treatment works in the United Kingdom, methane is collected and used to generate electricity – which is generally used to run plant on the site.

The Authority had run into a difficulty, however, because one of its generators had worn out and it proved too expensive to refurbish or replace. Switching to mains electricity, the Authority's engineers looked around for an alternative use for the methane. By mixing two parts of diesel to one of methane, they found, they could run a small fleet of vehicles, including a large sludge tanker. And, according to Professor James Picken, head of Leicester Polytechnic's department of mechanical engineering, the performance of the diesel vehicles had actually improved since the switch to the methane-blended fuel.

Among the scientists working on biomass gasification when I visited the Solar Energy Research Institute, meanwhile, was Dr Tom Reed, who pointed out that gas has historically been generated from a very wide range of materials, including 'biomass wastes from industry, and from feedstocks varying from camel dung to walnut shells, olive pits, rice hulls and sawdust'. He distinguishes between what he calls 'biomass mines' and energy farms, the latter having already been discussed in this chapter.

In fact, I had visited one 'biomass mine' several weeks before flying out to the States. Whereas energy farms produce energy, in whatever form, year after year, a biomass mine is defined as an accumulation of material which can only be used once for energy purposes. London Brick Landfill, which I visited that summer, has for some time filled its worked-out clay pits with municipal waste shipped in from cities like London. The problem here has been that the decomposing refuse produces methane and other gases, which can seep to the surface, causing explosive concentrations in any buildings, killing trees and imposing odour nuisances on nearby communities.

New methods developed by the industry, including higher compaction rates and refuse densities, have affected the water content and temperature of the fill material, sometimes resulting in higher gas yields – and aggravated environmental problems. At the time, there were already eleven sites producing methane from landfill material in the United States, and another thirty or so were expected to come on stream in the following year. Many of these sites are, in fact, vast when compared with European landfill operations, with refuse-input rates in excess of 5,000 tonnes a day. It has been estimated that such sites could meet perhaps 1 per cent of the United States' total energy needs.

London Brick was collecting gas from its Stewartby landfill site and pumping it to a nearby brick kiln. With the help of the Harwell Laboratory, which had originally started out in life as an atomic research facility, London Brick was monitoring gas flows at five separate wells across the site, and they so exceeded expectations that the site's gas-pumping capacity had to be constantly uprated. Analyses of the resulting gas indicated that air can be drawn into the gas stream if the ground is not properly consolidated, or if the cover material is porous. The presence of the air in the gas is significant because it increases the explosion risk, and it can also inhibit the production of methane by the anaerobic bacteria in the site. As a result, the waste-disposal industry has been thinking seriously of designing its landfill sites from scratch as giant 'bioreactors', with gas production very much in mind. One estimate produced by Harwell suggests that the UK industry as a whole could produce gas equivalent to 5,000 million tonnes of coal. Not, one might say, to be sniffed at.

The search is on, meanwhile, for new micro-organisms able to convert a wide range of feedstocks, whether purpose-grown or generated as a by-product of some other activity, for energy production. Cellulose, for example, would be an attractive source of energy, if micro-organisms could be persuaded to convert it enthusiastically and efficiently enough. Some scientists are working on a microbial route from cellulose to methanol, pointing out that the water content of biomass can prove something of a hindrance if you are using a pyrolysis gasifier, whereas it could well be advantageous in biological conversions – which typically do not need high temperatures or pressurized reactors, and tend therefore to be more energy-efficient.

And there are other applications of micro-organisms under development, like Professor John Pirt's algal bioreactor, which, he has claimed, can fix 18 per cent of the solar energy falling on it. Despite criticisms from other solar scientists, who argued that Pirt appeared to be rewriting the laws of photosynthesis, BP awarded him a £13,000 ($30,000) grant to continue his work. His tubular reactor carries a continuous culture of *Chlorella*, which is fed with ammonia, salts and 100 per cent carbon dioxide. The biomass produced has an exceptionally high starch content, which can be processed into liquid fuels and oxygen.

Using the reactor, Pirt estimated, 100 tonnes of coal equivalent could be produced each year in the form of algal biomass from one hectare of land. Sceptics argued that a more accurate figure might be 30–50 tonnes, but Pirt went on unabashed to predict that 100 million tonnes of coal equivalent – or 30 per cent of Britain's fossil-fuel requirements – could be produced on a land area of 10,000 square kilometres (3,860 square miles).

The main weight of photobiological investigation to date has focused on hydrogen production by complete organisms. When I visited the Solar Energy Institute, Dr Paul Weaver had just returned from a trip to a number of geothermal areas, where he had been hunting down suitable organisms to investigate for hydrogen production. Among the organisms exhibiting hydrogenase activity, which is associated with hydrogen production, are photosynthetic bacteria (e.g. *Chlorobium thiosulphatophilum, Rhodospirillum rubrum* and *Thiocapsa roseopersicina*), cyanobacteria (e.g. *Anabaena cylindrica, Nostoc muscorum* and *Synechococcus elongatus*), green algae (e.g. *Chlorella fusca, Scenedesmus obliquus* and *Ulva lactuca*), red algae (e.g. *Porphyra umbilicalis* and *Porphyridium cruentum*), brown algae (e.g. *Ascophyllum nodosum*) and non-photosynthetic bacteria (*Alcaligines eutrophus, Escherichia coli* and various strains of *Methanobacterium*).

If, David Hall argues, a photobiological system could operate at an overall efficiency of 10 per cent, 'then the world's total current energy needs could be met by turning over only half a million square kilometres to solar energy collection; only 0.1 per cent of the Earth's surface. This area,' he explains, 'is about that same as that of Morocco, Thailand or France, or twice the area of the UK, or one fifteenth that of Australia or Brazil, or three quarters of Texas. It wouldn't be necessary to take over agricultural land, and the sea could provide the water.'

In the UK, he believes, with the total incoming solar energy each year equivalent to 100 times the country's total primary energy consumption, 'we estimate that a tenth of the UK's land area would meet our total energy requirements. In other words, 2 per cent of the land would yield hydrogen equivalent to the country's natural gas consumption, while 4 per cent would match our petroleum or coal needs.' The UK, he notes, 'isn't likely to set aside such large areas for its energy needs, but the area of land needed to substitute for our natural-gas requirements is interesting.'

In the longer term, some photobiologists believe they could dispense with the whole organism approach – and with the problems associated with keeping vast collections of such organisms alive. Instead, they believe, we could use carefully selected components of such organisms. Take *Halobacterium halobium*, a micro-organism which flourishes in the Dead Sea, not far from where Israel's solar-pond work is taking place. *H. halobium* has been the subject of research projects in Britain, Holland, Hungary, West Germany, the USA and the USSR.

The main focus of attention has been the purple-patched membrane inside the micro-organism. This contains a pigment, bacteriorhodopsin, which harnesses sunlight to pump protons from one side of the membrane to the other. This pumping action also appears to take place efficiently even when the cells themselves have been destroyed and only the purple membranes remain. This fact suggests to some of the scientists working on the purple membranes that they might form the heart of low-efficiency, low-cost solar energy facilities for the Third World. According to S. Roy Caplan and Kehar Singh, who have been involved in the membrane research, 'small-scale purple-membrane solar energy converters located on the roofs of dispersed or isolated buildings, especially in the Middle East, where the level of radiation is high throughout the year, appear to be a distinct but distant prospect for the fulfilment of domestic energy needs'.

One somewhat speculative application of the purple membranes would be to produce hydrogen and oxygen via photolysis. If plant chloroplasts can do it, the argument runs, surely systems incorporating such membranes could do so too? But many photobiologists are far from convinced, believing, like Professor Hall, that the best approach may not be to use biological systems direct, but to study them to see how they operate and then to imitate them.

One scientist who takes this view is Lester Packer of the University of California, who argues that it will be 'a long haul to improve materially the existing systems. However, having the basic molecular information on the details of the light-energy conversion process could enable us to develop an efficient system patterned after bacteriorhodopsin. For example, knowing the structural features of the molecule, we could in principle synthesize a small segment that might exhibit the activity we desire'.

Indeed we could and it might. But, in the meantime, there are simpler ways of extracting solar energy from water. Both photobiological and photochemical techniques are still at the experimental stage, whereas our species has been harnessing the energy in the water cycle, which is driven by our solar fusion reactor, for at least 2,000 years. Today it supplies almost a quarter of the world's electricity – and is clearly worth looking at in more detail.

# 12 ⊙ *Turning Tides*

Figure 12.1: The NEL breakwater (source: National Engineering Laboratory).

Sleeping peacefully in their beds, one still night in 1969, the owners of the 'French mill' at Carew, Pembrokeshire, in South Wales, were rudely awakened by an ear-splitting racket coming from the direction of the nearby mill. Built in 1610, to harness the tides in grinding the corn of the lord of the manor and his tenants, the mill had finally been shut down in 1930, after three hundred and twenty years of operation. But then, nearly four decades later, it awoke in the middle of the night, as an exceptionally high tide swept in from the Atlantic.

The tide, rushing in past the mill's great wooden wheel, had dislodged the pin – and released the shackles – which had held it prisoner for so many years. By the time its owners arrived on the spot, it was roaring around and, inside the mill itself, every wheel, cog and shaft was revolving at top speed, with no load of corn to stabilize them.

The resurrection of the Carew tide mill showed that tidal energy is

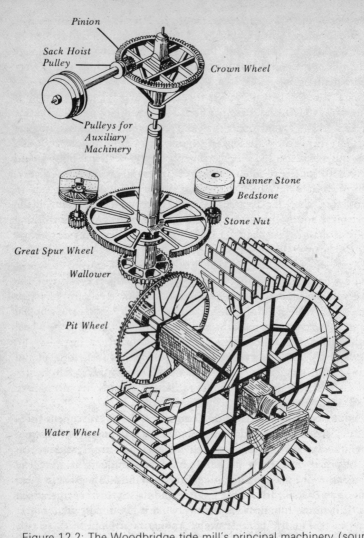

Figure 12.2: The Woodbridge tide mill's principal machinery (source: Woodbridge Tide Mill Trust).

as effective today as ever it was. Figure 12.2 shows how a similar mill, at Woodbridge, Suffolk, worked. The Woodbridge mill is billed by the Woodbridge Tide Mill Trust as the last remaining complete tide mill in the entire North Sea area, and it is certainly one of very few remaining.

The Woodbridge site was first recorded as having a tide mill as long ago as 1170, and there has been a succession of mills on the site ever since. Few lasted longer than 200 years, their foundation timbers rotting away in the waterlogged ground. The Carew mill, by contrast, was built of stone and has lasted accordingly. But both mills would have been subject to intense vibration from the grinding machinery, and fire would have been a constant risk at the Woodbridge mill in particular, where the dry timbers would have caught fire readily in the dust-filled atmosphere. The present Woodbridge mill was working until its main wheel shaft broke in 1957 – only sixteen years before OPEC burst upon the world scene.

At its simplest, a tide mill consists of a dam, together with sluices and a wheel, placed across a tidal estuary. As the tide races in, the reservoir (which may simply be the rest of the tidal estuary) fills with water and, once it is full, the sluices are closed, so that the trapped water is forced to run back through the mill sluice, turning the wheel and driving the mill machinery. Tidal power, in fact, has an impressively long history, with notable schemes in ancient Egypt and another, incorporating four 6-metre (20-foot) reversible water wheels, installed under the arches of the medieval London Bridge in 1580 to pump water. These wheels lasted until 1824.

As late as the Second World War, there were still scores of tide mills in operation around Europe. Indeed, there were over twenty in England alone in 1940, twelve of them actually in use – including the Woodbridge mill. Even in the United States, tidal mills were still working well into the present century. The odd thing about these mills, however, is that although they exploit a source of energy which is to all intents and purposes renewable, it is lunar in origin – rather than solar, like the bulk of the technologies covered in these two chapters on water and wind power. The ways in which solar radiation is translated into water and wind power were briefly covered in Chapter 2 (see pp. 34–5), and will be elaborated upon here. But, first, a few more words about lunar power.

## By the Light of the Moon

If you visit the Carew mill today, you will find its great wheel locked in place with a steel beam: its owners are taking no chances. But elsewhere the tides are being closely investigated as a potential energy source. In fact, while the Moon lights the midnight world, a growing number of people are living in homes lit and warmed by lunar power.

A £50 million tidal power scheme was built in 1967 at La Rance, on the Rance estuary in Brittany, which once boasted fourteen tide mills. The latest scheme has an installed capacity of 240 MW. Much larger schemes are now being considered, including a Russian project on the Arctic White Sea at Mezenskaya, with a very small experimental 400 kW unit already in operation near Murmansk. If built, the Mezenskaya project would involve building an 86-kilometre (53-mile) dam, enclosing a 2,200-square-kilometre (849-square-mile) basin, and generate an estimated 32 TWh (1 terawatt $= 10^{12}$ watts) a year, with an installed capacity of 10 GW.

In the East, a French consortium was brought in by the Korean government to assess potential tidal power sites, and the Indian government has also been thinking about exploiting such sites as the Gulfs of Kutch and Cambay (see Figure 12.3), with smaller schemes

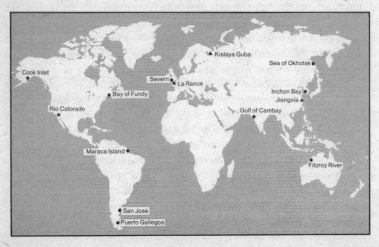

Figure 12.3: Tidal power plants (marked with triangles) and potential tidal power sites (dots) (source: Earthscan).

in the Bengal Sunderbans. Australia has also been considering two tidal schemes for the north-west part of the country at Secure Bay and Walcott Inlet.

The firm which carried out the feasibility study for the Australians, Binnie & Partners, was also involved in assessing the feasibility of the proposed Severn tidal barrage. The Severn estuary, like Canada's Bay of Fundy is an ideal site for a tidal power scheme, and certainly the best available in Britain. To understand why, it may help to look at lunar power in a bit more detail.

The smallest scheme proposed for the Severn estuary would harness something like thirty times more energy than does the La Rance facility. The basic resource which such schemes tap is provided by courtesy of the fact that the Moon is both constantly circling our planet and, at the same time, moving steadily, if almost imperceptibly, away from us. It has been estimated that the total amount of energy dissipated by the tides is about 3 TW ($3 \times 10^{12}$ watts) – or about 100,000 times less than the energy value of the incoming sunshine.

Nonetheless, the potential energy involved is very considerable indeed. Take China, for example. It has been calculated that China has a total tidal power potential of 110,000 MW – a tenth of the total world power demand – in the 500 or so bays in the seven provinces of Fujiang, Guangdong, Hebei, Jiangsu, Lisoning, Shandong and Zhejiang. China has been working on a 500 kW tidal station, working on both ebb and flow tides, at Jiangxia Creek on Yueqing Bay, which faces out on to the east China Sea. This scheme will eventually have six 500 kW turbines.

The tide in Jiangxia Creek rises to a maximum height of 8.39 metres (28 feet) twice a day, but there are many other areas which make sense in terms of tidal power: indeed, the Chinese have been operating another 280 small tide-driven pumping stations along the coast of Guangdong Province since the late 1950s.

Something like a third of the energy which is dissipated in this way is dissipated in a few shallow seas and major bays around the world. The so-called 'equilibrium tide', or the average tide set up by the Moon's influence, is well under a metre high. Tidal power only becomes attractive where this energy is focused or amplified by the topography of the shallow waters of the continental shelf. The Severn estuary is particularly attractive both because it is funnel-shaped (Figure 12.4) and its bed shelves, but also, more unusually,

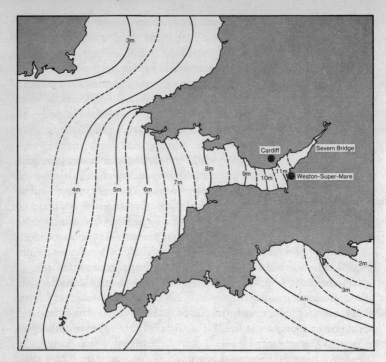

Figure 12.4: The tidal resonance effect in the Severn estuary
(source: Severn Barrage Committee).

because the tides are amplified by a 'resonance effect' deriving from
the fact that the length of the estuary is of the same order of magnitude
as a quarter of the tidal wave length.

The only difference between a tide mill and a tidal power scheme is
that the latter has a turbine – or turbines – where the tide mill has a
water wheel. The water turbine, in fact, currently produces something
like a quarter of the world's electricity. The water turbine was
invented by Benoît Fourneyron in 1820 and, as Daniel Deudney of the
Worldwatch Institute puts it, 'was to the water wheel what the
propeller was to the side paddle – a submersible, compact and more
efficient machine for energy transfer'.

While Britain, faced with major problems in fuelling the Industrial
Revolution with traditional energy sources such as wood and water,
switched to cheap coal, France was in a less happy position as far as

fossil fuels were concerned. Its most abundant energy source was *houille blanche* (literally 'white coal'), and the country's concentration on the development of improved technologies for harnessing hydropower therefore made a good deal of sense.

Tidal power plants, meanwhile, fall into three main categories of increasing complexity – and cost. First, there are the single-basin, single-effect schemes, where the turbine only generates when the water flows out of the basin, so that power is available for only perhaps 30 per cent of the time or less. Second, there are the single-basin, double-effect schemes, where the turbines generate as the basin is being filled by the tides as well as when it is drained. This approach approximately doubles the power produced, while the third approach, involving twin basins, can permit continuous production of power.

Both single-basin and double-basin schemes have been considered for the Severn estuary (Figures 12.5–8). The Severn Barrage Committee eventually recommended a single-basin generation scheme, estimated in 1981 as likely to cost £5.6 billion and produce 13 TWh (or 6 per cent of the current electricity demand in England and Wales), from an installed capacity of 7,200 MW. It rejected the proposed outer barrage (Figure 12.5), on the grounds that it would involve greater engineering risks and more serious environmental impacts, although overall the outer scheme would have provided 20 TWh a year from an installed capacity of 12,000 MW – at an estimated cost of £8.9 billion.

A third proposal involved a staged scheme (Figure 12.7), which would have cost more than the outer barrage, but would have

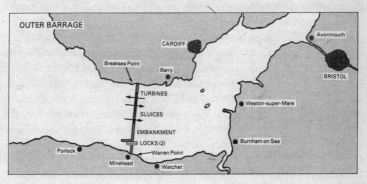

Figure 12.5: Outer barrage design (source: Severn Barrage Committee).

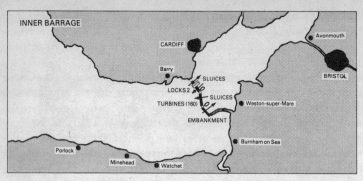

Figure 12.6: Inner barrage design (source: Severn Barrage Committee).

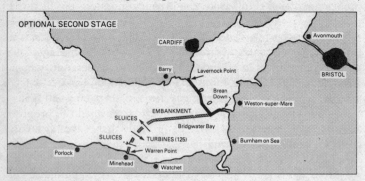

Figure 12.7: Optional second-stage scheme
(source: Severn Barrage Committee).

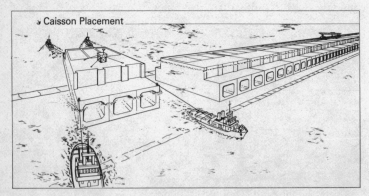

Figure 12.8: Caisson placement (source: Severn Barrage Committee).

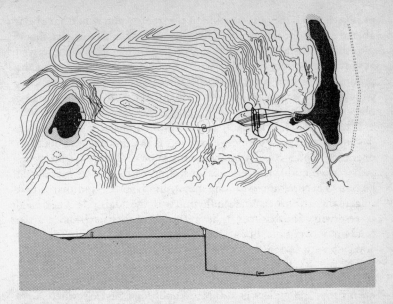

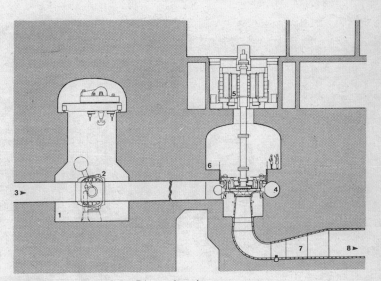

Figure 12.9: Plan of the Dinorwic scheme
(source: Central Electricity Generating Board).

produced about the same amount of electricity – and would have been able to do so sooner. An additional advantage would have been that if the scheme had been able to operate on flood-generation mode as well as on the ebb tide, then the two basins would have permitted the production of four main blocks of power through the 24-hour day, which would be more readily absorbed into the national grid than two blocks.

Whichever design is finally preferred (for things can still change), the Severn barrage's greatest attraction is that once it was built, an operation which could employ a workforce of 21,000 for up to ten years, it would have a very low operating cost – and its fuel would be free. There is, however, one major disadvantage and that is that tidal plant can only generate in rhythm with the tidal cycle. The design of reservoirs and basins can do a great deal to stretch out a given tidal input over time, but even so tidal power output will not always coincide with periods of high electricity demand.

The tidal cycle is 12 hours and 25 minutes, so that each high tide is 25 minutes later than the last. This varying, if unpredictable, cycle meant that the millers at Carew, Woodbridge and elsewhere were forced to work erratic hours. And, of course, there is a limit to how

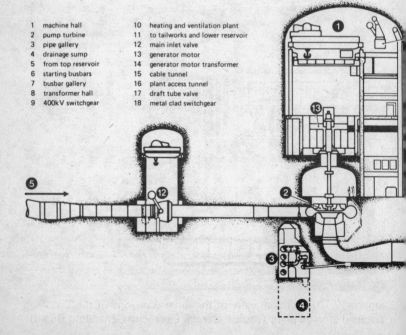

| | | | |
|---|---|---|---|
| 1 | machine hall | 10 | heating and ventilation plant |
| 2 | pump turbine | 11 | to tailworks and lower reservoir |
| 3 | pipe gallery | 12 | main inlet valve |
| 4 | drainage sump | 13 | generator motor |
| 5 | from top reservoir | 14 | generator motor transformer |
| 6 | starting busbars | 15 | cable tunnel |
| 7 | busbar gallery | 16 | plant access tunnel |
| 8 | transformer hall | 17 | draft tube valve |
| 9 | 400kV switchgear | 18 | metal clad switchgear |

long you can hold back the last tidal input if you want to capture the next efficiently. One possible solution to the problem is reminiscent of the Grand Old Duke of York's approach to military affairs: you march your water up to the top of a hill, and then you let it run down again.

## Selling Tidal Insurance

Back at La Rance, power output ranges from 300 MWh a day on spring tides to 740 kWh a day on neap tides. Because of the inevitable mismatch between tidal power production and the periods of power consumption, the La Rance plant has generally been used to displace output at oil-fired power stations. In the same way, the economics of the Severn scheme depends on the amount of conventional power-generating capacity it can replace.

Given that nuclear power stations have been seen as cheaper than coal-powered stations, the future prospects of the Severn scheme will depend on whether Britain relies most heavily on nuclear power or on coal-fired electricity-generating stations. The Severn Barrage Com-

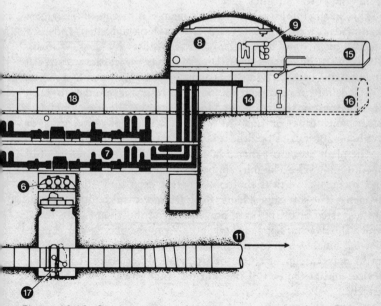

Figure 12.10: Sectional view of the inner workings of the Dinorwic pumped storage plant (source: Central Electricity Generating Board).

mittee pointed out that the prospect for nuclear power is cloudy and argued that tidal power would be a 'valuable insurance against the blackest kind of energy future'.

Where continuous power is needed, a number of energy-storage options are available – including the double-basin technique. Other methods include the storage of compressed air underground, with one relatively small plant (using gas turbine compressors) in operation at Huntorf, West Germany, and pumped water-storage schemes – an approach which has sometimes been used to stretch out the power available from the La Rance power station.

Europe's largest hydroelectric storage scheme at the time of writing is Dinorwic, in North Wales. Begun in 1974, the £460 million Dinorwic project involved the excavation of 3 million tonnes of slate rock to create a network of tunnels through the heart of Elidir Fawr, a mountain in the Snowdonia National Park. The tunnels link two lakes (see Figure 12.9), with water being pumped up from the lower reservoir (on the right of the diagrams) to the upper one, Marchlyn Mawr, on the left. The electricity used to pump the water up from the lower reservoir, Llyn Padarn, to Marchlyn Mawr comes from fossil-fuel and nuclear power plants – and could eventually come from tidal power facilities, too.

The chamber housing the station's main plant is one of the largest man-made caverns ever excavated, twice as long and half as wide as a football pitch – and higher than a sixteen-storey building. With six 313 MW turbine generators, Dinorwic has the capacity to reach an output of 1,320 MW in 10 seconds, by releasing water at a rate of 85,000 gallons per second from the upper reservoir into the labyrinth of tunnels inside the mountain. Once on stream, Dinorwic can inject a constant output of 1,680 MW into the national power grid for five hours, or it can stop dead and await the next peak in demand.

The plant uses more than 1,400 million gallons of water in a full operational cycle. The inlet tunnels are more than half-a-mile long and include a vertical shaft 440 metres deep and 10 metres in diameter. The sort of problems which Dinorwic was built to sort out are suggested by the peaks in power demand shown in Figure 12.11, which shows what happened when ITV ran the film *Dr No* in peak viewing time. Every time there was a commercial break, viewers got up to make a cup of coffee or use some other energy-consuming device, and at the end of the film the total power demand soared fiercely.

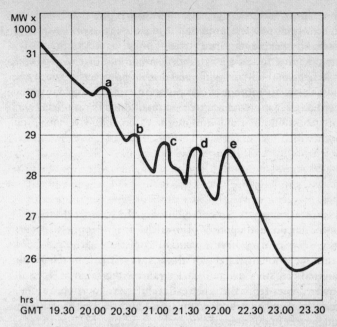

Figure 12.11: The impact of the film *Dr No* on UK electricity demand. The effect of a popular television programme on electricity demand is apparent in this curve, which shows demand peaks occurring during the evening of 28 October 1975 when the film *Dr No* was shown on all ITV Regions. Peaks a and e coincide with the start and finish of the film; peaks b, c and d with commercial breaks. (Source: Central Electricity Generating Board.)

Dinorwic helps to iron out those peaks without placing undue strain on conventional power production plants. It could also fill in for up to two power stations in the event of failures. But, as with any insurance policy, there is a premium to be paid. In fact, Dinorwic consumes more electricity in pumping water to the top of the hill than it generates in allowing it to roar back down through the turbines. For every three units of power it feeds into the grid, Dinorwic consumes four. 'We are not creators,' said Iorwerth Ellis, project manager at Dinorwic. 'We are a sponge. We will absorb what would otherwise be surplus electricity and then give it back to the grid – or three quarters of it – when it is most needed. Electricity,' he pointed out, 'is a fuel that has to be consumed as it is produced.'

But the Central Electricity Generating Board argues that Dinorwic would have been a success even had it never been used, because it enables other power plants to run at their optimum rate continuously, rather than having to undergo the costly wear and tear of repeated changes in pace and output. A far better idea, however, if you want to produce electricity rather than simply store it, is to have your water transferred to the top of the hill free – a task which the sun has been performing continuously and without major breakdowns since time immemorial.

## Water, Water Everywhere ...

'Falling water is the source of one-quarter of the world's electricity', Daniel Deudney pointed out in Worldwatch Paper 44, entitled *Rivers of Energy: The Hydropower Potential*. 'Whether harnessed by a slowly turning wooden water wheel on a tiny stream in Nepal or by a hundred-ton steel dynamo at Aswan on the mighty Nile, all hydropower comes from the ceaseless cycle of evaporation, rainfall and runoff set in motion by the sun's heat and the earth's pull. By harnessing water in one step of this cycle, as it flows back to the sea, water wheels and turbines convert this natural and endlessly renewable energy into a usable form.'

Indeed, as Deudney went on to say, 'the use of hydropower throughout history has been shaped more by social and political considerations than by the availability of a particular technology'. So, although the Romans knew all about water wheels, they did not make extensive use of water power because slavery and, later, under-employment removed any incentive to save on human labour. But the wars and famines which accompanied the collapse of the Roman Empire and, later, the Black Death (which killed perhaps a third of Europe's population) made water wheels much more attractive.

Water-wheel technology also spread to the New World, often flourishing where slavery failed to take root. By the end of the eighteenth century, for example, there were about 10,000 water wheels in New England alone. And then came the age of fossil fuels and of atomic energy.

Interestingly, Professor J. H. Fremlin of Birmingham University has argued that the water wheel killed far more people than has nuclear power. Colour televisions and luminous watches, he argued, present a cancer risk four times greater than that from pollution emerging from a plant like Windscale. Water power, he explained, involved the use of ponds into which people were in the habit of falling and, often, drowning. To use water wheels to produce the electricity generated by a single nuclear reactor, he had calculated, would result in 1,000 drownings a year.

Anyone taken in by this 'statistic' would be likely to believe that hydropower was a technology of the past, whereas today it supplies a quarter of the world's electricity, as we have seen, and 6 per cent of our total primary energy consumption – and its contribution shows every sign of growing significantly in the coming years.

Indeed, over thirty-five countries derive more than two-thirds of their electricity from the water which the sun has airlifted into the mountains. Ghana, Norway and Zambia, for example, all obtain 99 per cent of their electricity from hydropower, while other countries highly dependent on hydroelectricity are Mozambique (96 per cent), Sri Lanka (94 per cent), Zaire (90 per cent), Brazil (87 per cent), Portugal (77 per cent), New Zealand (75 per cent), Nepal and Switzerland (74 per cent), and Australia and Canada (67 per cent).

By the early 1980s, Europe was already exploiting 59 per cent of its total hydroelectric potential, while the Third World was using only 8 per cent of its estimated capacity (Table 12.1). Clearly, most of the world's hydropower potential is still untapped. Some countries, however, have consistently pursued an aggressive approach in this area. Austria, for example, is blessed with the river Danube, with a flow averaging out at about 2,000 cubic metres per second. In the late 1950s, the Danube Power Plant Company recognized a need to build a new hydroelectric power station every three years for the remainder of the century – and has completed a series of high-flow, low-head hydropower stations.

Some of Austria's neighbours who share the river have come to the same sort of conclusion. Along the 3,000-kilometre waterway, some 50 hydro-plants are planned, under construction or in operation in West Germany, Austria, Czechoslovakia, Yugoslavia and Romania. Indeed, in 1981, and against direct advice from the Kremlin (which prefers that its client nations do not co-operate independently), Yugoslavia, Romania and Bulgaria agreed to construct a series of massive hydropower stations along the Danube, with the expectation that some of the surplus electricity likely to be generated could be sold to Greece and Hungary.

*Table 12.1: World hydroelectric potential (source: World Energy Conference, 1980)*

| | Technically usable potential | | Present operating capacity | | Percentage of hydro potential at present harnessed |
|---|---|---|---|---|---|
| | $10^{12}$ kWh | % world total | $10^{12}$ kWh | % world total | |
| North America | 3.12 | 16 | 1.13 | 35 | 36 |
| Europe | 1.43 | 7 | 0.84 | 26 | 59 |
| USSR | 2.19 | 11 | 0.26 | 8 | 12 |
| Oceania | 0.39 | 2 | 0.06 | 2 | 15 |
| North | 7.13 | 36 | 2.29 | 71 | 32 |
| Africa | 3.14 | 16 | 0.15 | 5 | 5 |
| Latin America and Caribbean | 3.78 | 20 | 0.30 | 9 | 8 |
| Asia (excl. USSR)* | 5.34 | 28 | 0.47 | 15 | 9 |
| South | 12.26 | 64 | 0.92 | 29 | 8 |
| World total | 19.39 | 100 | 3.21 | 100 | 17 |

* It is not clear whether the Asia figures cover China. According to data supplied to UNERG by the Chinese, the country's usable hydro potential is $1.9 \times 10^{12}$ kWh, compared with its present capacity of about $0.05 \times 10^{12}$ kWh – implying that China is using only 3 per cent of its potential hydropower capacity.

It has been estimated that if all the energy in all the water flowing into all the world's oceans were to be harnessed, an inconceivable 73,000 TWh could be generated each year. Of course, only a small fraction of this total could ever be harnessed, with total current hydropower production running at about 1,300 TWh – or less than 2 per cent of the theoretical total yield. The World Energy Conference of 1980 estimated that the world's technically usable potential could be of the order of 19,000 TWh, over fifteen times the current output of the world's hydro-stations. These estimates may be open to dispute, but they do suggest that we have some way to go before we reach the physical limits of this particular solar resource.

## Some Flies in the Ointment

Inevitably, there are a number of obstacles in the way of any large-scale programme of investment in hydropower designed to harness this admittedly considerable resource. First, there are geographical problems, with many good potential hydro sites located well away from the main centres of population – a particular problem in a country like China, where the major proportion of the remaining un-tapped capacity lies in the far west of the country and the centres of population are in the east.

Second, and perhaps even more problematic, are the various environmental constraints. Apart from the loss of farmland and of wildlife habitat, a dam can raise the local water-table, waterlogging land, and waterborne diseases, such as schistosomiasis, can increase dramatically. Daniel Deudney mentioned the Aswan Dam. When I visited Aswan, during a project in which I was part of a team responsible for identifying and evaluating the environmental conse-quences of a range of major development projects in the Nile Delta, the incidence of schistosomiasis in the communities around Lake Nasser, which had formed behind the dam, was astonishingly high – although the disease had attracted less international publicity than had the ecological effects associated with the dam's construction.

One hydropower project which generated a great deal of adverse publicity for the Australian government was the proposed A$530 million (£329 million), 180 MW Gordon-below-Franklin dam. The Tasmanian Hydro-Electric Commission (HEC), which operates over 100 dams, wanted the new dam to supply power to energy-intensive industries, particularly in the basic metals sector. Conservationists fought the scheme fiercely, arguing that it would destroy a world-class wilderness – which had just been awarded a UNESCO World Heritage listing.

Hundreds of objectors were arrested, including Professor David Bellamy, the British botanist. 'I hope it is going to be a victory', he said, before being ushered into a Hobart lock-up. 'But if it is a defeat, the world has got to know that Australia has done a pretty bloody shady thing.' Interestingly, the HEC published its own assessment of the cost of rival energy schemes (Figure 12.12) – which suggested that solar energy could be ten times more expensive than hydropower.

Another obvious, but sometimes intractable, problem is that people have to be moved off sites which will be flooded by particular dam

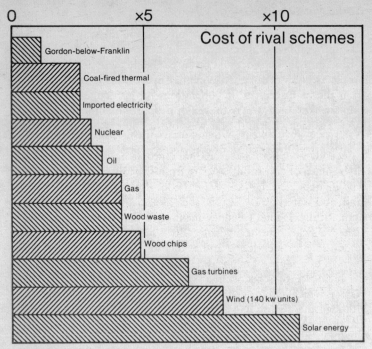

Figure 12.12: Comparison of costs for proposed Gordon-below-Franklin dam with those for alternative energy sources (source: Tasmanian Hydro-Electric Commission).

projects. On the other hand, the resulting reservoirs themselves become a magnet attracting inward migration. The explosive growth of population around many major reservoirs has gone hand in hand with accelerated deforestation, as the people seek out fuelwood, and with severe erosion and dam siltation problems. But even these problems could pale into insignificance beside the possible climatic and other environmental impacts likely to be associated with any major southward diversion by the USSR of the major rivers flowing into the Arctic Ocean.

Two years after I was in Egypt, I visited Iceland, where I found the country's hydropower programme coming up against environmental constraints of a rather different kind. Although Iceland had exploited only 11 per cent of its hydropower potential, the National Power

Company foresaw important constraints on the further development of hydropower projects. Many of the 100 or so potential sites are 'small and economically unattractive', it reports, 'and many others are beset with ecological problems.' Electricity was first introduced to Iceland less than eighty years ago, when a small stream was harnessed at Hafnarfjordur, south of Reykjavík.

Norway's Alta River, one of Europe's best salmon rivers, was the scene of a long-running, bitter battle between the Lapps and the Norwegian government, with hundreds of policemen being drafted in from all over the country to control the irate Lapps – who claimed that the construction and resulting works would ruin the grazing land for their reindeer. In spite of temperatures which fall below $-30°C$, hundreds of people demonstrated against the project, and some went on hunger strike.

A third major set of problems facing those charged with developing a country's hydro potential are political. With more than 200 river basins straddling international borders and other boundaries, international agreements have been essential in preparing the ground for major hydro schemes along such rivers as the Danube, Mekong, Nile and Rio Grande. But perhaps the best example of the political dimension of hydropower to date has been the Itaipu Dam, which should be the world's largest hydroelectric scheme by 1988.

A joint venture between Brazil and Paraguay, Itaipu will have a capacity of 12.6 million kilowatts – about 3.7 million kW more than the ultimate potential of America's Grand Coulee Dam, currently the world's most powerful dam. The plan for Itaipu triggered a flood of protest from Argentina. The Paraná River, which Itaipu is designed to harness, flows on southwards through Argentina – which feared that Itaipu would reduce the water level at its ports, interfering with shipping and spoiling its own hydroelectric plans. The various countries traded threats for a while, but then the dispute appeared to subside.

Seventeen thousand Brazilians and 11,000 Paraguayans have been toiling on the dam, which will be nearly a mile (1.6 kilometres) long and 620 feet (189 metres) high, and is estimated as likely to produce enough electricity to reduce Brazil's oil consumption by 100,000 barrels a day.

A different type of political problem, which has soured some of the major development agencies involved in big hydro projects, is illustrated by Indonesia's Asahan project, in north Sumatra, which was paraded as a shining example of President Suharto's New Order and has been south-east Asia's largest Japanese foreign-aid project. Critics have argued that the $1.8 billion project (1981 figures) is an expensive, low-employment showcase of little immediate benefit to Indonesia, many of whose 147 million people live in abject poverty.

In the early years, almost all of the 250,000 tonnes of aluminium produced by the associated smelter will be exported to Japan, with Asahan producing power at about a fifth the cost of electricity in Japan. The Japanese, worried by the criticisms the project has attracted, have said that they will avoid such gargantuan projects in the future. The experience, said one official, 'has led us to direct future aid at projects which meet basic human needs, or at small-to-middle scale industrial projects, which create more employment and are less open to the criticism of Japan as a selfish, raw-material-hungry giant.'

## An OPEC of Electricity?

Gargantuan the Asahan project may have been, but the statistics for Quebec's hydroelectric plans simply beggar the imagination. In an area the size of England, known as 'La Grande Complex' after the La Grande river, Quebec has been laying the foundations of a vast hydro scheme which will make Canada, in the words of one site worker, the 'OPEC of electricity'. Close to 17,000 workers at the peak of the construction effort will have built nine dams and 170 dykes to create a Connecticut-sized reservoir that could provide 85 years of water supplies to New York City.

Enough sand, gravel and rock are being quarried, it has been calculated, to lay a two-lane, foot-thick highway across the United States. In 1979, the first electricity surged southwards to Montreal and New York from the $16.2 billion undertaking – whose planned output will eventually be equivalent to the output of thirteen nuclear power plants the size of the Three Mile Island facility. When Phase 1 of the project was completed, in 1981, after thirteen years of construction work, enough electricity could be generated to light 171 million 60-watt light-bulbs.

The La Grande scheme had its roots in a decision taken by Robert Bourassa, then Quebec's premier, in 1971. The plan involved developing the James Bay water catchment, an idea which had earlier been rejected because nuclear energy seemed to be the wave of the future. Then after twenty-five nuclear reactors had been built along the St Lawrence River, Quebec declared a *de facto* moratorium on nuclear power in 1976, when new calculations showed that the James Bay project would produce electricity 16 per cent cheaper than the nuclear plants – a competitive edge which has been increasing ever since, for reasons described in Chapter 5.

The scheme, dubbed the 'project of the century' when it was first announced, has been developed by a specially created, semi-independent utility, the Société d'Énergie de la Baie James. Quebec is already planning further hydro schemes, even though the 11,400 M W project alone will almost double the province's installed electricity-production capacity, currently generated by about fifty power stations.

Phase 2 would bring a further 4,600 M W of new hydro capacity on stream by the 1990s, while to the north lie a potential 8,700 M W on the La Grande Baleins river. There has been remarkably little environmental opposition to the Canadian hydro schemes, and few serious environmental problems have yet emerged to compare with those experienced around such projects as the Aswan High Dam.

Provided the environmental aspects of hydro developments are properly assessed, and the appropriate action taken, there is every reason to believe that hydropower will continue to provide very cheap electricity, at least when compared with other generating options, both in the developed and the less-developed countries. The prospects

Table 12.2: *Projected increases in electricity generated from hydropower, 1976–2020 (figures given in exajoules = $10^{18}$ joules; source: World Energy Conference, 1980)*

|  | 1976 | 2000 | (*increase 1976–2000*) | 2020 | (*increase 1976–2020*) |
|---|---|---|---|---|---|
| O E C D countries | 3.78 | 5.37 | (× 1.4) | 7.80 | (× 2.1) |
| Centrally planned countries (incl. USSR and China) | 0.72 | 2.88 | (× 4) | 8.70 | (× 12.1) |
| Developing countries (excl. China) | 1.17 | 4.49 | (× 3.8) | 11.80 | (× 10.1) |
| World total | 5.67 | 12.7 | (× 2.2) | 28.30 | (× 5.0) |

seem particularly bright in the Third World, however, as Table 12.2 suggests.

But many of the schemes will be drastically smaller than La Grande Complex. Given that small or 'mini-hydro' projects in the 200–300 kW range can meet the electricity needs of a small Third World town, the prospects for small-scale hydropower, ranging from less than 1 kW to 10 MW, look very good. China, for example, has built something like 88,000 small hydroelectric stations, averaging 70 kW, although the 1980 schemes averaged 300 kW. Other countries which have surveyed suitable sites include Canada, Indonesia, Malaysia, Nepal, Papua New Guinea, the Philippines, Sweden, Tanzania, Turkey, the United States and Wales.

'The United Kingdom', said one government minister, reporting the findings of a study of the mini-hydro potential of Wales carried out by Salford University, 'although it has a strong tradition in the use of small hydropower, cannot look to this resource to make a large contribution to energy supplies. It can, however, make a worthwhile contribution.' The study had identified 560 sites, each with a potential installed capacity greater than 25 kW.

'The sites', said John Moore, then the parliamentary under secretary of state for energy, 'have been selected to take account of the impact on the local environment and on visual amenity, the topography, the engineering difficulties and the water flow conditions. If all the sites identified in this report were developed, they would produce enough electricity to save at least 80,000 tonnes of oil equivalent each year from an installed capacity of about 70 MW.' The greatest potential for energy production lay with 170 sites which fell in the capacity range 100–500 kW.

A survey in Sweden identified 1,300 sites in the 100–1,500 kW range, while France came up with 3,000–4,000 sites where mini-hydro schemes of up to 4,500 kW could be built simply with prefectural authorization. And the United States? 'America is in the cellar', said Commissioner Georgina Sheldon of the Federal Energy Regulatory Commission in 1981. 'By 1984', she continued, 'Quebec's hydro will light 12 per cent of New York City'. Yet, she implied, the United States was resting on its laurels. Certainly the Grand Coulee Dam still ranked as the world's largest, but nationwide the best hydro sites had already been used and the smaller schemes now required looked like being rather more expensive.

That said, however, those remaining, if small, sites could provide

11–13 per cent of America's electricity, scarcely a contribution to be dismissed out of hand. A survey carried out by the US Corps of Engineers found 2,100 possible mini-hydro sites: 1,400 dams which either had no hydropower plant installed so far or else were fitted with hydro-generators too small for the resource, and 700 totally un-developed prospects.

A major boost for mini-hydro investment in the United States came with the passage of the 1978 Public Utilities Regulatory Policies Act (or, for those enthused by acronyms, PURPA) which required, *inter alia*, that the power utilities buy electricity from the owners or operators of small plants. Furthermore, the utilities were directed to buy in that power at the 'least avoidable' cost. What this means is that if, by using hydro plant, a utility can reduce its output from an oil-fired plant, it has to buy in electricity from anyone wishing to sell the output of their own small-scale plant at a unit cost equal to that of the oil which is saved. So the mini-hydro operator may, in effect, be paid as though he had used oil to generate the power he is selling to the utility.

Elsewhere around the world, the inducements may not have been quite so sweet, but the pressures were such that a growing number of countries were taking the hydro option very much more seriously. Two of the countries listed above as deriving more than two-thirds of their electricity from hydropower, Nepal and Norway, will serve as examples of the trend.

In Nepal, cross-flow turbines, which can generate power from moderate water pressure, are increasingly being used for rural electrification. Electricity derived from flowing water is used to pump more water into irrigation systems, or, alternatively, the water's energy is exploited by means of hydraulic ram pumps. One of the most pressing reasons for the interest in hydropower, as explained in Chapter 10, is the rapid deforestation taking place through vast tracts of the Himalayas. To take just one example, if you want to dry a kilogram of ginger, it can take 10 kilograms of fuelwood; so hydro-power can significantly slow the progress of deforestation. The problem is that the development of Nepal's hydro potential is simply not proceeding at a sufficient pace to keep track with, let alone out-pace, the demand for fuelwood.

Developments in the microprocessor field promise to cut the cost of mini-hydro schemes. A group of British companies, for example, has been demonstrating a new electronic load control device which could halve the cost of constructing mini-hydro schemes. The micro-processor-based system regulates the output of power from the turbines to the grid, regardless of the flow through the turbines. When there are flow surges, the excess power is switched to a 'ballast' circuit – a miniature version of pumped storage. Intermediate Technology Industrial Services (ITIS), Evans Engineering and GP Electronics believe that their system could help countries like China to exploit their hydro resources. China, which already has over 100,000 mini-hydro stations but has only tapped about 3 per cent of its potential mini-hydro resource to date, apparently agrees – it promptly placed a number of orders, having seen the system perform successfully in trials.

In Norway, meanwhile, over 1,000 small hydro schemes have been abandoned since the 1930s, because of competition from cheap oil, while at least 750 have been abandoned in the United States since the Second World War. But Switzerland, in a programme which gives some sense of the shape of things to come, has been refurbishing many of its abandoned hydropower plants.

Mini-hydro projects may be increasingly important in the coming decades, but the headlines will continue to be seized by the big projects – and there is still no shortage of these. Indeed some of them, when built and then eventually abandoned, will make impressive ruins. Israel, for example, has proposed a 110-kilometre (68-mile) canal from the Mediterranean to the Dead Sea, much of its route running far underground, at an estimated cost of some $700–800 million – seen as wildly conservative by some of the project's critics (indeed, the estimated cost had risen to $1.3 billion by early 1983).

The canal idea would exploit the 390-metre (1,300-foot) difference in height between the two seas. Israel's plan has proved to be political dynamite, with various Arab and African delegates storming out of the UNERG Conference when the Israeli delegate got to his feet to speak. Jordan argued that its huge $500 million potash plant on the Dead Sea would be flooded, while others saw the scheme as a ruse to hold on to occupied territory, given that some of the associated works would need to be built on such land and, presumably, would require long-term defence against sabotage.

The project, however, has been warmly received in many quarters in Israel, and could produce in the region of 570 MW (though 1983 estimates suggest 850 MW), perhaps supplying 15 per cent of the country's electricity needs by 1990. Israel does not have the capital resources itself to carry the project through, but there are many who would see such a project as a vital contribution to the country's long-term security, particularly the American Jewish community – so that it would be foolhardy to predict that it will never get off (or under) the ground. If – and when – it does, it will fulfil the prophecies made in a novel written in 1902 by Dr Theodor Herzl, which followed imaginary travellers through Israel in the late twentieth century. 'Before them,' Herzl wrote, 'stretched the broad blue expanse of the Dead Sea, and an ear-splitting din was heard there, the sound of the waters of the canal brought here in tunnels from the Mediterranean pouring down the valleys.'

Egypt, too, has been thinking seriously about tapping the Mediterranean, proposing to construct a canal from the coast into the Qattara Depression in the Western Desert, creating a lake 300 kilometres by 100 (190 by 60 miles), about 60 metres (197 feet) below sea-level. As in the Dead Sea scheme, it is expected that the water reaching the Depression would, in the main, evaporate, so that the water-level would not increase indefinitely. The canal would need to be about 75 kilometres (45 miles) long.

As with other Western Desert depressions, a steep scarp marks the Qattara Depression's northern edge. By exploiting this drop, it has been calculated that 3–5 billion kilowatt hours could be generated every year – a welcome contribution to the 88 billion kilowatt hours which some expect the country to be consuming each year by the end of the century. Advocates of the project argue that it would bring all sorts of side-benefits, including tourism, new fisheries and even improvements in local climate. But there was considerable relief when Egypt announced in the autumn of 1982 that it would excavate the canal by conventional means rather than by using nuclear explosions. In spite of the possible advantages, this scheme could just as easily sour the region's underground water resources, although its environmental implications could well be dwarfed by those likely to be associated with an even more grandiose scheme, designed to exploit the hydro potential of a totally different – if equally hostile – environment.

The idea involves tapping the glacial runoff from the Greenland ice-cap, with summer melt-water being channelled into natural lakes in south-west Greenland. By the time one is talking of projects on this sort of scale, statistics become meaningless, but it has been suggested that such a scheme might provide 120,000 MW of generating capacity, with the electricity being used to produce liquid hydrogen for shipment to the major energy markets – or sent direct via an undersea cable. When compared with the probable obstacles confronting such a scheme, the mountains facing the pioneers of wave power begin to look like the proverbial mole-hills.

## The Wave of the Future?

'Stop lying there looking sorry for yourself', Mrs Margaret Salter is reputed to have told her husband at the height of the first oil crisis; 'Why don't you solve the energy crisis?' Stephen Salter, an engineer at Edinburgh University, was suffering from an attack of flu at the time, but was sufficiently galvanized to repair to his study and begin work. 'What she wanted,' he later told David Ross, author of what was billed as the 'first-ever book on wave energy', *Energy from the Waves* (Pergamon, 1979), 'was something which would provide the vast amounts of energy needed, would be clean and safe, would work in winter in Scotland and would last for ever. It is a good thing,' Salter noted drily, 'to have the design objective clearly specified.'

The idea of extracting energy from the waves was not a new one, although Salter, his colleagues and his competitors have taken the various technologies into areas scarcely dreamed about by earlier pioneers. The first patent covering wave energy, it appears, was filed on 12 July 1799 in Paris by the Girards, father and son. Their idea, according to the patent application, was to construct a gigantic lever, whose fulcrum was to be located ashore, while the wave energy 'pick-up' end of the contraption would be secured to a pontoon, which would rise and fall with the waves.

Since then, some 340 patents have been filed in Britain alone. As far as Salter was concerned, 'the obvious extraction mechanism was something like a lavatory ball-cock, bobbing up and down.' But when he tried out this sort of mechanism, he found that it only captured about 15 per cent of the energy in a wave. If the hinge was placed beneath the water, however, it appeared that the energy-capture rate could be boosted to about 60 per cent. After trying a number of different designs, he finally hit upon the idea of the 'Duck' – a mechanism shaped somewhat like a pine cone, with a pointed end and a rounded end. Bobbing up and down, such mechanisms can extract up to 90 per cent of the energy in waves, with smooth water emerging behind a line of such devices.

The initial response to Salter's ideas in Whitehall was not enthusiastic. The Department of Energy had, in fact, carried out a brief desk study in 1972, but the resulting report had been shelved. Then Salter wrote to Peter Walker, at the time the minister responsible for energy. 'We get a lot of oddball inquiries and schemes into this department,' the civil servant who was asked to deal with the letter later recalled, 'and most of them come my way. We frequently get perpetual motion schemes. Lots of people want to do something about using sawdust. Or painting the Moon another colour. And during the oil crisis there were some very strange suggestions. Salter's letter was from a peculiar address: the School of Artificial Intelligence, Bionics Research Laboratory, Edinburgh University. The letter had been photostated at some stage on its rounds and the thought crossed my mind that if someone was trying to do a hoax it would be easy to cut up a potato and "print" a heading and send off a letter like this.'

The civil servant, Gordon Goodwin, had himself been responsible for carrying out the earlier wave-energy study, and had been surprised at the quantities of energy which might possibly be extracted by suitable devices. It has been estimated, for example, that there are 10 kW of energy in every square metre of ocean. Salter, it soon transpired, was no crank, and neither was Sir Christopher Cockerell, the inventor of the hovercraft, whose 'raft' concept had its roots in the hovercraft experience, where wave damage had been a major consideration in designing the craft's 'skirts'.

The Cockerell Raft was rather like a naval architect's nightmare. As Sir Christopher himself put it, the Raft was like 'a ship that had broken its back. The naval architect goes to school to find out how to design a ship that doesn't do that. Now we have to reverse the drawings.' The Raft was designed as a number of articulated pontoons, following the contours of the waves as they surged in towards the shore.

When David Ross published his book in 1979, during the second oil shock, the Cockerell Raft was still among the front-runners, but by the time the Department of Energy came to assess the various competing systems several years later, the Raft had been overtaken by a number of other systems – although elements of Sir Christopher's design lived on elsewhere. Stephen Salter, for example, had adapted the Raft's power-generating hinge to produce a joint to link a string of Ducks together.

One proposal which was patented during 1979, and therefore was not mentioned in *Energy from the Waves*, was devised by two Lockheed scientists, Leslie Wirt and Duane Morrow. In their design, a dome-shaped structure, some 76 metres (250 feet) in diameter, was built in such a way that it would float just beneath the surface of the water. This device had only one working part, a turbine, which extracted energy (in theory, at least) from waves which, entering openings at the top of the device and being guided thereafter by vanes, spiralled into a vortex inside an 18-metre (60-foot) deep central core. Because the resulting facility combined elements both of an atoll and of a dam, it was dubbed the 'Dam-Atoll' – and little has been heard of it since.

Wave-energy systems can be classified into three main categories: coastal, offshore floating and offshore submerged. The attractions of having your wave-energy facility ashore are obvious. Like an onshore OTEC plant (see Chapter 8), it would be easier to build and maintain, posing less of a hazard to shipping and being less likely to founder in a violent storm. And it would be much easier to feed power from a shore-based facility into the national grid – or into an associated energy-consuming facility – than from an offshore plant.

One onshore scheme was first mooted in 1959, twenty years before David Ross published wave energy's first book. Designed by the British Crown Agents for Mauritius, where south-westerly trade winds provide an almost continuous supply of waves, the idea was to cap a coral reef with a sloping concrete wall, over which the waves would pour. The resulting sea-water would accumulate behind the reef and, given that the lagoon would be some 1.5–2 metres above sea-level, the trapped water could be allowed to drain back into the sea through a turbine. The power provided might not be that great, but a more elaborate scheme involved using the water in the lagoon to pump water uphill into a pumped storage reservoir – affording a much greater head of water.

The Mauritius scheme may yet be built, affording a 20 MW capacity and producing electricity costing only a few pence per kilowatt-hour. Meanwhile, in Norway, another coastal scheme had been developed by the Central Institute for Industrial Research. The basic science involved in the scheme is similar to that in the Mauritius proposal, but the Norwegians added a further refinement which promises a dramatic improvement in the efficiency of wave-energy capture by such onshore schemes.

Led by Philos Even Mehlum, the Norwegian team worked out how to focus waves in very much the same way that an optical lens focuses light waves. Given that the wavelength, and thus the speed, of waves is proportional to the sea's depth, Mehlum's team calculated that a number of horizontal plates, moored or anchored at different depths in about 30 metres of water, would have the desired focusing effect. Two different approaches had been tried; one increased the amplitude of the waves towards a focal point, while the other 'shaped' the waves by shifting the phase of different parts of a wave, just as a lens shifts the phase of different components of a beam of light. Instead of using a lens, however, the experiments used concrete blocks to focus the waves.

The Norwegians were confident that they could extract 80 per cent of the energy in the waves by focusing them from 10 kilometres out at sea on to a single 400-metre strip of coast, building up waves of between 15 and 30 metres in height. To convince sceptics, they were planning at the time of writing to build a pilot facility on the Norwegian coast.

In contrast, both the Duck and the Raft (Figure 12.13) were conceived right from the start as offshore structures, exposed to the mercy of the elements. Other offshore technologies include the Lanchester Polytechnic 'SEA Clam' and the Lancaster Flexible Bag, invented by Professor Michael French of Lancaster University. Belfast University's 'oscillating water column' device, designed to power a large marine navigation buoy, was one of several designs stemming from the work of Professor Yoshio Masuda – whose original proposal consisted of a simple canister floating in the sea, with a couple of holes in the top, allowing air to be sucked in and pushed out through a turbine.

Professor Alan Wells had, in fact, developed a turbine able to generate both on the 'blow' and 'suck' parts of the cycle, and the resulting combination produced by Belfast University was licensed in 1980 by the Ryokuseisha Corporation, based in Tokyo, for use in navigation buoys. Ryokuseisha had sold almost a thousand wave-energy buoys during the previous fifteen years to, among others, Trinity House and the Commissioners for Irish Lights. The Belfast

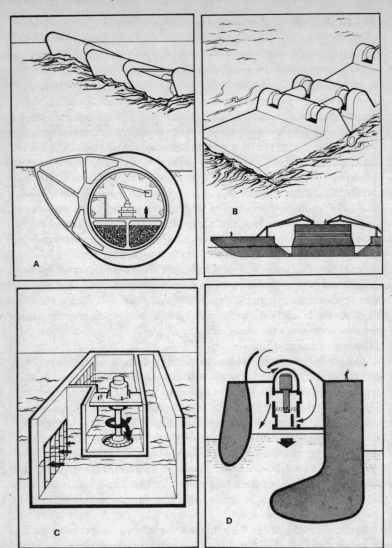

Figure 12.13: Artist's impressions of various wave-energy devices (the human figures on each device are realistically to scale).
A = 'Salter's Ducks'. B = 'Cockerell's Rafts'. C = Hydraulics Research Station (HRS) Rectifier. D = NEL Oscillating Water Column (OWC). (Source: ATOM.)

technology represented an improvement on that previously used by the Japanese, involving a conventional one-way flow turbine and a complicated system of flap valves.

The most successful wave-energy device, however, was Japanese – and it embodied Professor Masuda's concept. If Cockerell's Raft

Figure 12.14: Possible locations for wave-energy devices, with available energy estimates in kW/m annual average (source: Department of Energy)

looked like a ship with a broken back, what was one to make of the *Kaimei*, a ship with large holes intentionally cut in its hull at water-level? The 80-metre ship, built at a cost of $50 million by the Japanese government and the International Energy Agency, converted the fluctuating air pressure generated by the relatively small waves of the Sea of Japan into electricity by passing it through a series of slow-speed turbines.

While the 2 MW *Kaimei* was busy generating, the 'Bristol Cylinder', which was one of the technologies falling into the offshore submerged category, was still on the drawing-board, but it too showed a good deal of promise. Held underwater by chains attached to power generators, the cylinders oscillated in the underspin generated by the waves overhead. Another submerged technology was Vickers' sea-bed generator, a variant of the oscillating water column idea, in which the air that drives the turbine moves around a closed circuit. By contrast, the National Engineering Laboratory's oscillating water column involved a massive structure rather like a breakwater, with the waves entering the structure from its seaward side, driving air through a turbine, and then pouring out the back.

Britain's 'wave climate' is particularly attractive as far as wave energy is concerned, with a number of suitable sites stretched out between Cornwall and the Outer Hebrides (see Figure 12.14), but it was by no means clear, as oil prices plummeted during 1982 and 1983, that the Department of Energy was going to continue its support for the various research projects. In an atmosphere of mounting tension, the competing teams argued their respective cases wherever and whenever an opportunity afforded itself.

## The Simple-minded Engineer

Salter's Duck was, by anyone's standards, a far more complicated piece of engineering than were most of its competitors. It used gyroscopes to capture and store energy, and, unlike some other technologies, it was best suited to mass-production techniques rather than once-off construction techniques. Concerned that this apparent complexity was in danger of losing him the race, Stephen Salter took time off from his research to challenge the notion that simple solutions work best.

While admitting that the Duck was a twenty-first-century technology, he cited the bicycle as an example of the fact that simple solutions are not necessarily the best engineering solutions. The bike may look simple, but, to succeed, cycle technology 'needed the invention, development and production of ball bearings, sprockets, roller chains, the free-wheel and gear-changing mechanisms. The pneumatic tyre required advances in the processing of rubber. Lightweight frames needed thin-walled drawn steel tubing. The most expensive bicycles today,' he argued, 'use tubing with carefully graded wall thickness to give extra strength near the ends. If you think that bicycles are simple', he concluded, 'try building one with the tools and materials in a blacksmith's forge.'

All true, of course; but the immediate question in the minds of the politicians was 'which technology is ready for scaling up?' Only three wave-energy technologies were ready at the time: the SEA Clam, the Lancaster Flexible Bag and the NEL's oscillating water column. And of these three, only Norman Bellamy's team at Lanchester Polytechnic believed that it was ready to go the full hog and build a spine some 180 metres long, 10 metres high and 8 metres wide. The spine, it was estimated, would displace 18,000 tonnes, providing a 2.5 MW capacity, and cost £10 million. Backed by Sea Energy Associates (SEA), made up of Ready Mixed Concrete, Cawood and Fairclough Construction, the Clam team calculated that a full-scale device would involve 320 units, each 275 metres long, would weigh 44,000 tonnes and would generate 2,000 MW.

As long ago as 1980, in fact, consultants Rendell, Palmer and Tritton had reported to the Energy Technology Support Unit (ETSU), which was responsible for running the Department of Energy's renewable-energy programme, that both the Bristol Cylinder and the Lancaster Flexible Bag could produce electricity at less than 5 pence per kilowatt-hour (or 'unit'), within the cost range of power produced by oil-fired and coal-fired generating stations. By 1982, Rendell, Palmer and Tritton had also accepted that the Clam could meet this target, based on the performance of a one-tenth scale model on Loch Ness.

Interestingly, by that time the Clam no longer looked like a clam, although it had been decided to keep the name. It had lost the original steel 'shells', designed to take the full force of the waves, for reasons of economy – their elimination cut the Clam's costs by about 20 per cent. Now it is a relatively simple structure, with a series of flexible Kevlar fabric air-bags mounted along a long, hollow spine of reinforced concrete. Passing waves would push the bags in towards the spine, it was argued, forcing air out and through a turbine. It was, in many respects, a very similar technology to the Lancaster Flexible Bag, except that the Flexible Bag had ducts to feed air to big central turbines, while the Clam had a small turbine for each of its air-bags.

It was estimated that a full-scale 10 MW generating unit would have ten clam bags attached to a 275-metre spine, moored at an angle to the approaching waves. The full 2,000 MW (or 2 giga-watt) scheme, which would be equivalent in power output to a coal-fired station like Drax B, was costed (at 1981 prices) at £3,400 million.

The National Engineering Laboratory's oscillating water column (as embodied in the breakwater: see Figure 12.1, p. 281) may yet be the first wave-energy technology to achieve scale-up. Convinced that there will be an important market for wave-energy devices, the UK Department of Industry decided in 1982 to part-fund a feasibility study, costed at £675,000, for a £12 million, 4 MW oscillating water column demonstration plant off Lewis in the Outer Hebrides. Such a plant would produce power at twice the cost of existing diesel plant, but later, larger stations should be 40-per-cent cheaper than diesel generators.

Among the questions which have been asked about such wave-energy capture devices, one which has surfaced constantly, is whether they can cope with the continued buffeting they would receive over a period of, say, twenty years. Remembering that a 17-metre wave is about the same height as a six-storey block of flats, it is chasten-ing to think that the weather-ship *Weather Reporter* in 1971 en-countered a 26-metre wave in the North Atlantic – and higher waves still have been reported. This was one reason why NEL switched from a moored, floating oscillating water column to the breakwater design, which sits directly on the sea-bed.

Some critics also ask whether it will be possible to convert the high-torque, low-angular-velocity power of waves into the low-torque, high-angular-velocity power used in running most machines. And, they suggest, the problems of getting the power ashore may well prove rather more difficult than the enthusiasts imagine.

Wave-energy technology will inescapably be capital-intensive, and relatively few countries have access to the appropriate 'wave climate'. But for those that do, and Britain is a prime example, the prospects may yet prove sufficiently attractive to launch a major programme of construction and deployment. Surprisingly, though, we still have a good deal to learn about the waves which ceaselessly pound our shores.

Few people, for example, realize that a wave can travel a thousand miles without a single gallon of sea water moving further than a few hundred metres. One analogy which has been dreamed up to illustrate the phenomenon is that of a carpet: lift a corner and shake it, and a wave travels across the floor – but the pile stays where it was when the wave has passed through. In just the same way, the fact that a wave travels, say, from the Atlantic to Cornwall does not mean that a cold current of water has sliced through the middle of the Gulf Stream. But there are many areas where science still has some way to go in coming to grips with wave energy – and, since we have mentioned the Gulf Stream, in coming to grips with current power.

## Submarine Windmills

Dive into the sea between Orkney and Shetland, in the English Channel or near Alderney, in the Channel Islands, and the chances are you will end up some way from your starting-point – provided you can stay afloat. All around the world, fierce currents sweep through the ocean waters, representing a significant potential source of energy. As usual, however, the problem is: how to harness it?

A 4-knot (2.1-metres-per-second) current can contain about 4.4 kW of energy per square metre. An obvious, though by no means simple, way to tap this power is to suspend an underwater version of the windmill in the current. It has been estimated, for instance, that a vertical-axis machine with 100-metre (330-foot) blades would have a power output of 10 MW in a 4-knot current. But what would such a scheme look like in practice? Scientists working on a plan to tap the energy of the Gulf Stream think they have a pretty good idea.

'This is no blue-sky scheme,' project director Peter Lissaman told *Omni*. 'It isn't a Buck Rogers flight of fancy. It really will work. The materials to build the thing are available today – we're not waiting for the development of any exotic controls or superstrong structures. The design is based on well-understood hydrodynamics. Constructing and installing it involves standard marine and offshore oil-rig engineering and practice. And the electrical and transmission components are all off-the-shelf items.'

Lissaman's involvement in the *Coriolis–1* project took some people by surprise, given that he had earlier been involved in the pioneering flights mounted by Dr Paul MacCready, and particularly in the design of the *Gossamer Condor* and *Gossamer Albatross*. However, Lissaman thought it made sense, pointing out that his work on current power came directly out of research he had carried out earlier in Sweden, where he had looked at the ways in which a collection of windmills interfere with each other's supply of wind – or, to put that a bit more positively, at how close windmills can be placed to each other without damping the performance of downstream machines.

In 1973, the same year Stephen Salter was sent packing to his study, Professor Bill Mouton, a New Orleans engineer and architect, stood on the flooding banks of the Mississippi and wondered how all the energy in that mighty river might be put to good effect. The idea of a submerged windmill occurred to him, but the more he thought of it, the more he was convinced that the Gulf Stream represented a far better prospect.

Just 32 kilometres due east of Miami, for example, the Gulf Stream surges past at about 2.5 metres per second – or 7 kilometres an hour. But Mouton's first published proposal attracted a good deal of scepticism. The turbines, he was told, would be torn apart by underwater stresses. If they survived those, then they would provide less than a tenth of the energy he expected. And, even if they managed to produce energy, he was told, the giant turbines would slow the Gulf Stream, causing changes in the climate. The circling blades would mince fish, and the structures would sink unwary shipping. Apart from which, they told him, the whole thing would cost the earth.

Not so, said Lissaman, when he carried out an intensive study of the concept. 'I showed that the Gulf Stream is a massive energy system,' he recalls, 'more powerful than anyone had believed. It contains fifty times as much energy as all the rivers in the world put together. Taking out ten thousand mega-watts would be an *Augenblick* – a blink of the eye – compared to the total amount of energy in the system. In all likelihood you won't even know the turbines are out there.'

Mouton, in fact, had come up with two strokes of genius in the meantime. First, he decided to make the turbine blades limp, not rigid. They would be catenary or free-hanging blades, taking their shape from the passing water – just as the suspension cables of, say, the Golden Gate Bridge take their shape by hanging in gravity. Such blades are very strong indeed, since they do not have to withstand twisting or bending forces. And his second idea was equally striking. Whereas energy is usually taken off from an axle, Mouton saw that the sort of axle which would have been required would have needed to be impossibly strong.

Instead, he suggested that the power could be drawn from the outside tips of the blades and that, to keep the whole structure steady in the water, there should be two sets of blades for each turbine, rotating in different directions. But what about the environmental impact?

Lissaman's calculations, in fact, showed that 230 *Coriolis*-type turbines arrayed between points 32 kilometres east and 192 kilometres north of Miami would slow the Gulf Stream by less than one per cent, and would change the temperature by less than a couple of millionths of one degree Celsius – both small fractions of the natural variation in the Gulf Stream's speed and temperature.

As for the effect on shipping, Lissaman reported that there would be 'none whatsoever. These turbines will be moored some hundred feet below the surface, far below any ships and, incidentally, protected from even the worst storms on the surface. Only the boys in a ship's sonar room will know anything's down there. As for the impact on the Gulf Stream, I've calculated that merchant shipping is already putting much more energy and more heat perturbations into the water than the entire *Coriolis* Project will.'

But what about the fish – or whales? Lissaman is convinced that a whale could push the blades aside. 'Remember,' he pointed out, 'these blades are spinning *very* slowly, about three or four metres per second. You try catching a trout by moving your net through the water at three or four metres per second and see how well you do. The biggest fish in the ocean could swim through these blades without even being touched, much less injured, which is to say that the little fish probably won't even know the turbine is there.'

Japan, Peru and South Africa are among the countries that could harness major currents, which are, in effect, solar power twice removed – given that solar energy (coupled with the earth's shape, rotation and tilt) makes the winds blow as they do, and the winds (coupled with the direction of the earth's rotation) produce the currents.

Perhaps the most important obstacle facing Mouton and Lissaman is the simple problem of visualizing the scale of their project. Each turbine, for example, would be encased in a circular aluminium hull which would (Lissaman would say *will*) be 168 metres across. Or, to put it another way, you could just about take three Boeing 747 jets and stick them wing-tip to wing-tip across the mouth of each turbine. If and when the full set of 230 turbines are moored in the Gulf Stream, it is estimated that they could produce 10,000 MW, equivalent to the output of ten nuclear power stations or the electricity needs of Florida.

And the cost? Lissaman calculates that it would cost $10 billion to construct and deploy all 230 turbines, which, given that they would produce something like 10 billion watts of power, would work out at one dollar a watt – which, if it were achievable, would be cheaper even than nuclear energy is argued to be. 'I have no doubts that there will be problems and heartbreaks,' said Lissaman, 'as there always are in any plan of this scope. I honestly compare this with the building of the Suez Canal. It's that big, that costly, with the same interesting legal international ramifications. Who owns those waters? Who owns the ocean bottom where these engines will be anchored? How will we distribute the power to the different states?'

Given these problems, the faint-hearted are likely to say that if we have to capture wind energy, we may as well do it direct rather than at second-hand, via the currents or waves, and we could keep our feet dry the while by building our windmills on solid ground, rather than stringing them out in the ocean depths. But there is nothing faint-hearted about the windmills which Boeing has been building near Goldendale, Washington State.

# 13 ⊙ Wind Farmers

Figure 13.1: An artist's impression of a wind farm
(source: U K Atomic Energy Authority).

'Did I not tell your worship they were windmills?' the loyal, if slightly confused, Sancho Panza asked his battered master shortly after Don Quixote de la Mancha had charged a collection of thirty or forty windmills on the plains of Montiel. When Don Quixote's lance lodged in the great circling sail of one windmill, which the knight had mistaken for a giant, both he and his mount were lifted off the ground – and then rudely dumped when the lance shivered into pieces. 'And who,' Sancho Panza observed, 'could have thought otherwise, except such as had windmills in their head?'

Today, when a small but growing number of scientists and engineers might be said to have windmills on the brain, it is hard to imagine how important such machines once were. Introduced to medieval Europe from the Arab world, via Persia, the windmill is thought to have been used first in Babylon, for irrigation. The concept probably arrived in Europe, as did a great deal of value, in the impedimenta of the returning Crusaders. By the end of the twelfth century, in fact, windmills were increasingly common, and by 1400 the wind had become such an important source of energy that the Vatican, in the shape of Pope Celestine III, was laying claim to a tithe on all windmills.

In their heyday, during the late eighteenth and early ninteenth centuries, there were something like 10,000 windmills operating in Britain, with another 10,000–12,000 in the Netherlands, and perhaps 1,800 in Germany. They were used for pumping water for drinking and irrigation purposes, as in ancient Babylon, but also for grinding grain, crushing oil-seed, sawing wood, and making paper.

The typical Dutch windmill, with its great sweeping sails, could deliver an estimated 30 kW in a wind blowing at about seven metres a second (or Force 4). As indicated in Chapter 11, a windmill in an exposed location might achieve an output of about 10 kW on average, which over a full working day might be worth about 240 KWh. 'The traditional Dutch windmill,' says wind-power engineer Dr Peter Musgrove, of Reading University, 'could do the work of more than two hundred men, or several tens of horses or oxen: hence its importance for so many centuries.'

It is very unlikely indeed, however, that a latter-day Don Quixote would find windmills like those on the plains of Montiel if he returned several years hence. 'Despite the very substantial cost increases over the last decade,' Dr Musgrove points out, 'energy is still relatively inexpensive when seen in a historic perspective. One can still purchase the energy equivalent of a man working hard all day, in the very convenient form of a kilowatt-hour of electricity supplied to one's home, office or factory, for approximately four pence. The output of a traditional Dutch windmill would conse-quently be valued at only about £10 per day, insufficient to pay the attendant's wages, and with no surplus to provide any return on the capital that would need to be invested in the windmill's con-struction.'

As with tidal power or hydropower, the fuel may be cheap or free, but the initial capital costs can be very substantial indeed. But Dr Musgrove is only one of those who believe that we are either at (or even past) the point at which investing that capital in wind-energy machines makes real commercial sense. The machines they have in mind, however, are radically different to those which Don Quixote so rudely encountered. But, first, where does this free fuel come from?

## The Answer's Blowing in the Wind

Only a very small proportion of incoming solar radiation is converted into the kinetic energy of the winds, although this small proportion still represents a massive total amount of energy, far more than our industrial societies consume each year. As usual, however, the problem lies in converting even a small fraction of that energy into useful work.

'Two basic meteorological phenomena give rise to the bulk of the world's winds,' says senior Worldwatch Institute researcher Christopher Flavin in *Wind Power: A Turning Point* (Worldwatch Paper 45). 'One large pattern of global air circulation stems from cool polar air being drawn towards the tropics to replace lighter, warmer air that rises and then moves towards the poles. Areas of high and low pressure naturally develop and the force of the earth's rotation causes air to circulate clockwise in the southern hemisphere and counterclockwise north of the equator. These broad patterns are responsible for major weather features such as the persistent trade winds in the tropics and the prevailing westerlies found in the northern temperate regions.'

The second major factor influencing the world's winds tends to be rather more local in effect. Given that the air over the oceans is not heated up as much as that over the land, cooler air is drawn in towards the land as the warmed air there rises. 'The net result,' says Flavin, 'is dynamic, unstable weather systems of enormous complexity. The thermal energy of sunlight is constantly converted to the kinetic energy of the winds, but wind energy is simultaneously dissipated via friction with the earth's surface and within the wind itself. Only a very small portion of the wind's energy can actually be used,' he stresses. 'Most winds occur at high altitudes or over the oceans and are therefore inaccessible. Even the most ambitious wind-energy schemes would tap only a small fraction of the total resource, somewhat akin to occasionally lifting a bucket of water out of the Amazon River.'

Given that the power extractable from the wind is, as the scientists would say, proportional to the cube of the wind speed, relatively small variations in the annual average wind speed can produce very significant variations in the energy produced by a windmill – or aerogenerator, as the newer wind-energy machines are called. As Table 13.1 shows, doubling the wind speed increases the available power

*Table 13.1: Average wind speeds and power densities*
*(source: Earthscan)*

| Average wind speed: metres/sec. | miles/hr | Power density in wind (watts per square metre) | Output (in watts per square metre of sail) at three levels of efficiency: 5% | 15% | 30% |
|---|---|---|---|---|---|
| 2 | 4.5 | 10 | 0.5 | 1.5 | 3 |
| 3 | 7 | 35 | 1.7 | 5.2 | 10 |
| 4 | 9 | 82 | 4.1 | 12.3 | 25 |
| 5 | 11 | 160 | 8.0 | 24.0 | 48 |
| 6 | 13.5 | 276 | 13.8 | 41.5 | 83 |
| 7 | 15.5 | 439 | 22.0 | 65.9 | 132 |
| 8 | 18 | 655 | 33.0 | 98.0 | 197 |
| 9 | 20 | 933 | 47.0 | 140.0 | 280 |

eight-fold. A 5-per-cent efficiency (see the third column from the right) is characteristic of a relatively unsophisticated multi-bladed wind pump (drawing 4 in Figure 13.2), millions of which were in use during the nineteenth and early twentieth centuries. A 10-per-cent efficiency might have been achieved by a well-designed and carefully located traditional sail mill (drawing 1 in Figure 13.2), while a modern aerogenerator or wind turbine can readily achieve a 30-per-cent efficiency.

A great deal obviously depends on how constant the winds are, and on their speed, but their timing in relation to the periods when work needs to be done or when electricity is consumed is also vitally important. As Flavin puts it, 'wind power may be more economical in northern Europe, where peak electricity demand coincides with higher winter winds, than in parts of the eastern United States, where the greatest need for electricity occurs during the summer doldrums. Geographically speaking, wind energy is of course most valuable in areas where people live and where energy use is high. The enormous

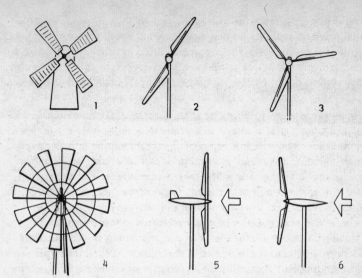

Figure 13.2: Horizontal axis windmill designs (source: Earthscan).

wind-energy potential of the Himalayas, for example, is unlikely ever to be tapped to a large extent.'

Windmills have been erected during a number of anti-nuclear demonstrations, most notably at what is intended to be the largest nuclear power plant in Europe, at Plogoff, in Finistère, France. In fact, although France has been investing tremendous sums in nuclear energy, it has also been tinkering with windmills. The French state electricity company, Électricité de France, has been experimenting with a 100 kW windmill on the island of Ouessant, off the Brittany coast. And, between 1958 and 1962, a 800 kW wind-powered plant was connected to the grid at Nogent-le-Roi, near Paris. In the mid-1960s, a couple of windmills (one rated at 132 kW and the other at 1,000 kW) were built at Saint-Rémy-des-Landes, in the south-west of the country. These experiments, however, were abandoned when France turned to inexpensive oil in the 1960s and to nuclear energy in the 1970s.

But a country which perhaps best meets the twin characteristics of wind availability and concentrations of population and energy demand is Holland, often thought of as the 'land of windmills' and, in fact, picked in 1975 by the International Energy Agency as the lead country for wind-energy research.

## Energy Polders Need Dutch Courage

It is extraordinary to think that as late as 1900 one quarter of Holland's industrial energy came from windmills. While countries like Britain, where the invention of the steam engine and the availability of abundant coal gave a massive boost to the Industrial Revolution, left their tide mills, their water wheels and their windmills to rot, the Dutch had a much poorer fossil-fuel base and concentrated instead on the improvement of the windmill. And Holland has been at the cutting edge of the new efforts to harness wind energy.

During the early 1980s, for example, the Dutch government was debating whether to combine two of the country's oldest technologies, dyke-building and windmills, in a revolutionary scheme designed to convert intermittent wind energy into a firm, reliable source of power.

This, the so-called 'Lievense plan', was named after Lukas Lievense, a private engineering consultant who suggested the basic concept to the government in 1979, and envisaged a huge 'energy reservoir' set within a new dyke, which would rise up 30 metres (98 feet) out of a vast lake north-east of Amsterdam. Whereas electricity normally has to be consumed as it is generated, pumped storage schemes such as Dinorwic mean that energy can be stored until it is needed, and the Lievense plan, which is designed around the idea of an 'energy polder', is a development of the pumped storage principle.

An advisory committee, after a year-long study for the Dutch Ministry of Science Policy, came out with a forceful endorsement of the plan, concluding that it should be started as soon as possible. The committee suggested that the government begin with a 55-square-kilometre (21-square-mile) reservoir enclosed by a 30-kilometre (18.6-mile) dyke – itself contained within the Afsluitdijk (or 'enclosing dyke') with which the Dutch turned the former Zuider Zee into the Ijsselmeer lake.

If construction of the dyke, which would include two hydroelectric stations fitted with reversible turbines (each providing about 800 MW), were to begin by 1985, the committee said, the first station could begin producing power by 1990, and the second could be on stream by 1995. The final phase, if it was thought economically worthwhile, would involve the construction of a 110-square-kilometre (42.5-square-mile) reservoir in addition to the earlier 55-square-kilometre reservoir, this time enclosed within a 55-kilometre (34-mile) dyke. This would include another power station, bringing the total projected electricity output by the year 2000 to 2,400 MW (or 2.4 gigawatts).

Ultimately, it is thought, some 1,050 wind turbines would be needed, each rising some 80 metres (262 feet) into the sky – a fact which critics of the scheme say will lead to 'horizon pollution', arguing that modern aerogenerators bear no resemblance whatever to the traditional Dutch post mill. Lukas Lievense retorted that the alternative was to rely on nuclear power and imported fossil fuels. He also believed that such environmental problems as possible interference with bird migration routes could be resolved by the careful siting of the windmills.

The scheme's supporters, including the advisory committee, have compared the price tag of $3.2–5 billion with the potential energy savings and suggest that it could show a profit of $400 million by the end of the century. The project could, moreover, cut Holland's oil consumption by perhaps 1.5 million tons a year, worth between 1 and 2 billion guilders if fuel prices rose by an average of 2–4 per cent a year. The electricity utilities would need to import less oil, estimated at 8-per-cent less, while the project development programme would provide something like 71,500 man-years of work and, once the scheme was built, 1,650 full-time jobs.

Dutch scientists have, in fact, calculated that if 5,000 wind turbines were placed along the country's 250-mile (402-kilometre) west coast, they could yield about 20 per cent of the electricity currently produced in Holland. The experimental 300 kW wind turbine at the national energy research centre at Petten, a small town on the west coast, has provided a good deal of experience with the operation of large windmills.

Although the Dutch wind-energy research programme has been fairly modest, the co-ordinator of the Petten research, Gijsbrecht Piepers, stresses that Holland's scientific approach has paid dividends. The Petten wind turbine was packed with monitoring equipment to assess the stresses on the 25-metre (82-foot) rotor blades and on the axle which drives the generator. The Dutch opted for a two-bladed design for reasons of economy, and built the turbine to operate at wind speeds of between 5 and 17 metres a second, which would provide power for nearly 200 full days a year. They picked a horizontal-axle machine (all the designs shown in Figure 13.2 are horizontal-axle designs) because the technology is further developed than is the vertical-axle technology pioneered by Peter Musgrove and others, even though the latter is independent on wind direction and the rotor blades can be cheaper to make.

The Petten scientists had originally hoped to build two comparable turbines, one with a horizontal axle and the other with a vertical axle, but their budget failed to stretch sufficiently. A small vertical-axle machine, with 5.5-metre (18-foot) blades, was built by the Fokker Aircraft group, at its Schiphol Airport headquarters, but, after tests, this was later dismantled. Some vertical-axle configurations are shown in Figure 13.3.

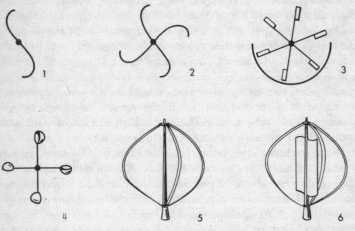

Figure 13.3: Some vertical-axis windmills. Unlike horizontal-axis machines, which have to be pointed into the wind, vertical-axis windmills will work whatever direction the wind comes from. Drawings 1–4 are viewed from above. The single-bladed (1) and double-bladed (2) Savonius rotors are proven designs. The flat-plate rotor (3) is easier to make, but requires a windshield. The cupped rotor (4) is often used for wind-speed indicators, while the phi-Darrieus rotor (5), looking like an egg-whisk, was invented in France in 1927. The final drawing shows a hybrid Savonius–Darrieus rotor. (Source: Earthscan.)

At this stage it is perhaps appropriate to point out that, while there are two basic types of windmill, the horizontal- and vertical-axis configurations, there are also two different modes of operation: *drag*, where the rotors (like the sails on a ship) cannot move faster than the wind, and *lift*, where, with the use of aerofoil blades, high rotational speeds and efficiencies can be achieved.

Whereas Holland chose two-bladed wind turbines, Denmark, whose Department of Energy had estimated that 10 per cent of the nation's electricity could be generated from the wind by the late 1990s, has tended to favour three-bladed designs, like the third drawing in Figure 13.2, arguing that the two-blade designs tend to be less stable and efficient. The three-blade design dates back in Denmark to a 24-metre (78.7-foot) diameter machine, rated at 200 kW, built at Gedser after the Second World War. This ran for ten years, until competition from oil forced it out of business. It was revived in 1978, however, for two years of experimental work – and was claimed to be the world's only large aerogenerator to have survived a life-time of normal service.

Having developed the first aerogenerator, as long ago as 1890, the Danes' interest in windmills spans all sizes of machine, from the Trind 2 MW (54-metre-diameter) machine – once the world's largest, and built in 1977 with volunteer labour – through to much smaller models, including those generating less than 100 kW. Among the designs which have been tested at the Risø National Laboratory are Ulrik Poulsen's Innoventic, a 30 kW machine built like a crane with a two-bladed aluminium rotor held at the end of a long jib slanted at 30° to the horizontal, and the so-called 22 kW 'blacksmith's mill', a design which has been promoted by the Danish Blacksmiths Association – which was initially attracted by the simplicity of the design and by the fact that it can be built by local tradesmen using inexpensive steel angle struts.

As far as larger wind turbines are concerned, the Danish experience has not been entirely happy. Two 40-metre (131-foot) diameter turbines, built to slightly different designs but both having a rated output of about 630 kW, have been tested at Nibe, near Aalborg, but have been plagued with problems. Project leader Mogens Johansson argued that these difficulties would not slow down the country's wind-energy programme, even though some parts of the turbines apparently needed radical modification. In prospect is a programme of between 1,500 and 2,000 50-metre (164-foot) diameter machines meeting 10 per cent of Denmark's electricity needs by the late 1990s.

The Danes have been encouraging the use of windmills with 30-per-cent government grants, and over 500 have been built. They are still expensive, though, and only the windiest sites have been showing a return on the initial investment within five years.

In Sweden, meanwhile, the conclusion is that large horizontal-axis wind power plants with two or three blades currently have the best potential, with the result that research there has focused on two such machines, having rated outputs of 2 MW and 3 MW. At the time of writing, what was claimed to be the world's largest wind generator (260 feet high and weighing 452 tonnes) was being lifted into place at Maglarp, near Trelleborg. The present objective of the wind-energy programme in Sweden is to provide a factual base for a parliamentary decision by 1985 on whether to go ahead with the large-scale introduction of wind energy into the Swedish power system. One asset enjoyed by the Swedes is their totally integrated national electricity grid, which was built up to transmit hydro-electricity from the northern provinces.

But, just as with Sweden's biomass energy programme, reviewed in Chapter 10, a good deal of attention is being paid to the environmental implications of wind energy. Indeed, it is interesting, in the context of the concern of some Dutch critics of wind power about 'horizon pollution', that when the British Central Electricity Generating Board's predecessor, the Central Electricity Authority, proposed to erect a small prototype wind generator on the Lleyn peninsula, in Wales, over thirty years ago, the plan was stalled by local opposition.

## Wading into the Waves

'I have a mental target of generating a tenth of Britain's electricity supply by the year 2000,' says Dr Peter Musgrove of Reading University. 'I think that it is technically attainable and I think that it is economic.' The CEGB appears to be increasingly of the same mind. Early in 1981, for example, David Howell, then secretary of state for energy, announced that Britain's first big wind-power generator (see Figure 13.4) would be built on top of a hill in the remote Orkneys, where the wind speed averages about 18.6 kilometres (30 miles) per hour.

Orkney Wind Turbine spec:–
Diameter .........................20m
Rated power .....................250kw
Rated wind speed.............17m/sec
Rotational speed .............88r.p.m.
Blades ..........................⎰ Fixed pitch
⎱ NACA 44xx series
Control ..............................Variable pitch tips

Transmission ....................2 stage shaft mounted
Generator.....................⎰ Synchronous
⎱ 440v. 3 phase
Orientation .......................Servo drive
Tower ...............................Steel
Controller..........................Microprocessor
Annual energy ................700,000 kwh at
10m/sec site

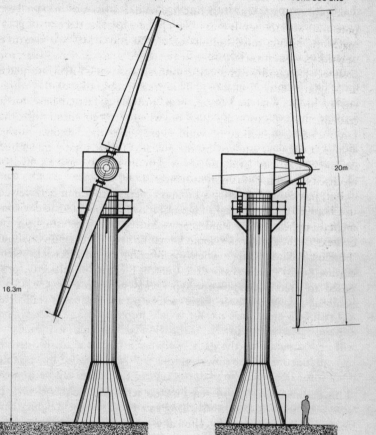

Figure 13.4: Design for the 250 kW Orkney machine
(source: Taylor Woodrow Construction).

The machine, which, it was thought, would cost about £6.2 million and generate 3 MW of electricity, represented the most ambitious renewable-energy project undertaken to date by the British government, with the funding coming from the Department of Energy and the North of Scotland Hydroelectric Board. The Board had, in fact, run into considerable political problems in the Orkneys – which at that time were predominantly supplied with electricity from expensive diesel-powered generators. In 1980, the Board had tried to impose a fuel surcharge on the islanders, but was forced to back down in the face of fierce local opposition.

As a direct result, the Board said that it expected to lose something like £8 million in providing energy to the Orkneys, the Shetlands and the Western Isles. Two wind turbines were proposed to provide cheaper power, one a 250 kW machine and the other the 3 MW machine, both to be built atop 525-foot (160-metre) Burgar Hill. The smaller machine was designed to be 86 feet (26 metres) high, from its base to its rotor tip. The rotor itself will be 66 feet (20 metres) long, and the machine's output was seen as sufficient to supply about eighty homes.

The larger machine will be 250 feet (76 metres) from its base to the tip of its 197-foot (60-metre) rotor. The rotor will be mounted on a rotatable steel nacelle high atop a 150-foot (46-metre) hollow concrete tower, almost as high as Nelson's Column in London's Trafalgar Square. The complete machine was projected to weigh 195 tons, and working at full capacity it was expected to meet the power needs of 1,000 of the 8,000 domestic power consumers.

The 3 MW machine's nacelle is held in place by four pads which grip the outside of the tower. As the wind veers around, so the nacelle will be reoriented by the pads 'walking' around the tower, driven by hydraulic rams. The power output will be controlled by variable pitch rotor tips – the outer 20 per cent of the rotors can be rotated in such a way as to provide increasing levels of reverse thrust, stopping the rotors (with the help of a giant set of disc brakes) when the wind speed exceeds 60 miles (96.5 kilometres) per hour. This 'feathering' mechanism is controlled by a microprocessor which is constantly fed with information about wind speeds.

But why stop the rotors at all? The answer is that if they were designed to cope with all the wind speeds they might encounter, they would be hopelessly over-designed in relation to the winds they would be required to harness for the bulk of the time. Throwing away the wind energy available when wind speeds exceed 60 miles per hour is, in fact, a small price to pay for the ability to design the machines more economically. And, indeed, such high wind speeds are not experienced too often, even up in the Orkneys. Dr David Lindley of the Wind Energy Group, a Taylor Woodrow subsidiary, estimates that by operating the machine at wind speeds between 37 and 60 miles per hour, it should be possible to capture between 70 and 80 per cent of the energy available. The smaller machine will operate at wind speeds ranging between 16 and 60 miles per hour.

When the two machines are operating in tandem, they should supply up to 15 per cent of the island's annual electricity needs. And, according to the Hydroelectric Board's chief engineer, Alex Murray, 'if the development programme is successful, the Board hopes to be able to order MW-size aerogenerators on a commercial basis in 1985–6, and thus begin to bring the rising costs of generating electricity with diesel fuel under control.'

Next, the CEGB announced plans for the UK's first windmill 'farm', an array of up to ten giant machines up to 400 feet (122 metres) high, with three sites under investigation. First, though, the CEGB planned to gain operating experience by building a medium-sized machine beside the Carmarthen Bay coal-fired power station at Dyfed, South Wales. The Dyfed windmill, standing 150 feet (46 metres) high and generating 50–200 kW of electricity is a horizontal-axis machine and, if successful, will be the precursor of a cluster of up to ten 1–4 MW windmills, to be built by the mid-1980s, with larger-scale wind-energy investments starting perhaps three years later. Three lowland sites were being considered for the windmill cluster or 'wind farm' – Bradwell in Essex, Richborough in Kent and Wigsley, near Lincoln. The larger machines could well include some vertical-axis designs, it is thought, with Peter Musgrove's designs among the prime contenders.

'I can't think of any other energy source which has a smaller environmental effect,' he says. 'No chimney stacks spewing pollution, no waste disposal, and I couldn't care less if a bunch of terrorists were let loose among an array of windmills.' Ornithologists have expressed their concern, though, about 'bird strikes', although the evidence to date suggests that this is unlikely to be a significant problem. The spinning rotors can also reflect television and radio signals, causing interference, although their influence is unlikely to extend much beyond perhaps two kilometres. Another reason for keeping the machines away from areas where people live is that they can shed their blades or, in winter conditions, ice.

Noise problems may prove rather more significant, although most existing machines seem to be more or less inaudible beyond 200–300 metres (656–984 feet). Occasionally, nearby hills or valleys can focus the sound, causing pockets of noise problems, although there is no reason why these problems should not be resolved by careful siting of the windmills. So far, public acceptance of the prototype wind-mills has been good, although more opposition must be expected when larger concentrations of machines begin to appear on land.

A more pressing area of concern has been the shedding of rotors by some experimental machines. The 100 kW aerogenerator installed by EdF at the Île d'Ouessant, for example, hurled one of its 58-foot (18-metre) blades over 200 yards (183 metres). To quote Michel Hug, the EdF director responsible for building new plant, it ended up looking 'like a bent paperclip'.

A basic problem with large horizontal-axis aerogenerators is that the stresses exerted on the blades as they turn end over end can be very considerable indeed. One official at the US Department of Energy commented that today's aerogenerator is 'like a fatigue testing machine that, as a sideline, produces energy'.

Early in 1981, for example, Alcoa's 46-metre (150-foot) high experi-mental 500 kW wind turbine, designed to withstand winds of up to 160 kilometres (99 miles) per hour, was caught by a 65-kilometre-per-hour gust while starting up during tests at Southern California Edison's Palm Springs wind-energy centre – and collapsed. A Darrieus or 'egg-whisk' vertical-axis machine (see drawing 5 in Figure 13.3), it lost at least one of its blades, which, shearing outward, sliced through the guy-lines supporting the machine. Despite this setback, however, Southern California Edison's vice-president for advanced engineering, Larry Papay, said he was still optimistic about the future of wind energy. Such accidents, he pointed out, are 'an important part of the learning process'.

Aerodynamically, the Darrieus wind turbine operates in a very similar way to a horizontal-axis machine, but the curved blades extract power from the wind twice in each revolution, first as they sweep across the wind upwind of the tower and, second, when they pass across the wind downwind of the machine. Although a small amount of energy is dissipated as the blades move upwind or down-wind, research has shown that vertical-axis machines provide overall efficiencies at least as high as their horizontal-axis competitors.

One of the main advantages of the Darrieus design, or of the Musgrove development of the concept, is that they are able to extract wind coming towards them from any direction. Unlike all the windmills in Figure 13.2, for example, they do not need to be pointed into the wind. Furthermore, as Peter Musgrove argues, 'the vertical shaft also allows one to mount heavy items of equipment, such as the speed-increasing gearbox and the electrical generator, close to ground level, reducing the cost of the support structure and improving access for maintenance.'

But how large can we expect wind energy's contribution to be? 'It is probably realistic to estimate a potential contribution of at least 10 per cent towards our electricity needs from land-based wind-energy systems,' says Musgrove. 'This would require about 3,600 wind turbines like Mod–2 and, in groups of 25 with each group within an area of four kilometres by four kilometres, the total land area involved is about 2,300 square kilometres, approximately 1 per cent of the rural land area in England and Wales. It is, however, important to recognize,' he points out, 'that with wind turbine arrays one can continue normal agricultural activities right up to the base of the wind turbine towers.'

Even so, the prospect of 3,600 very large windmills (and more of the Mod–2 design in a moment) may prove too much for the public and their planners to accept. If so, one solution is to put your wind farms offshore. 'I hadn't realized,' Peter Musgrove says, 'until I started looking at charts how shallow much of the North Sea is. You can go all the way to Holland without going deeper than 100 feet (30 metres).' The United Kingdom has an edge on the rest of the European Community in that it is surrounded by very extensive areas of shallow sea and now has very considerable experience in the engineering and construction of major offshore structures, thanks to North Sea oil.

That said, however, the cost of offshore installations tends to be substantially higher than for their onshore counterparts. According to Taywood Engineering, the cost of the support structure for a single wind turbine (i.e. excluding the turbine itself) would be about £3 million. Maintenance costs would be higher, at some £34,000 a year, and the onshore support facilities for a 200-machine cluster might cost £25 million.

The Taywood study, carried out for the Department of Energy, looked at three possible offshore sites: Burnham Flats in the Wash

Approaches; Shell Flat off Morecambe Bay; and Carmarthen Bay. These sites were chosen from a short-list of seventeen sites, although Taywood stressed at the time that they should not be seen as automatic choices for future projects.

Clusters of up to 200 offshore aerogenerators, spread over an area of about 60 square kilometres (155 square miles), could provide 600 MW to the national grid, the study concluded. Their main economic value, like that of the proposed Severn tidal barrage, would be in the savings they would contribute to the burning of fossil fuels. Machines with 100-metre rotorspans located in areas with an annual mean wind speed of 10 metres a second (i.e. higher than anything shown in Table 13.1) could generate electricity at a cost of 3.4 pence per kilowatt-hour, compared to the then current cost of about 1.5 pence for electricity from a coal-fired power station. A similar field of 80-metre-diameter machines operating in an area with annual mean wind speeds of 9.5 metres per second could generate electricity at a cost of 5.1 pence, it was thought.

If wind power were to be developed vigorously, Dr Musgrove (who helped in the Taywood Engineering study) argued, it would match the development of nuclear power over the previous twenty-five years

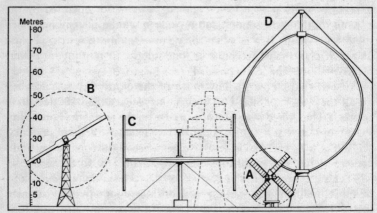

Figure 13.5: Comparative scale of a number of different modern aero-generators. A = typical traditional British windmill. B = large horizontal-axis wind turbine (modern design). C = large vertical-axis wind turbine concept (British design – Musgrove); in background – 400 kV electricity pylon. D = large vertical-axis wind turbine concept (US design – ERDA). (Source: ATOM.)

and contribute up to 20 per cent of Britain's electricity supply by the year 2000. He forecasts that each cluster of 200 windmills will be equivalent to one 1,000 MW power station, whether fossil-fuel-fired or nuclear, operating at 35-per-cent load factor. The drawings prepared by such consortia as that including Taywood Engineering showed horizontal-axis machines, while Musgrove (co-operating with a consortium led by Sir Robert McAlpine & Partners) clearly favoured vertical-axis machines (see Figure 13.5 for a hint of the scale) – although at the time of writing his funding had enabled him only to get as far as designing a 100–150 kW vertical-axis machine. The world's biggest windmills, as I found when I visited Boeing's Goodnoe Hills site in Washington State, were still horizontal-axis machines.

## 'An Overspeed Condition'

Sad to relate, all three of Boeing's Mod–2 wind turbines were temporarily out of service when I arrived at the Goodnoe Hills site, near Goldendale. Eleven days after Senator Henry Jackson threw a switch tying the machines into the regional power grid, operated by the Bonneville Power Administration, one of the machines had been damaged during testing of its emergency feathering system. To use the words of Boeing spokesman Joe Holmes, it went into 'an over-speed condition'.

What he meant was that the failsafe systems failed to engage when the rotor began to speed up and, as a result, the accelerated drive train burned out the generator. The rotor, nacelle (see Figure 13.6) and tower were unaffected by the accident, and there were no injuries. The 37-foot (11.3-metre) nacelle contains the drive train, generator and associated electronic equipment. The nacelle itself rests high atop a 200-foot (61-metre) tubular steel tower, the foundations of which have been made resistant to seismic shocks and extreme wind conditions.

The computer-controlled Mod–2 design was developed with un-attended operation in mind – and the windmills have a design life of thirty years. Built on a 2,600-foot (792-metre) high ridge over-looking the Columbia river, 127 miles (204 kilometres) east of Port-land, Oregon, what Boeing called the world's 'first wind farm' is an extraordinary sight. Each windmill is 350 feet (107 metres) high

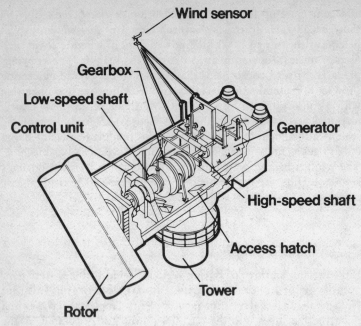

Figure 13.6: Mod–2 nacelle (source: Boeing Engineering and Construction).

from its base to its rotor tip (see Figure 13.7), with a single 90-ton, 300-foot (91.4-metre) rotor.

At maximum capacity, each machine can generate 2.5 MW, and together the three machines can supply about 2,400 homes. Power from these demonstration systems came out at about 10 cents per kilowatt-hour, which was not competitive with other forms of generation, but Boeing was confident that wind farms of 100 or more such units could bring the cost down to 4 or 5 cents per kilowatt-hour.

The Mod–2 turbines begin producing power when the wind reaches 14 miles (22 kilometres) per hour, equivalent to about 6 metres per second. They reach their rated output at 27.5 miles (44 kilometres) per hour and continue at that output until the wind speed reaches 45 miles (72 kilometres) per hour, at which point the blade tips feather and rotation ceases. The wind speed at Goodnoe Hills averages about

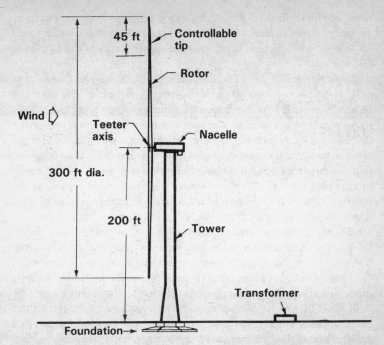

Figure 13.7: The Mod–2 design (source: Boeing Engineering and Construction).

16½ miles per hour through the year, with speeds ranging between 14 and 47 miles per hour for about 60 per cent of the time – measured 33 feet (10 metres) above the ground.

Boeing started on its first windmill for a commercial customer, Pacific Gas & Electric (see Chapters 5 and 6), during 1980. Total project costs were estimated at $10 million, according to PG & E. While the three Goldendale machines were expected to supply 30 million kilowatt-hours annually to the Bonneville power grid, the PG & E machine, located in the windswept hills of Solano County about 40 miles (64 kilometres) north-east of San Francisco, was designed to generate about 7.4 million kilowatt-hours a year.

'That's a tiny fraction of the 60 billion or so kilowatt-hours that PG & E customers use annually,' said Nolan Daines, PG & E's vice-president for planning and research. 'The significance of this project is that it is the essential first step for PG & E in the development of this resource.' PG & E, which has also been investing in geothermal power plants for some time, plans to install an additional 80 MW of wind-turbine capacity, requiring 32 units of the Goodnoe Hill variety.

These windmills are radically different from the old Dutch post mill, not just in terms of scale (Figure 13.5) but in terms of the technology used. It is significant that most of the companies which have become interested in wind energy have been either aerospace or helicopter companies. As Peter Musgrove, who himself trained as an aeronautical engineer, points out, 'it is important to recognize that the blade of a wind turbine functions in a way that has much in common with the way the wings of an aeroplane function.' As he puts it, 'it is equally important to recognize that the traditional windmill represents the technological state-of-the-art about the year 1800 – more than a century before the first aeroplane flew. And,' he stresses, 'one has only to compare modern airliners, such as the Boeing 747 or European Airbus, with their flimsy predecessors of the 1910s and 1920s to recognize the enormous strides that have been made in aircraft design and construction in the last seventy years.'

In West Germany, Messerschmitt–Bölkow–Blohm of Munich has been working since 1978, with the help of the Federal Ministry of Research and Technology, on a very large wind generator called Growian II. The company, which has considerable experience in developing helicopter rotors, was considering using a single 75-metre blade, with its rotational axis 120 metres above the ground. Meanwhile, at Stuttgart University, Professor Franz Wortmann's team had come up with a one-blade windmill which defied all the laws of symmetry – but still managed to sweep up 4.4 kW of power from a circular area of 50 square metres in an 8-metre-per-second (Force 5) wind. 'We found that by avoiding the turbulence of two rotors', Professor Wortmann explained, 'we were able to achieve a rotor speed of 450 kilometres per hour at the tip – the fastest in the world.' West Germany, in fact, had been taking wind energy seriously: by the end of 1980, for example, it had spent some £20 million, compared with £100 million in the United States and a mere £2 million in Britain.

The US federal wind-energy programme was initiated in 1973, under the auspices of the National Science Foundation. It was incorporated into the Energy Research and Development Administration when ERDA was formed in 1975 – and into the Department of Energy when that was set up in 1977. In 1974–5, a 100 kW (Mod–0) experimental wind generator was built for ERDA by NASA's Lewis Research Center at its Plum Brook test site, near Sandusky, Ohio. After developing and testing the 100 kW turbine, an experimental 200 kW system based on the original design was developed. The first of the four 200 kW (Mod–0A) test units was installed at Clayton, New Mexico, and began operating in early 1978. The third of these Mod–0A machines was installed at Block Island, Rhode Island, in 1979, while the fourth appeared at Kahuku on the island of Hawaii during 1980.

The next main step in the federal programme was a 2 MW wind turbine with a 200-foot (61-metre) rotor, the Mod–1 machine, built by General Electric and installed high atop Howard's Knob, a 4,400-foot (1,341-metre) mountain overlooking Boone, in North Carolina, during 1979. Each successive model has shown improved performance, greater output and a progressive reduction in the relative unit weight. The Mod–2 design, for example, generates twice as many kilowatt-hours each year as does the Mod–1 design, while weighing 20 per cent less.

Boeing also started work for NASA during 1980 on the Mod–5 design, which is intended to be about the same size as Mod–2 but, it is hoped, will generate electricity for less than 3 cents per kilowatt-hour – measured in 1977 dollars and based on production quantities of machines, representing a 20–30-per-cent improvement on the Mod–2 machines.

One major area of improvement, and one which Dr David Lindley feels the British wind-energy people have been able to skip entirely, is in the materials used in the rotors. The Mod–0A machines were designed to deliver their maximum output in a slightly higher wind than was the Mod–0 design, and had two blades – mounted downwind of a steel lattice-work tower (6 in Figure 13.2). Now after many thousands of hours of operation, generally unattended, the Mod–0A series has shown up a number of failings with such early rotor materials as aluminium. Later versions of the Mod–0A had wooden blades. Elsewhere in the US wind-energy programme, steel or glass-fibre blades have been used. The Orkney machine, incidentally, like the Goodnoe Hills machines, will use steel.

## Small May Be Beautiful

One small American company which believes that it has the answer and that, not to put too fine a point on it, companies like Boeing have taken the wrong turning, is US Windpower. This company, in fact, had completed a pilot wind farm of twenty windmills before Senator Jackson threw the Goodnoe Hills Switch, and decided that the way to develop wind energy economically was to crowd lots of small windmills on to a site. At its Crotched Mountain wind farm, in New Hampshire, US Windpower was using 40-foot (12-metre) rotorspan machines mounted on 60-foot (18-metre) steel tripods.

Each of these relatively small windmills can generate 30 kW in winds of 25 miles (40 kilometres) per hour, and the company has also built a 50 kW test windmill at Burlington, Massachusetts. It plans to build 200 of these 50 kW windmills, at a cost of $50,000 apiece, and locate them in clusters of forty a time on sites in New England, Oregon, Washington, Montana and California.

While Boeing was talking about driving the price of wind-generated electricity down from $10 to $1 per peak watt, US Windpower was claiming that its machines had been built at a capital cost of $1 per peak watt. The main reasons for this low cost was the use of off-the-shelf components such as a 50-horsepower motor, run backwards as a generator, and of commercially available transmission equipment. The only custom-made bits were the fibreglass blades and a microprocessor used to control the entire operation – including feathering the windmills when wind speeds exceed 50 miles (80 kilometres) an hour.

General Electric, meanwhile, which had built the Mod–1 machine for $7.5 million, or $3.75 a peak watt (excluding, of course, the cost of all the R & D work which went into the machine), was hoping that its next prototype, a 4 MW machine with blades 350–400 feet in diameter, could be put into mass-production and that after 99 of them had been built the capital cost of the 100th machine would represent a mere 65 cents per peak watt (in 1980 dollars) – compared with the 70 cents target set for solar cells (see Chapter 9).

The company which has plans to build the 'world's largest wind farm', appropriately called Windfarms Ltd, had a strange genesis. Wayne van Dyke, who set up the company in the late 1970s, is a former mergers and acquisitions specialist who moved to San Francisco in 1970, spending his time turning companies around. At thirty-three, van Dyke retired. Then, as fate would have it, a snow-storm felled a power-line to his all-electric house and started him thinking about alternative energy sources.

It is an indication of just how successfully he pursued his thinking that in 1981 he sold off 60 per cent of Windfarms to Standard Oil of California and Sigma Resources, an oil company which invests in a wide range of energy projects, for $16 million. He had landed an initial $250 million contract with the Hawaiian Electric Company to build twenty-six wind turbines in Oahu (see Chapter 14). And he had also landed a $700 million contract with PG & E to build a 146 wind turbine scheme, designed to generate about 1 billion kilo-watt-hours a year – or about one sixtieth (less than 2 per cent) of the energy consumed by PG & E's customers.

A profitable black-out, at least as far as Wayne van Dyke was concerned. But elsewhere power black-outs and brown-outs have become a way of life. Take Turkey, where daily power cuts of up to three hours have been common – and where energy is described as the country's No. 1 problem. Time is running out for the country's oil-wells: 'With the existing fields, we are essentially flog-ging a dead horse,' said the head of the state planning agency. The World Bank was investing in a $70-million scheme for secondary oil recovery, using carbon dioxide injection, at the Bati-Raman field, and the oil companies are being encouraged to explore the country's remote regions for new deposits – but Turkey's energy planners are not counting on an oil bonanza.

The country has what is described as the world's largest lignite-fired thermal power plant, but its construction has been considerably slowed by labour relations, terrorism and funding problems. Al-though Turkey gets something like 40 per cent of its energy from hydropower, oil still accounts for over 40 per cent of the country's energy – and about 85 per cent of that oil has to be imported. Although Turkey's oil consumption, which has been running at 18 million tonnes a year, is modest by the standards of many developing countries, it is caught in something of a vice, having allowed itself to become hooked on cheap oil for its industrial expansion during the late 1960s and early 1970s. Its oil bill in 1980, for example, totalled $3.2 billion, considerably more than the $2.9 billion earned by Turkish exports that year.

But, whereas Turkey has hydropower, at least 6.5 billion tonnes of lignite reserves and, it is estimated, uranium reserves of 4,500 tonnes or more, many developing countries are in a far more pre-carious position. It is a strange fact, then, that despite the obvious attractions of wind pumps, such as those which dotted North America in the past and still do in many places today, they are not widely used in the Third World.

Observers agree that this is because there is a lack of awareness about the potential energy to be had from the wind, and, more seriously, because most wind pumps are too difficult to manufacture in poorly equipped village workshops. The materials are often too expensive for subsistence farmers, while the relatively modest repair and maintenance activities required, ranging from the lubrication of the bearings once a year to the refurbishment of the blades, may over-tax the technological resources available in such countries.

New generations of multi-bladed windmills have, however, been developed by groups such as Britain's Intermediate Technology Development Group and by the Dutch Steering Committee for Wind Energy. ITDG set up its wind-pump development programme towards the end of 1975 with two main objectives in mind: the design should be suitable for economic low-volume production in developing countries from widely available standard steel sections; and, second, the system should be adaptable through minor modifi-cations for either high-volume low-head pumping, as in irrigation, or for the more traditional low-volume high-head bore-hole pumping function.

The ITDG team, which included Peter Fraenkel, had come up with a number of very exciting new ideas, one of which actually involved using a Darrieus wind turbine to extract energy from river and canal currents – for use in water pumping and electricity genera-tion. This type of machine is ideal where there is no head of water available to drive a conventional turbine, and tests on the river Thames at Reading showed that the Darrieus turbine rotor can convert 25 per cent of the energy which flows through its swept area into useful shaft power. The Dutch government provided funds for the manu-facture and field testing of a prototype. The machine was in operation from January of 1981 on the White Nile, at Juba in Southern Sudan. In a current speed of 1.2 metres a second, a 200-litre oil-drum 5 metres above the river level was filled in less than one minute, representing 300 cubic metres of water over 24 hours.

More conventional windmill designs developed by organizations such as ITDG are now undergoing tests in countries such as India,

Kenya, Pakistan, Peru, Sri Lanka and Tunisia, although there is concern that even these machines are too complicated and expensive for most of their potential users. Some countries have been trying to develop the sail windmill, even though its sails need replacing every two years or so, because it can be put together in the average village workshop. But case studies carried out in many developing countries show that, whatever the machine used, wind power is often more economical than the alternatives – including, in some cases, bullock power.

Even in relatively advanced countries like Britain, there are those who are trying to build very cheap windmills. Hugh Piggott, of Scoraig Wind Electric, is one such. He recommends building your windmill from scrap materials, and he has been building scrap windmills for most of his neighbours in Scotland. 'It is actually easier,' he says, 'to design the windmill after – or even during – a visit to the scrapyard, rather than before. It all depends on what you can find.'

We are still a long way from the day when the Pope tries to tax the wind again, however. Even so, the Vatican is not unaware of the potential of solar energy, it appears. 'It seems obvious that the sun, our chief and richest source of energy,' Pope John Paul II told one group of energy experts, 'should figure largely in the search for new energy resources. This should become one of the main objects of research.' The following year, the Pope was the victim of an assassination attempt carried out by a Turkish terrorist, and his mind, inevitably, became otherwise occupied. But the question we shall address in the final chapter of this book will be: how long will the Vatican (and, for that matter, the rest of the world) have to wait before it can economically plug into renewable energy?

# Beyond the Rehearsals

# 14 ⊙ Renewable Futures

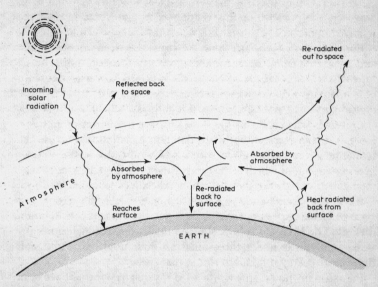

Figure 14.1: Fate of solar radiation reaching the earth
(source: Earthscan).

*Question:* We know which were the world's top ten energy sources in 1980; but how is their ranking likely to change through the remaining years of the twentieth century? *Answer:* It's anyone's guess, but read on. Although the previous chapters have looked at the ways in which the various energy supply technologies work, or might work, with a welter of detail on who has been doing what and where, there has been no attempt as yet to rank-order their present and potential future contributions to the world's energy budget.

Recalling the comments of Exxon president Howard Kauffman on the acute difficulties involved in forecasting oil demand in the current energy climate (quoted on p. 59), it is worth stressing that there is nothing more uncertain than the future. Indeed, as we shall see below, the West German government has actually given up trying to forecast energy demand in any detail. 'Forecasting is the art of knowing where to scratch before it starts to itch,' one West German official said, recognizing that his country had more than once been caught scratching itself in the wrong place since 1973. That said, however, the purpose of this chapter is to give some idea of the relative importance of the various renewable-energy technologies.

But, first, a new balance must be struck between energy supply and energy demand, between horsepower and energy horse-sense. Interestingly, two scientists based at the Harvard University Museum of Comparative Zoology were recently surprised to discover that the typical horse uses no more energy if it gallops a mile in four minutes than it does when it walks the same distance in quarter of an hour. Horses, it transpires, adopt three different gaits tailored to use the minimum of energy at given speeds. These are the walk, the trot (a faster variant of which is the canter) and the gallop. Horses change their gait at exactly the speed at which it becomes economic to do so.

If, on the other hand, you train a horse to use the wrong gait at a particular speed, you will find that its energy consumption rockets. The Harvard results showed that a horse which normally walked at a little under three miles an hour used one and a half times more energy if it had to trot at that speed.

Like so many horses, the world's 165 sovereign countries have been moving at different speeds, often in different directions, and will continue to do so. This fact, taken with their dramatically unequal endowments of renewable and non-renewable resources, suggests that there is no single energy palliative for the problems which have emerged since the first oil shock. Coal cannot be *the* alternative to oil, any more than nuclear fission or renewable energy can. Those who have rehearsed the transition away from oil, in whichever direction, have found that most of the glib formulas which surfaced after the OPEC breakthrough simply do not work.

Big may not always be best, but small is certainly not uniformly beautiful. The growing recognition that the only way forward is to consider all the component needs which go to make up the larger energy-demand picture has led many early renewable-energy enthusiasts to qualify their claims and shift their targets. Their increasing sophistication has been demonstrated by the succession of national 'low-energy strategies' which have appeared in recent years. By stressing energy efficiency and the careful matching of the various forms of energy to end-use needs, such strategies have aimed to reduce per capita energy demand – while often allowing for continued economic growth.

Energy efficiency, unquestionably, is now the name of the game. Indeed, if you were looking for a symbol of the new era of energy consciousness it would not be the *Solar Challenger*, for all its ingenuity. Instead, suitable candidates might include two other aircraft in the news at about the same time, both designed to fly non-stop, without refuelling, around the world. The *Free Enterprise*, built by American Tom Jewett at a cost of some £170,000 and designed to fly at 24,000 feet, taking full advantage of the prevailing winds, carried less than 370 gallons of fuel and, at a fuel-consumption rate of 60 miles per gallon, had a range of 22,800 miles – compared with the 28,000-mile range planned for rival Dick Rotan's *Voyager*, a giant flying trimaran with massive outrigged fuel tanks. The basic idea in both cases was to stretch fuel to the limit. Suitable symbols indeed for the economies of the 1980s and 1990s.

The low-energy strategies published to date have been attempts to identify the economic, technological and social 'gaits' whose adoption will help given countries to do more with less energy. In the United Kingdom, for example, Gerald Leach of the International Institute for Environment and Development (IIED) and others were responsible for *A Low Energy Strategy for the UK* (IIED/Science Reviews, 1979), which argued that the UK's gross domestic product could be trebled with little or no growth in total energy demand. Fundamental to the argument was the idea that there is no hard and fast link between growth in GDP and growth in total energy demand, a conclusion which Leach followed up by examining energy use in considerable detail in each sector of industry, in commercial and public buildings, in housing and transport. In the industrial sector alone, for example, the study considered almost 500 categories of fuel end-use.

Two years later, the US Solar Energy Research Institute (SERI) produced its study of the prospects for making significant energy savings through energy-conservation measures and the increased use of renewable sources of energy. The resulting report, entitled *A New Prosperity: Building a Sustainable Energy Future* (Brick House, 1981), promptly became the subject of intense political infighting, with the Department of Energy trying hard to prevent its publication, arguing that its methodology was suspect. Having your methodology questioned by the DOE, said outgoing SERI-director Denis Hayes, was 'like being called ugly by a frog'. In the event, however, Representative Richard Ottinger sidestepped the DOE by having the report printed by the House of Representatives Energy and Commerce Committee.

More to the point, however, the report argued that through increased energy efficiency the United States could achieve a full-employment economy, with per capita income increasing 45 per cent over the next twenty years, while reducing national energy consumption by nearly 25 per cent. Tables 14.1 and 14.2 summarize the study's main conclusions on the desirable trends in fuel and power demand – and the potential contribution of renewable energy by sector. 'Efficiency and sustainability will be the hallmarks of the new prosperity', the study concluded, with the major renewable-energy contributions coming from hydropower and from biomass, which it was estimated were already supplying 6 per cent of the nation's energy.

But the SERI report proved very much out of line with the plans

*Table 14.1: The SERI forecasts of US end-use energy demands (source: SERI)*

| | (Including no renewable contribution) (Quads* of oil equivalent) | | | | | |
| | 1977‡ | | | 2000 potential | | |
| Sector | Fuel | Electric | Total | Fuel | Electric | Total |
|---|---|---|---|---|---|---|
| Buildings | 13.2 | 13.4 | 26.6 | 5.5 | 12.3 | 17.8 |
| Residential | (8.8) | (7.8) | (16.2) | (3.8) | (7.1) | (10.9) |
| Commercial | (4.7) | (5.6) | (10.4) | (1.7) | (5.5) | (7.2) |
| Industry | 19.8 | 9.3 | 29.1 | 18.7 | 10.7 | 29.4 |
| Agriculture | 1.3 | 0.3 | 1.6 | 1.4 | 0.3 | 1.7 |
| Transportation | 19.5 | — | 19.5 | 12.6–16.5 | † | 12.6–16.5 |
| Personal | (15.1) | — | (15.1) | (6.9–10.5) | † | (6.9–10.5) |
| Freight | (4.3) | — | (4.3) | (5.7–6.0) | † | (5.7–6.0) |
| Totals§ | 53.8 | 23.0 | 76.8 | 38.2–42.1 | 23.3 | 61.4–65.4 |

* One Quad per year is approximately equal to 500,000 barrels of oil per day.

† Aggressive rail-electrification and electric-vehicle programmes could create between 0.75 and 1.15 Quad (primary equivalent) demand for electricity in the transportation sector, with the displacement of 0.46–0.76 Quad of petroleum (fuel) demand.

‡ 1979 total consumption was roughly 79 Quad.

§ Not including about 2 Quad of fuel saving possible through co-generation.

( ) = Not additive within end-use sector.

*Table 14.2: The potential renewable-energy contribition to US energy demand by the year 2000 (source: SERI)*

(Oil equivalent displaced in Quads)

| Sector | Solar thermal | Biomass* | Wind | Photo-voltaics | Hydro | Total |
|---|---|---|---|---|---|---|
| Buildings | 1.9–2.3 | 1.0 | 0.8–1.1 | 0.4–0.7 | | 4.1–5.1 |
|   Residential | (1.6–1.9) | (1.0) | (0.8–1.1) | (0.3–0.45) | — | (3.7–4.45) |
|   Commercial | (0.3–0.4) | — | — | (0.1–0.25) | — | (0.4–0.65) |
| Industry | 0.5–2.0 | 3.5–5.5 | — | — | — | 4.0–7.5 |
| Agriculture | — | 0.1–0.7 | — | — | — | 0.1–0.7 |
| Transportation | — | 0.4–5.5 | — | — | — | 0.4–5.5 |
| Utilities | — | — | 0.5–3.4 | — | 3.4–3.7 | 3.9–7.1 |
| Total | 2.4–4.2 | 4.8–10.5† | 1.3–4.0† | 0.4–0.7 | 3.4–3.7 | 12.3–22.5† |

*Biomass estimates are given in terms of oil displaced, rather than primary biomass supply.

† These columns do not add; high end of penetration is limited to less than total of potential applications in end-use sectors.

( ) = Not additive within end-use sector.

of the incoming Reagan administration, as did Denis Hayes (see Chapter 3). Nonetheless, the solar industry's prospects in the United States are still seen as bright, as is discussed later. Indeed, many private corporations have been continuing to make significant breakthroughs in renewable-energy technology at a time when government funding has been cut back fiercely. However, before turning to look at the market prospects for the individual renewable-energy technologies after the 'solar eclipse' of the early 1980s, we take a brief look at two 'miracle' economies whose continuing energy vulnerability is pushing them in rather different directions: West Germany and Japan.

## Jugular Veins

Even with the respite afforded by slackening oil prices, West Germany still considered – and considers – energy to be a front-rank problem. Whereas energy outgoings accounted for only 1 per cent of the country's gross national product (GNP) in 1972, by 1981 the proportion had risen to about 5 per cent. This may not represent quite as great a problem as that faced by the developing countries, whose raw-material exports have been buying less and less oil (Chapter 1, p. 26), but West Germany was still having to set off 20 per cent of its 1981 export earnings against energy imports, compared with 11 per cent in 1978 and 6 per cent in 1972.

As Table 14.3 shows, West Germany managed to cut its oil imports between 1973 and 1980, but its total energy import bill rose from D M 8 billion in 1972, through D M 31 billion in 1978 to an estimated D M 75 billion by 1981. A current-account surplus of D M 18.5 billion in 1978 was converted into a deficit of nearly D M 30 billion by 1980, with the Bundesbank attributing more than half of this swing of D M 48 billion to rising energy prices.

*Table 14.3: West Germany's energy sources in 1973 and 1980 (source: West German Coal and Industry Federation)*

|  | (million tonnes of coal equivalent) | | (% share of total energy) | |
|  | 1973 | 1980 | 1973 | 1980 |
| --- | --- | --- | --- | --- |
| *Domestic* | | | | |
| Coal | 74.7 | 66.5 | 19.7 | 17.1 |
| Lignite | 31.7 | 37.3 | 8.3 | 9.5 |
| Natural gas | 21.9 | 19.9 | 5.8 | 5.1 |
| Oil | 9.6 | 6.8 | 2.5 | 1.7 |
| Others | 6.4 | 7.7 | 1.8 | 2.0 |
| Total domestic | 144.3 | 138.2 | 38.1 | 35.4 |
| *Imports* | | | | |
| Oil | 199.3 | 178.7 | 52.7 | 45.8 |
| Natural gas | 16.6 | 44.4 | 4.4 | 11.4 |
| Nuclear | 3.9 | 14.4 | 1.0 | 3.7 |
| Coal | 9.5 | 10.7 | 2.5 | 2.7 |
| Others | 4.9 | 3.8 | 1.3 | 1.0 |
| Total imports | 234.2 | 252.0 | 61.9 | 64.6 |
| Total | 378.5 | 390.2 | 100.0 | 100.0 |

The federal government has been investing in renewable energy, as discussed in Chapter 3 (p. 46), but the early 1980s also saw a marked hardening of the government's resolve to push through its nuclear-energy programme – despite widespread resistance at nuclear sites such as Brokdorf. The country's industrialists, and particularly those in the chemical industry, have been complaining for some time that the poor record of the nuclear industry in getting power plants on stream is having major implications for their own competitiveness. They estimated, for example, that France's success in the nuclear field (p. 105) had given the French chemical industry a 25-per-cent competitive edge, thanks to cheaper energy prices there.

Slower economic growth rates than expected had meant that the country had not suffered as disastrously as some industrialists had predicted, but considerable pressure was clearly being exerted on the federal government to boost nuclear power. The economics ministry was convinced that there was little chance of expanding hydroelectricity or lignite-fuelled power station capacity. The federal government therefore concluded that the only really viable alternative, given that the German coal industry had become something of a lame duck, was nuclear energy. It did not, however, set any public targets, having been burned several times previously. In 1974, for instance, it set the very ambitious nuclear target of 45,000–50,000 MW to be installed by 1985. By 1982, it had some 9,000 MW of nuclear capacity in operation, generating something like 13 per cent of its electricity and accounting for about 4.8 per cent of primary energy requirements. A further 11,200 MW of capacity were under construction, with work halted on the 1,300 MW reactor at Whyl pending the outcome of court hearings begun in 1977. So it looked as though, if everything went unusually well, it might manage something less than half the target figure set in 1974.

And, as though the nuclear industry's problems were not enough, Chancellor Schmidt's government had been wrestling with the political backlash from the United States over the contract West Germany signed in November 1981 with the Soviet Union for natural gas – to be supplied through the controversial pipeline (Chapter 4, p. 63). Having cut the proportion of its oil imports coming from OPEC from 96 per cent in 1973 to 73 per cent by the early 1980s, West Germany saw the pipeline as one way of further diversifying its energy options. The Soviet Union's share of gas used in the country might rise from about 17 per cent to a possible 30 per cent by the late 1980s, it admitted, but was this likely to be any more dangerous than relying on the volatile Middle East as a major oil supplier?

Another option which was being urgently explored, and it has been featured in many of the low-energy strategies published in recent years, was the use of waste heat from industry and power stations in district heating schemes. A few weeks after signing the gas-supply contract, the federal and state governments announced a DM 2.1

billion ($948 million) scheme designed to boost the country's use of waste heat over the following five years. At the time, nearly 8 per cent of all West German space and water heating came from district heating, and the government was planning to increase this proportion by the end of the century to perhaps 25 per cent – at a total cost (in 1981 DM), of perhaps DM 120 billion compared with an annual DM 80 billion oil import bill.

Such schemes are inevitably expensive. For comparison, Dr Walter Marshall's report on the prospects for combined heat and electrical power generation (called co-generation in the United States) in the UK concluded that it could meet up to 30 per cent of the country's space heating and hot-water needs (equivalent to 30 million tonnes of coal a year). To exploit CHP fully, the Marshall report concluded, 'would take a good many decades. And the cost will be high. To meet 30 per cent of the domestic, commercial and institutional heating and hot water load after the year 2000 could cost £17bn when using coal as the primary fuel or £20bn when using nuclear power.'

In conventional power stations, about 63 per cent of the energy originally contained in the fuel is effectively thrown away as waste heat. In 1980–81, for example, the UK Central Electricity Generating Board's power stations, including its nuclear stations, supplied 211.5 terawatt-hours of electricity from a total consumption equivalent to 97.6 million tonnes of coal. The energy dispersed as heat was itself equivalent to 67 million tonnes of coal – or nearly 100 times the amount of heat produced by all the world's solar collectors in 1980.

Clearly, this sort of energy resource is a much more attractive target than most renewable-energy sources at the moment, and West Germany's funding levels reflect this fact. But there are a number of drawbacks with district heating which will constrain its development, including the fact that it is only economic in the big industrial areas, with high-density populations. An effective energy-conservation strategy can make the economics involved look rather less attractive in some areas. And the hot water can only currently be piped about 8–10 kilometres from the heat-source. Nuclear stations, by contrast, could produce hot water which could be economically piped over distances of up to 25 kilometres, but the idea of siting nuclear reactors in heavily populated areas is politically highly contentious.

The best indicator of West Germany's success in dealing with its energy problems, and in covering up the jugular vein exposed by the successive energy crises which struck this otherwise thriving economy through the 1970s, is the changing relationship between energy consumption and GNP. From 1973 to 1980, for example, primary energy consumption increased by only 3.1 per cent, while the Federal Republic's GNP grew, in real terms, by 17.5 per cent.

In Japan, meanwhile, energy consumption per unit of GNP had been falling at a rate of 3.4 per cent a year since 1973. Japan's GNP had grown by 35 per cent while its total energy consumption had gone up by only 15 per cent – and its oil consumption had actually fallen by 8 per cent. Energy use in the energy-intensive iron and steel industry had fallen, when measured per unit of production, by 43 per cent; in the cement industry, it had fallen by 32 per cent; and the chemicals industry had achieved a 17-per-cent improvement.

'Energy conservation has become a matter of national survival for Japan', said one energy expert. The country has very little in the way of domestic energy resources and was importing about 88 per cent of its energy needs. It has been the world's third largest importer of oil, and by far the most vulnerable to any upheavals in supply. Between 1978 and 1979 alone, its fuel bill trebled. Again, Japan is better-placed to pay such bills than are most developing nations, given its success in international markets with its high-technology products, but this sort of economic haemorrhaging has become a major political concern there.

By exporting ever more, Japan has managed to pay its oil bills, but it has also been developing a number of alternatives to oil. Apart from ensuring that its stocks of oil are built up to the equivalent of 140 days' consumption, it has set its sights on cutting its dependence on oil to about 43 per cent by 1995. Coal's share of the Japanese market is planned to rise from about 11.6 per cent to 16.5 per cent, while it is hoped that the country's embryonic nuclear industry will be able to boost its share from 2 per cent to 14.3 per cent.

One of the most impressive features of Japan's industrial success has been the use of 'quality circles', which draw on the worker's experience and interest to identify and push through product-quality improvements and cost-cutting measures – with energy conservation now a central issue under consideration. By using forty quality circles throughout one factory employing 750 people, Suzuki produced three ideas which cut its energy costs by 20 per cent during 1981 alone.

Sanyo received 4,500 energy-efficiency ideas from its workers when it sought their advice, and other factories have instituted 'no days' – on which nobody uses the lifts, the telephones or some other piece of energy-consuming equipment.

Japan has also, as Chapter 3 (p. 42) indicated, been investing steadily in renewable-energy R & D. The National Sunshine Project has been responsible for the 10 M W Nio plant (Chapter 3, p. 43), and a 100 M W solar power station is on the drawing-board for 1991. Another key area on which Japanese scientists have been working is energy storage. Initial tests carried out by Professor Zenichi Yoshida of the engineering department at Kyoto University showed that 2.2 pounds of a yellow crystal could store 92,000 calories – suggesting that a solar heater with a surface area of one square metre could store 85 million calories of energy a year. The crystal was made by combining a petroleum derivative, norbornadiene, with methyl radicals and a substance named cyano. Sunlight changes the compound's molecular structure, a change which can be reversed releasing the latent heat of crystallization, by the addition of a silver catalyst. One problem, however, is that the compound is sensitive only to ultra violet light, which accounts for no more than a fraction of incoming solar energy.

The Japanese government is also heavily supporting a project designed to extract uranium from sea-water, in the belief that it will probably be worth paying the cost premium for the degree of energy independence likely to be achieved in the process, while a number of companies are developing and exploiting the O T E C technology described in Chapter 8. And, as we shall see later, Japan has its eyes on the US solar market, too.

## The Ubiquitous Microprocessor

One of the most interesting and hopeful trends, however, is that some of the new technologies, such as biotechnology and micro-electronics, offer much improved energy efficiencies in conventional applications. Microprocessors, as we have seen, are being used in an increasing number of energy supply applications, as in the control of aerogenerators or mini-hydro turbines, and they also promise increasing sophistication in the monitoring and control of energy consumption. In Chapter 8, for example, we looked at Honeywell's

20,000 square feet (1,858 square metres) of solar collectors atop its Minneapolis headquarters (p. 195), one of the largest solar installations in the United States. But Honeywell has been approaching solar energy from a rather different angle. 'We are not as interested in selling solar-energy systems as we are in being conversant with the nature of the beast we will want to control', said Neil Sher, director of the Honeywell strategy centre.

The company's revenues from the controls and instrumentation market have been growing at 15 per cent a year, and energy conservation has represented an increasingly important target. By applying the latest microelectronics technology to thermostats and control systems, Honeywell was forging ahead: in 1980, for example, it sold as many set-back thermostats (i.e. those that turn the heat up or down automatically at pre-set times) in two weeks as it did in the whole of 1973 – and it estimates that at least 50 per cent of its controls end up in energy-conservation applications.

Britain's Central Electricity Generating Board, meanwhile, was embarking on what was described as 'the biggest revolution that the electricity supply industry has had'. For the first time, microprocessor technology was on the verge of creating a true market for electricity, with supply and demand balanced from minute to minute. We have seen, in Chapter 12 (p. 293), that electricity consumption shoots up during times when the activities of consumers are synchronized – as by the showing on television of a popular film. During the wedding of Prince Charles and Lady Diana Spencer in 1981, the national power grid had to cope with sudden surges in demand of 2,000 MW as critical points in the ceremonies passed and viewers turned on kettles and other appliances. One way of dealing with this problem is to use old power stations, held on standby, as the CEGB did that summer. Another approach is to use pumped-storage schemes like Dinorwic (p. 292) to supply peak electricity.

But the microprocessor approach, dubbed 'CALMS' (Credit and Load Management System), looks like a long-term winner. By using advanced microelectronics, the CEGB can constantly inform the energy-consuming equipment in each household of the present price of electricity. The messages, transmitted by radio, telephone or through the electricity supply system itself, would be used by a microprocessor-based control system in each household to decide when to turn on and off non-essential appliances. The freezer or water heater, for example, might be switched off for half an hour at a time, and the overall effect, the CEGB believes, would be to cut peak demand by at least 10 per cent. This could save England and Wales an estimated £1 billion a year, equivalent to £50 off the electricity bill paid by consumers living in the average three-bedroomed house.

But this technique, which is still very much in its early days, is only one example of a new trend in power-supply and energy-demand management. Another is the exciting energy-planning experiment which has been taking place in the Pacific Northwest – involving states such as Idaho, Montana, Oregon and Washington. By the late 1960s, almost all the accessible and economic hydropower resources of this region had been harnessed, so the power utilities turned to nuclear power. The ill-fated WWPPS programme (see p. 107) took the shine off nuclear power there, and boosted rates throughout the region, aggravating its economic problems.

Now, under the provisions of the Pacific Northwest Electric Power Planning and Conservation Act, any power utility receiving power from the Bonneville Power Administration must adhere to the Regional Conservation and Power Plan – which requires that *only* the most cost-effective conservation and power generation resources be used. Even better, as far as the proponents of energy conservation and renewable energy are concerned, the Act requires the utilities to consider all investments in the following order of priority: conservation, renewable resources, co-generation, and nuclear or coal plants. In short, as the Northwest Conservation Act Coalition points out, 'the Northwest enjoys the first legal mandate for a "soft energy path".'

For the first time in the United States, the utilities can 'purchase' energy-conservation and renewable resources as they would any other energy source. And, as Mark Reis, director of the NCAC, puts it, 'if home weatherization or solar industrial process heat is found to be the most cost-effective source of needed energy, [the Bonneville Power Administration] must acquire these resources as it would a coal or nuclear plant.' The Coalition has prepared a Model Plan analysing the end-use energy needs of the region and showing how it can eliminate the need for eleven planned thermal power stations.

Of course, conservation and renewable energy may well turn out to be less cost-effective than the more conventional alternatives, such as coal or nuclear energy, but at least in the Pacific Northwest they are in with something of a head start. The time has come, however, to look at the prospects for the various energy sources covered in

*Sun Traps* – and to look, in particular, at the contribution which the renewable-energy sources are likely to make in the remaining years of the century and beyond.

## The Renewable Forecast

'I do not believe that the events of the 1970s resulted from a temporary aberration or that the energy problem has gone away,' said Shell chairman Sir Peter Baxendell in the midst of the 1982 oil glut. He dismissed as 'simplistic and dangerous' the idea that market forces had reasserted themselves in the oil market and that OPEC's power had been undermined. The supply of oil, he pointed out, is still highly vulnerable to political action, particularly with the oil industry being dependent on a single source, Saudi Arabia, for up to 30 per cent of its needs.

High interest rates and the economic recession have damaged the prospects for many of the alternative-energy programmes launched in the wake of the first oil shock, as we have seen in earlier chapters, but the International Energy Agency was also warning that the industrialized nations could well be in for another oil price shock in the late 1980s. In its review of the energy policies and programmes of its twenty-one member nations, the IEA warned that the oil price rises of 1979–80 had reduced incomes in the OECD countries by 13 per cent, producing a total loss of income of almost $1,000 billion – or about $1,250 per person. The complacency which had closely followed the oil glut, it said, could well prove at least as great a threat as the problems of dealing with a tight energy market before the glut.

The OECD, in its *World Energy Outlook*, has warned that there will be less oil available to OECD countries in the 1990s because OPEC countries will be consuming more, Third World countries will need more to fuel their own development programmes and, unless synfuel plants are coming on stream, oil production in the OECD region will be falling. The net result, according to the OECD and the International Energy Agency, could be an 'excess demand' for oil of anywhere between 9 and 21 million barrels a day – an excess which could translate into significant price rises or, in the event of a supply distribution, into a price explosion.

BP, meanwhile, was suggesting that oil demand in the leading western industrialized nations is likely to continue falling for the remainder of this century, rather than growing. But, it warned, this decline will be offset – or probably even exceeded – by striking growth in the oil demands of Third World countries, including members of OPEC (see Table 14.4). BP's projections suggest that, whereas oil demand will fall at rates of up to 1.6 per cent per annum in Western Europe, the annual growth rate is likely to be between 1.5 and 4 per cent in the OPEC, Middle Eastern and African countries.

Table 14.4: *Oil demand growth rate ranges, 1980–2000 (source: BP)*

|  | % per annum growth |
| --- | --- |
| OPEC, Middle East, Africa | 1.5–4.0 |
| South-east Asia | 1.5–3.5 |
| Latin America | 0.3–3.3 |
| Japan | 0.5–1.2 |
|  | % per annum decline |
| Western Europe | 0.1–1.6 |
| Australasia | 0.2–1.5 |
| North America | 0.8–1.3 |

These estimates are slightly different from those produced by the Washington-based Worldwatch Institute, which predicts a slight fall in world oil consumption by the end of the century, but the assumptions used by the Institute include a rather more significant input from renewable energy than did those adopted by BP. While the forecasts for renewable energy in Table 14.5 may err slightly on the side of optimism, they certainly are consonant with the analysis of the current status of the various technologies contained in earlier chapters, and some interesting pointers emerge.

Firstly, while coal will not be *the* alternative fuel, it could well take over the number-one slot in the energy top ten. The Worldwatch Institute sees coal use rising by some 80 per cent by the year 2000. By 1990, coal will meet 35 per cent of the world's energy needs, according to Worldwatch. This compares fairly well with the International Energy Agency's prediction that coal will meet about 44 per cent of the predicted growth in total energy demand in the various OECD countries during the 1980s – and that by the end

Table 14.5: *World non-renewable and renewable energy consumption in 1980, with projections to 2000\* (source: Worldwatch Institute)*

| Energy source | 1980 | 1985 | 1990 | 1995 | 2000 | Rank† | Chapter |
|---|---|---|---|---|---|---|---|
| | (million tonnes of coal equivalent) | | | | | | |
| Coal | 3,149 | 3,831 | 4,660 | 5,145 | 5,680 | 2/1 | 4 |
| Oil | 3,908 | 3,810 | 3,712 | 3,526 | 3,322 | 1/2 | 4 |
| Natural gas | 1,807 | 1,850 | 1,900 | 1,875 | 1,850 | 3/3 | 4 |
| Cow dung | 57 | 60 | 60 | 55 | 45 | | 11 |
| Crop residues | 100 | 110 | 110 | 100 | 100 | | 10 |
| Energy crops | 3 | 16 | 30 | 45 | 55 | | 10 |
| Waste-to-electricity and steam | 10 | 12 | 15 | 20 | 25 | Total bio-mass 4/4 | 10 |
| Waste-to-methane | 4 | 10 | 30 | 53 | 90 | | 10 |
| Wood | 1,015 | 1,100 | 1,220 | 1,410 | 1,640 | | 10 |
| Hydropower | 600 | 710 | 850 | 1,020 | 1,200 | 5/5 | 12 |
| Nuclear | 244 | 445 | 645 | 720 | 730 | 6/6 | 5 |
| Geothermal | 13 | 27 | 52 | 87 | 140 | 7/7 | 6 |
| Solar collectors | 1 | 5 | 18 | 49 | 100 | 8/8 | 7 and 8 |
| Wind | 3 | 5 | 17 | 90 | 200 | 8/9 | 13 |
| Photovoltaics | 0 | 0 | 2 | 20 | 40 | 10/10 | 9 |
| Total | 10,914 | 11,991 | 13,321 | 14,215 | 15,217 | | |
| Renewables | 1,806 | 2,055 | 2,404 | 2,949 | 3,635 | | |
| Renewable % | 16.5 | 17.1 | 18.0 | 20.7 | 23.9 | | |

\* Electricity from all sources calculated in terms of coal required to produce equivalent amount.
† First ranking is for 1980, the second for the period 1985–2000.

of the decade coal could account for 27 per cent of all energy use, compared with 22 per cent in 1980.

There are a number of environmental problems which will need to be tackled before this sort of growth can be accommodated, however. First, there is the problem of 'acid rain', with sulphur dioxide generated by burning coal being washed out of the atmosphere as sulphuric acid – and having a devastating effect on ecological systems and, indeed, on the fabric of our cities and the state of our own health. Canada's environment minister calculated in 1980 that controlling acid rain would cost Canada $8 billion by the end of the century, while the United States would pay $80 billion.

The CEGB, meanwhile, was estimating that if it used limestone desulphurization to control the sulphur-dioxide problems generated by its power stations, the annual cost could be £1 billion and the resulting sludge at a single power station complex, at Drax, would be enough, over the life-time of the complex, to fill a lagoon of 2.5 square miles (6.5 kilometres) to a depth of 20 feet (6 metres). And the cost of electricity, the CEGB originally argued, would go up by some 30 per cent – although it now believes that the cost need not be so high.

But the acidification problems found throughout regions like Scandinavia are real – and likely to become more troublesome if a major transition back to coal occurs. The evidence could hardly come stronger than the acid rain dumped by one storm on Wheeling, West Virginia. With a pH value of 1.5, the rain was more acid than lemon juice. The acid rain and snow which falls in Scandinavia, Poland, Nova Scotia or on the Canadian shield country may not be as strong as lemon juice, but many lakes in Norway and Sweden are now lifeless, and the Canadians have stressed that an estimated 48,000 of their own lakes will be imperilled within a decade. Polish trains, meanwhile, must slow down on acid-corroded rails, and even the Statue of Liberty is under attack. During the March 1983 election in West Germany, Chancellor Kohl announced that if his coalition was re-elected (and it was), he would introduce new controls on industrial plants and coal-fired power stations, a programme which would require an investment of £3.3 billion. This, however, was substantially less than the £16 billion crash programme the Greens had promised if they ever held the balance of power.

Ultimately, however, the carbon-dioxide issue could prove an even more serious threat to those who see coal as the fuel of the future. Figure 14.2 shows that we have so far actually consumed, typically by burning, only a small fraction of the earth's fossil-fuel reserves – of which about 90 per cent is coal. But these fossil fuels will get harder to come by as we exhaust the easily accessible reserves, and, in their burning, we will contribute to the marked increase in atmospheric carbon dioxide recorded since 1860 (see Figure 14.3).

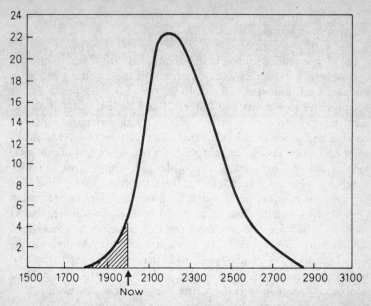

Figure 14.2: Proportion of fossil-fuel reserves burned to date (in thousand million tonnes; source: Earthscan).

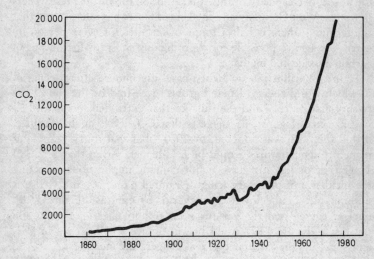

Figure 14.3: Man's contribution to $CO_2$ levels (in millions of tonnes, excluding forest burning; source: Earthscan).

The figures in Figure 14.3 do not include carbon dioxide ($CO_2$) deriving from burned forests.

The earth's atmosphere as a whole operates very much like the glass in a greenhouse, trapping solar radiation. When it hits the atmosphere, between 35 and 50 per cent of the incoming radiation bounces back into space. Some 10–20 per cent is absorbed by the atmosphere, as we saw in Chapter 2, and the balance (40–50 per cent) reaches the earth's surface. These rough estimates, however, conceal variations in the behaviour of the different wavelengths of solar radiation. Visible sunlight accounts for 46 per cent of our solar income, while 7 per cent is ultra-violet radiation – most of which is screened out by molecules of nitrogen, oxygen and ozone. The other major component of our solar income is infra-red radiation or heat. Most of this heat is captured by the atmosphere, thanks to the so-called 'greenhouse effect', and $CO_2$ contributes to this effect.

Given that atmospheric $CO_2$ levels have risen by something like 8 per cent since 1957, and by perhaps 25 per cent since 1860, scientists have been questioning what would happen if this trend continued unabated? Given long enough, the oceans might absorb much of this $CO_2$ and the world's forests act as an important 'carbon sink' – but the rapid rate of deforestation around the world is reducing the absorptive capacity of this sink. And, on top of this, researchers in Kenya, West Germany and the United States have discovered that the termite – there is half a tonne of termites for every person on earth – is also responsible for a prodigious and growing output of carbon dioxide and methane.

Figure 14.4 illustrates a 'worst-case' greenhouse effect scenario, in which world energy demand grows seven-fold by the end of the twenty-first century and the bulk of that extra demand is met by burning coal. Figure 14.5 suggests that $CO_2$ levels might stabilize, if this approach was adopted, by 2070 – but that thirty years later planetary temperatures would be 8°C higher. Given that a rise of 1 per cent or less can have major climatic implications, affecting the incidence of planetary icing or rainfall patterns, an 8°C rise is unthinkable. In the low-$CO_2$ scenario, by contrast (Figure 14.6), nuclear energy and the various solar technologies take over, and the result (Figure 14.7) could be very much smaller rises in $CO_2$ emissions and the associated global temperature increases.

This issue is infernally complex, like that centred around the effect of chlorofluorocarbon aerosol propellants on the earth's atmospheric

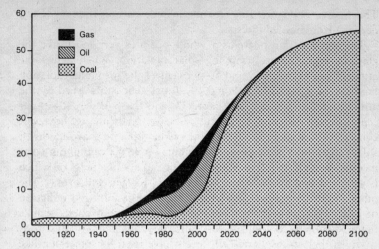

Figure 14.4: 'Worst-case' CO₂ scenario, involving greatly increased coal-burn (vertical scale in terawatts, or million watts; source: Earthscan).

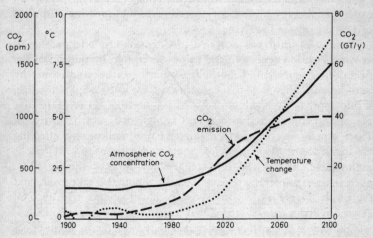

Figure 14.5: CO₂ impact of 'worst-case' scenario (source: Earthscan).

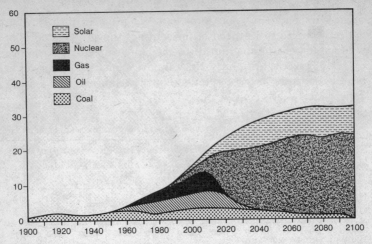

Figure 14.6: Low-CO₂ scenario, involving low coal use and high nuclear and solar contributions (vertical scale in terawatts; source: Earthscan).

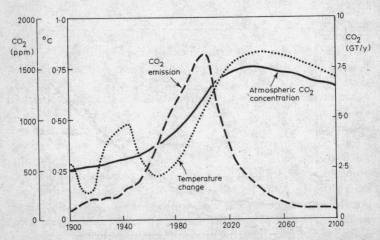

Figure 14.7: CO₂ impact of low-CO₂ scenario. Note: the vertical scale here is different from the one in Figure 14.5 (source: Earthscan).

ozone layer, but if $CO_2$ does turn out to be a problem, then growing notice will need to be taken of the statistics shown in Table 14.6, with natural gas turning out to be the most parsimonious emitter of $CO_2$ among the fossil fuels. Nuclear power and solar energy could prove even better in this respect, although the burning of biomass-derived fuels clearly emits $CO_2$.

*Table 14.6: $CO_2$ emissions from different fossil fuels (source: Earthscan)*

|  | Giga-tonnes of carbon emitted when producing 100 Quads of heat | Ratio of $CO_2$ produced |
| --- | --- | --- |
| Natural gas | 1.45 | 1.0 |
| Oil | 2.0 | 1.4 |
| Coal | 2.5 | 1.7 |
| Synfuels (coal converted to oil or gas) | 3.4 | 2.3 |

Countries like West Germany and Japan, as we have seen, still see nuclear power as a fundamentally important component of their energy strategies, and the Worldwatch Institute assumes that nuclear energy's contribution to world energy supplies will increase three-fold by the end of the century, which could make the nuclear industry a somewhat happier place to work. But nuclear energy, as we saw in Chapter 5, is still closely associated with the problems of proliferation. The nuclear industry in Britain, for example, has a good (though not spotless) safety record, even if the US industry does not. But there also remain a number of very difficult problems to be resolved in the radioactive-waste-disposal field – and no nuclear expert has yet convincingly demonstrated that this problem will ever be safely and economically resolved. Technology moves on, of course, and we may come up with some excellent solutions. But we are making a big assumption if we take this for granted. There are also the problems associated with decommissioning nuclear plants, although these at least seem technically feasible – at a very considerable cost, possibly equivalent in some cases to the cost of building the power station in the first instance. And we shall be sterilizing large areas of land for what, in human terms, will be eternity.

Nuclear fission has enough attractions for us to be relatively sure that fission reactors will continue to be built. The USSR, for example, envisages at least doubling its nuclear-power capacity by the year 2000 (Table 14.7). Indeed, whatever the anti-nuclear lobby may anticipate in the way of nuclear catastrophes, the tripling of world nuclear-power capacity predicted by the Worldwatch Institute seems quite plausible.

And the fast breeder reactor, for all the very real problems it will bring in respect of proliferation, will also be built in increasing numbers – because the energy locked up in the spent fuel from conventional nuclear stations is too great to ignore. Estimates of how much energy Britain's stored nuclear wastes could be expected to produce in breeder reactors have ranged from a high $50 \times 10^9$ tonnes of coal equivalent to figures less than half that amount. But these figures, if they are moderately within range, put this option on a level with Britain's coal – which is said to be good for another 300 years at present levels of consumption.

These estimates, however, are inevitably suspect, given that the spent fuel would have to be reprocessed a considerable number of

Table 14.7: *Energy balance in the USSR, 1980–2000, in million tonnes of oil equivalent (source: International Energy Agency)*

|  | 1980 | 1985 | 1990 | 2000 |
|---|---|---|---|---|
| *Energy production* |  |  |  |  |
| Oil | 603 | 560–620 | 540–620 | 520–615 |
| Natural gas | 365 | 520 | 640 | 810–865 |
| Coal | 337 | 335 | 350 | 480 |
| Nuclear and other | 125 | 135 | 170–200 | 260–330 |
| Total | 1,430 | 1,550–1,610 | 1,700–1,810 | 2,070–2,290 |
| *Energy consumption* |  |  |  |  |
| Oil | 450 | 485 | 500–525 | 510–580 |
| Natural gas | 322 | 440 | 530 | 660–700 |
| Coal | 331 | 332 | 343 | 473 |
| Nuclear and other | 124 | 133 | 167–197 | 257–327 |
| Total | 1,227 | 1,390 | 1,540–1,585 | 1,900–2,090 |
| *Net energy surplus* total | 203 | 160–220 | 160–215 | 170–210 |
| *Growth trends* (in % per year) | 1973–80 | 1980–85 | 1985–90 | 1990–2000 |
| *Energy consumption* | 3.9 | 2.4 | 2.0–2.8 | 2.2–2.8 |

times to extract even half the level of energy suggested. The promises made on behalf of nuclear fusion may well also look inflated in retrospect, but again the potential contribution, as we saw in Chapter 5, is such that fusion research will continue to be funded. Companies like General Atomic may indeed make their breakthrough, but fusion is not going to be a significant energy source in this century – and its long-term contribution must still be open to question.

Geothermal systems, by contrast, are already producing a useful amount of energy, equivalent to some 13 million tonnes of coal in 1980 (see Table 14.5), and are becoming increasingly important in a relatively small number of specially favoured countries. By 1980, geothermal energy accounted for 7 per cent of the renewable-energy budget worldwide, and the Worldwatch Institute expects this contribution to grow nearly eleven-fold by the year 2000. This forecast ties in well with that made for geothermal electricity by UNERG (see Table 6.2, p. 135). Overall, renewable energy accounted for an estimated 16.5 per cent of the world energy budget in 1980, with biomass energy contributing over 65 per cent of the renewable-energy budget (Table 14.5). By the end of the century, this proportion is forecast to have slipped to about 54 per cent, although the total renewable contribution will have grown considerably by then: the Worldwatch Institute predicts that it will have doubled – and will account for 23.9 per cent of the world's total energy needs by the year 2000.

Hydropower, which ranks second among the renewable-energy sources, is also expected to double its contribution, while wind power is forecast to contribute well over 60 times as much energy by the end of the 1990s. But look at the figures for solar collectors and photovoltaics. Even if we combine their contributions, we are told that they will be providing less than 1 per cent of the world's energy by the end of the century. Can this be true?

## A Future for Sun Trappers

'If he thinks solar energy is only for the future, he's living in the past', declared the *Sun Times* in the midst of the fight to prevent the Reagan administration's cuts in renewable-energy funding (see Figure 3.4, p. 50) going through Congress. It was referring, of course, to President Reagan (Figure 14.8). But what would the President's

# SUN TIMES

PUBLISHED BY SOLAR LOBBY • 1001 CONNECTICUT AVENUE, NW • WASHINGTON, DC 20036 • MAY/JUNE 1982

**If he thinks solar energy is only for the future, he's living in the past.**

Figure 14.8: If he thinks . . . (source: Solar Lobby).

energy advisers have thought if they could have seen the apparently poor showing of the direct solar technologies covered in Chapters 7–9 in terms of the share of the world's total energy needs they would meet by the year 2000? The answer is that they had already seen much more pessimistic figures, prepared by government agencies and on behalf of the nuclear-power lobby, for example.

Indeed, it is interesting to note that solar collectors will need to multiply their contribution *one-hundred-fold* and the photovoltaics industry must expand *forty-fold* if they are to meet even this 1-per-cent target! All the indirect solar technologies, such as biomass energy, hydropower and wind energy, seem to have relatively bright futures – is this all we can hope for the direct solar-capture technologies? Here the answer is almost certainly yes. But consider what is already happening in the solar-energy field, despite the government cut-backs.

Prophets of the 'solar age', like Hazel Henderson, talk as though this dawning age of renewable-energy and minimum-waste economies is just around the corner – and of course, in historical terms, it is. If the human race survives the next century or so in good order, despite all the omens, then the chances are that we will be tapping into most of the forms of renewable energy discussed in *Sun Traps* – and more besides. But a century is a long time for beings who find it hard enough to think several years ahead, let alone decades.

So what is happening to the solar industry today? The US market for solar collectors was probably worth about £100 million by 1982, while Japan's market had reached about £50 million and Britain's just over £10 million a year. The world photovoltaic market was perhaps worth a total of £50–70 million, although it was growing very fast indeed.

A 'solar profitability' survey carried out that year by the Solar Lobby came up with results which flew in the face of most people's expectations. Defining the companies surveyed as either 'pure solar companies' (i.e. 75 per cent or more of their sales came from solar products) or 'hybrid solar companies' (less than 75 per cent solar sales), the Solar Lobby found that 72 per cent of the 'pure' solar companies reported sales gains in 1982 – and 90 per cent of the 'hybrid' companies did so, too. Even more significant, 41 per cent of the 'pure' companies recorded increased profits, and some companies turned in extraordinary performances: Nova Energy, for example, boosted its profits by 266 per cent, while A. T. Bliss & Company registered a 98-per-cent increase in profits.

The solar market was still small by most standards, but some areas were growing very rapidly indeed. The number of passive solar homes in the United States grew from perhaps 500 in 1977 to 60,000–80,000 by 1982. Active-solar-collector sales there increased from $17 million in 1975 to an estimated $400 million by 1981, sales which translate into fuel savings equivalent to 1–1.5 million barrels of oil a year. The number of US solar-collector manufacturers had increased from 50 in 1975 to more than 300, while the number of buildings with active solar-energy systems, such as those described in Chapters 7 and 8, increased from 30,000 in 1978 to 400,000 – better than a thirteen-fold increase.

Between 1975 and 1980, sales of active solar systems, passive solar designs and photovoltaics grew at an annual rate of 155 per cent, according to the Solar Lobby. When wind energy, hydropower, biomass conversion and geothermal systems were included, annual US renewable-energy sales reached $4.5 billion in 1980. Sales of co-generation and waste-heat recovery equipment (including heat pumps) reached $4.3 billion, and renewable fuel sales represented a further $1.7 billion. Alcohol fuels, however, were severely depressed by the slumping oil prices, and companies like Texaco, Standard Oil of California and Phillips Petroleum were cutting back on their commitments in this area.

In Brazil, however, the world's first industrial-scale ethylene-from-ethanol plant came on stream late in 1981, with Petrobrás predicting that it would take some 30 per cent of the ethanol obtained from energy crops in the state of Alagoas in the 1981–2 season. Indeed, a growing number of companies, including the American firm Iotech, see the main immediate payoffs from ethanol R & D coming in the production of chemicals from ethanol derivatives and by-products.

The US solar industry was beginning to get a little nervous about Japan's solar enthusiasm, however. The Japanese bought about 800,000 solar water heaters in 1980, compared to sales of perhaps 100,000 in the United States. Japanese manufacturers had expressed the view that their domestic market could level off at about the 1 million water heaters a year mark, and the implication is that they will then turn their eyes to the export market – and to the United States in particular. With market consultants Frost & Sullivan forecasting that world sales of photovoltaic products would pass $16 billion by 1990, American manufacturers were beginning to look to their laurels.

The EEC Commission had also identified photovoltaics as a potential growth market, a fact reflected in its 1979–83 solar budget (Table 14.8). One EEC country which is pursuing this market very seriously is Italy. Early in 1982, a newly-formed company called Pragma announced a five-year, $50 million photovoltaic programme. As usual, Pragma has substantial backing from more conventional energy suppliers, being 75-per-cent owned by Agip Nucleare. It hopes to have a production capacity of 6–8 MW of photovoltaic cells by 1986. Italy, in fact, will almost certainly be a good market for this technology, having plenty of sunshine and a host of remote mountain and island settlements needing power.

In contrast to Frost & Sullivan, however, Mike Starr of Sir William Halcrow & Partners suggested that the photovoltaic market would be worth $5–10 billion by the end of the century, rather than $16 billion by 1990.

*Table 14.8: EEC solar budget, 1979–83 (source: Commission of the European Communities)*

| Project | Budgeted* | Spent* |
|---|---|---|
| A: Solar energy in dwellings | 8.2 | 8.3 |
| B: Thermo-mechanical solar power plants | 4.7 | 4.7 |
| C: Photovoltaic power generation | 15.91 | 15.9 |
| D: Photochemical, photoelectrochemical and photobiological processes | 2.65 | 2.6 |
| E: Energy from biomass | 8.2 | 7.4 |
| F: Solar radiation data | 1.8 | 2.0 |
| G: Wind energy | 1.18 | 1.0 |
| H: Solar energy in agriculture and industry | 0.6 | 0.7 |
| Programme management | 2.76 | 3.4 |
| Total | 46.00 | 46.00 |

* In European Currency Units, worth £0.57, D M2.45 or $1.10 in January 1982.

But, whatever the market forecast, exciting developments are very much in prospect. A company based in New York State, Solar Technology Associated Research (STAR), has announced that it has developed a new design of photovoltaic cell which will generate three times as much power from an array one third the size of currently available arrays. Without support from either the US government or the big oil companies, STAR claims that it has developed a cell well able to meet the goal of 70 cents per peak watt – and well before the target date.

The new cell, which employs 'micro-corduroy, thin-film' technology, and can be made either from polycrystalline silicon or gallium arsenide, has been designed for easy mass-production. At the time, STAR had only laboratory test cells to show, with six-inch diameters, but computer studies showed that there should be no limit to the ultimate size of the cell once mass-production begins.

Mass-production, in fact, will be the key to the solar future, a fact the Japanese were quick to recognize. Purists may debate whether Boeing should build windmills – or whether this task should be left to Dr Schumacher's Intermediate Technology Development Group (see Chapter 13). Both approaches, the big and the small, clearly have their place, but the experience of companies like Boeing in tooling up for mass-production runs will be crucial. And in this sense, at least, it is good to see companies like Ford developing products like the integrated solar-energy package for small communities which it developed for NASA and the Jet Propulsion Laboratory – or Fiat involved in building a wind farm of ten 50 kW aerogenerators in Sardinia.

This recognition is also at the heart of the proposals advanced by West Germany's AEG-Telefunken for the construction of vast photovoltaic arrays, 'solar plantations', in the world's desert areas – to produce hydrogen for use as a substitute for oil. Dr Reinhard Dahlberg, a top researcher for the financially troubled company, West Germany's second largest electronics company, has been trying to persuade the financial world to invest $12 billion in an extra-ordinarily ambitious scheme (and this will only take it to 1990), designed to develop self-reproducing photovoltaic plantations.

Stripped to its bare essentials, the idea is that over 100,000 planta-tions (see the example in Figure 14.9), with a total generating capacity of 10,000 GW, would be built over the next fifty years in ten specially selected tropical locations – including seven deserts in Africa, Australia, and North and South America. In such locations, Dahlberg argues, each 140-square-metre array could produce hydrogen equiva-lent to a tonne of oil a year. Altogether, he estimates, the complete programme would produce hydrogen equivalent to 15 billion tonnes of oil a year by 2040, and there would still be enough surplus power to run the assembly plants which would manufacture all the components required – so that the scheme would make no extra demands on the world's existing supplies of conventional energy.

With an average photovoltaic cell efficiency of 14 per cent, cell costs of 0.15 cents a peak watt and water-to-hydrogen electrolysis

Figure 14.9: A solar hydrogen 'plantation'
(source: AEG-Telefunken).

efficiencies around 85 per cent, all levels which Dahlberg believes
are achievable in the near future, the project's cost to 2040 would
total about $27,000 billion at 1980 prices, although if cell and water
electrolysis efficiencies only reach 10 and 70 per cent respectively,
the final price tag could leap to an astronomical $50,000 billion.
Dahlberg admits that the scheme is 'wildly ambitious', but points
out that the cost of burning oil over the next twenty years will amount
to some $20,000 billion worldwide.

By contrast, the campaign mounted by Roger Billings of the Billings
Energy Corporation, based in Missouri, seems unduly modest.
Billings has converted all sorts of vehicles to run on hydrogen, including a bus (Figure 14.10) and a US Postal Service Jeep. His 'Project
Liberty' aims to give the United States energy independence by converting it from imported oil to hydrogen derived largely from coal.
In 1980 he moved his company to Independence, Missouri, to begin
the first phase of the project, a hydrogen-powered community. He
is converting twenty houses and something like 100 vehicles, including
the Jeep, in the process. The next step is a wholly hydrogen-powered
town, Forest City in Iowa. Iowa coal is so cheap that Billings has
estimated that he could produce fuel at the equivalent of 50 cents
a gallon, and he hopes to have the project operating by 1984 as a

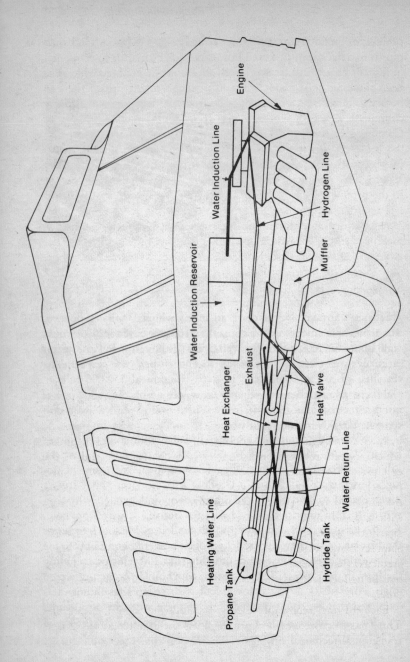

Figure 14.10: The Billings hydrogen bus (source: Billings Energy Corporation).

prelude to building a much larger complex to gasify coal and then pipe it to a hydrogen-powered Los Angeles. The hydrogen economy, in fact, has many attractions, and Canada is one country which has been thinking hard about ways in which it might bridge the gap before it embarks on a full-fledged hydrogen conversion. An all-party committee of MPs tabled a report in the Canadian House of Commons early in 1981 arguing that alcohol fuels would provide the bridge, whereas the tar-sands developments in Alberta would prove a costly diversion. They may yet prove to have been right. They also argued strongly in favour of Canada's developing its expertise in the production of methanol from wood – a resource of which it has an abundant supply.

A great deal will depend on the success of hydrogen scientists in making their hydrogen production processes more efficient. One hopeful announcement came from Texas A & M University, where two important breakthroughs had been achieved by Dr Marek Szlarczyk and Dr A. Q. Contractor. Working independently, they had achieved significant improvements in the photoanodes and photocathodes used when converting solar energy into hydrogen. Their two refinements could boost conversion efficiencies from less than 1 per cent to about 10 per cent. Even so, the commercial application of water electrolysis is still probably decades away, rather than years.

The renewable-energy field, as previous chapters have shown, has also had its share of technical fiascos. We have heard of Citibank's skyscraper, which provided space for a technology which did not exist by the time the building was completed; of Dornier's plant in Jordan which appears to have been hopelessly over-designed; and of the collapse of America's kelp scheme and Kenya's Kisumu ethanol project. Yet who, ten years ago, would have thought that Sweden, the 'land of the midnight sun', would now be experimenting seriously with a wide range of solar technologies? Who would have predicted the opening, early in 1982, of the Solar One 10.8 MW plant at Barstow, in the Mojave Desert? And who would have predicted that a newly independent Zimbabwe would meet 15 per cent of its fuel needs with alcohol derived from home-grown sugar-cane?

Each of the renewable-energy technologies described in *Sun Traps* has its environmental problems, its social implications and its transitional technical problems. The notion that renewable-energy technologies are intrinsically benign in environmental terms has occasionally attracted critical comment in the environmental press (Figure 14.11), but any critical analysis of the likely impact of such technologies by environmental organizations still occasions incredulity among some renewable-energy stalwarts. The National Audubon Society, for example, published a report in 1983 which warned that many of these technologies are far from benign. Among the potential side-effects identified were air and water pollution caused by the conversion of biomass into energy; urban sprawl resulting from the increasing use of solar collectors, which are best suited to detached, single-family houses; the depletion of woodlands by the fuelwood industry; and the increased risk of earthquakes generated by major dams.

'Symbolically, it's like someone in the nuclear industry saying nukes are dangerous', said one environmental consultant, while Scott Sklar, as acting director of the Solar Lobby, argued that the report 'hurts renewable energy'. Others were not so sure: William Brown, an energy analyst at the Hudson Institute, commented that 'What was once black and white among environmentalists is now a shade of grey.' Meanwhile, back at the national Audubon Society, senior energy scientist Jan Beyea explained. 'We're trying to say, "Make good choices early on in developing large-scale energy technologies".'

But, with some 9 per cent of everyone who has ever lived alive at the moment, and all of us consuming energy at much higher rates than has been the norm for our species to date, we shall need to harness new energy sources, whether renewable or non-renewable, wherever we can find them. The nature of the energy crisis, meanwhile, is changing. The developed countries will still experience major problems with energy supply and pricing, but the problems of the developing countries are far more serious – and deserve our urgent attention. As President Fidel Castro of Cuba put it at a summit meeting of non-aligned nations in 1983, 'in 1960, 6.3 tons of oil could be purchased with the sale of a ton of sugar. In 1982, only 0.7 tons of oil could be bought with the same amount of sugar.' This problem was described in detail in Chapter 2 (p. 26).

If the renewable-energy industry can indeed supply a quarter of the world energy budget by the end of the century, as is suggested in Table 14.5, then it will have made a major contribution to resolving some of these problems. But the structure of the industry is causing concern in a number of the organizations which are keen to see a

"Come here this instant, or the Wave Power Generators will get you."

Figure 14.11: A jaundiced view of the renewables (source: *The Ecologist*).

major stimulus given to the under-developed nations, along the lines suggested in the Brandt Commission's reports. The International Institute for Environment and Development (IIED), for example, carried out a study of the problems and opportunities associated with transfers of solar-energy technology from the developed to the under-developed or developing countries.

The generation of know-how to manufacture these technologies requires considerable investments in research and demands substantial scientific and technological skills,' IIED concluded, 'neither of which are often available to developing countries.' Worse, as far as IIED was concerned, 'the generators of know-how are concerned to protect their proprietary information through legal measures, like patents.' And, it continued, 'the research activities related to these technologies are today concentrated within a few Western countries and, in these countries, within a few transnational companies.'

But, politics aside, IIED needs no convincing that renewable-energy technologies *will* be vitally important for the developing world. 'While preferential access to oil would help many developing countries to meet their immediate and near-term energy needs and smooth their transition to renewable energy sources,' its report concluded, 'the development of renewable-energy technologies and reasonable access to them alone will help to solve their long-term energy problems – and ensure that the energy transition will indeed take place.'

Meanwhile, there is a great deal developing countries can do for themselves. In Zimbabwe, for example, one highly appropriate project involved turning a barn into a solar collector by painting the roof black and installing a thin ceiling, with the warm air trapped between the roof and ceiling blown by electric fans through grain or tobacco. Or consider the activities of the Solamatics Company there. It designed a series of relatively cheap solar water heaters for low-cost housing. Although the system cannot store heat overnight, it does provide it when it is most needed. According to Professor David Hall, 'the water is warm enough by 11 a.m. for the morning laundry; by 2 p.m. there is plenty for after-lunch washing up; and the system is at maximum efficiency between 4 and 7.30 p.m., when most after-work and after-dinner washing is done.'

Around the world, we can safely predict, the oil tankers will continue to sail, coal will continue to emerge from deep and open-cast mines, and nuclear power plants will continue to come on stream behind their bristling security fences. But at any given moment the weight of photons hitting our planet, after their 8-minute journey from the sun, is thought to be equivalent to the weight of a large ocean liner. In renewable-energy terms, at least, our ship is constantly coming in.

Ultimately, a number of island communities around the world may prove to have been our energy pathfinders. Located more than 2,000 miles from its nearest neighbour, Hawaii, for example, has no oil, no coal, no natural gas and no other conventional energy resources of its own – so it must import something like 90 per cent of the energy it needs. With strong memories of their isolation after the attack on Pearl Harbour, the Hawaiians have been pressing ahead with an ambitious renewable-energy programme.

The OTEC project may be under review (see Chapter 8), but energy planners in the fiftieth US state are hoping to meet 10 per cent of its electricity needs from wind power by 1990. The Hawaiian Electric Company, for example, has been turning into the wind, spending $240 million to build thirty-two aerogenerators. Sitting in the middle of the trade winds, Hawaii has some of the best winds for power generation in the United States. Biomass already supplies about 40 per cent of the electrical power on Hawaii itself, and 38 per cent on Kauai. And the geothermal site at Puna, in a region rich in volcanoes, could eventually produce enough power to meet all the islands' needs.

'We were scoffed at then,' recalls Hawaii's energy research co-ordinator, Dr John Shupe, thinking back to the 1960s, 'but we were able to convince the legislature that this was vital to the future, that they didn't *need* to go on spending a billion a year on OPEC oil. So we started out with a shoestring budget of $200,000 and it's all gone from there. In the early 1970s I was a voice in the wilderness: today we're criticized for not moving fast enough.'

But, while Dr Shupe's political ally, Senator Spark Matsunaga, expressed the hope that Hawaii would become an 'energy pathfinder for the globe', the fiftieth state's circumstances are, if not unique, at least unusual. Elsewhere, renewable-energy research and development expenditure has been under pressure as the world recession, coupled with the success of some national energy conservation programmes, sent oil prices spiralling downwards. Where some renewable-energy technologists had feared that OPEC would cut oil prices just as new alternative energy schemes came on stream, to scuttle them, they now found that the natural operation of the market could have an equally devastating effect as far as the economic justification for their activities was concerned.

'Sure, I feel vindicated,' said Professor Peter Odell, sometimes considered the high priest of energy unorthodoxy, who had argued throughout the 1970s that the oil industry was being unduly pessimistic about its prospects – and had consistently dismissed the consensus opinion that there must be 'an inevitable, near-future scarcity of oil'. Indeed, he soon concluded, he had himself been guilty of a degree of pessimism. Far from the Age of Oil being over, he asserted, the world oil industry will not hit its peak of production until the year 2017 at the earliest, and is unlikely to return to present production levels until the 2050s. As Chapter 4 indicates, new oil-fields remain to be found, new enhanced oil-recovery techniques promise to boost production from existing and new fields, and, while the shock-waves resulting from the collapse of so many oil shale and tar sand ventures are still ringing around the world, the energy potential of such unconventional oil resources remains vast.

Although one should always take the oil industry's figures on alternatives to oil with a pinch of the proverbial salt, it is worth recalling the comparative technical production costs for a range of energy sources produced by Shell and quoted on p. 14. Middle East oil was by far the most attractive economically, followed by North Sea oil, oil from shale, substitute natural gas made from coal in north-west Europe, crops grown for fuel, electricity from solar, wind or tidal sources, and finally, in this listing at least, solar heat. Of course, it is simplicity itself to pinpoint regions or applications where this order of priority is effectively reversed, with renewable energy outperforming oil, but they remain special cases.

Yet these special cases, such as Brazil, Hawaii, Israel or Japan, guarantee that technological evolution will continue to take place at a surprisingly rapid pace in much of the renewable-energy field. This is important because if oil prices are going to rise less rapidly than many of us had expected, then renewable-energy technologies are going to have to become cheaper, more efficient and easier to use if they are to compete effectively. The entry into the solar-energy field of such companies as Matsushita and Sharp, both skilled in mass production and based in a country which recognizes its vulnerability as far as fossil fuels are concerned, suggests that the cost of some renewable-energy technologies will tumble in the next few years.

Japan's sail-assisted merchant ship, the *Shin Aitoku Maru*, attracted a great deal of publicity when it was launched in 1980, with its plastic-coated unconventional sails controlled by micro-computer. In Britain, too, the Prudential Assurance Company announced that it intended to underwrite a study of wind-powered cargo ships by Walker Wingsail – a company which had developed an aerofoil sail able to give double the thrust of a windjammer's rig and save at least 20 per cent of the ship's fuel bills. 'We are applying the latest marine and aerospace technology to design fully computerized wingsail systems,' said John Walker, the company's founder and managing director.

In many ways, this type of development symbolizes the way forward for the renewable-energy technologies. In some circumstances, some renewable-energy technologies will make sense as freestanding sources of energy, generally supplying isolated communities, whether in the Outer Hebrides or Hawaii. Elsewhere, such technologies will initially be adopted in an auxiliary, support role, diversifying the energy mix for communities and countries with the foresight to see that, even if the Age of Oil is going to last longer than most of us expected, the political uncertainties will remain.

No one with any sense of the ways in which technologies develop will sniff at these sorts of opportunities. Instead, they will recognize that such applications represent proving grounds for technologies which are still, in most cases, fairly low down on what promises to be an exponential development curve. Ultimately, we shall have renewable-energy technologies which are relatively simple to use and yet which, as Stephen Salter has pointed out, are the product of some highly sophisticated systems engineering – like the Wingsail or Salter's Duck.

The early 1980s were a period in which a number of conservative governments, most of them with a strong prejudice in favour of nuclear energy, fought inflation and then recession with varying degrees of success. Inevitably, some areas of longer-term research and development, particularly support for renewable-energy work, were cut back severely. Yet there is every reason to expect that our economies, like some cargo ships, will be supplying at least 10 per cent of their energy needs from renewable resources by the end of the century. If, however, energy prices prove more volatile than expected, for whatever reason, then support for the renewable-energy industry will grow – and so will its energy contribution.

At the end of Chapter 3, we asked whether venture capital outfits like the Egg Co. should invest in renewable energy. The evidence suggests that, while some investors may well go 'down the tubes with well-meaning investments', the investment opportunities are likely to be very significant indeed. Much of the start-up or pump-priming funding must come from the public sector, and, by the late 1980s, many of the renewable-energy technologists now operating on the margin of the economy will find themselves increasingly part of the economic mainstream. From being voices in the wilderness, like Dr Shupe in Hawaii, they will once again find themselves under pressure to come up with the renewable goods – and being criticized for not moving fast enough.

Governments, like Britain's, have tended to shrug off requests that they publish comparative assessments of the energy return likely to be generated by investing, say, £1 billion in nuclear power, energy conservation, district heating or renewable energy. However, one important study which concluded that an energy future based predominantly on improved energy efficiency and renewable energy would have an economic edge on Britain's official energy plans was published in 1983 by Earth Resources Research. The underlying research had been sponsored by the Department of Energy's Energy Technology Support Unit, the Commission of the European Communities and Shell UK.

As the economic picture begins to brighten, conservatism in politics will increasingly be supplemented or replaced by a recognition that conservation and sustainability are likely to be key factors underpinning the successful economies of the 1990s and beyond. The sun is not *the* answer to our energy problems, but it is going to be a key element in successful energy strategies. Our local star is so vast that we can miss a comet colliding with it and generating enough energy in the process to power the United States for a thousand years; but its actual and potential energy contributions, both in the developing and the developed countries, are now also so great that even the most antediluvian governments will find it increasingly impossible to turn a blind eye.

# Index